TECHNOLOGY AND WOMAN'S WORK

TECHNOLOGY AND WOMAN'S WORK

Elizabeth Faulkner Baker

COLUMBIA UNIVERSITY PRESS
New York and London

Elizabeth Faulkner Baker is Professor Emeritus of Economics at Barnard College, Columbia University.

To My Sister,

OLIVETTA FAULKNER

ABBREVIATIONS

ESR	Employment Security Review
JPE	Journal of Political Economy
MLR	Monthly Labor Review
U.S. BLS	United States Bureau of Labor Statistics
U.S. WB	United States Women's Bureau

Preface

Technological advances from steam engine to automation have altered the lives of all workers, but for American women they have uprooted the past and redirected life. It has been an intriguing and rewarding experience to follow woman's new and uncertain course through more than 160 years, and to venture a suggestion for her future. We shall find it a zigzag road in man's domain, beset with obstacles—social, economic, physical, and psychological. For women have been contending not only with the difficulties of the new work itself, but also with the problems of establishing their right to have it, particularly when jobs have been scarce during economic depressions.

But circumstances were on women's side. Our modern economy needed them. As markets expanded, production methods had to be improved and costs lowered. A major solution was mass production aided by Yankee ingenuity—more machines and diluted skills to take the place of a small amount of capital and a large amount of skilled labor. Hence, as women were accepted in the labor force they have been used to reduce costs. Being less intent upon improving their status because of home responsibilities, the majority of them have remained at the broad employment base while men were rising to the narrow top.

A multitude of women have nevertheless made their mark in the professions and arts—as teachers, nurses, social workers, entertainers. Without sacrificing femininity they are everywhere in the office, at the switchboard, behind the counter; some in highly responsible and well-paid positions. More women are entering the field of science, and now we have witnessed a Russian woman astronaut orbiting the globe 42 times. Coeducation in America has gained almost complete public acceptance; and in many directions the sex line is blurred.

Today we witness more than one out of every three women of working age employed outside their homes—some 24 million of them. Their average (median) age rose from 26 years in 1900 to 41 years in 1962, and close to two thirds of all are 35 years or more, 942,000 being 65 years and over. The emergency of World War II prompted both government and industry to encourage married women to enter the labor market as never before, and today for the first time in history more than half of the women at work are married and living with their husbands. There are well over 13 million of them, a third of their total number and nearly a fifth of all persons at work. The heads of between four and five million families are women, more than half of them in the labor force. The over-all employment of women rose 35 percent in the last decade and only 8 percent for men. Almost half of the additional workers predicted for 1970 will be women—an increase of 25 percent as compared to 14 percent for men.[1]

Thus the throng of "unoccupied ladies . . . ready to work, but finding no field," who distressed the editors of *The Economist* a century ago, appear to have found more than a few outlets for their ambitions and abilities. And economic pressures upon them do not slacken.

These conclusions are evident despite certain irregularities in the data upon which they rest. The census record of people at work extends back to 1820, but the reports were necessarily sketchy, and up to 1870 all "female hands" were included regardless of age. From 1870 to 1930 paid workers ten years of age and over were included, and beginning in 1940 the minimum age has been 14 years. In that year a major shift was made in census classifications. From 1890 to 1940 the count was of "gainful workers"—those who reported a gainful

[1] *U.S. WB Bull. 285*, pp. 4, 10, 34, 39, 42–46; U.S. Department of Health, Education, and Welfare, *News Release*, November 25, 1962; *American Women*, p. 6.

occupation whether or not they were employed at the time the census was taken. In 1940, the term "labor force" was introduced for the first time. Hence we now have reports of those who were employed or were looking for work during the week before the census was taken whether or not they may have worked at gainful occupations at other times of the year. Accordingly, many seasonal and other part-time workers were not reported, and these included a large but unknown number of women. On the other hand, new workers are now counted among those in the labor force but not in the occupational classifications.

The Census Bureau has worked out adjustment factors to make the earlier figures more comparable with those of 1940 and after, and this has made it necessary to regroup some occupations, the content of which is constantly changing. One result is that the number of occupational titles varies from one census to another. For example, in 1940 there were 451 detailed occupations and now there are 479, and women are found in all of them. Nevertheless, according to the President's Commission on the Status of Women, only a little over three and a third million of them are in labor unions.[2]

No work of the proportions of this volume can be entirely free from error, and for any errors noted by the reader the author takes full responsibility. Reliable published and unpublished sources have been consulted wherever they could be found, some far richer than others, so that the treatment is necessarily uneven in places. But this account could not have been prepared with the authority it is hoped it has achieved without the appraisal and advice of critics in their various

[2] For explanations of census reporting and adjustments for comparability, see John D. Durand, *Labor Force in the United States, 1890–1960* (New York, Social Science Research Council, 1948); Gertrude Bancroft, *The American Labor Force; Its Growth and Changing Composition* (New York, John Wiley & Sons, 1958); *U.S. WB Bull. 218*, pp. 12–14; *American Women*, p. 35.

fields, as well as of friends and colleagues. It is a great pleasure
to identify them:

My greatest obligation is to Professor Felicia Johnson Dey-
rup of the New School for Social Research, who read the entire manuscript and made inspiring suggestions for improving
both content and arrangement. This is a far better book as
a result of her patient and scholarly advice.

My next obligation is to Professor Jack Barbash, a national
authority on labor unions at the University of Wisconsin, who
generously gave me the benefit of his long experience in a re-
assuring and informative appraisal of the chapter on White
Collar Unionism.

Other colleagues and professional people to whom I am indebted are Professor Theresa Wolfson of Brooklyn College for
stimulating comments on the earlier chapters, and Barnard
College Professors Clara Eliot and Mirra Komarovsky for their
critical reviews of chapters 16, 17, and 19 on professional
women; Adele Herwitz, Evelyn B. Moses, and Virginia L.
Bauknecht of the American Nurses' Association for advice and
information on the status of nurses, Chapter 18; Dr. Herbert J.
Lahne for suggestions for the revision of Chapter 9 on Women
in the Textile Industries and for wise general comments; Professor Ray L. Trautman for help in Chapter 8 on Women on
the Farm; and Professor Hunter Wright for pointers on expres-
sion and style.

I am under obligation to the following others who gave information and criticism in the field of education. On the technology of education, Chapter 17, T. Wilson Cahill, Administrative Assistant, Board of Education of Washington County,
Maryland; Raymond W. Graf, New York Supervisor, State Aid
Program for Classroom Television; and especially to P. Kenneth Komoski, President of the Center for Programmed Instruction, Inc., for his illuminating advice and information on

teaching machines and the other new teaching devices. I also thank Eleanor G. Coit, Director of the Labor Education Service, for information on the unionization of office workers, Chapter 20; and Lawrence L. Williams, Survey Research Center at the University of Michigan, on office automation. The instructive articles by Fred M. Hechinger, education editor of the New York *Times*, have been useful many times.

From the business and industry sector of the economy, I received expert advice from Dr. Alfred N. Goldsmith of the Radio Corporation of America on the technical aspects of the electronic computer in chapters 11, 12, and 13; from Emil Hamma, Assistant Vice President of the Chemical Bank New York Trust Company on automation in banking, Chapter 13; from the American Telephone and Telegraph Company, Peter B. Howell, Force Conditions Supervisor, Patrick J. Ewing, Revenue Information Supervisor, and his successor, Robert L. Varner, for very generous and expert assistance in the preparation of Chapter 14, Women at the Switchboard, and again in a section of Chapter 20 on white-collar unionism; from an anonymous representative of the tobacco division of the American Machine and Foundry Company in Chapter 10; from Mrs. Marilyn Cooke, Director of Public Relations at Lord and Taylor's and Mrs. G. G. Michelson, in charge of Macy's New York division, on Chapter 15, Women Behind the Counter; and from Don Taylor, Secretary of the New York Employing Printers Association, on women in the composing room, Chapter 10.

Dr. Ewan Clague, United States Commissioner of Labor Statistics, and Robert J. Meyers, Chief of the Division of Productivity and Technological Developments, gave valuable assistance on office automation in Chapter 13. And the United States Women's Bureau has given continuous cooperation.

Among the union officers who have contributed in important

ways to chapters 9 and 10 on production and unionism in the textile and clothing industries, I am especially indebted to Dr. Lazare Teper, Director of the Research Department of the International Ladies' Garment Workers' Union, who gave much critical advice as well as information, and his Senior Research Assistant Walter Mankoff. Further help came from Howard Samuel, Assistant General President of the Amalgamated Clothing Workers of America, and Milton Fried, Research Director; and from Andrew Janaskie, General President of the Federation of Hosiery Workers. Solomon Barkin, Director of Research of the Textile Workers Union of America, also made a few useful comments.

On unionization in printing and publishing in Chapter 10, these members of the International Printing Pressmen and Assistants' Union were most helpful: Fred Roblin, Editor of *The American Pressman,* Walter M. Allen, Research Director, the late George L. Googe, Secretary-Treasurer, Walter J. Turner, Vice-President in charge of specialty printing, and Sol Fishko, President of Printing Specialties and Paper Products Union No. 447. Union President Anthony J. DeAndrade and Edward Kilheffer also read the manuscript critically. Informative members of the International Typographical Union were John J. Pilch, Vice-President, and Bertram Powers, President of New York Typographical Union No. 6. Officers of the International Brotherhood of Bookbinders and President James Moore of New York Bookbinders Local 25 also contributed information.

Howard Coughlin, President of the Office Employees' International Union, and his secretary, Dorothy Kroeber, answered questions on women in their union for Chapter 20; and I received generous help from Max Dombrow of the Community and Social Agency Employees' Union Local 1707 of the American Federation of State, County and Municipal Employees.

My sister, Olivetta Faulkner, and my friend, Marcus Heyman, read many of the chapters and made incisive comments which were carefully followed. I also pay tribute to Barnard College on the occasion of its seventy-fifth anniversary.

Finally, I wish to express a heartful of thanks to the Columbia University Business and General Reference librarians for their indefatigable assistance and their many courtesies beyond the call of duty throughout this long undertaking.

E.F.B.

Contents

Part I *A Century of Change*

1 Alexander Hamilton and the Eighteenth Century   3
2 Women at Work in the Textile Mills   8
3 Women at Work at Other Manufactures   24
4 Women at Work Away from the Factories   53
5 A Summary of a Century of Women's Work   75
6 The Status of Women in 1900   80
7 Early Protective Labor Legislation for Women   88

Part II *Six Decades of Change in Factory, Office,*
          and Shop

8 Traditional Occupations   99
9 Women in the Textile Industries   113
10 Women at Work on Other Nondurable Goods   148
11 Durable Goods and the Advent of Electronics   194
12 Twentieth Century Manufactures—the Advance
     of Automation   206
13 Women in the Office and the Electronic Computer   212
14 Women at the Switchboard   238
15 Women Behind the Counter   247

Part III *Change in Women's Professions*

16 Broadening Opportunities   259
17 Teachers and the Technology of Education   279
18 Nurses   312
19 Professional Women Since 1900   325

Part IV   White-Collar Unionism

20   Can White-Collar Workers be Organized?   335

Part V   Our Economy's Adjustments to Women's Work

21   Protective Labor Legislation   395
22   Summation, Adjustments, Special Problems   425

Bibliography   443

Index   451

PART I
A Century of Change

CHAPTER 1

Alexander Hamilton and the Eighteenth Century

In the early days when men hunted and fished for food, and in the agricultural age when they tilled the soil, their womenfolk performed the never-ending "motherhood occupations"—attending to the needs of the household, preparing the food, making the family clothing, rearing the children. And almost every family owned a loom, a spinning wheel, a reel, and knitting needles. Some families produced hundreds of yards of "homespun" in a single year.[1]

Then under the domestic system when winter prevented work in the fields, the men stayed at home and took over the weaving of yarns which the women and children had carded and spun. When there were not enough spinners in the family to keep the looms busy (especially after Kay's flying shuttle in 1733 that enabled one man to handle a wide loom more rapidly than two persons could operate it before), a homeless woman from the neighborhood would be employed to help. No matter how humble the living quarters, the man was the independent master and the woman learned both the forebearance and the persistence that were to serve her in paid occupations.

Indeed, women probably never worked harder than under the domestic system. In his classic report on manufactures in 1791, Secretary of the Treasury Alexander Hamilton expanded on the "vast scene of household manufacturing, which contributed more largely to the supply of the community than could be imagined, without having made it an object of particular inquiry." This "pleasing result" of his investigation, he said, was

[1] Meyer, p. 276.

"applicable as well to the southern as to the middle and northern states":

Great quantities of coarse cloths, coatings, serges, and flannels, linsey-woolseys, hosiery of wool, cotton, and thread, coarse fustians, jeans, and muslins, checked and striped cotton and linen goods, bedticks, coverlets, and counterpanes, tow linens, coarse shirtings, sheetings, toweling, and table linen, and various mixtures of wool and cotton, and of cotton and flax, are made in the household way, and, in many instances, to an extent not only sufficient for the supply of the families in which they are made, but for sale, and even in some cases for exportation. It is computed in a number of districts, that two-thirds, three-fourths, and even four-fifths of all the clothing of the inhabitants, are made by themselves.[2]

Ironically enough in view of her homebound traditions, the inventions which gave American factory production its start toward the end of the century were precisely those which served to call woman out of her home to seek a living—Hargreave's spinning jenny, Arkwright's throstle frame, Cartwright's power loom, and others. And after the War of the Revolution Watt's steam engine, which had sparked England's industrial advances, rapidly replaced the water wheel that required location on a stream, so that now where coal could be supplied New England textile mills could be built and operated near large towns where workers were plentiful.[3] Furthermore, Eli Whitney's cotton gin, invented in 1793,[4] greatly increased the supply of American cotton and prompted rapid develop-

[2] Alexander Hamilton, *Report on the Subject of Manufactures,* Vol. I, 1791 (New York, Williams and Whiting, 1810), pp. 210–11.

[3] Wright, p. 120.

[4] It has been held that the cotton gin was really invented by Catherine Littlefield Greene, widow of General Greene; that she intrusted its construction to Whitney, who was boarding with her at the time; and that when wooden teeth would not do the combing work it was she who suggested wire. She did not take out the patent in her own name, it was explained, because "to have done so would have exposed her to the ridicule and contumely of her friends and a loss of position in society, which frowned upon any attempt at outside industry for women." (Matilda Joslyn Gage, "Woman as an Inventor" in *North American Review,* May, 1883, pp. 482–83; *U.S. WB Bull. 28,* p. 5.)

ment of the textile industry with its need for improved machinery. And this need was also met, as we shall see, when Whitney invented machine tools which turned out standardized, interchangeable parts—an advance which would make division of labor possible and give rise to other occupations that would call for more and more women.

It was in 1789 that Samuel Slater, a mechanic who well knew textile machinery in the old country and became known as "the father of American cotton industry," came to the United States and built the first plant for carding and spinning yarn in Pawtucket, Rhode Island, for use of Arkwright's water-power spinning frame.[5] Owing to Britain's refusal to export machines and operators, Slater was obliged to reproduce the models from memory, and to train his own workers, whom he employed in families as in England—men, women, and children. By 1800, 15 mills in Massachusetts, Rhode Island, and Connecticut represented the organized cotton industry of the new nation, and New England appeared destined to be its center. Until 1814, however, when the power loom was introduced, the yarn was sent out to be woven in homes on hand looms. Now women and girls increasingly took on the weaving job.[6]

Along with his satisfaction at finding a "vast scene of household manufacturing," Secretary Hamilton hailed factory employment for women because it made development of the new system possible without taking men from the fields. In "the cotton mill invented in England, within the last twenty years," he reported:

All the different processes for spinning cotton, are performed by means of machines, which are put in motion by water, and attended chiefly by women and children; and by a smaller number of per-

---

[5] Kaempffert, II, 230, 322; Beverly, Massachusetts, is said to have been the citc of America's first cotton mill, built in 1787. (Bogart, pp. 245, 391.)

[6] Abbott, pp. 36, 45–46, 93–94; Clark, I, 535; *U.S. BLS Bull. 604*, pp. 84, 86.

sons, in the whole, than are requisite in the ordinary mode of spinning. And it is an advantage of great moment that the operations
of this mill continue with convenience, during the night, as well as
through the day.

Factories also, Hamilton urged,

afford occasional and extra employment to industrious individuals
and families, who are willing to devote the leisure resulting from
the intermissions of their ordinary pursuits to collateral labours, as
a resource for multiplying their acquisitions or their enjoyments.
The husband-man himself experiences a new source of profit and
support, from the increased industry of his wife and daughters; invited and stimulated by the demands of the neighbouring manufactories.

Beside this advantage of occasional employment to classes having different occupations . . . [is] the employment of persons who
would otherwise be idle, (and in many cases a burthen on the
community,) either from the bias of temper, habit, infirmity of
body, or some other cause, indisposing or disqualifying them for
the toils of the country. It is worthy of particular remark, that, in
general, women and children are rendered more useful, and the
latter more early useful, by manufacturing establishments, than
they would otherwise be. Of the number of persons employed in
the cotton manufactories of Great-Britain, it is computed that four-
sevenths nearly are women and children; of whom the greatest proportion are children, and many of them of tender age.

[The] scarcity of hands [is also diminished] by the vast extension
given by late improvements to the employment of machines, which,
substituting the agency of fire and water, has prodigiously lessened
the necessity for manual labour.[7]

Public moralists, too, acclaimed the factory employment of
women. In these men's views women who did not respond to
the call would be "doomed to idleness and its inseparable attendants, vice and guilt." But men like Tench Coxe, Gallatin,
and Mathew Carey shared Hamilton's thought that it was

[7] Hamilton, Report on Manufactures, I, 175–77, 192.

mainly to meet the nation's economic problems that women must be summoned to the factories.[8]

Woman's place was thus not in the home, according to our founders, but wherever her "more important" work was. She was not unschooled for her new duties in either temperament or discipline, and society would somehow have to make the necessary adjustments.

[8] Abbott, *pp.* 57, 321.

CHAPTER 2

Women at Work in the Textile Mills

Economic and political conditions kept women employed in their homes for more than a dozen years after Hamilton's exhortations. Agriculture and commerce were the profitable enterprises during the war between England and France and up to the time of the Embargo Act of 1807. Hence capital and labor were engaged in farming and shipping. But when that period had passed, and during the Anglo-American War of 1812, manufacturing arose:

as if by enchantment—on every stream she [the nation] formed for herself spacious dwellings, and collected in them many thousands who in no other way could contribute to the general weal. Those too young or too old to bear arms, who had no strength for agricultural labours—the female, whose domestic services could be dispensed with in her family, found here a means of individual gain, and of adding to the public prosperity.[1]

The Rise of Textile Manufacture

As early as 1815, therefore, 140 cotton manufacturers had set 130,000 spindles in operation in the general vicinity of Slater's mills.[2] And the large proportion of female workers in the "infant industries" became a major basis for protectionist arguments to prevent throwing back on the community for support "thousands of poor women and children for whom the ordinary business of agriculture [supplied] no opportunities for earning a livelihood."[3]

In accordance with Hamilton's thesis, home duties were thus

[1] George S. White, *Memoir of the Father of American Manufactures* (Philadelphia, 1836), p. 200.
[2] Kaempffert, II, 208.
[3] Abbott, p. 52.

considered of secondary importance, and economic, political, and technological magnets drew women into paid occupations. With their families they formed new communities where manufacturers chose locations near power and markets. Towns grew in size and household gardening and sheep raising tended to be abandoned as housewives found it cheaper and easier to buy clothing, food, soap, and other provisions at the stores than to prepare them at home.[4] In turn, as family tasks lessened many women became available for factory work for self-support or to contribute to the family income. In 1831, former Treasury Secretary Albert Gallatin pointed out in his "Memorial for the Free-Trade Convention" that although agriculture was more productive than manufactures, the employment of women in cotton and woolen industries was "much more productive than if applied to the ordinary occupations of women." He calculated that the annual value product of 200 females in a single cotton mill was $14,000.[5]

In that year a New York Convention of the Friends of Domestic Industry reported that 39,000 females were employed in the country's cotton mills, and that the immense sum of $4,000,000 in wages which they received annually could be considered "so much clear gain to society." For until these and other domestic manufactures were established the womenfolk were almost without employment. But now, daughters became a blessing to the farmer. In brief, as Mathew Carey put it, women were now "a source of wealth, rather than an incumbrance."[6]

THE LOWELL COTTON MILLS

Meanwhile a more complete type of cotton manufacture had been organized. In 1814—the year of the peace declaration

4 *U.S. WB Bull. 115*, p. 3.
5 Abbott, pp. 53–54.
6 *Ibid.*, pp. 54–56; Sumner, p. 55.

with England—Boston merchant and Harvard graduate Francis
Cabot Lowell and associates had formed the Boston Manufacturing Company. At Waltham, Massachusetts, they built the
world's first factory to perform all the operations of converting
raw cotton into cloth by the power loom which Lowell had designed from memory and imperfect drawings after close study
of textile machinery in Lancashire. Soon, Waltham became the
pattern for a group of cotton mills in and near the town named
after Lowell, which became known as the "City of Spindles." [7]

As early as 1816, therefore, the Committee of Commerce and
Manufactures reported to Congress that an estimated 66,000
women and girls were employed in the cotton industry, as
compared to 34,000 males, some two thirds of whom were
boys under 17. By 1832, females were thought to outnumber
males by more than 110 percent. Woman and child labor outside the home had really begun, with its characteristics of monotonous work and low pay for "women's jobs." [8]

Both machinery and morals at the Lowell mills were
planned for the employment of farmers' daughters who wanted
to earn money. To do this two British customs were broken.
The first was that at Waltham the Lowell mills adopted frame
spinning instead of mule spinning, which was awkward for
women because skirts interfered with following the yards-long
sliding carriage that moved back and forth on rails.[9] Women's
slacks would of course have been shocking in those days. In
a second innovation a paternal system of factory boarding
houses was established to protect the girls from the "horrible.

[7] Sumner, p. 50; Wright, p. 131; Bogart, p. 394.
[8] Sumner, pp. 50, 54–55; Abbott, pp. 89, 95.
[9] Quite a different "school" of cotton manufacture that followed English
precedent was established at Fall River, Massachusetts, in 1817. There, foreign
labor was introduced early and mule spindles operated by men were used.
Paid in goods instead of money, the employees were hired by families—men,
women, and many young children who were housed in company tenements
—a plan which appears to have spread to the factories of New York, Pennsylvania, New Jersey, and Maryland. (Sumner, pp. 53, 57; Abbott, pp. 121, 272;
Ware, p. 74; Bogart, p. 436; U.S. BLS Bull. 604, p. 88.)

experiences" of British factory women in the "dark Satanic Mills" of which William Blake wrote, which were coming to light at the time.[10]

Doubtless the scarcity of male operatives was also a factor. After being patriarchs in their own family domains under the domestic system, men preferred the independence of farm life to tending machines in a factory. To them the frontier was a refuge. Hence at the Waltham and Lowell mills they were employed only as overseers, painters, machinists, teamsters, card coverers, general laborers, and the like; and even these were probably English immigrants some of whom had small farms of their own where they could enjoy the fresh air while gardening and clearing and improving their property. In 1827, therefore, an estimated nine tenths of the 1200 persons in the Lowell mills were women and girls, only 20 of whom were as young as 12 and 14 years of age, the others ranging from 16 to 18.[11]

One way of recruiting the buxom daughters was to send out agents to county districts and pay them a stipulated price per head. Some firms added a premium when a girl was brought from such a distance that she could not easily get back. For it seems that one of the Lowell rules was that, once hired, an operative must remain at work for 12 months in order to receive what was termed "honorable discharge"; and she must give two weeks' notice of intention to leave. Absences from work were permitted only by consent of the overseer and only "in cases of absolute necessity" unless there were spare hands to take the places.[12]

On the other hand Lowell factories were carefully planned

[10] A favorite current argument against tariff protection for American manufacture was that the factory system produced a depraved and ignorant laboring class. (Sumner, p. 79; Ivy Pinchbeck, *Women Workers and the Industrial Revolution, 1750–1850* [London, George Routledge & Sons, 1930], pp. 194, 310–11.)

[11] Abbott, pp. 46, 89, 95, 121; Sumner, p. 52.

[12] Sumner, pp. 80, 97; Ware, p. 107.

to attract the young women by being organized to resemble as nearly as possible big boarding schools in which supervisory care was provided. All operatives were required to live in the company boarding houses, and one of the strict house rules was that doors were locked every evening at ten o'clock. The "house mothers" were carefully selected women "of perfectly correct and moral deportment," some of them widows whose own daughters worked in the mills. In sum, we are told that "abundant evidence exists to show that 'from the beginning, Lowell had a high reputation for good order, morality, piety, and all that was dear to the old-fashioned New Englander's heart.' " [13]

Employment in the Lowell group of factories before the middle of the century, as recorded by Edith Abbott, was therefore a socially respected occupation. All types of women had been dispossessed of their home carding, spinning, and weaving activities, and factory work and a few months of teaching were about the only occupations open to them. Thus the line between "working women" and "middle-class women" which would emerge in the second half of the century was scarcely discernible in the first half; and a girl who had worked at Lowell became a person of importance when she rejoined her rural neighbors. "Her fashionable dress and manners and her general air of independence were greatly envied by those who had not been to the metropolis and enjoyed its advantages." [14]

Many of these girls were sisters of young men who were "going west" to the prairie country, and they themselves were not without some pioneering spirit. A great many of them had attended the common schools and some were saving money to enter the women's academies or seminaries of the day. In 1837, Mary Lyon's Mount Holyoke Female Seminary for training teachers "broke upon the thoughts of many of them as a

13 Sumner, pp. 79–80, 85; Abbott, pp. 114, 116.
14 Abbott, pp. 110, 121.

vision of hope." [15] "For what were we?" questioned Lucy
Larcom in retrospect:

Girls who were working in a factory for the time, to be sure; but
none of us had the least idea of continuing at that kind of work
permanently. Our composite photograph, had it been taken, would
have been the representative New England girlhood of those days.
We had all been fairly [sic] educated at public or private schools,
and many of us were resolutely bent upon obtaining a better education. Very few were among us without some distinct plan for bet-
tering the condition of themselves and those they loved.

And she continued toward the end of the century:

For the first time, our young women had come forth from their
home retirement in a throng, each with her own individual purpose. For twenty years or so, Lowell might have been looked upon
as a rather select industrial school for young people. The girls
there were just such girls as are knocking at the doors of young
women's colleges to-day. They had come to work with their hands,
but they could not hinder the working of their minds also. Their
mental activity was overflowing at every possible outlet. [16]

Mill operatives thus often replenished the ranks of country
school teachers while the underpaid school mistresses did factory work when they could. [17]

Under these circumstances Lowell operatives were not inclined to chafe over long hours of work—12 to 13 a day; nor
to resent sleeping from four to eight in a small, badly ventilated room. They were near schools and circulating libraries;
many attended the Lyseum lectures of John Quincy Adams,
Edward Everett Hale, John Pierpont, and Ralph Waldo Emer-

[15] *Ibid.*, pp. 111–12; Newcomer, p. 11.

[16] Lucy Larcom, *A New England Girlhood* (Boston, Houghton's, 1889), pp.
222–23. Miss Larcom was one of eight children who worked on and off at
Lowell from 1825 to 1850 to help her widowed mother keep the "wolf from
the door," and contributed poems to the mill girls' *Lowell Offering*. At several
intervals during those years and after, she taught school. John Greenleaf
Whittier became interested in her poetry and eventually they collaborated in
making anthologies.

[17] Sumner, pp. 88–89; Abbott, pp. 111, 116–17, 120, 131–32.

son. Some were reading Dickens, Longfellow, Whittier, Hawthorne, Margaret Fuller, and others. In fact, these alert young women strove for "improvement of head and heart before that of situation . . . with all New England beckoning them back to their native hills." [18] Probably most of them expected to marry, and if not, there was the family home to which to return. Factory life was thus an episode and the Lowell girls colored it with their own hopes and ambitions, kept flowers in the factory windows and bits of poetry or passages from the Bible pasted up over their looms to be committed to memory. This was the "golden era" for factory girls and the factory was the "alma mater" for such women as Lucy Larcom and her associates.[19] Thirty years later Lucy Larcom had them speak out in poetry:

> In plain words
> I am a school ma'am in the summer time
> As now I am a Lady of the Loom,
>
> Character is not the stuff inside those factory walls
> That circumstances can spoil,—my gospel reads.
> And if it were, the daughters of our honest yeomanry,
> Children of tradesmen, teachers, clergymen
> Their own condition make in mingling.[20]

But the impression must not be left that all was sweetness and light in the Lowell mills. In fact there was a great deal of public, political, and medical discussion and protest against the long, hard hours of labor, the injurious cotton dust, and the bad ventilation in both boarding houses and factories. Moreover, "hundreds of thousands of girls," Larcom recalled, cared nothing for books but worked at Lowell as they would have

[18] Sumner, pp. 62, 87–88, 103; Abbott, "History of the Employment of Women in the American Cotton Mills," Part III, "Early Mill Operatives," cont'd., *JPE*, XVII (January, 1909), 19, 22.

[19] Sumner, pp. 89–90.

[20] Lucy Larcom, *An Idyl of Work* (Boston, R. Osgood & Co., 1875), pp. 18, 53.

worked earlier "at the family sewing or at any household toil at home" at the domestic arts, which were theirs for life.[21]

Hence in 1836 these Lowell operatives turned out on strike against a reduction in their already low wages; and in 1845 Sarah Bagley, calling herself "a common-schooled New England female factory operative," organized her Lowell associates into the Female Labor Reform Association, which took over the *Voice of Industry* under her editorship. In that labor paper, Miss Bagley accused the *Lowell Offering* of being "under the fostering care of the Lowell corporations, as a literary repository for the mental gems of those operatives who have ability, time, and inclination to write, and the tendency of it ever has been to varnish over the evils, wrongs, and privations of factory life." [22] Her vigorous campaign for a ten-hour day, combined with that the New England Working Men's Association, resulted in a Massachusetts legislative appointment of the first of several commissions to investigate working conditions in the textile mills. The final result of this, as we shall see, was that a quarter of a century later Massachusetts was the first state in the Union to enact an enforceable law limiting the working hours of women and children.

It was also during the fermenting forties that the character of the cotton-textile industry was undergoing rapid change. Control had passed from the original owners, wages were lowered, an influx of male immigrants prompted wider introduction of mule spinning, and weaving processes were speeded up so that the operatives were tending four looms instead of two.[23] Finally, the industrial depression of 1848–49 and the discovery of gold in California abetted the forces that marked a second turning point in woman's emergence from unpaid homework—this time away from the textile mills. As thousands

<hr>

[21] Sumner, pp. 100–108; Abbott, "Early Mill Operatives," *JPE*, pp. 24, 32n.

[22] Sumner, p. 90; Ware, "Sarah Bagley," *Encyclopaedia of the Social Sciences*, II, 385.

[23] Ware, p. 115; Abbott, pp. 96, 107–08.

of girls left Lowell and other mills to take manual occupations elsewhere, or to be teachers, nurses, missionaries, or wives, immigrant Irish women who had come as domestic servants gradually drifted into their places.[24] Thus by 1850, Sarah Bagley's following had so degenerated that the Female Labor Reform Association disappeared.[25]

As a result of these changes, women and girls formed only 69 percent of the working force in Lowell factories in 1848 as compared to 90 percent 20 years earlier. Before the middle 1850s one half of the operatives were Irish men and women, many of them refugees from the long famine in their country; and in the next decade Lowell lost its place as America's "Spindle City." [26]

After 1870, weaving was done on faster and more complicated looms that required more adjusting. Coarse, plain goods gave way to those that were bleached, dyed, and printed; and a new machine called a "slasher" was introduced for sizing the yarns in intense heat. The increased need for technical competence thus tended to increase the proportion of men and boys.[27] The overseers at Lowell and sister mills in Maine, New Hampshire, and Vermont thus imported families from Canada and Europe for work formerly done by American women, whom the Massachusetts governor had advised to go west.[28] Women were wanted as nurses and to fill teaching posts left

[24] Abbott, "Early Mill Operatives," *JPE*, pp. 27–28.
[25] Ware, "Sarah Bagley," p. 385.
[26] Abbott, "Early Mill Operatives," pp. 27–28; Sumner, p. 82; Clark, II, 105.
[27] Sumner, p. 57; Abbott, p. 99.
[28] According to a recent account, when the University of Washington's first president, Asa Mercer, discovered in the 1860s that Seattle's population was so masculine that it was "almost wholly beyond the reach of feminine influence and wholesome restraints," he journeyed to New England and brought back 57 "mill-working maidens" and Civil War widows who were greeted by the town bachelors and found homes or took up occupations such as school teaching and dressmaking. (Anne Grosvenor Robinson, "Seattle, City of Two Voices," *National Geographic Magazine*, April, 1960, p. 498; see also Sumner, p. 83; Lahne, pp. 3–4, 103.)

by men who had gone to the front; also, as we shall see, for various clerical positions.[29] By the end of the century, therefore, while the number of women cotton-mill workers aged 16 years and over had reached its heighest point—nearly 127,000 —the proportion women were of all employees had fallen to its lowest point—42 in 100.[30]

Recording what had occurred, the Twelfth Census noted that "the operation of some of the modern machines requires the care of men, because it is beyond the physical and nervous capacity of women"; that female mule spinners were even fewer in number than before; and that more men were themselves able to support their families, or else their wives and elder daughters had found employment in the shops and offices. The Census of 1905 added that

the number of places in which women can profitably be employed in a cotton mill in preference to men or on an equality with them, steadily decreases as the speed of machinery increases and as the requirement that one hand shall tend a greater number of machines is extended. Accordingly we find that without any concert of action—perhaps unconsciously to the general body of manufacturers— there is a slow but steady displacement of women by men.[31]

WOOL MANUFACTURE

Women were less numerous in the manufacture of wool than of cotton, but toward the close of the century the proportion of women to all wage earners in these two branches of the textile industry became almost the same. When woolen and worsted goods are taken separately, however, we find interesting differences. The American manufacture of worsted

[29] Abbott, "Early Mill Operatives," *JPE*, p. 29.

[30] Sumner, p. 251. When girls 10 to 16 years of age were included the number was some 148,000, or 49 in each 100. (Abbott, p. 102.)

[31] Sumner, p. 58; *U.S. Census Reports, 1900*, IX: *Manufactures*, Part III, pp. 32–33; *U.S. Census Reports, 1905*, *Manufactures*, Part III, "Special Reports," pp. 29, 30.

goods got its start in men's wear just after the Civil War, and it not only employed more women than did woolen goods but, unlike the cotton sector, it employed more women than men. In 1870 women constituted 55 percent of the workers on worsted, men 30 percent, and children 15 percent. In 1900, the respective proportions were 45.3, 44.8, and 9.7. In woolens and worsteds combined, the proportion of women in 1900 was little more than 40 in each 100 employees compared to a little less than 42 per 100 in cotton.[32]

The reason for the difference in the employment of women in woolen and worsted goods appears to have been mainly technological. In the manufacture of both, the wet and dirty preparatory processes of sorting and securing the wool were performed by men; and more men than women did the dusty, greasy job of carding. But then, whereas the short fibers used for woolen goods were ready for spinning, extra and intricate mechanical processes were necessary for the long-fiber worsteds before the yarn was spun. Here the "roving" (small strands wound on a jack spool) was combed—by machine after 1890—to extract the long fibers or "tops," and to lay them straight and parallel so that they emerged in a long, soft strand or rope fiber. By 1900, some 1,450 combing machines were in use in various states. Although the process required considerable reaching and stretching as well as constant standing, the operatives were largely women. It was a hot job but not dusty because the wool had been oiled. Another hot and humid woman's job was that of operating drawing frames in which the strand was more finely drawn out ready for the spinning.[33]

Then came the spinning and more twisting of the worsted yarn, handled also by women and children because it was usually done on a cap frame, while the woolen yarns were

[32] Sumner, pp. 59, 251–52; *U.S. Census Reports, 1900,* IX: *Manufactures,* Part III, p. 102; Clark, II, 422.

[33] *U.S. Census Reports, 1900,* IX: *Manufactures,* Part III, p. 83; U.S. Bureau of Labor, *Woman and Child Wage-Earners,* XVIII, pp. 331–32.

spun by men on a great spinning mule which, as in the cotton industry, was not for women because of their skirts.[34]

The weaving processes were practically the same for woolen and worsted goods. When the hand loom gave way to power about 1870, more women than men did the weaving. In the last decade of the century, however, many improvements increased the speed of the looms—from 100 to 115 pick per minute and in some classes of work to as much as 150 a minute—and this caused an increase in the proportion of men. The work of burling, mending, specking with ink, and kindred operations was largely for women, but, as in the preparatory processes, the wet and heavy finishing jobs of fulling, scouring, dying, shearing, and the like required men.[35]

Like cotton textiles, the wool industry was concentrated in the New England and eastern states, with smaller mills scattered throughout the Mid-west and South; but unlike cotton they reached as far as the Pacific coast. In a study of 46 mills just after the turn of the century, the United States Bureau of Labor found that the extent to which women and children were employed varied from mill to mill and from state to state —the proportion of women ranging from 12 to 77 in each 100 workers and the proportion of boys and girls from practically none to nearly 27 percent of all, with averages of 42 percent and 7 percent respectively. The Bureau's findings proved to be very near those for the industry as a whole as reported by the Census of 1905: of about 180,000 wage earners nearly 95,000 or 53 percent were men and 64,000 or 40 percent were women, the rest being children.[36]

In summing up its report on the wool industry at the turn

[34] U.S. Bureau of Labor, *Woman and Child Wage-Earners*, XVIII, 328, 331, 332; *MLR*, January, 1938, pp. 86, 89.

[35] *U.S. Census Reports, 1900*, IX: Manufactures, Part III, p. 79n; Sumner, p. 59; U.S. Bureau of Labor, *Woman and Child Wage-Earners*, XVIII, 330–31.

[36] U.S. Bureau of Labor, *Woman and Child Wage-Earners*, XVIII, 322–23, 332; Clark, II, 428–30; *U.S. Census Reports, 1900*, IX: *Manufactures*, Part III, pp. 83–85, 87; *U.S. Census Reports, 1905, Manufactures*, Part III, p. 90.

of the century, the Census Bureau noted that, since combing machines replaced hand combing, the woolen branch—broadcloths, doeskins, cassimeres, jeans, flannels, woolen and cotton mixed dress goods, and the like—appeared in danger of taking a place second to the worsted branch, including suitings, dress goods, unholstery goods, and braids, and large quantities of yarns for carpets. "The introduction of the worsted cloth for men's wear and the wonderful development of the knit-goods manufacture," said the Bureau, "have made great inroads on the consumption of carded wool goods which formerly were necessities, substituting combed wool fabrics for men's wear and knitted underwear in place of flannels." [37]

KNIT-GOODS MANUFACTURE

The knit-goods industry differed from the other branches of textile manufacture by making the garments as well as the fabrics. And although women's monopoly was broken at the end of the eighteenth century when men took over the knitting on hand looms, and on factory power looms in the 1830s, this is the only one of the major textile industries in which women's employment expanded as compared to that of men. Many women followed their work into the factory, and before 1850 the *Workingman's Advocate* noted that "a girl can make, with a power loom, 20 pairs of drawers a day." Men appear to have retained the actual weaving while women, in and out of their homes, sewed and finished various articles to make "leisure hours add to the income and comforts of their families." [38]

In those days the industry was producing "half-fashioned goods" in which the product of the machine was passed along to be cut to pattern and sewed on the sewing machine. The Civil War decade stimulated the industry both by heavy demands from the quartermaster and by a mechanical device

[37] *U.S. Census Reports, 1900,* IX: *Manufactures,* Part III, pp. 99, 101.
[38] Sumner, pp. 59–60.

that turned out seamless goods automatically. And well before 1900 machines were producing full-fashioned goods, including ribbed underwear and long, full-fashioned cashmere hose for women.[39] In a study of hand and machine methods, the United States Commissioner of Labor discovered that machines in this trade had quickened production by as much as four to 280 times. "Power machinery has come in as a magical assistant to the power of muscle and mind," Commissioner Wright commented.[40]

Full-fashioned knitting machines were complex and "invariably" operated by men of several years training; but the other machines required only semi-skilled work which could be learned in two to six weeks. Here was work for women, as well as in the sewing-machine operations and on light handwork such as mending, stamping, sorting, folding, and boxing, which called only for dexterity, exactness, and willingness to repeat a series of simple movements all day long. Thus, whereas in 1870 women numbered 8,000 or 54 percent of all hands, by 1900 the industry was absorbing more than 53,500 women— back to the 64 percent of all employees which they had attained in 1850 when the total number of women and girls was not quite 1,500.[41]

SILK MANUFACTURE

When silk factories began to appear after 1829 it was expected that raising silkworms and reeling and preparing the silk would provide "healthful, profitable, and pleasant" employment to vast numbers of women and children at their own homes. More females than males were employed on the power loom for weaving silk, which began to displace the hand loom

[39] Clark, II, 443–45.
[40] Carroll D. Wright, U.S. *Commissioner of Labor's Thirteenth Annual Report, 1899,* "Hand and Machine Labor," I, 289; Wright, p. 335.
[41] U.S. Bureau of Labor, *Woman and Child Wage-Earners,* XVIII, 197, 199; Sumner, pp. 60, 252.

before the middle of the century, and had rendered it practically obsolete by 1900. By 1860 more than six out of ten workers in the manufacture of silk, silk goods, sewing, and twist were women and girls. In fact this preponderance of females was one reason for the rapid development of the industry during the Civil War and Reconstruction periods.[42] Paterson, New Jersey, became known as the "silk city" of the country, not only because it had a large supply of water power and sufficient clean water to process the silk and was near consuming and distributing centers, but also because it supplied cheap labor from the families of men employed in the city's machine shops and locomotive works.[43]

Furthermore, improved machinery in the mid-seventies for "throwing" silk (the spinning process of twisting the filaments from the cocoons into weft threads for weaving) speeded up spindle revolutions from 3,500 to an optimum of 10,000 per minute; and the operation could be managed by two attendants, one on each side. Still further advances in throwing machinery in the last decade of the century enabled unskilled females to replace males, with the result that for this operation alone broadsilk and ribbon mills opened annexes in the mining towns of Pennsylvania, where they employed miners' wives and daughters who until then had been without industrial employment. This in turn tended to attract other branches of the industry, perhaps especially when the increasing adoption of the power loom also enabled women and girls to replace men. On the other hand wherever there was a change from the "Swiss motion" to the "heavy and arduous" work of "horizontal warping," men displaced women.[44]

The effects of technological change in opening up new op-

[42] U.S. Bureau of Labor, *Woman and Child Wage-Earners*, IV, 34; Sumner, pp. 60–61.
[43] Clark, II, 118–19; Alderfer and Michl, p. 417.
[44] Sumner, p. 61; Clark, II, 453–54; U.S. Bureau of Labor, *Woman and Child Wage-Earners*, IV, 18–20, 35–40, 205.

portunities for women in the silk and silk-goods industries were thus noteworthy. By 1900 nearly 35,000 women were so employed as compared to less than 2,000 women and girls 40 years before; but it is worth noting that the proportion of women in 1900—53 percent—was the same as in 1870. Technology had pushed men in at the top, women down, and children out.[45]

ANOTHER TURNING POINT FOR WOMEN

The shifts in the distribution of workers in the silk industry appear to have followed the trend for the textile industry as a whole, heavily weighted as it was by the cotton sector, which first took women out of their homes, then saw many of them leave for other occupations. In 1850, the nearly 87,000 female hands were half of all those employed in the textile industries, while a half century later the nearly 303,000 women 16 years of age and over were scarcely 41 percent of the total.

The Civil War period seems to have been the turning point for women in textiles. The shutdown of cotton factories at that time caused women to seek other factory and nonfactory employment from which they did not return when the mills reopened. Hence the men of imported Canadian and European families were employed to do much of the work formerly done by women.[46]

[45] U.S. Bureau of Labor, *Woman and Child Wage-Earners,* IV, 31; Sumner, pp. 61, 252.
[46] Sumner, pp. 83, 250, 251–52.

CHAPTER 3
Women at Work at Other Manufactures

The Principle of Interchangeable Parts

Probably no single technological advance had a more radiating impact upon women's work than the invention and adaptation of the principle of interchangeable parts, which made possible what Europeans called "the American system of manufacture." Only a few years after the great contribution of the cotton gin and in time for the War of 1812, Eli Whitney perfected a system by which he produced musket parts that were so exactly alike—and therefore interchangeable—that they could be assembled automatically into quantities of completed weapons for the government. Here was the key to mass production in industry, in which women were to have an important role. For here, in a system of processes, automatic power-driven machines which could usually be tended by "cheap labor" would be turning out textile machinery, sewing machines, agricultural implements, watches and clocks, locomotives, typewriters, telephones, automobiles, and many other products, as well as the tools that make the machines, all of which must otherwise have been fashioned one by one, if at all, by skilled craftsmen.

Thus, as we shall see, when toward the end of the century electricity made it possible to drive mass-production operations with electric energy, women were also to be drawn into a relatively new world of durable-goods manufacture. Meanwhile, let us witness the effects of new machines upon their traditional occupations.

Manufactures—Nondurable Goods

THE SEWING MACHINE AND CLOTHING MANUFACTURE

An early application of the principle of interchangeable parts—and a pivotal instrument of social change—was the production of Elias Howe's sewing machine in 1846 with its eye-pointed needle, which in the improved Singer machines became a revolutionary force in clothing manufacture. Whether by hand or machine, sewing had always been woman's work, and now the new device made it possible to sew on heavier materials such as leather. But we are reminded that, in general, machinery and the division of labor in the clothing trades did only to a lesser degree what machinery and division of labor did in the textile trades. It transferred the woman worker from home to factory, but less completely because of the relative simplicity and inexpensiveness of the sewing machine.

The Singer machines, with their foot treadle, improved tension, double-pointed shuttle, and lock stitch, were ready for clothing makers to fill orders for uniforms for Civil War soldiers. For example, a single New York establishment in 1862 is said to have used 400 sewing machines and produced some 10,000 shirts in a week. When the conflict was over, returning soldiers wanted ready-to-wear civilian clothes, and European immigrants chose American clothes to replace their peasant costumes. Hence, by 1870, Clark tells us that "the mass of the male population of the United States was clad in ready-made clothing." [1]

Soon a new cutting knife made it possible to cut several layers of cloth at a time, which required greater strength than cutting a single ply with shears. There was, therefore, a gradual replacement of women cutters by men. Wholesale shops now put the pieces to be made into garments into the homes of the tailors, who worked under the family system, with their wives and children. The woman ran the sewing machine and did the less important handwork of finishing and bottom sewing, also the buttonhole making until in the late seventies a buttonhole machine mechanized that process. These contrivances were run by foot power, and clumsy and heavy though

[1] Clark, II, 431; Kaempffert, II, 381, 385, 390–91, 393–94; Meyer, p. 285; U.S. Bureau of Labor, *Woman and Child Wage-Earners*, II, 486.

they were, they were usually operated by women in the small shop as well as at home. Payments were made by the piece, which often induced serious overstrain because the operators could control output by controlling the machine.[2]

Beginning about 1880, other revolutionizing changes entered the men's clothing industry which in one way or another were to have special effects upon the employment of women. An influx of new immigrants began to crowd out English, Irish, and German tailors; the shop or factory began gradually to replace the home; steam, gas, and electricity supplemented foot power for driving the machines. For example, on a power-driven machine a girl could make more than 3,000 buttonholes a day as compared to the 100 a day that a skilled tailor could make by hand.[3] The work, however, was often done under far worse conditions than before—to the extent that this has been called "the darkest period in the clothing industry." It was the prelegislation period of sweatshops under the contract system, with the accompanying evils of low wages, long hours, seasonal employment, unsanitary, overcrowded, and ill-ventilated workrooms—all intensified by constant immigration. The nearly 81,000 women over 15 years of age who were employed on the factory product and customwork constituted more than half of these "sweated" workers.[4] We shall see in Chapter 7 that state legislation for the special protection of women and children began in these years.

The influx of immigrants, especially the Russian Jews in New York City, is said to have reduced the employment of women in this industry: first, because there were more men than women among them; second, because of "a general racial opposition" to employing women; third, because the pace set

[2] Sumner, pp. 177 ff.; Lazare Teper, *The Women's Garment Industry, an Economic Analysis* (Educational Department, International Ladies' Garment Workers' Union, 1937), p. 11.

[3] Clark, II, 447.

[4] Abbott, p. 234; Meyer, pp. 287–88; U.S. Bureau of Labor, *Woman and Child Wage-Earners*, II, 487–91.

in some branches of the trade was considered too great for women to maintain; and fourth, because legislation after 1892 tended to force work from home to outside shop. Hence, while the number of women at work on men's clothing rose to nearly 90,000 in 1900, their proportion fell to 47 percent of the labor force compared to 64 percent in 1860. When men's shirts and other furnishing goods were added to factory and custom-made suits, the Census of Manufactures counted 146,000 women, or 57 in every 100 employees in this field.[5]

Women's apparel was largely a household product as late as 1880, with the exception of cloaks, which were being ready-made in factories almost entirely by women, even including the skilled work of cutting. Then as women's tailored suits came into vogue, followed by shirtwaists and ready-to-wear undergarments, more men came into the picture, with the result, according to the Twelfth Census of 1900, that although the number of factory women in this branch of the trade had more than doubled, the nearly 57,000 of them formed only 68 percent of all workers. In other words a goodly number of men were doing what had formerly been "woman's work"— that of dressmakers and seamstresses, occupations which the *Boston Courier* had cynically suggested for men back in 1830 when times were "out of joint"—because woman was encroaching upon "the exclusive dominion of man." [6]

BOOTS AND SHOES

In sharp contrast to soft clothing and cotton-cloth manufacture, the boot and shoe industry proved to be an almost en-

---

[5] Sumner, p. 253; Abbott, pp. 229–34; Abbott and Breckinridge, p. 34; Willett, p. 72.

[6] Sumner, pp. 14, 253; Her table shows, however, that nearly 41,000 women still formed 90 percent of all employees in nonfactory "dressmaking." And we shall note in Chapter 6 that on high authority the census method of classifying dressmakers, seamstresses, tailors, and tailoresses in 1900 was so inadequate as to render the statistics "of very questionable value," because no one knew the nature of the work they included (Abbott and Breckinridge, p. 33); Abbott, pp. 240–41.

tirely new field of work for women, though fluctuating, narrowly defined, and requiring no skill. By machinery and the factory system, the binding of shoes was rescued for women from the "degradation of the other sewing trades." Moreover, wages were higher than in the cotton mills, and competition from the foreign born was not so great as in the textiles.[7]

Women had no part in shoemaking before the end of the eighteenth century. There was first the village cobbler, and in the Revolutionary War period the boot was made by a "team" of men. Then by 1800 it was recognized that women and children in the family could well be used to "stitch and bind," and this part of the operation became "women's work" as the industry grew large and prosperous. In those days, in nearly every home there was "Hannah, sitting in the window, binding shoes."[8]

The manufacture of ladies' shoes became a specialty in Lynn, Massachusetts, where many women were employed because the work was lighter and less fatiguing than on men's shoes. While the skilled male in the shop served an apprenticeship of seven years and learned the whole trade, the female did her unskilled work of stitching and binding at home along with her domestic duties; and in the coast fishing villages where shoemaking occupied fishermen during the winter, wives and daughters did the binding during the rest of the year. As early as 1829, Lynn's 62 shoe factories employed some 1,500 women binders and trimmers and 1,500 "mechanics," while in large cities shoebinders became victims of the sweating system under "garret bosses." Both skilled and unskilled work was done by hand.[9]

It was in the seminal forties that the primitive methods of shoemakers' shops and binders' homes began to be replaced by machine operation. The leather-rolling machine of 1845

[7] Sumner, pp. 116, 174.
[8] Abbott, pp. 149–52; Andrews and Bliss, p. 42.
[9] Abbott, pp. 152, 155–56, 163.

saved men's labor, and a few years later there was a radical change in women's work when it was discovered that the sewing machine could be successfully used with dry thread for stitching and binding.[10] In 1852 a "Singer patent" for stitching shoe uppers was installed in a Lynn factory and a woman was engaged to run it. Stitching shops were set up in various parts of the city and, as steam power was substituted for foot power, the women moved from home to factory. But in a single decade the wider use of heavy sewing machines and waxed thread reduced the proportion of women employees in Massachusetts to 31 percent; and in the nation as a whole their number fell from 33,000 to 28,500—from 31 to 23 percent of all workers.[11]

The sewing of shoe uppers to soles had always been done by men; but just when men were going off to war in 1862 the McKay sole-sewing machine—which did in one hour what the journeyman had done in 80—was introduced and women were put to operating it to help meet the enormous demand for soldiers' footwear. It proved too heavy for them to manage, however, as was the Goodyear welt machine that soon followed, so by the 1870s it appears that, despite the radical changes in the nature of the work, the division of labor between the sexes had been little altered. Women and girls continued to fit linings and sew shoe uppers while men did the cutting, the sewing of uppers and soles, the "heeling," "finishing," and kindred things—all by mechanisms not belted to steam. Women assisted in the preparations for "lasting," or putting the shoe together.[12]

By 1900 the Twelfth Census reported a remarkable increase in the number of women and children employed in boot- and shoemaking and a slight drop in the number of men. The explanation was that "women are largely taking the places of

[10] *Ibid.*, p. 163.
[11] *Ibid.*, p. 166; Sumner, p. 171.
[12] Abbott, pp. 173–74; Commons, "American Shoemakers," p. 73.

men . . . in the operation of the lighter kind of machinery, and children are, to a considerable extent, succeeding to the places made vacant by women." The nearly 47,000 women thus formed a third of all employees as compared to 30 percent ten years earlier. In the stitching room alone there were 49 processes instead of the single one done by one woman before the advent of the sewing machine; and in the industry as a whole the census noted 126 different classes of operations—perhaps a more minute division of labor than in any other industry. The dividing line between "men's work" and "women's work" was still only slightly dimmed, however, but native-born women seemed to have found a permanent place in this man's trade.[13]

THE DAUGHTERS OF ST. CRISPIN

Women were more active in this industry than in other trades, but not as strikebreakers for the reason that mechanization had not enabled them to do the men's work as we shall see that it did in cigar making. In 1833, supported by the Men's Cordwainers Union, women formed the Female Society of Lynn and Vicinity for the Protection and Promotion of Female Industry. There they expressed the conviction that "women as well as men have certain inalienable rights," and resolved to establish a uniformity of prices for their work and "to form other salutary regulations . . . relating to their common welfare." In the same decade New York shoebinders formed at least a temporary organization, also in Philadelphia, where during a strike the men's society resolved "to flourish or sink" with them.[14]

In 1860, 1,800 Lynn shoe stitchers joined the journeymen in a vigorous strike against reduction of wages following the financial crisis of 1857, and by the end of the decade the only women's national trade union in the country was formed—the

[13] Abbott, pp. 177–78, 180–82, 184.
[14] Andrews and Bliss, pp. 41–45.

Daughters of St. Crispin—initiated by the Grand Lodge of the Knights of St. Crispin, which rose (1868–72) in protest against the "new menace of cheap labor and green hands" that chalgened their status. The Daughters held four annual conventions—1869–72—at the second of which they condemned "one sister's making a percentage on another sister's labor" and assured "our fellow-citizens that we only desire to so elevate and improve our condition as to better fit us for the discharge of these high social and moral duties, which devolve upon every true woman." [15]

The Daughters called two strikes against the "boss stitchers" in 1872. The more important and successful one was in Lynn against wage reductions for the highest paid stitchers in order to increase the wages of the lowest paid ones—again "to establish more uniform prices." With the support of the Knights, they resolved at a special meeting to protect their "rights and privileges, as free-born women . . . to the fullest extent of our ability." [16] In common with other national unions, however, the Daughters practically disappeared in the industrial depression that began in 1873. Three years later some 200 persistent women shoeworkers attempted to reorganize a Lynn local. It did not prosper, but "many of its members carried with them into the assemblies of the Knights of Labor a knowledge of unionism that greatly aided the leaders of that movement." At the close of the century the newly formed Boot and Shoe Workers' Union was urging all classes of men and women to unite in a single industrial union.[17]

TOBACCO

Cigar Making and Union Activity. Technological innovation was only one of four major forces that drew women into cigar making, for even at the end of the nineteenth century this

---

[15] *Ibid.*, pp. 16, 108–09; Commons, "American Shoemakers," pp. 73, 74.
[16] Abbott, pp. 171–72.
[17] Andrews and Bliss, pp. 16, 110; Commons, "American Shoemakers," p. 75.

sector of the tobacco industry was still in transition between handicraft and machine production.[18] The other forces were the nature of the industry itself, extensive immigration, and strikebreaking.[19]

Cigar making was one of the early household industries in Connecticut, Pennsylvania, and other tobacco-growing states, and by 1905 it had spread into every part of the country. The first very inferior cigars, we are told, were rather generally sold or exchanged for dry goods and groceries at the country store; and women seemed particularly qualified to make them because the work was not heavy, and skill depended upon manual dexterity and a sensitive touch.[20]

Farmers' wives continued to roll cigars until, in 1862, the imposition of the federal revenue tax prompted an exodus of the trade from home to factory and the employment of men who made a superior product. The best cigar was entirely handmade by a single craftsmen who shaped his own "bunch" in his hand, bound it, and put on the wrapper.[21]

The cigar maker's craft was twice challenged in 1869 when his work was subdivided: first, by the use of the wooden "mold" from Germany in which women who learned the trade in a year or less could shape and bunch under artificial pressure; second, when the first of thousands of immigrant Bohemian women cigar makers, after the destruction of their factories in the war between Prussia and Austria, introduced a "team system" in which young girls could be employed to prepare and roll the bunches.[22]

In the eighties there was rapid introduction of tools and

[18] Meyer Jacobstein, *The Tobacco Industry in the United States* (New York, Columbia University Dissertation, 1907), p. 140.

[19] Sumner, p. 198.

[20] Abbott, pp. 187, 190–91; U.S. Bureau of Labor, *Woman and Child Wage-Earners*, XVIII, 90.

[21] Sumner, p. 199; Jacobstein, *The Tobacco Industry*, p. 84.

[22] Sumner, p. 198; Jacobstein, *The Tobacco Industry*, pp. 83–84; Abbott, pp. 198–200, 202.

machinery for the production of cheap cigars—for stripping and bunching the tobacco and for cutting leaf-wrappers on a metal sheet with a perforated plate in the center, known as a suction table. These changes caused the beginning of a transfer of woman's work from tenements to large factories, and handwork on cheap cigars almost disappeared.[23]

Were women members of the union in this industry? Apparently the cigar makers believed at first that it was better to have them in the union than outside it. So in 1867, only three years after its formation, the Cigar Makers' International Union altered its constitution to admit women to membership. And in 1875 a clause was added which prohibited local unions from refusing membership applications "on account of sex or system of working." More than that, the *Cigar Makers' Journal* admitted that once women became members they were as faithful as men to the principles of unionism. But the International's demand for equal pay for equal work for women proved to be the opening for strikebreakers. This was because the competition of unskilled women pulled all women's wages down to less than half those of men, which were also not high.[24]

The 1870s thus became a crucial decade for organized cigar makers. Women and boys came into the Cincinnati trade with the introduction of molding devices as a result of a long strike against wage reductions, and the union retaliated by refusing membership to any women. The officers explained that they had tried to get them into the union, but had decided that "if they would not work with us, we would work against them." In 1877 a big general strike occurred in which many women joined the strikers in "the spirit of the struggle," while a large

23 Abbott, pp. 199, 203–04; Sumner, p. 199; Lucy Winsor Killough, *The Tobacco Products Industry in New York and its Environs* (New York, Regional Plan and its Environs, 1925), p. 21.

24 Andrews and Bliss, pp. 92–94; Sumner, p. 205; Jacobstein, *The Tobacco Industry*, p. 165; Abbott, p. 208.

number of others were employed as strikebreakers. In New York City more than half of the cigar makers are said to have been women working in crowded and filthy tenement houses, small shops, and large factories. Hence when Bohemian women joined the strikers, several hundred American girls who had been taught the trade were ready to take their places.[25]

In the light of all this experience what was the International Union to do about the woman problem? The answer is that it advocated "protective" legislation! In 1878 the Baltimore local sent the defiant message to Union President Adolph Strasser that "we have combatted from its incipiency the movement of the introduction of female labor in any capacity whatever, be it bunch maker, roller, or what not." And in the very next year Strasser gave voice to his solution:

We can not drive the females out of the trade, but we can restrict this daily quota of labor through factory laws. No girl under 18 should be employed more than eight hours per day; all overwork should be prohibited; white married women should be kept out of factories at least six weeks before and six weeks after confinement.[26]

We shall see in later chapters that the Cigar Makers were unsuccessful in their scheme to hold the trade for themselves by legislation against employment of women, but that New York tenement-house labor began to be regulated in 1892. At this point it is enough to note that women were increasingly drawn into the cigar trade by machinery in large factories that turned out the cheaper cigars; and also that both foremen and manufacturers were said to have testified that "the highest possible skill" in handmade cigars was attained by some women who were "equal to any man." Moreover, since it was an unwritten law of the trade that the cigar maker always

[25] Abbott, pp. 200–201; Sumner, pp. 201–202; Andrews and Bliss, pp. 92–94.

[26] Andrews and Bliss, pp. 92, 94.

"gets his smokes off the boss," it was a considerable saving to employ women because they did not smoke.[27]

This may have been prophetic testimony for the twentieth century. For we find the Census of Occupations in 1900 recording that the percentage of married women in the manufacture of cigars and tobacco was larger than in any other occupational group except that of seamstresses. Competent women said they could earn enough to "make it pay" to continue on the job and "hire a cheaper woman" to help at home with the children. "It's a trade you always come back to." [28]

But aside from the Bohemians, who had been thoroughly trained in their own country, relatively few women acquired the skill of cigar makers. Unlike boys, they were usually unwilling to serve their apprenticeships in view of the hope of marriage, and parents were even less willing to undergo the necessary sacrifices. Employers also deemed it not worthwhile to teach a girl who was likely to leave the trade soon. Nevertheless, organized cigar makers in 1894 considered themselves "confronted with child and female labor to an alarming extent." More than that, since the industry continued to turn out handmade as well as mold-made and cheap cigars, the Union asked the American Federation of Labor in 1901 for passage of resolutions opposing employment of both machinery and women.[29]

MANUFACTURED TOBACCO

In contrast to cigar making, the domestic system of manufacturing plug, chewing, and pipe tobacco gave way early to factory production with semiautomatic machines operated by

[27] Abbott, pp. 202–04; Sumner, p. 201.
[28] Abbott, pp. 210–11, Killough notes, p. 26, that some cigar manufacturers made special efforts to locate their factories where married women were available and arranged working hours so they could meet family needs and start the children off to school.
[29] Abbott, pp. 207, 213–14.

unskilled men, women, and children, largely in industrial centers and in southern states. Much of the work was tending and feeding the machines where only deftness and quick motion were required; and a few more highly skilled workers wrapped, made twists, and spun roll. By 1880 more than half of the working force were women and children who received "incredibly low wages." In general the occupations were fairly clearly defined by sex, but where unions had a foothold men and women are said to have received the same pay for the same work. It may be noted, however, that the 25,000 membership of the Tobacco Workers' International Union, organized in 1895, had fallen to 4,000 in 1901 as a result of absorption of many of the independent tobacco factories by the Tobacco Trust, which had been formed in the cigarette industry in 1890.[30]

The manufacture of snuff was the most complicated and oppressively odorous of all tobacco occupations, and women took no part in it except in the packing and labeling rooms.[31]

CIGARETTES

Cigarette making was a relatively minor industry up to the twentieth century, and the product was reported by the Census Bureau only in combination with cigars. In its modern form it was mechanized almost from the first, however, and beginning in the 1870s it grew more than eightyfold from some 40 million to some 3,260 million cigarettes in 25 years.[32] Men were employed where physical strength was needed and in a few skilled occupations such as adjusting the machines. Women tended the lighter machines, carried cigarettes to

---

[30] Jacobstein, The Tobacco Industry, pp. 40–41, 141–45, 202–03.

[31] U.S. Bureau of Labor, Woman and Child Wage-Earners, XVIII, 315–16.

[32] U.S. Census Reports, 1900, IX: Manufactures, Part III, pp. 671–72. Much of the popularity of cigarette smoking, the Census Bureau noted, originated in business and social circles where for many years there had been an increasing demand for a short, inexpensive smoke that produced immediate results.

packers, put on the revenue stamps, packed and labeled the cartons. If the leaves had not been stripped before they arrived at the factory, this was other work for women. By 1900, therefore, the number of women in cigar and cigarette making had risen to nearly 38,000 or 36 percent of all employees compared to but 3,000 or 11 percent thirty years earlier.[33]

As the twentieth century opened tobacco had become a fixed charge in many American budgets; and in the industry as a whole the census reported employment of well over 53,-000 women, or 38 in every 100 wage earners compared to only 2,000 women and girls—14 percent of all—in 1850.[34]

PRINTING AND PUBLISHING

Like cigar making, but unlike boot and shoe manufacture, printing was a family enterprise in the eighteenth century. Also like the cigar trade and unlike that of boots and shoes, women in the printing industry were used as strikebreakers in the nineteenth century. But unlike cigar making, technological changes in printing as in shoemaking failed to draw many women into men's jobs.

In the small family office of the eighteenth century one or more women were found operating presses and setting type in the eight states of Massachusetts, Connecticut, Rhode Island, Pennsylvania, New York, Maryland, Virginia, and South Carolina; and some of them became proprietors in printing offices.[35] By 1815, Isaiah Thomas noted that women and girls were "not infrequently" employed as compositors in printing houses, and that two women at the press in Philadelphia performed "their

[33] U.S. Bureau of Labor, *Woman and Child Wage-Earners*, XVIII, 77–79, 88; Sumner, p. 256.

[34] Sumner, pp. 250, 256. A picture of a long cigarette-making machine in the New York State *Industrial Bulletin* for August, 1961, suggests that cigarette manufacture anticipated the phenomenon of automation when in 1894 this single device began to produce cigarettes automatically—shredded tobacco and paper being fed in at one end and the completed cigarettes emerging at the far end.

[35] Barnett, p. 309; Abbott, p. 246; Sumner, p. 213.

week's work with as much fidelity as most of the journeymen."
In 1831 young girls were said to be "very adroitly superintend-
ing the printing of sheets by a press worked by horse power." [36]

Even at that time, however, woman's path was not smooth.
She had both friends and enemies. For example, in 1830 the
Boston *Courier* denounced employment of women in book
printing as "an evil of recent growth" because the number
was "sufficient to lessen very considerably the calls for journeymen and to dishearten all who, as apprentices, were ambitious
of distinguishing themselves as faithful and skilled printers."
Concurrently it was asserted in Philadelphia that "in consequence of the improved machinery . . . in printing, and by the
substitution of boys and girls for men in . . . printing offices,
there are . . . between two and three hundred journeymen
printers who have been able at best to obtain but occasional
employment in the occupation in which they have been educated." And in the following year it was estimated that 200
women were employed in printing in Boston.[37]

In Philadelphia women were receiving encouragement from
the *Banner of the Constitution,* which congratulated Boston
printers for having found female labor a means of lowering
costs of production. This paper attributed the destitution of
20,000 females in northern cities to "the American system,"
which it said had thrown their husbands and fathers out of
work; and now there was no reason why the printing business
should not be turned over to women. Moreover, since "the
labor of females can not command more than half the wages
that men can," their employment "would have a powerful influence in reducing the expenses of printing." [38]

Printing in those years seems in fact to have been a rather

---

[36] Sumner, p. 212; Abbott, p. 247.
[37] Sumner, p. 213.
[38] *Ibid.,* p. 214. The allied printing trades of Boston were reported to be
employing 687 men at about $1.50 a day and 395 women at about 50 cents a
day—the rate which 215 boys received. (Abbott, p. 249.)

important occupation for women. So much so, we are told, that striking shoebinders in Lynn in 1834 considered it a possible alternative employment to shoebinding. And in the same decade Harriet Martineau listed typesetting and bookbinding as two of seven occupations she found open to women.[39] In 1845 the New York *Tribune* reported that girls were operating most of the light-powered presses in book offices; and in the fifties in Philadelphia, where power presses had been installed in all leading establishments, many of the employees who tended them were reported to be females. Also in the sixties typesetting in many New York printing offices was said to have been done largely by women, and except for the offices of the morning daily newspapers, which required night labor, "the work that they are able to do equals both in quantity and quality that done by men." In a number of smaller cities forewomen were being employed.[40]

THE COMPOSING ROOM AND UNION ACTIVITY

But printing did not become a trade that women could make their own, as did cigar making. For one reason it was and continued to be largely skilled work which required apprenticeship. For another reason, which Abbott attributed to "jealousy," men wanted the trade for themselves; and by strong union policy they discouraged ambitious girls from learning it. Hence the girls learned what they could and got jobs in nonunion shops or as strikebreakers.[41]

In his classic book on *The Printers*, Professor Barnett recorded that as early as 1832 the Philadelphia Typographical

[39] Sumner, p. 213; Abbott, "Harriet Martineau and the Employment of Women in 1836," in *JPE*, XIV (1906), 615.

[40] Sumner, pp. 212, 219–20.

[41] Abbott, pp. 250–51. During a compositors' strike in New York in 1869, Susan B. Anthony is said to have appealed to employing printers for aid in organizing a school to teach typesetting to girls. "Give us the means," she pleaded, "and we will soon give you competent women compositors." Perhaps because of opposition by the International Typographical Union no such school was founded. (Sumner, p. 221.)

Society was disturbed by a report that Mathew Carey, economist and publisher, had promised a foremanship to a nonunion printer if he would agree to employ women as compositors.[42] Three years later the Columbia Society of Washington
was struck with dismay when members learned that some
Philadelphia women were to be taught typesetting, then to
be brought to Washington to work for General Duff Green; and
in that year girls were employed to break a Philadelphia newspaper strike. It seems, however, that there is no contemporary
evidence that women were employed as journeymen printers
in either Philadelphia or Washington; but in 1836 a committee
of the National Trades' Union, which included pressmen and
bookbinders as well as compositors, referred to printing in
New England as "in a certain measure governed by females." [43]

At the mid-century the Census of Manufactures, without
specifying whether in the skilled or less-skilled operations, reported more than 1,400 women and girls employed in printing
and publishing (including lithography and copperplate),
which was 16 percent of all workers.[44] Hence, after long de-
bate on the "woman question" at its convention in 1854, the
young National Typographical Union resolved that it should
not "encourage by its acts the employment of females as compositors." Whereupon, it handed the problem over to the local
unions, and Philadelphia responded by instructing its delegates to the next convention "to oppose any recognition of the
employment of females as compositors." The Boston union,
however, while not admitting women to membership, resolved
that "all females be allowed to work at all branches of the

42 Barnett, pp. 309–10; Abbott, p. 251. Carey is said to have denied the
charge, but to have admitted interest in finding more desirable employment
for women who were drudging in the sewing trades. (Ethelbert Stewart, "A
Documentary History of Early Organizations of Printers," in U.S. Bureau of
Labor Bull. 61., 1905, p. 884. See also Carey's crusade against women's low
wages, Sumner, pp. 123–33.)
43 Barnett, p. 310; Stewart, "A Documentary History," p. 884n.; Sumner, pp.
213–14.
44 Sumner, p. 258.

business," but with the protective—and in fact prohibitive—proviso that "they receive the scale." [45]

Late in the sixties the National Typographical Union was forced by circumstances to reconsider the policy of exclusion. Women were being employed at "notoriously low" wages on several large daily newspapers, notably the New York *World* and the Brooklyn *Eagle;* and in several strikes local unions had been defeated by women strikebreakers. Moreover, organized printers were keenly feeling the criticism from Susan B. Anthony and other advocates of equal rights who were working to widen the field of employment for women.[46]

Promptly, in 1867, the National Union authorized a committee to "report a plan to regulate and control female compositors, so that ladies in the business may benefit themselves and inflict as little injury as possible upon printers." [47] Hence, during a strike in New York in the following year, New York Typographical Union No. 6 organized a union of 40 women typesetters, and Women's Typographical Union No. 1 applied for a charter from the newly named International Typographical Union, which it received. The much-agitated outcome was that the constitution was amended to permit chartering women's unions of typesetters with the consent of the men's local unions and with their approval of the women's scales. Philadelphia and Chicago unions admitted women in 1870, and the next year the International urged all locals to affiliate women either in separate unions or by admitting them into their own organizations.[48] Although the New York women's local was the only one formed, many women were affiliated to membership

[45] Barnett, pp. 311–12; Stewart, "A Documentary History," p. 884n.; Abbott, pp. 252–53. Meanwhile there was disaffection among some pressmen's locals that complained of being no more welcome than women. (Baker, *Printers and Technology,* p. 61.)

[46] Barnett, p. 312; and see Israel Kugler, "The Trade Union Career of Susan B. Anthony," *Labor History,* Winter, 1961, pp. 90–100.

[47] Barnett, p. 312.

[48] Baker, *Printers and Technology,* p. 61n.

with the men, and Augusta Lewis of New York was selected corresponding secretary of the International.[49]

Nevertheless, the New York women's local did not prosper. According to Barnett, the advocates of "equal rights" failed to give the anticipated support by refusing to pay the union scale. Even Susan Anthony, proprietor of the *Revolution,* was paying less than the scale by a previously signed contract with nonunionists. The women's union complained, moreover, that union plants discriminated against its members.[50]

Aside from union pressure, employers' preference for men may have been because women were less well trained, less adaptable, and less strong physically than the average man. Nearly all were hand compositors who rarely learned any part of the trade but the setting of "straight" matter; and even here they were more often than not said to have been inferior to men. Rarely were they employed to set "display" matter, or to make up the forms or impose. For, different from the boys who learned the trade of typesetter by working four years at its various branches, and at very low wages at first, the great majority of girls were immediately put to setting type because they wanted to earn as much money as possible in the hope of leaving the trade in a few years to be married. Furthermore, aside from their reluctance to serve the four-year apprenticeship, girls could not be asked to do the many "odd jobs" that boys did, and at times there was too much physical exertion for women.[51]

For these and probably other reasons, women who asked equal wages with men discovered that they invited discharge. Hence, with some exceptions they accepted lower pay in nonunion shops for the simpler work of setting straight matter after a six-week training course, or more often just learning as

[49] Barnett, p. 313.

[50] *Ibid.*, p. 314; Kugler, "The Trade Union Career of Susan B. Anthony," pp. 98–100.

[51] Barnett, p. 316.

they worked.[52] The mass of women compositors could not earn the union rate, reported Barnett, and the union preferred to leave them unorganized rather than permit them to work for less than the men.[53]

When Augusta Lewis made her report to the International Union in 1871, she stated the conditions as she saw them:

We refuse to take the men's situations when they are on 'strike'; and when there is no strike, if we ask for work in union offices we are told that there are no conveniences for us. We are ostracized in many offices because we are members of the union, and although the *principle* is right, the *disadvantages* are so many that we cannot much longer hold together, and I trust our want of success will be attributed to the true cause.[54]

The fact that the women could not find employment except at lower wages also deeply concerned the New York men's local, but it did not succeed in having their charter revoked until 1878.

Then in the decade of the 1880s the policy of the compositors' union regarding women became fixed: first, women typesetters were not to be employed at a lower rate than was paid to men; second, in order to enforce this principle separate unions of women were not to be allowed; third, a local union must admit women on the same terms with men, and foremen, unions, and chapels were ordered to "make no distinctions on account of sex in persons holding travelling cards." The ITU was thus able to boast being an advocate of the "equal pay" doctrine.[55]

Whether or not this doctrine was aimed to keep women out

---

[52] Andrews and Bliss, p. 189. New Work employers were an exception in dealing with women, Abbott records. (Abbott, pp. 255–56.) They followed the policy of refusing to employ a woman who could not "perform the work just as well as a man," and one employer was reported to have said that if he was compelled to reduce women's wages in his composing room he would not employ them at all.

[53] Barnett, pp. 315–16.

[54] *Ibid.*, 314.

[55] *Ibid.*, p. 315; Abbott, pp. 253–54.

of the composing rooms has been a much debated question. In any case it resulted in keeping most of them out of the union. Theoretically there was no reason why they should not become journeymen compositors and receive the same wage rates as men. Typesetting was a skill that required intelligence and training, it was light work for the most part, and women had nimble fingers. But as a matter of fact their work was not identical with that of men. They did not lift heavy forms of set type, for example.

At this pont it should be noted that, although other branches of the printing industry had been mechanized, all these composing-room questions had occurred while typesetting was essentially what it had been in Gutenberg's day; and both the number and proportion of women compositors who set straight matter by hand increased considerably with a rising demand for printing.

Then came the Mergenthaler Linotype, which some held could be operated by female typists. But while the ITU president is said to have admitted that women were quicker than men to learn to operate the Linotype, he insisted that they lacked the "endurance to maintain for any length of time the speed on a machine" of which a man was capable. Hence the powerful union acted promptly and vigorously to save composition for its members, not by advocating "protective" legislation for women, as the cigar makers had done, but by demanding that the new machines were to be operated only by "journeymen printers trained in the trade as a whole." [56] Furthermore, it is important to note, Barnett observed that nonunion employers in this and other countries employed journeymen to operate their typesetting machines. He concluded, therefore, that the technical character of the Linotypes required "the skill of the superceded handicraftsman" to handle

[56] Abbott, p. 257.

them most efficiently and with the necessary speed; and the Linotype operators themselves held that machine work was far more exhausting than hand composition.[57]

Competition between men and women compositors was thus more seeming than real, it was discovered, for the men "almost invariably" did the more difficult work while the women did the simpler kinds—the "straight composition" and distributing type. At the close of the century, therefore, only 1,300 out of more than 15,000 women 16 years of age and over were union members—8 percent compared to 32 percent of the men; and by 1908 only 3 percent were women. Women formed 10 percent of all composing-room employees, and only 713 of them out of nearly 12,000 were operating typesetting machines. The conclusion was that

the printing trades furnish a striking example of a large body of intelligent and more or less skilled women almost universally outside of the union organization of their trade, and when within it playing a wholly passive part.[58]

THE PRESSROOM

But by no means was this the extent of women's employment in printing and publishing. The composing room was only one branch of the industry. There were also the pressroom and the closely associated bindery, with their highly varied occupations [59] which were largely mechanized before the advent of typesetting machines.

We have seen that women were tending hand presses in

[57] Barnett, pp. 202, 206–08. At the turn of the century the ITU also ruled that proofreaders in union offices must be union members and that all members who read proof must be "practical printers." (Barnett, pp. 247–48.)

[58] Andrews and Bliss, pp. 138, 188, 191.

[59] Beginning with the secession from the ITU of the pressmen in 1889, followed by the bookbinders in 1892, the stereotypers and electrotypers in 1902, and photoengravers in the years 1900–04 (Baker, *Printers and Technology*, pp. 73, 81), the once all-inclusive organization became a compositors' union whose members do no printing even though they have continued to call themselves "the printers."

the eighteenth century. They were employed on power presses in the 1850s, and they were hand-feeding paper into the presses throughout the nineteenth century.[60] In fact, according to the Aldrich Report to the United States Senate in 1893, almost all pressfeeders from 1842 to 1874 were females, and where a male or two was employed he received the same wage. Beginning with 1875 and through 1891—the last year of the investigation—male and female feeders were about equally divided; and while no female received as high a wage rate as a few of the males, none received as low a rate as some males. More often the rates were the same.[61]

Feeding sheets of paper—hundreds a day, one by one—was monotonous work, and on slow machines boys and girls who acquired dexterity had been adequate for the job. But after 1885 the faster and more complicated presses required more skill and experience, and their rapid introduction created a demand for men instead of women because men could assist the pressman in setting up the press and preparing the "make-ready" as well as feeding the sheets. These men were really press *assistants* who were learning to operate the machines as they worked, and from their ranks emerged future pressmen. In 1895 the pressmen formerly recognized the assistants by changing the name of their organization to the International Printing Pressmen and Assistants' Union.[62] While the union seems to have had no women members, women continued to feed presses in small, unorganized shops; and we shall see in Chapter 10 that, even after automatic feeding machines were installed after the turn of the century, many girls continued to be employed.

In the broad field of "paper and printing," 7,000 females of all ages were 32 percent of the labor force in 1850, but by

[60] Sumner, pp. 212–213.

[61] Nelson W. Aldrich, *Aldrich Report to the 52nd Congress, 2nd Session, 1892–93*, III, Part 2, 344–48.

[62] Baker, *Printers and Technology*, pp. 147, 175.

1900, after heavy machinery had been installed, the 74,000 women 16 years of age and over were only 25 percent.[63]

THE BOOKBINDERY

Bookbinding, it will be recalled, was one of the seven occupations in which Harriet Martineau found women employed when she visited America in 1836. As in the boot and shoe industry there seems always to have been a division of labor between men and women—the women and girls doing the semiskilled work of collecting, folding, pasting, and sewing the signatures (groups of pages) which required manual dexterity, while skilled men apprenticed to the trade did the heavy work of covering and backing the books. Records of the wages women received indicate that they were little above those in the sewing trades, and less than half the wages paid to men.[64]

Both folding and stitching were done by hand until a book-folding machine was introduced in the late fifties, and a book-sewing machine sometime later. Both mechanisms were relatively light so that, although they reduced the number of girls needed to operate them, female workers were still used. In fact, both bookbinding and blank-book making seem to have employed a larger number of women than any other branch of work connected with printing and publishing. In 1850 the 1,700 women and girls were 49 percent of all employees, and in 1900 the nearly 8,000 women 16 years of age and over were also 49 percent. When girls under 16 were included the number was more than 14,000 and constituted slightly more than half of all employed.[65]

[63] Sumner, p. 250. Bishop records that with the introduction of Fourdrinier machinery in Springfield, Massachusetts, about 1835, the largest paper factory in the country was "employing twelve engines, and more than one hundred females, besides the usual number of male hands." (Leander J. Bishop, *A History of American Manufactures, 1608–1860* [Edward Young & Company, 1868] II, 303.)

[64] Abbott, pp. 248–49; Sumner, pp. 209–10; Andrews and Bliss, p. 182.

[65] Sumner, pp. 210–11, 257; Baker, *Displacement of Men by Machines*, p. 6; Andrews and Bliss, p. 182.

Since there was so very little competition between the sexes in this trade, the policy of the International Brotherhood of Bookbinders was to organize women in separate unions, and by 1908 about a fourth of all bindery women were union members.[66]

SUMMARY ON WOMEN IN PRINTING AND PUBLISHING

To sum up the effects of technological change upon women in printing and publishing occupations, we find that they were complicated, various, and discouraging to women. Machines in both composing room and pressroom had reduced the opportunities for their employment; and in the bindery, while nearly half of all employees were women, machines did not draw them into men's work.

Newspapers and book and job printing were employing nearly 29,000 women in 1900 compared to little more than 1,400 in 1850, and they comprised 18 percent of the labor force. Moreover, by 1905 the number of women in these occupations had increased to well over 37,500 or one fifth of all employees.[67]

FOOD AND OTHER NONDURABLE PRODUCTS

In the preparation of food women partly retrieved their traditional place which they lost when many of the processes moved out of their homes. By 1900 factories making "baker's bread," which was produced by men, were employing some 10,400 women in the production of "bread and other bakery products"—more than 17 percent of all. And the entire group of "food and kindred products" employed about 64,600 women or nearly 21 in each 100 compared to a mere 919 or 2 per hundred 50 years earlier.[68]

Improved methods of hermetically sealing cans, together

[66] Andrews and Bliss, pp. 138, 182–83.
[67] Sumner, pp. 221, 258; Abbott, p. 259.
[68] Sumner, pp. 189, 255.

with the California gold rush and the Civil War, gave great impetus to the canning industry. At first the cans were made by tinners—a man's trade. But with the introduction of automatic machinery in the early eighties women were taken on to tend and feed the machines for making the cans and for painting, labeling, and wrapping them after they were filled. These were the only occupations for women in the meat-packing industry. On the other hand the canning and preserving of fruits and vegetables employed well toward 20,000 women in 1900, or 54 percent of all so employed. And by that time more than 40 in 100 oyster canners were women. Of those who put up pickles, preserves, and sauces, women constituted 45 in 100. These were light, unskilled jobs which demanded dexterity, and there seems to have been little or no competition between the sexes.[69]

Candymaking employed the second largest number of women in the food industries at the close of the century— nearly 16,000 or 47 percent of all compared to less than 350 or one in five in 1850. But few women were engaged in producing malt liquor; and men had displaced women and dairymaids in the making of dairy products. However, 2,800 women—44 in 100—were employed in producing coffee and spices compared to only 12 or 3 percent at the mid-century.[70]

Manufactures—Durable Goods

WATCHES, CLOCKS, AND SOME OTHER PRODUCTS

With few exceptions employment in watch- and clockmaking appears to have been women's introduction into a new world of durable-goods manufacture where they were to flourish in the twentieth century—a development directly attributable to the system of interchangeability of parts that brought new

[69] *Ibid.*, pp. 189, 190, 255; U.S. Bureau of Labor, *Woman and Child Wage-Earners*, XVIII, 55.
[70] Sumner, pp. 190, 191, 255.

automatic machinery and quantity production. In fact, before
the Civil War this formerly highly skilled man's trade was pronounced "admirably adapted to the female sex," and by 1868
half of the 250 employees at the Elgin Watch Company were
women and girls—chiefly farmers' daughters from the neighborhood. By 1880, the Tenth Census reported that women
were 36 percent of all watchmaking workers, compared to 15
percent 20 years earlier; and Professor James C. Watson was
quoted as follows on their employment at the American Watch
Company:

There are many important operations in the manufacture of watches
by this method where the delicate manipulation of female hands is
of the highest consequence, and . . . the amount of wages paid by
the company is determined by the skill and experience required,
not by the sex of the operative.

Watson noted further that either men or women could be employed on many of the watchmaking operations, but that
women's work was usually that of

the cutting and setting of pillars, the drilling of pin- and screw-
holes in plates, the cutting of the teeth of wheels and pinions, the
leaf-polishing, the gilding, the making of hair-springs, the setting
of springs, the making of pivot jewels and balance screws, the
putting of movements together, and the fitting in of roller jewels
and jewel pins.[71]

Further subdivision of labor in the next 20 years and the increasing adaptability of women to the intricate operations of
automatic machinery and to the assembling of parts, which
had been almost exclusively men's work and required expert
watchmakers, resulted in an increase in the number of women
and a decrease in the number of men. Hence, by the end of
the century half of 7,000 employees in watch manufacture
were women; and well over 1,000—close to 23 in every 100—

[71] *Ibid.*, 224, 225; U.S. Census Office, *Tenth Census, 1880*, II: *Manufactures*, "Report on the Manufactures of Interchangeable Mechanism," p. 678.

were at work on clocks, where the men's job of making the cases was still an important feature.[72]

In the entire group classified as "metals and metal products other than iron and steel," the number of women and girls rose from 738 at the mid-century to more than 25,800 in 1900. In addition to watch- and clockmaking, more than 6,000 were making jewelry—nearly a third of all workers. And women were commonly employed in the manufacture of nails and tacks, and in weighing and filing coined money in the mints. In general, their work was that of polishing, filing, soldering, weighing, and packing all kinds of lighter metal articles, and of tending the lighter machines.[73]

Glass was another durable product which by 1900 attracted more than 3,500 women to make light and fancy articles under a system of divided labor, largely in finishing, decorating, and packing departments. Although they comprised less than 7 percent of all workers, this was a marked advance over the mid-century count of only 97 women and girls who formed less than 2 percent of all.[74]

Summary of a Century of Change in Manufactures

There were of course numerous other occupations we have not mentioned in which women found work during this century of change. In fact, United States Labor Commissioner Wright reported that by 1890 only nine out of 369 general groups to which the country's industries had been assigned did not employ women—"Their employment, therefore, as clerks, operatives, or apprentices, may be considered universal." [75]

[72] Sumner, pp. 225, 258; *U.S. Census Office, Twelfth Census, 1900,* IX: *Manufactures,* Part IV, p. 486.
[73] Sumner, pp. 223–24; 250, 258.
[74] *Ibid.,* pp. 226–27, 258.
[75] Wright, p. 209.

It is noteworthy that in every census year far more than half of all females at work for pay were in textiles and the seasonal clothing industry—household occupations from time immemorial. Less than a third were in industries other than textiles, clothing, food, liquors, and kindred products. In some instances these women had followed the machine into old trades which were men's sphere by tradition, such as cigar making. But for the most part it was some of the newer occupations which they entered almost if not quite from the beginning, and in which they successfully held their own.[76] The proportion of all employees who were women rose or fell according to the nature of the work. Relatively few were employed on durable goods, but they had made their start.

Other nondurable industries which employed few in number but large proportions of women at the close of the century included paper boxes—more than 18,000 women, or two in every three workers; paper bags and matches, where women were over a fifth of all employees; and rubber and elastic goods, where more than 7,000 women were at work—about two in five.[77]

In manufacturing and mechanical pursuits as a whole the average number of women rose from somewhat more than 225,000 in 1850 to well over a million in 1900. But in those 50 years the proportion of women to men dropped from 23 to 19 in each 100. And they composed less than a fourth of all gainfully employed women and girls.[78] Where were all the others? We shall soon know the answer.

[76] Sumner, pp. 19–20, 28, 195.
[77] *Ibid.*, pp. 257, 259.
[78] *Ibid.*, p. 250.

CHAPTER 4
Women at Work Away from the Factories

In the first year that gainfully employed women and girls were counted by the federal census—1870—four fifths of them were engaged in their traditional occupations on the farm or in domestic service, but by 1900 their proportion had dropped to 58 percent. Technological developments had played a significant role in the change.

ON THE FARM

Prior to the Civil War women who worked for pay on the farm were not often employed in the field, or "put into the ground" as the saying went, but were hired to look after the dairy or the poultry.[1] But as the steel moldboard plow of 1833 and the Marsh harvester of 1858 began to win the approval of farmers during the scarcity of labor in the sixties, horse-drawn machinery was adopted—greatly stimulated by the homestead movement. Then it was that women farmers and agricultural laborers were taken on to the extent of about 397,000, and 30 years later, 977,000—about 18 percent of all employed females.[2] In the last decade of the century—after the Census Bureau had announced the passing of the American frontier—the number of these women and girls had increased by 27 percent while the number of men and boys rose 12 percent.[3] Of the more than 770,000 females 16 years of age and over in what the census termed "agricultural pursuits," 456,000 were grouped with agricultural laborers, including family members; nearly 308,000 were classified as farmers, planters, and overseers; and about 6,000 in "other agricultural pursuits."[4]

[1] Abbott, p. 12; *U.S. WB Bull. 218*, p. 191.
[2] Sumner, p. 246.
[3] Abbott and Breckinridge, p. 25.
[4] U.S. Bureau of the Census, *Statistics of Women at Work*, 1900, p. 32; U.S. Bureau of the Census, 1900, Table 1, p. xxiii.

DOMESTIC AND PERSONAL SERVICE

Compared with agriculture, domestic service is an example
of the effects of changing technology acting in reverse, for
while the number of women and girls reported in this group
rose from one to two million in the 30 years before 1900,
other occupations were opened to them and their proportion
of all employed females fell from 58 percent to 39 percent.[5]
Furthermore, domestic service was the only one of the five
major occupational census groups in which the last decade
of the century brought an increase of men and boys considerably greater than that of women and girls.[6] The census threw
no light on the cause of this change. Perhaps it was a demand
for waiters in restaurants and hotels.

Women "hired out," doubtless, before Alexander Hamilton's
exhortations to draw them into cotton mills. And we are told
that the opening of these mills, especially at Lowell, caused
a marked rise in the wages of women domestics. Nevertheless,
while factory girls sometimes bemoaned their low wages, the
din of the machines, the poor ventilation, and the monotony
of their work, they were reluctant to go out as "hired help"
who lacked both social position and personal independence.
One woman's rebellious comment was that a girl who went
into the kitchen was called a bridget, "But if she goes behind
the counter she is escorted by gentlemen to the theater, dined,
and called a lady." But it is nothing but "false pride which will
not permit them to serve a mistress, but keeps them slaves to
masters," commented the New York *Times* in 1868.[7]

It should be noted, too, that domestic and personal service
was a sort of catchall census classification during those years
when women at work were only beginning to be reported systematically. It was not until 1880 that teachers were classified

[5] Sumner, p. 246.
[6] Abbott and Breckinridge, pp. 25, 32.
[7] Sumner, pp. 182–83; Lucy Larcom, *A New England Girlhood* (Boston,
Houghton's, 1889), p. 199.

under "professional service," and even at the end of the century nurses along with midwives were grouped as domestic servants.

By 1900, nearly 40 percent of all the nation's gainfully employed women 16 years of age and over were reported in domestic and personal service—more than 1,950,000 of them; but with the growth of the hotel and restaurant business many had been attracted into that sector where servants and waitresses worked a fixed number of hours, as did saleswomen and clerks. In fact, about three out of four of all servants and waiters 16 years and over were women.[8]

TEACHERS

At the time in the 1830s and 1840s when technological change and the influx of immigrants at the Lowell cotton mills began to prompt those respected farmers' daughters to look elsewhere for employment, Jeffersonian liberals were introducing free elementary schools. And despite tradition, local authorities were ready to hire young women as teachers for the reason that, since they had no other professional openings, they could be had at half, a third, or even a quarter of what was paid to men. In Pennsylvania in 1835, for example, the "female teacher" would accept $9.00 a month.[9] In the next year Harriet Martineau listed teaching as another one of the

[8] Sumner, pp. 18, 247, 254.

[9] Newcomer, p. 14. It is worth recalling that by tradition teaching was a masculine calling and that up through the first quarter of the nineteenth century most teachers were men. In colonial days many New England towns appear to have considered admission of girls to their schools as "inconsistent with the design" thereof. Marriages at 13, 14, and 15 years of age were common, and an educated wife was deemed "an infringement upon the domain of man." (Woody, I, 92, 93, 95.)

Women held "dame schools" for little children (Lucy Larcom, A New England Girlhood, p. 140, recalled that she was "only a baby" of two years when she began to go to a dame school); and they were often assigned to teach in the common district schools during summer months, when males were at a premium. Also, women taught in Quaker schools in Pennsylvania; and wives of southern planters sometimes taught in the "old Field Schools," which stood where tobacco and cotton raising had been abandoned. (Elsbree, pp. 68–70, 199.)

seven occupations which she found open to women, though
more authoritative records listed more than 100—practically
all in manufacturing except for those in agriculture and domestic service.[10] Teaching was the only real profession.

In the 1840s Henry Barnard and Horace Mann spoke up for
women as teachers. Barnard, Secretary of the Connecticut
Board of Commissioners of Common Schools, deprecated the
miserable compensation women received and the lack of a
place of their own to live. Horace Mann embellished his report
to the Massachusetts Board of Education in 1845 by noting
that

four fifths of all women who have ever lived, have been the slaves
of man,—the menials in his household, the drudges in his field, the
instruments of his pleasure; or at best, the gilded toys of his leisure
days in court or palace.

The Boston Board of Education declared, moreover, that
women were "incomparably better teachers for young children
than males . . . [inasmuch as] the whole forces of the mind are
more readily concentrated upon present duties." [11]

These early arguments for opening the teaching profession
to women were doubtless in line with the only practicable
course. Men were being attracted by business opportunities
and skilled trades, and the phenomenal growth of public
schools created an alarming shortage of teachers. The annual
reports of state school superintendents were urgent on the
subject. They recommended women for their peculiar qualifications, their superior character, their greater permanence in
the profession, and, most of all, for the economy of employing
them.[12] From Queens College in London as early as 1849 came
the advice that when you "educate women . . . you educate
teachers of men." And a dictum from North Carolina educator

[10] Abbott, "Harriet Martineau and the Employment of Women in 1836,"
JPE, 1906, pp. 617, 620.
[11] Elsbree, pp. 199–201.
[12] *Ibid.*, p. 205.

Charles McIver was that you "educate a man and you have educated one person; educate a mother and you have educated the whole family." [13] All this pressure resulted in an increase in the number of women teachers in Massachusetts alone by more than 1,600 in the nine years 1838–47 while only 67 men were added.[14]

But relief from the scarcity of men teachers of course required that girls as well as boys be taught, and tradition was cracked again when girls began to receive high school education. Worcester, Massachusetts, had opened what seems to have been the first public high school for girls as early as 1824. Two years later New York City started a Female High School. A Boston public school "for the instruction of girls in the higher departments of science and literature" was also opened in 1826 with 130 pupils, half of whom were from private schools. But this innovation proved to be so immensely popular that it was considered "an alarming success," and after two years it was abolished "because it was found that a single school of this description would not accommodate more than one fourth part of those who ought to attend such an institution." [15]

From these strange years up to the Civil War period free elementary and secondary schools sprang up throughout the nation; and it appears that girls were admitted to them from the first because most neighborhoods were so sparsely settled that there were not boys enough for one grammar school and one high school.[16] There were also normal schools and seminaries in many parts of the country. Then in the wake of five years of war that drained the northern and western states of men, the National Bureau of Education reported that fewer men than women were teaching in the public schools; and

13 Newcomer, p. 32.
14 Abbott, p. 140.
15 Woody, I, 519–21.
16 Thomas, "Education of Women," in *Monographs on Education in the United States,* Nicholas Murray Butler, ed. (Albany, J. B. Lyons Co., 1900), I, 321–22.

after that time, as men went west, both elementary and secondary schools went largely into the hands of women.[17]

Women's eligibility as teachers in the common schools was thus being considered in a new light: their low salaries were balm to taxpayers; women of marriageable age in New York outnumbered men by nearly 39,000 and in Massachusetts by 27,000; and the leaders of the women's emancipation movement held that women were natural teachers of the young and would eventually receive equal pay with men.[18] "It is WOMAN who is to come in at this emergency, and meet the demand," Catharine Beecher had written in 1851, "woman, whom experience and testimony have shown to be the best, as well as the cheapest guardian and teacher of childhood, in school as well as in the nursery." [19]

Even higher education for women had early beginnings. Emma Willard presented her "Plan" to New York's Governor Clinton in 1818 to put women's education "on an equal footing with that of men," [20] and Catherine Beecher also strove for instruction for women on the college level. We have noted the "vision of hope" that Lowell cotton-mill girls saw in Mary Lyon's Mount Holyoke Female Seminary of 1837. New York had chartered a number of academies and seminaries by that time, and before the Civil War more than 50 women's "colleges" were listed, though few of them offered an A.B. degree. Meanwhile, also in 1837, Oberlin College admitted women to its courses four years after its founding, and seven years later Hillsdale College in Ohio did likewise, followed by Antioch in 1853, and the universities of Utah and Iowa in the same decade.[21] From that time, as universities opened in the western states, they admitted women inasmuch as women teachers had

17 *Ibid.*, p. 323.
18 Woody, I, 460; II, 1.
19 Catharine E. Beecher, *The True Remedy for the Wrongs of Women* (Boston, Phillips, Sampson & Co., 1851), pp. 240–41.
20 Woody, I, 113, 305–12.
21 Newcomer, p. 12.

become firmly established in the secondary schools. As M. Carey Thomas reminds us, they had to receive higher education "if only for the sake of the secondary education of the boys of the country." [22]

Doubtless the woman's rights movement, launched at Seneca Falls in 1834 by Elizabeth Cady Stanton, Lucretia Mott, Susan B. Anthony, Lucy Stone, and others, had played a part in the educational and occupational advancement of women and girls, as did John Stuart Mill's famous *Subjection of Women* in both England and America 35 years later. Moreover, girls like those at Lowell, as well as housewives, were reading some 60 ladies' magazines, including *Godey's Lady's Book,* edited by Sarah Hale, who had been tutored by her Dartmouth College brother. The brother waged hard campaigns for higher education for women and for their admission to the professions of medicine and nursing after adequate training. He urged more physical education for women and deplored the menace of corsets.[23]

Women were also being freed from much of their household drudgery by early labor-saving inventions such as the cookstove, and often a hot-air furnace in the cellar, the sewing machine, and the match. And gas light and improved oil lamps enabled them to read more comfortably in the evenings before the open fire.[24] At the ninth National Woman's Rights Convention in 1859, Caroline Dall thus offered her resolution:

That it is our bounden duty to open, in ever possible way, new vocations to women, to raise their wages by every advisable means, and to secure to them an education which shall be less a decoration to their persons than a tool to their minds.[25]

By 1870 the teaching profession employed some 5 percent

[22] Thomas, p. 324.

[23] Newcomer, pp. 8, 16; Eleanor Flexner, *Century of Struggle: The Women's Rights Movement in the United States* (Cambridge, Massachusetts, 1959), p. 65.

[24] Newcomer, p. 16; Catharine E. Beecher, *A Treatise on Domestic Economy* (Boston, Thomas H. Webb & Co., 1842), p. 260n.

[25] Woody, II, 441.

of the working women of the country. The paucity of available men, the growing belief in the special qualifications of women, and the economy of employing them, together with the great increase in school enrollments owing to population growth and to technological advances that released many children from work in field and factory, all these had increased the number of women teachers in the public and private schools to more than 84,000, or two thirds of all teachers. (There seems to be no record of the number who were married at that time, but it is probably safe to guess that there were very few, if any.) Some 11,000 women were enrolled as students in institutions of higher learning—about one for every four men; and by the turn of the century these women numbered some 85,000—more than one for every three men.[26]

At that time more than 327,000 women were teachers—73 in every 100.[27] Among women's professional occupations they ranked first—76 in every 100, and fifth among all women's occupations—outnumbered only by servants and waitresses, agricultural laborers, dressmakers, and laundresses.[28]

NURSES

Nursing the ill and wounded became another outlet for aspiring New England cotton-mill girls and for women who had to support themselves or their families when technological innovations took away so much of their homework. The Friends of Philadelphia made early attempts to establish schools of nursing, but the development of the profession was by no means smooth and we must turn to older countries for the setting.

[26] Newcomer, pp. 19, 46; *U.S. WB Bull. 218*, pp. 158–59.

[27] Approximately, musicians and teachers of music were 57 percent of all men and women in that profession; artists and teachers of art, 44 percent; literary and scientific persons, 32 percent; physicians and surgeons, 6 percent; other professional service, 3 percent. U.S. Bureau of the Census, *Statistics of Women at Work*, p. 32.)

[28] *Ibid.*, 109.

Female nursing is as old as Christianity, Cook reminds us, but before Florence Nightingale appeared on the scene the occupation everywhere was regarded as a menial service—ill-paid and little respected. For example, Miss Nightingale wrote to a friend in 1851, after she had lived as an inmate at the Kaiserworth School on the Rhine, that the account which a young surgeon in a London hospital had given of its nurses "beats everything that even I know of. This young prophet says that they are all drunkards, without exception, Sisters and all, and that there are but two nurses whom the surgeon can trust to give the patients their medicine." [29] Again in 1854 she wrote to her father that the head nurse in a certain London hospital had told her that "in the course of her large experience she had never known a nurse who was not drunken, and that there was immoral conduct practiced in the very wards, of which she gave me some awful examples." Also from Paris a report on the *clinique obstétrical* at the Écòle de Médecine was that "the *élèves* have the reputation of being pretty generally the students' mistresses." [30]

It was during the terrible event of the Crimean War in the mid-fifties that Florence Nightingale—with her "razor-like brain" and her "legendary lamp"—set a heroic example of administrative genius "that was to save the British Army from destruction more effectively than all the siege guns that Lord Raglan could muster." [31] And it was in 1880—"a date . . . the most memorable in the history of nursing"—that a Nightingale School was opened at St. Thomas's Hospital in London, designed to train nurses rather than to provide menial services for hospitals. Here was the birth of the nursing profession.[32]

[29] Sir Edward Cook, *The Life of Florence Nightingale* (New York, Mac-Millan, 1942), I, 109, 113, 116–17, 440, 445.

[30] *Ibid.*, p. 61n.

[31] Peter Gibbs, *Crimean Blunder* (London and New York, 1960), p. 245.

[32] M. Adelaide Nutting and Lavina L. Dock, *History of Nursing* (2 vols., New York and London, G. P. Putnam's Sons, 1907, 1935), II, 181.

In the United States in 1852 the American Women's Education Association had urged that the "care of the human body in infancy and sickness" was one of "the true professions of women." Hence in the war between the states—before which men had often done the cooking and nursing as well as the fighting—Clara Barton, despite "bitter opposition," led northern women to cook and nurse in the field hospitals behind the battle front; and in the South Mrs. Jefferson Davis said that "the exception" among her Richmond friends "was the woman who did not nurse at a hospital." [33]

In the following decade Linda Richards became America's first graduate nurse—a product of the country's first modern school of nursing at the New England Hospital for Women and Children in Roxbury, Connecticut. Patterned after the Nightingale and Kaisersworth institutions, other nursing schools were founded in New York, New Haven, Boston, and Philadelphia; and with advances in medical science and the development of hospitalization the nurses' training period was expanded to three or more years. The Johns Hopkins School of Nursing raised the academic standards further by admitting only high school graduates as pupils.[34]

Building on these foundations, the American Nurses' Association was formed in 1896, uniforms were adopted, the principle of state examination and licensing of nurses was accepted; Lillian Wald introduced the civic spirit into the nurses' settlement; Teachers College of Columbia University opened courses in hospital administration and public health; and the American Red Cross—organized by Clara Barton in 1881—received its first federal charter in 1900.

In that year about 11,000 of 108,691 nurses and midwives

[33] Woody, II, 73; Nutting and Dock, *History of Nursing,* I, 101; Charles A. and Mary R. Beard, *The Rise of American Civilization* (New York, Macmillan, 1930), II, 76.
[34] Nutting and Dock, *History of Nursing,* II, 347–51; Anna J. Haines, "Nursing," in *Encyclopaedia of the Social Sciences,* XI, 406.

had become graduate nurses. Unfortunately, however, many who sent census returns failed to specify whether they were "trained" or "practical" nurses, so all were listed as midwives under domestic and personal service.[35]

SALESWOMEN

In contrast to teaching and nursing for the more educated women, employment in retail stores became a new occupation for "working women" who may have chosen it instead of manual labor such as domestic service, or sewing and other congested trades, or factory work itself. Its relative attractiveness —away from the din of machinery—lured women and girls despite very low wages.[36] "White-collar" jobs, as we call them today, were greatly limited, and a low wage or salary was better than none.

As early as the 1830s Mathew Carey, that champion of working women, urged relief from low wages for tailors and seamstresses by employing them in retail shops for which "they are admirably calculated." In the forties New York newspapers— the *Herald, Sun,* and *Tribune*—published articles on the subject; let men "go out to the fields and seek their livelihood as men ought to do and leave the females their legitimate employment" for which "females alone are suitable and intended." "It is a shame that fine, hearty lads, who might clear their 50 acres each of western forest in a short time, and have a house, a farm, a wife, and boys about them in the course of ten years, should be hived up in hot salesrooms, handing down tapes and ribbons, and cramping their genius over chintzes and delaines." And if these lads knew no better, the *Tribune* thought women "of intelligence and means" should boycott shops that did not

[35] Haines, p. 406; *U.S. WB Bull. 218*, p. 161; U.S. Bureau of the Census, *Statistics of Women at Work*, pp. 32–33.

[36] Carroll D. Wright, *U.S. Commissioner of Labor's Fourth Annual Report*, "Working Women in Large Cities," 1888, p. 9; Ralph M. Hower, *History of Macy's of New York, 1858–1919* (Cambridge, Howard University Press, 1943), p. 196.

employ women.[37] Here was early seed for a consumers' league, which was to take root a half century later.

Employment of women in mercantile establishments was still being advocated in the 1850s with little effect. The New York *Times* was saying that particularly in retail dry-goods stores women's employment "would properly enlarge their sphere of action and occupation and it is a business that they can do better than men. . . . It would give employment to a great many young ladies, and would be degrading to no one willing to earn a living." [38] Comparing America and England with Europe on employment of women in stores, one paper stated that "50,000 retail stores in our large cities and towns ought to afford employment and good wages for 100,000 women." During the Civil War women and girls responded so numerously to the demand for "saleswomen" that they were pathetically exploited. For example, Philadelphia stores were said to have taken them on for six months for no pay under the pretense of teaching them the business, to have given them $2.00 a week for the second six months and $3.00 during the second year, then to have discharged them to make room for newcomers on the same terms.[39]

Macy's, on New York's Fourteenth Street, was a pioneer in establishing saleswomen. A recent writer tells us that in the early sixties a woman cashier and bookkeeper was made store superintendent and proved to be highly successful, and that in the postwar years an average of only 12 percent of all Macy employees were men and boys. Sales clerks accounted for the largest number of women, followed by a great many 12- to 14-year-old cash girls who seemed willing also to sweep floors and dust counters at $1.50 a week in the hope of becoming stock girls or even clerks.[40]

[37] Sumner, pp. 234, 235.
[38] Abbott, p. 3.
[39] Sumner, pp. 235, 237.
[40] Hower, pp. 65–66, 193, 196–97. Hower (p. 193) tells us that A. T. Stewart, who had the largest New York department store, used very few

While there was no union action among the main body of
Macy employees at this time,[41] by 1870 the men in Broadway
stores had formed the Clerks' Early Closing Association and
had won a 7 P.M. closing time, except for Saturday nights.
Meanwhile the saleswomen employed in Sixth and Eighth
avenue stores and on Grand and Catherine streets had also
organized, and they appealed to the men's association to induce their employers to follow the Broadway example. Their
special complaint was that they were not permitted to sit down
at any time throughout the long day because sitting would
make it appear that trade was dull.[42]

After the 1870s, as new customer demands encouraged suc-
cessive introduction of large department stores, mail-order
houses, and chain stores, a greater division of labor gave employment to more women, or more precisely, girls. According
to the United States Commissioner of Labor, reporting in 1888,
75 percent of employed women were between 14 and 25 years
of age, the average being 22 years. Commissioner Wright
noted that there was immorality among the girls who had to
travel long distances after dark, especially on Saturday nights,
when they worked until ten or eleven o'clock; also among those
friendless young women who lived in city tenements without
home restraint, "suffering every conceivable discomfort, subject to long periods of idleness, which they often enter upon
with an empty purse." [43]

In the final decade of the century some women in retail
shops organized again, this time forming the Working Women's
Society, which was the forerunner of the Women's Trade Union League. They hoped to unionize shopwomen, but decided
that it was even more necessary to organize shoppers. The

women to wait on customers, but rather "the handsomest men he could obtain
. . . because he had noticed that ladies . . . liked to gossip and even to flirt
with them." And other stores followed his example.

[41] *Ibid.*, p. 306.
[42] Sumner, pp. 237–38.
[43] Wright, *Working Women in Large Cities*, pp. 21, 62–63; see also U.S.
Bureau of Labor, *Woman and Child Wage-Earners*, Vol. V.

immediate outcome of their efforts was the formation of the
Consumers' League of the City of New York in 1891 with
Josephine Shaw Lowell (Mrs. Charles Russell Lowell) as
president; and the league promptly prepared a "white list" of
shops which paid minimum wages and provided reasonable
hours, suitable seats, and decent sanitary conditions.[44]

In her report for 1895 the league's president expressed grat-
itude to and pity for working women "because of their helplessness and the peculiar hardships to which they are exposed.
They are helpless because they are women . . . because they
are young, and . . . exposed to peculiar temptations from the
fact that, when wages fall below the living point, the 'wages
of sin' are always ready for them." [45]

The consumers' league movement extended to Brooklyn,
Philadelphia, and Boston, and state leagues were organized in
Illinois, New York, Pennsylvania, and Massachusetts. Then at
a convention in 1898 these bodies federated to form the National Consumers' League and elected John Graham Brooks
president and Florence Kelly executive secretary. Only five
years later 64 branches of the national league had been formed.[46]
In Chapters 7 and 21 we shall note the legislative action
which they pursued for special protection of women.

By 1900 the number of women 16 years of age and over,
classified as "saleswomen" by the Census of Manufactures, had
grown from some 7,500 to more than 142,000 in 20 years, and
this occupation ranked eighth in the nation as a field of employment for women.[47] But by no means had men been either
ridiculed or frightened away by the newspaper chidings of the
forties—perhaps as a result of A. T. Stewart's example for at-

[44] George Soule, "Consumers' Leagues," in *Encyclopaedia of the Social Sciences*, IV, 291; Nathan, pp. 15–21, 25–30, 131–33.

[45] Consumers' League of New York City, *Annual Report*, 1893, p. 8.

[46] Soule, "Consumers' Leagues," p. 291; Nathan, pp. 60, 68–69.

[47] There were nearly 146,600 women 15 years of age and over by report of
the U.S. Census Bureau, *Statistics of Women at Work*, pp. 39, 91–92; Sumner
pp. 238, 259.

tracting customers. For whatever reason, the numbers of men had kept pace with the development of large department stores, and at the close of the century the proportion of "saleswomen" among all "salesmen and saleswomen" in the country as a whole remained practically stationary—at 23 percent. However, in major cities, including Baltimore, Boston, New York, Philadelphia, and Washington, women formed as much as a third or more of the total sales force.[48]

TELEPHONE AND TELEGRAPH OPERATORS

"WHAT HATH GOD WROUGHT?" In today's perspective this first message that Samuel F. B. Morse tapped out over his new electric telegraph on May 24, 1844, after more than a decade of experimentation based upon earlier inventions,[49] seems to have envisioned a day for women. For electric energy was to play a dominant role in technological changes both outside and inside the home. We have seen that women entered the professions of teaching and nursing in the second half of the century, and that during and after the Civil War occupations for "working women" expanded to include employment in retail stores. Now also the dawn of other commercial and clerical occupations was breaking, implemented by the telegraph and telephone, the typewriter, and other office machines that would lure many "middle-class" women and girls into paid employment for the first time.

Telegraphy was not to create the woman-employing occupation that the telephone created, although girls were employed as telegraph operators almost from the beginning. The Western Union Telegraph Company became an entity in 1856, and three years later it cooperated with Cooper Union in offering free instruction to women, who were said to have been "a great success" as operators. By 1870 the Census of Occupations re-

[48] Sumner, p. 238; U.S. Census Bureau, *Statistics of Women at Work*, pp. 92, 93.
[49] Kaempffert, I, 298.

ported 355 women employed not as operators but in the general service of the telegraph companies; and business colleges began teaching the subject. By 1886 New York City was thus reported to have "about two hundred ladies engaged in this occupation," some in the service of brokers.[50] It is not possible to note further progress of women in this first of the new arts of communication because telegraph and telephone operators were combined in the census reports.

And now for a great and lasting employer of women—the telephone. It was the voice of Alexander Graham Bell calling his assistant over his "harmonic" telegraph on March 10, 1876, that said, "Mr. Watson, please come here, I want you." Soon crude switchboards were built on the plan of telegraph switchboards. But unlike the telegraph, the operators were not girls but boys who, we are told, soon became so impudent, noisy, and inattentive that girls were taken on to replace them.[51] Telephone operation was thus on its way to becoming a feminine monopoly.

Why did telephone service become "women's work" and telegraphy "men's work"? An Englishman undertook to get below the surface of this question. There was no part of the work of "telegraphists" that a woman performed better than a man, he wrote, and women were employed because of their cheapness and their "relative docility":

Steady work at low pressure, and more or less mechanical in character, necessitating little or no judgment, seems to be admirably performed by women, but where these conditions are lacking they are generally inferior to men.

The writer quaintly added that woman's "lack of judgment

50 Sumner, p. 241; *U.S. WB Bull. 50*, p. 40; Woody, II, 69; As usual, women were paid about half what men received, and one of three objectives in a nationwide strike of telegraphers in 1883, which was unsuccessful, was equal pay for like work between the sexes, the other two being an eight-hour day and extra pay for Sunday work. (Wright, pp. 306–07.)

51 Kaempffert, I, 320, 326, 334–35.

may be due—in part at least, to educational disability, but there seems to be something more fundamental in the inability to work at high pressure." He noted that the "artificial social prejudice" which banned night duty for women prevented reliance upon them for irregular work to meet emergencies. Moreover, because either law or custom required them to leave when married, their work was not undertaken *con amore* and with a desire to excel, a fact which militated against highest efficiency.[52]

The United States Bureau of the Census explained in 1902 that "while women have found a limited employment in telegraphy . . . telephony, with its simpler, narrower range of work to be performed at the central office, has provided opportunity for a large number of young girls at a low rate of pay, comparing in this respect with the factory system." The Bureau added that "many young women of education" were attracted to telephone operation because their duties were more varied than when watching machinery, hours were shorter, surroundings more agreeable, and they came in contact with the personalities of subscribers. Moreover, "opportunities of preferment" that were offered, especially in private exchanges, and at higher wages, had become so numerous in New York City with the growth of business that they employed more than all of the "great exchanges of the local telephone company." [53]

It is interesting to find, furthermore, that telephone companies in large cities seemed to have taken a leaf out of Lowell textile-mill records to attract "well-bred women"—"young women above the average in ability and ambition." Almost at once they began to provide comfortable rest rooms as well as parts of their lunches, the Census Bureau informs us. Around the turn of the century the operators in one company were

[52] Charles H. Garland, "Women as Telegraphists," *Economic Journal,* XI (June, 1901), pp. 251, 258, 259.

[53] U.S. Bureau of the Census, Special Reports, *Telephones and Telegraphs,* 1902, p. 49.

lectured to and given materials on accuracy and general improvements of methods. Competitive scrapbooks on the subject won money prizes, which by popular vote were used to buy books. The result was that, with the cooperation of the company, "excellent circulating libraries" were established in 11 city exchanges. In several exchanges reading clubs were formed, in others flower and vegetable gardens, and a women's athletic club in another. To recruit girls the exchanges gave operators money premiums for each recommended applicant who remained in the training school two weeks, and more when she was graduated and had stayed on the job three months.[54]

Introduction of the automatic "girless central"—the dial system—was to raise the danger of "technological unemployment" in the 1930s, but it did not materialize, as we shall see, because of the company's careful planning and the growth of the industry. For New York had only begun to talk to Chicago by telephone in 1892, and by 1900 telephone service had expanded so rapidly that the number of telephone and telegraph operators had risen to some 22,000, of whom 29 percent were women 16 years of age and over. Only two years later female telephone operators numbered well over 37,000, compared to some 2,500 males, while commercial telegraph companies were employing a little less than 3,000 women and more than 10,000 men—and the railroad companies almost all men.[55]

OFFICE WORKERS

And then the typewriter. "Father Sholes, what a wonderful thing you have done for the world!" said a daughter-in-law at the bedside of Christopher Latham Sholes near the end of the century when telegraph and telephone wires were busy. "I don't know about the world," was the response, "but I feel that

54 *Ibid.*, p. 51.
55 *Ibid.*, p. 50; Kaempffert, I, 343; Sumner, pp. 241–42, 259.

I have done something for the women who have always had to work so hard. This will help them earn a living more easily." With the use of an old telegraph key, Sholes had invented a practical "writing machine" in 1867 which he named a "typewriter," and the first typist was one of his own daughters.[56]

This "great-grandfather of office machinery," which was introduced to the public in 1873, was destined to mark the entrance of women into the business and commercial office work of the nation almost as abruptly as textile machinery had done in the manufactures. Sholes took his crude invention to Remington's mechanical experts, whose skilled machinists turned out the parts so accurately that they were interchangeable. Typewriters could then be built by the dozens, hundreds, or thousands if people wanted them, and Mark Twain is said to have bought one of the first ones on which he copied his *Tom Sawyer*. Before 1900 Underwood "visible" machines, on which the operator could see what he was writing as he struck the keys, were being produced by the tens of thousands.[57]

Office work, like retail selling, had always been men's occupation, yet some women were so employed before the invention of the typewriter. As clerks and copyists in Washington, they clipped or trimmed notes in the Treasury Department [58] and copied speeches and other documents for members of Congress. Their first experience as stenographers seems to have been transcription of notes on legislative debates and court cases taken down by men. And as far back as the "roaring forties," when newspapers were urging that selling in stores was "suitable and intended" for women, a New York speaker had declared that there were "hundreds of females"

[56] Kaempffert, I, 268, 275–76.

[57] *Ibid.*, pp. 273–74, 276, 278, 280.

[58] Francis Elias Spinner, U.S. Treasurer, 1861–75, is reported to have said, "The fact that I was instrumental in introducing women to employment in the offices of the government, gives me more real satisfaction than all the other deeds of my life." (*Life*, March 24, 1961, Letter to the Editor by Temple R. Hollcroft.)

in the city who could keep the books "as well as any man in it." A few years later a contributor to the New York *True National Democrat* held that "as accountants and bookkeepers, females would stand unrivaled." [59] Nevertheless, it was not until the advent of the typewriter that women were to be received in these positions.

The corporate form of business had been largely limited to railroads and other public utilities, and to banks and insurance companies before the Civil War, but in the seventies a surge of new business combinations swept away small manufacturers who had become too competitive to break even. The first transcontinental railroad had been completed in 1869, and by 1900 there was a railroad net of 193,345 miles. Population had risen to more than 76,000,000, or two and a half times that of 1860; and the value of manufactured products had soared to six and a half times its 1860 level.[60] The nation was indeed ready for large-scale production and trade in widely scattered markets, which required a tremendous increase in business correspondence, record-keeping, and general office work. The typewriter and the telephone were thus indispensable new tools that drew young middle-class women into the labor market.

How were these girls made ready for office work? To begin with, since they helped their mothers at home after school while boys had the alternative of a paid job, more girls than boys were high school graduates. And in the decade of the eighties the New York Young Women's Christian Association and Cooper Union opened classes in typewriting, stenography, bookkeeping, commercial arithmetic, and kindred subjects.[61] By the end of the century nearly 19,000 girls were taking courses of this kind in the public high schools—almost half of all such pupils; and nearly 24,000 or more than half of the

[59] Sumner, pp. 238–39, 240.
[60] U.S. Twelfth Census, *Manufactures*, 1900, Part I, p. xlvii.
[61] Newcomer, p. 46; Meyer, p. 290.

commercial- and business-school students were female. Meanwhile, as early as 1870 women had been encouraged by an act of Congress which required that those employed as clerks in government offices should be graded like men and receive the same salaries.[62]

Furthermore, the fact that the girls had received technical training, together with the probability that business executives may have decided they liked to have trained and attractive young women around, appears to have resulted in a change of mind about which sex office people should be. So by 1900 the Twelfth Census reported that stenographers and typists constituted one of the 11 occupational groups in which more than three fourths of all employees 16 years of age and over were women. There were 85,000 of them; and when 15-year-old girls were included the number was 86,000—a 30 percent increase in a single decade. Nearly two out of three of these were between the ages of 15 and 24; more than nine out of ten were under 35; four out of five were single and living at home; and more than half were of native parentage.[63]

In numbers the women in two other office groups advanced almost as much as stenographers and typists, but by no means had they kept pace with the men, to say nothing of outnumbering them. However, 81,000 women clerks and copyists were 13 percent of all so employed, and the nearly 73,000 women bookkeepers and accountants were 29 percent.[64]

The decade of the seventies had thus opened a new world of employment to women and girls who had not worked for pay before. They had received more schooling than those in

[62] Woody, II, 70; Sumner, pp. 239–40.

[63] U.S. Bureau of the Census, *Statistics of Women at Work*, pp. 102, 105–08; Sumner, p. 259.

[64] U.S. Bureau of the Census, *Statistics of Women at Work*, p. 97; Sumner, 259. When 15-year-old girls were included, clerks and copyists numbered almost 84,000 and bookkeepers and accountants nearly 73,000, which marked increases over 1890 of 33 percent and 167 percent respectively. (U.S. Bureau of the Census, *Statistics of Women at Work*, p. 39.)

the traditional occupations of domestic and personal service and manufacturing, and they seemed to be held in better social repute. In other words the advent of "paper work" was offering an alluring alternative to domesticity. Altogether, in 1900 the saleswomen, telegraph and telephone operators, stenographers and typists, clerks and copyists, bookkeepers and accountants who were 16 years of age and over numbered more than 403,-000—33 in every 100 so employed. Women seemed to be especially suited as typists and switchboard operators because they were tolerant of routine, careful, and manually dexterous.

CHAPTER 5
A Summary of a
Century of Women's Work

The accompanying table reveals some of the end results of a century of change in women's work:

Gainfully Employed Women in 1900

	10 years of age and over	16 years of age and over	Percent of all employed women		Women as a percent of all employees 16 years and over
			10 years and over	15 years and over	
Total	5,319,397	4,833,630	100.00	100.00	17.7
Agriculture	977,336	770,055	18.4	16.2	8.3
Professional service	430,597	429,497	8.1	8.6	34.2
(teachers and professors in colleges, etc.)		(327,206)		(6.5)	(73.4)
Domestic and personal service	2,095,449	1,953,467	39.4	40.2	36.8
Trade and transportation	503,347	481,159	9.4	9.9	10.4
Manufacturing and mechanical pursuits	1,312,668	1,199,452	24.7	25.1	17.6 *

Female population 10 years and over: 28,246,384—18.8 percent employed
Female population 16 years and over: 23,485,559—20.6 percent employed
Male population 16 years and over: 24,851,013—90.5 percent employed

Sources: Sumner, *Women in Industry*, pp. 18, 246, 247, 254, 259; U.S. Bureau of the Census, *Statistics of Women at Work*, pp. 9, 10, 32, 109; Abbott and Breckinridge, p. 25.
* In the foregoing text summary on manufacturing, pp. 51–52, 19 percent was given from Sumner, who included some differently classified occupations.

The table reveals first of all that, although in 1900 women were "a new economic factor"—marginal members of the nation's labor force, more than five million, or about one in every five in the female population ten years of age and over, had become paid employees, and that nearly 18 in every 100 wage earners were women 16 years and over. This means that the number of employed women had tripled in 30 years.

Much the largest proportion of these women and girls were still in domestic and personal service—more than 2,000,000 or about 40 in every 100. But it should be noted that the proportion had dropped from 58 in 100 in 1870, and that in the last decade of the century more males than females entered this form of employment. It is also well to recall that even in 1900 nearly 12,000 graduate nurses were reported as domestic and personal servants, and that hotels and restaurants had drawn many women and girls away from household work.

The second largest number of working women and girls after a century of change were in manufacturing and mechanical pursuits—more than 1,300,000, approaching one fourth of all, which was four times as many as in 1870. This is where women's paid work began, it will be recalled. They had been dispossessed of their work at home by textile machines that stimulated investment for private profit in an ambitious new country rich in natural resources. Thus "doomed to idleness," they worked in cotton mills to earn a living or to help support a family, and to free men for work in the fields. In varying degrees women were also desirable workers in the manufacture of woolen and worsted goods, silk goods, and hosiery and knitwear.

The early invention of the principle of interchangeable parts that brought mass production by semiskilled and unskilled workers at specialized machines marked a second great step in women's work. Even if they had been accepted as apprentices to the skilled trades, most girls were reluctant to spend four years in training because they expected to be married and have children. In other words they were said not to take their work *con amore,* but they could learn to tend machines in a short time, and they were quick and dexterous.

An early and highly important product of the application of the principle of interchangeable parts was the sewing machine, which did for women in the clothing trades what machines had done in the textile industry—transferred their work from home to factory. In fact, we have noted that in every census year considerably more than half of all employed women and girls were in the cloth and clothing trades, including the binding of boots and shoes, which was new to them. Their work had changed in character, but not in amount or even in intensity.

As automatic machinery and quantity production made division of labor possible in other industries, and as immigration increased at a time when textile machines were becoming heavier and more complicated, women were drawn into numerous other occupations which they had not known before. For example, the manufacture of clocks and watches and other metal products was considered "admirably adapted to the female sex" because of nimble fingers and sensitive touch. And we may recall that in 1890 the United States Commissioner of Labor reported that women were employed in all but nine out of the 369 groups of manufacturing and mechanical industries.

For the most part, men in labor unions resisted the entrance of women into their trades because they associated women's occupations with the coming of machines, which threatened their security as craftsmen. Moreover, women accepted jobs as strikebreakers at times, and took what wages they could get. An outstanding example of such a conflict was in the manufacture of cigars and cigarettes, the result of which was that by the close of the century 53,000 women and girls were at work in the tobacco industry—38 in each 100 wage earners. Women fared far less well in the organized printing trades, however, except for the semiskilled operations in bookbinding, where they comprised about half of all in that trade.

The third largest group of employed women and girls at the turn of the century were on the farm—977,000 ten years of age and over, or 18 percent of all employed females, more than 770,000 of them at least 16 years of age. The number of women and girls had increased twice as fast as the number of men and boys. However, less than nine in every 100 farm workers were women in 1900.

Coming to the Twelfth Census report on women in the professions we find that, while only one in three persons in the entire division was a woman, more than 73 in each 100 teachers were women. Consider this outcome in the light of the earlier assertion that an educated wife was "an infringement upon the domain of man."

Finally, we look at the Trade and Transportation Census for 1900 where 10 percent of all employees 16 years of age and over were women. But our table cannot reveal that in the last thirty years of the century the number of women and girls in this division soared from 19,000 to more than 503,000—some 2,700 percent. More than nine out of ten of these "white-collar" workers were saleswomen, telegraph and telephone operators, stenographers and typists, clerks and copyists, bookkeepers and accountants. The 140,000 saleswomen may otherwise have been domestic servants, seamstresses, or "working women" in some other congested occupation. But the commercial and clerical jobs—especially those created by the invention of the telephone, the typewriter, and other office devices—drew "middle-class" women and girls away from domesticity into paid work. These young women had had more schooling than other employed females except for those in the professional services. More girls than boys were high school graduates, and many of them also received special training so that business executives found themselves both surprised and pleased to have them around.

Looking back over the century, then, we witnessed in the early decades women and girls of all classes—"educated" and uneducated—entering the factory because machines had taken much of their work away. Again in the final decades we found all classes at paid work, but with the difference that four fifths of them were employed outside the factory. As railroads and business combinations expanded production and trade throughout the nation, new office and commercial devices had seemed to answer the prayers of those who had been asking what to do with daughters. In addition, nursing had become "woman's work," and more women than men were teachers. "The advance of women, during the last hundred years or so, is a phenomenon unparalleled in history," wrote a prominent feminist and reformer.

Never before has so large a class made as much progress in so small a time. From the harem to the forum is a long step, but she has taken it. From the ignorant housewife to the president of a college is a long step, but she has taken it. From the penniless dependent to the wholly self-supporting and often other-supporting business woman, is a long step, but she has taken it. She who knew so little is now the teacher; she who could do so little is now the efficient and varied producer; she who cared only for her own flesh and blood is now active in all wide good works around the world. She who was confined to the house now travels freely, the foolish has become wise, and the timid brave.[1]

Nevertheless, woman's place in American society was one of the great unsolved questions of the day, some aspects of which it is important to consider along with the changing attitude of the courts.

[1] Charlotte Perkins Gilman, *The Home: Its Work and Influence* (New York, McClure, Phillips & Co., 1903), p. 324.

CHAPTER 6
The Status of Women in 1900

The low wages paid to women have been in evidence throughout our account of the effects of nineteenth century technological changes upon their work, and in some instances the causes seemed obvious. What were disinterested observers saying?

Why Were Women Paid Less than Men?

Insofar as it was true that women received lower wages than men for the same kind of work, the United States Commissioner of Labor stressed the fact that woman had come into industry from a "general subjection to man . . . as an entirely new economic factor," which he thought was enough in itself to keep her wages low; that the pressure to secure work in the limited occupations open to her created supplies of workers greater than demands for them, so that the employer was relatively free to determine what he would pay; that her standard of life both physically and mentally was lower than man's; that her low wages were a result of "inefficient equipment for life work" owing not to lack of skill or ability but to the hope of matrimony, so that she did not feel warranted in spending years to equip herself for the best service; [1] that a woman, therefore, did not fill a good position "with the same assiduity" as a man, and her usual lack of responsibilities "either of family or of society" left her without ambition to achieve the best results.[2]

[1] "It is obvious," Abbott and Breckinridge noted, "that, for processes requiring less skill and dignity, the untrained and casual laborer will be employed. . . . And if, because of lack of training or the prospect of a temporary stay in the industrial world, women are the casual laborers, these tasks will fall to them, unless taken from them by the still less skilled and dignified labor of children" (*JPE*, 1906, p. 37.)

[2] Wright, "Why Women Are Paid Less Than Men," *The Forum*, July, 1892, pp. 634–35.

The commissioner added that woman lacked the influence that came from "combination and association" with others, except as man helped her when his object was "too selfish to be of any practical benefit to her"; that she did not become a political factor in society—and she could not vote. Hence where men who exercised economic and political power were able to get a work week of ten hours or less without legislation, both in England and America protective laws had to be enacted for women who were grouped with children.[3]

In a summary of the findings on the *Condition of Woman and Child Wage-Earners in the United States* after intense investigation early in the century, the United States Bureau of Labor made three revealing comments on the causes of differences in men's and women's earnings: first, that "to a very large degree" there was a difference in the work done; second, to a lesser degree there was a difference in the strength, swiftness, or skill when doing the same work; and third, that in so few instances as to be considered negligible there seemed no reason for the lower wages except that women were willing to accept them in order to be employed. "Almost everywhere," said the report, "women predominated in the unskilled work, probably because they could be secured for this at wages which would not attract men. . . . Women were rarely, if ever, paid less than men for doing exactly the same work." [4]

As an example of the first cause, investigators in the glass industry cited the grinding of glass tumblers. While both men and women were called "grinders," they were rarely engaged in handling the same class of ware. In all the shops studied, women were grinding tumblers and small, cheap articles, while practically everywhere men were grinding heavy and fine glass.[5] The labor commissioner also reported in 1895 that "in many cases . . . in which the same occupation admits of two

[3] *Ibid.*
[4] *U.S. BLS Bull. 175*, pp. 23–24.
[5] U.S. Bureau of Labor, *Woman and Child Wage-Earners*, III, 313.

grades of work, there is no doubt that women and children perform the lighter while the men perform the heavier grades." [6]

Another observer also noted that, even though an occupation itself may be identical, men and women were paid differently because the men and boys did subsidiary work that called for greater strength. Male press feeders, for example, not only learned the trade, which women did not, but they could be asked to lift and carry things that women could not.[7]

Conditions such as these led to the conclusion which Abbott and Breckinridge drew from the Census of Occupations, from which much of the information on women's work has necessarily been taken. Analyzing the Twelfth Census of 1900 they remarked that the report should have been presented as a census of occupational groups rather than of occupations because it did not explain the *nature* of employment. "From it," they wrote, "we can learn *how many, who, in connection with what general industries*, but NOT *what*." In particular they cited the census methods of classifying dressmakers, seamstresses, tailors and tailoresses as being so inadequate as to render the statistics "of very questionable value" because no one knew what was meant by them. Were the skilled employees in a shirtwaist factory dressmakers? Was a home finisher in a tenement a seamstress or a tailoress? The authors noted that, while the Census of Manufactures in 1900 reported 40,835 dressmakers, the Census of Occupations tallied 344,794! [8]

As for the demand for "the same wage for the same work," these commentators held that such a claim could be based only on the fact that it really was the "same work," and they asked, "Where is the same work to be found under present conditions?" The general conclusions of their penetrating

[6] Carroll D. Wright, U.S. Bureau of Labor, *Eleventh Annual Report*, "Wages of Men, Women and Children," 1895–96, p. 26.

[7] Elizabeth Beardsley Butler, *Women in the Trades, Pittsburgh, 1907–08* (N.Y. Charities Publication Committee, Russell Sage Foundation, 1909), p. 342.

[8] Abbott and Breckinridge, pp. 28, 33, 39–40.

analysis was that, in the absence of a rational system for the division of labor between men and women based upon what they were peculiarly fitted to do, "the only plan compatible with the continued self-respect of working women is evidently free competition . . . in those processes in which both can engage, which means that women must enter upon industrial life in a workmanlike spirit, have opportunity to acquire necessary skill, and overcome the obstacles to the practice of a craft after it has been acquired." [9]

In about the same vein, long-experienced and sagacious Commissioner Wright told how he thought equality of wages between men and women might be achieved:

The growing importance of woman's labor, her general equipment through technical education, her more positive dedication to the life-work she chooses, the growing sentiment that an educated and skilful woman is a better and truer life companion than an ignorant and unskilful one, her appreciation of combination, and the general uplifting of the sentiment of integrity in business circles, her gradual approach to man's powers in mental work, her possible political influence—all these combined, working along general avenues of progress and of evolution, will bring her industrial emancipation, by which she will stand, in those callings in life for which she may be fitted, on an equality with man. As she approaches this equality, her remuneration will be increased and her economic importance acknowledged.[10]

We shall see that it was more than seven decades later before Congress passed an equal-pay-for-equal-work law.

Woman's "Place"

What shall we say of "woman's place" during the century after Alexander Hamilton declared that it was in the factory instead of in the home? Contrary opinions on the subject were aired at least as early as 1829, when a writer in the Boston

[9] *Ibid.*, p. 40.
[10] Wright, "Why Women Are Paid Less Than Men," p. 636.

Courier announced that "powerful necessity is rapidly breaking down ancient barriers, and woman is fast encroaching, if the assumption of a right may be deemed an encroachment, upon the exclusive dominion of man." Asserting that the times were "out of joint," this paper cynically suggested that soon "our sons must be educated and prepare to obtain a livelihood in those dignified and more masculine professions of seamstresses, milliners, cooks, wet nurses, and chambermaids." [11]

In the next decade the National Trades' Union declared that "the system of female labor" was "the most disgraceful escutcheon on the character of American freemen, and one, if not checked by some superior cause, will entail ignorance, misery and degradation on our children to the end of time." [12] And a speaker before the Philadelphia Trades' Union hoped that the time might soon come "when our wives no longer doomed to servile labor, will be the companions of our fireside and the instructors of our children; and our daughters, reared to virtue and usefulness, become the solace of our declining years." He urged women who were obliged to work for a living to form trades' unions and get their wages raised so they could work less and finally be free from "that kind of labor which was designed for man alone to perform." [13]

Moreover, as late as 1875, when Carroll D. Wright was chief of the Massachusetts Bureau of Labor Statistics, he was saying in connection with a recently enacted law in that state which restricted women's daily hours to ten, that "Married women ought not to be tolerated in the mills at all . . . for it is an evil that is sapping the life of our operative population, and must sooner or later be regulated, or, more probably, stopped." [14]

On the other hand, woman suffragist Mary Livermore, lec-

[11] Sumner, p. 14.
[12] *Ibid.*, p. 28.
[13] *Ibid.*, p. 14; and see *U.S. BLS Bull. 175*, p. 48.
[14] Wright, *Sixth Annual Report of the Massachusetts Bureau of Statistics of Labor*, 1875, p. 183.

turing and writing on what to do with daughters, asked why continue the theory that "all men support all women" when it does not fit the facts. Many women who had husbands, she noted, were compelled to help earn the living or to "earn the entire livelihood of the whole family." Also many were widows. And the response to Horace Greeley's exhortation to "Go west, young man," had left an excess of women in the eastern states which, in Massachusetts alone, exceeded 60,000. For this and many other reasons "no girl should be considered well-educated, no matter what her accomplishments, until she had learned a trade, a business, a vocation, or a profession." Livermore found support for her theories in an address by a University of Berne professor who attributed the decline of marriage in Europe to the fact that "a woman is less able than formerly to help her husband on account of the extent to which corporate manufacture has superseded domestic industry." [15]

All in all, technological and economic forces proved stronger than the warnings and yearnings of those who looked back, but social adjustment was slow—a phenomenon which the late Professor Ogburn named the "cultural lag." [16] Hence, while at the end of the century some five million women and girls were producing "exchange values" for the market instead of "use values" for the home, the "sphere" of woman was anomalous and confused. With some exceptions women themselves were confused no less than society at large about what they could and should be doing. For this unsolved riddle, John Stuart Mill had suggested a solution in 1869, when he advised that

one thing we may be certain of,—that what is contrary to women's nature to do, they never will be made to do by simply giving their

[15] Mary Livermore, *What Shall We Do With Our Daughters?* (New York, Charles T. Dillingham, 1883), pp. 60, 61, 65, 138, 144.

[16] William Fielding Ogburn, *Social Change* (New York, B. W. Huebsch, 1922), pp. 200ff; "Cultural Lag as a Theory," *Sociology and Social Research* (January–February, 1957), pp. 167–74.

nature free play. . . . What women by nature cannot do, it is quite
superfluous to forbid them from doing. What they can do, but not
so well as the men who are their competitors, competition suffices
to exclude them from; since nobody asks for protective duties and
bounties in favor of women; it is only asked that the present bounties and protective duties in favor of men should be recalled.[17]

That some progress along these lines had been made was
attested by the Twelfth Census of 1900, which reported only
eight out of 303 separate employments in which women were
not at work.[18] Moreover, only a few years later the United
States Bureau of Labor discovered that "the married woman
is by no means an exceptional figure in the industrial world";
that in 24 out of 27 industries studied, married women constituted 10 percent or more of all women 20 years of age and
over, and in some occupations the proportion ran up to two
or three fifths of all.[19]

"The age of invention must be held accountable for this
entrance of woman into spheres entirely strange and unknown
to her," wrote Commissioner Wright 20 years after his argument against the "evil" of employing married women.

For under the hand-labor system she was used to home duties, to
field drudgery, and to the work necessary for the assistance of her
husband or father in the hand labor which he performed, and under
that system she lived a narrow, contracted, unwholesome life in the
lower walks of industry, and she was not known or recognized in
the higher . . . but with the establishment of the new system, the
attraction to women to earn more than they could earn as domestic
servants or in some fields of agricultural labor, or to earn something
where before they had earned nothing, constituted them an economic force, the result of which has been that women have assumed

[17] Mill, pp. 57–58.
[18] These were soldiers, sailors, marines; street-car drivers; firemen in fire
departments; apprentices and helpers to roofers and slaters; helpers to steam-
boiler makers and helpers to brass workers—occupations which required physical strength. (Abbott and Breckinridge, p. 24.)
[19] U.S. BLS Bull. 175, pp. 17–18.

the position and are obliged therefore to submit to all the conditions of a new economic factor.[20]

Wright pushed his thoughts further in an attempt to foresee the effects of this change upon woman herself, upon society, and upon man "as her companion and friend." That woman was in open rebellion against the old doctrine of "woman's sphere" he was certain; also that she had become "an important economic factor." For as a teacher her power was unquestioned, and she held a secure position in the arts and sciences. One temporary effect of her advance, he prophesied, would be a decrease in the marriage rate and an increase in the divorce rate. But he thought both of these results would place the family on a more sacred and enduring basis; and this in turn would enhance the morals of the community. Wright believed woman would act wisely in her new industrial freedom so that she would be "on true social equality with man," and

with such social equality her loveliness will become more lovely, she will make man's life happier and better, and with increased influence over his intellectual being, she will lead him to higher attainments, and with her intense psychic force she will be able to become a power in the world that we have not yet fully seen nor yet fully comprehended.[21]

And now that women have become a less immature economic and political factor in the twentieth century, we shall attempt to trace some effects of some of the more recent technological innovations upon their further employment and status. But first it is important to see what state legislators had been doing on behalf of those who were at work.

[20] Wright, p. 203.
[21] Wright, "Why Women Are Paid Less Than Men," pp. 637–38.

CHAPTER 7

Early Protective Labor Legislation for Women

Our story of a century of change in technology and woman's work would be incomplete without noting that the cotton mills, which first drew women out of their homes, were first to have their hours effectively limited by law, though not for several decades. Earlier protective legislation applied only to children or to men as well as women, and it was largely unenforced.

The unimplemented principle that factories should be regulated on behalf of all operatives had been established as early as 1802 in England under the influence of the great textile manufacturer Sir Robert Peel and his associates. First action in America was directed against child labor that interfered with the education of children, and it seems to have been the efforts of Horace Mann that led the Massachusetts legislature in 1842 to regulate the hours of children under the age 12.[1]

It was also in 1842 that Lowell, Massachusetts, petitioners sought to prevent manufacturing corporations from employing persons more than ten hours a day. The stated reasons were: 1. it would "serve to lengthen the lives of those employed, by giving them a greater opportunity to breathe the pure air of heaven, rather than the heated air of the mills"; 2. that "they would have more time for mental and moral cultivation"; and 3. that "they will have more time to attend to their own personal affairs, thereby saving considerable in their expenditures." [2] And it was in the midst of public and medical criticism of the long hours and bad ventilation in the Lowell mills in 1845 that

[1] Wright, pp. 266–68.
[2] Clara M. Beyer in U.S. Women's Bureau Bull. 66, Part I, p. 13.

Sarah Bagley's Female Labor Reform Association, aided by the Workingmen's Party, agitated for a ten-hour day that led to the first governmental investigation of labor conditions in the country.

From that time efforts to shorten the working day were almost continuous in Massachusetts, against opponents who pointed to the fact that girls did not stay long in the factories, as they did in England, and that factory work was no more injurious than other kinds of labor. A legislative committee was instructed in 1850 to consider the fact that Lowell mills were running 12 hours a day, 14 hours more a week than English mills; and perhaps it was this prod that influenced manufacturers in the state to lengthen the meal time by fifteen minutes [3]—a remote beginning of the "coffee break" of today!

Meanwhile, the men of organized labor, who could of course vote, had become strong enough to be a factor in state politics, and leaders conducted ten-hour conventions, delivered speeches, and wrote pamphlets. Then with the exodus of thousands of New England operatives from the mills and the influx of thousands of foreigners, political leaders became less concerned about restricting hours and more interested in aiding their own careers.[4] Organized workmen thus elected or defeated legislators according to their position on the hours bills, with the result that New Hampshire passed the first general law in 1847 that made ten hours the legal working day. Maine and Pennsylvania followed the next year, then New Jersey, Ohio, Rhode Island, and Connecticut in 1855. So with one ear lawmakers heeded the demands of workmen by putting these acts on the books, while with the other ear they listened to manufacturers by making the measures ineffective. The method was to include such unnoticed declaratory provisions as "where there is no contract or agreement to the contrary," or "nor shall any person be prevented by anything herein contained from work-

[3] Wright, p. 269; Sumner, p. 70.
[4] Beyer, p. 15; Ware, p. 154.

ing as many hours overtime as he or she may agree." And if
he or she refused to sign "special contracts," he or she was
likely to be blacklisted.[5]

MASSACHUSETTS

In Massachusetts, however, the more sophisticated petitioners insisted upon an effective act if any at all; and this so
alarmed the manufacturers of that state that in 1853 they reduced the working day to 11 hours in the hope of preventing
legislation.[6]

Following the Civil War, organized labor moved for an
eight-hour day for women, and Wisconsin passed such a law [7]
—still-born as the others had been. But again Massachusetts
moved differently. The legislative commission told workmen
that their desires could be met better outside than inside the
legislature; and attention was called to the fact that "a permanent body" of factory operatives was being created at Lowell,
composed only in part of American stock and largely of Irish
and French Canadians. Then by maneuvers that have never
been quite clear to historians, the newly proposed bill, which
became law in 1874, was restricted to "women and children
employed by woolen, cotton, linen and all other incorporated
companies"—Massachusetts workingmen having decided, as in
England, to "fight the battle behind the women's petticoats." [8]

Perhaps the major force that brought enactment of this bill
was the nation's first State Bureau of Labor Statistics created
in 1869, which began at once to urge action with the support
of spirited citizens and both political parties. Governor Washburn had argued in vain that "the limit of a day's work to
three-fourths of the laboring class in this Commonwealth being

---

[5] Sumner, pp. 69–70; Andrews and Bliss, pp. 69–70.

[6] Sumner, p. 73; Beyer, p. 15.

[7] U.S. WB Bull. 66, Part 2, p. 267.

[8] Abbott, p. 144; Beyer, p. 16; Elizabeth Brandeis, "Labor Legislation," in
History of Labor in United States, III, 462.

10 hours, I am not able to see that any great deteriment would result if the same limit should be extended to the other fourth. ... I know of no reason why it should not apply as well to male as to female operatives." But the response had been that the contemplated act was "for the protection of the health of a large class of women of the Commonwealth," and for the aid of children—objects which "have ever been recognized as proper subjects for legislative action." [9]

The Massachusetts factory law of 1874, provided with penalties for violations, thus limited the hours of women and of minors under the age of 18 to ten a day. Two years later the state supreme court decided that "there must be no doubt that such legislation may be maintained either as a health or police regulation if it were necessary to resort to either of those sources of power." [10] And in 1879–80 legislative amendments materially strengthened the act.[11]

But this was not all that Massachusetts achieved in the way of protective legislation before the century ended. The 64-hour week had been so generally established in the New England textile industry by 1890 that, during a business depression two years later, organized labor induced the legislators, against the opposition of manufacturers, to pass a 58-hour bill for all women, assuming that in practice it would apply to men as well. Also, after a campaign of more than 17 years, nightwork for women and minors in manufacturing was forbidden between the hours of 10 P.M. and 6 A.M.[12] And in 1882 the Commissioner of Labor, supported by medical men, had deplored "the barbarous practice of keeping shop-girls all day upon their feet," and induced the lawmakers to require seats for females in factories and stores. Following that the State Consumers' League, with the support of the American Federation

[9] Beyer, p. 19–20.
[10] Commonwealth v. Hamilton, 120 Massachusetts 383 (1876).
[11] *U.S. WB Bull. 66*, Part 2, p. 181.
[12] Beyer, pp. 28–29, 49.

of Labor, succeeded in 1900 in bringing women in stores under the protection of the maximum-hours law.[13]

New York State

New York was far behind Massachusetts in regulating women's factory hours. First attention was given to mercantile businesses and to tenement-house labor. An act of 1881 required seats in both factories and stores, but it was loosely drawn and generally ignored. Not until the Working Women's Society became aroused and the Consumers' League of the City of New York was formed in 1891 was there concerted action. At that time, as noted in Chapter 4, the league drew up a "white list" of shops which observed fair standards; and when a legislative committee received the bill it declared that "female employees . . . themselves regard the necessity of sitting down at unemployed times during the day as imperative. The testimony of physicians [also of some employers] is corroborative of the truth of these statements of employees." In 1896, therefore, when an hour law was enacted for stores it also required one seat for every three female employees.[14]

The New York mercantile hour law of 1896 was the result of five years of effort on the part of the Working Women's Society, which had hopelessly abandoned attempts to organize store employees, and aside from the Consumers' League they had interested a hundred clergymen in their cause. The act applied to women under 21 years of age and allowed a maximum of 60 hours a week. More than ten hours a day was prohibited unless it was to shorten one work day in the week. It

[13] *Ibid.*, pp. 44–45, 64–65.
[14] *Ibid.*, pp. 117–18. Mrs. Charles Russell Lowell, president of the league, had testified before an investigating committee in the previous year that Macy's was already putting seats behind "a great many of the counters; four or five seats—a very good, reasonable number." (New York State Legislature, *Report on the Condition of Female Labor in the City of New York*, I, 69–70.)

also excepted holiday shopping days from December 15 to January 1. Fines or imprisonment were the price of violations. League members had urged inclusion of all women, but they were less disconsolate at the outcome when an investigation indicated that 70 percent of the girls were under the age of 21. The act also prohibited young women from night work between the hours of 10 P.M. and 7 A.M. except on Saturdays and during the Christmas holidays.[15]

In the meantime, although the Cigar Makers' International Union had not succeeded in realizing the proposal of its president in 1879 for "protective" legislation for women to curb their competition in the trade, it was able to induce the New York legislature to pass a law aimed to abolish tenement-house cigar making by persons in the employ of manufacturers who were also landlords. However, when the board of health insisted that the act was "not a sanitary measure" it was promptly annulled by the state's highest court.[16]

In 1892 a new law called for regulation rather than abolition of New York tenement-house labor. Homework on 24 specified groups of articles—clothing and artificial flowers as well as tobacco products—was limited to workers who were members of the family, and a license for use of the apartment for the work was required.[17]

The measure tended to cause transfer of the work from home to factory, and a doctor's dissertation on women in the clothing trade stated with no little satisfaction that

it is generally conceded that the legal protection afforded women workers in shops and factories in New York State is ample, and

[15] Brandeis, p. 469; Beyer, pp. 68–70, 103–04. In its report for 1895, pp. 13–14, the Consumer's League of the City of New York stated that upon investigation it had discovered that 16 of the largest dry-goods houses in the city during the holiday season had filched the equivalent of 60,020 working days of 10 hours each, "which is 191 years and some months."

[16] In re Jacobs, 98 NY 98 (1885); Baker, *Protective Labor Legislation*, pp. 26, 104–05.

[17] Baker, *Protective Labor Legislation*, p. 106.

no radical change in the fundamental regulations is soon to be expected.[18]

The writer sugested that enforcement of the law in small shops could be improved, but she concluded that the constant influx of immigrants would continue to present the double problem of trying to protect buyers of the products while affording work opportunities for industrious wives and mothers.[19]

New York State's first factory-hour law was more conservative than that of Massachusetts. Enacted in 1886 following agitation by the Workingmen's Assembly in cooperation with the Society for the Prevention of Cruelty to Children, it also applied only to women under 21 and to male minors under 18—prohibiting them from working more than 60 hours a week. And although only two inspectors were provided, with no clerical help and no office space, their dedication to the aims of the act during the next ten years resulted in enforcement procedure, which, according to an official observer, made it "one of the most effective labor codes in the country." In 1889, in accordance with the inspectors' recommendation, the law was amended to prohibit nightwork by young people between the hours of 9 P.M. and 6 A.M.[20]

But a more extensive factory law was on the way. The inspectors had soon begun to recommend inclusion of all women, and they finally achieved their goal in the factory act of 1899. Primarily to aid the enforcement of the nightwork prohibitions for the younger women and minors, all females were included in the new act. In presenting their case the inspectors called attention to more stringent laws for women and children in some other states, and noted the hardships women endured because of their inability to organize. As an example they cited the fact that, while nonunion women cigar makers were working ten hours a day, members of the cigar makers' unions

[18] Willett, pp. 198–99.
[19] *Ibid.*, p. 206.
[20] Beyer, pp. 66–67, 103.

worked only eight hours.[21] Organized labor was of course glad
to join the State Bureau of Labor Statistics in supporting the
inspectors' appeal, but the validity of the nightwork prohibition for adult women was so questionable that violations were
permitted rather than to run the risk of a test case, which was
not made until after 1900.

A Turning Point

By 1900, 14 states had women's hour laws on their statute
books in addition to some other regulations [22] and the Massachusetts court decision of 1876 stood unchallenged for 19
years—until 1895.

In that year legislative skies were clouded by a verdict of
the Illinois State Supreme Court, which annulled an enforceable eight-hour law for women and children in manufacturing.
The act had been leveled primarily at sweatshop work on
ready-made clothing, with Florence Kelly—an early Hull House
resident—a vigorous supporter. Under both state and federal
constitutions, however, the Illinois court declined to follow
the Massachusetts decision on the ground that the basis of the
new law was "not the nature of the things done, but the sex
of the persons doing them," and this was discrimination against
both factories and women—therefore untenable. Women "have
a natural equality with men," the court held, "and no distinction may be drawn between them with respect to power
of engaging to labor." Moreover, there was "no reasonable
ground . . . for fixing upon eight hours in one day as the limit
within which a woman can work without injury to her phy-
sique, and beyond which, if she work, injury will necessarily
follow." [23]

But despite the Illinois decision, proponents of hour regula-

21 *Ibid.*, pp. 71–75, 103–04.
22 *U.S. WB Bull. 66*, Part 2.
23 Ritchie v. People, 155 Ill. 98 (1895).

tions for women went right on with their cause and succeeded in getting a new law in Pennsylvania as well as in New York. The Pennsylvania act permitted adult women to work as much as 12 hours a day and 60 a week, but it was an advance over legislation in other states in that it included not only factories and stores but also laundries, workshops, renovating works, and printing offices; and provisions for its enforcement were included.[24]

Moreover, at the exact turning point of the century—1900—the Superior Court of Pennsylvania validated the law of that state on grounds of physical inferiority of women and their special grouping because of potential motherhood. "Surely an act which prevents the mothers of our race from being tempted to endanger their life and health by exhaustive employment can be condemned by none save those who expect to profit by it," the court remarked, adding that

it is undisputed that some employments may be admissable for males and yet improper for females, and regulations recognizing and forbidding women to engage in such would be open to no reasonable objection. . . . Adult females are a class as distinct as minors, separated by natural conditions from all other laborers, and are so constituted as to be unable to endure physical exertion and exposure to the extent and degree that is not harmful to adult males.[25]

Thus out of the national confusion over what to do about the "new economic factor," the seed of a new judicial philosophy had been sown concerning her protection by law. That this seed took solid root in the first decade of the new century we shall see in Chapter 21.

[24] *U.S. WB Bull. 66*, Part 2, p. 244.
[25] Commonwealth v. Beatty, 15 Pa. Super. 5 (1900).

PART II
Six Decades of Change in
Factory, Office, and Shop

CHAPTER 8
Traditional Occupations

In 1900 two thirds of the American people still lived on farms and much of their family consumption was manufactured in the home by the wife and other members of the family. Since that time, technological change and improvements in productivity have caused a shift in much of the economic activity from farm to factory and shop. Today there is relatively little manufacturing carried on in the rural household. As with non-farm families, an increasing proportion of consumption goods is obtained through purchase in stores—in part a result of the movement of farm women into other employment which enables them to buy more goods instead of producing them at home.

Women on the Farm

Incredible as it may seem to us in the 1960s, although the Census Bureau announced the passing of the American frontier in 1900 we are told by a survivor that two thirds of all the homesteading occurred in the first three decades of the present century. Not afraid to work, here were "resolute bearded men and brave sun-bonneted women living in sod houses on the high, dry lonesome land so long possessed by the buffalo, the Indian and the cattlemen." They swapped butter and eggs for salt and flour and coffee. Droughts destroyed crops and starved many families out. Then the Great Depression and dust storm of the thirties put an end to the old days and marked the beginning of the new. Since that time technological advances have largely recreated the American countryside. Automation is reaching the fields as well as the factories. The size of profitable farms has thus necessarily increased to get full use of machinery, and intensive cultivation such as home gardens has been disappearing.[1]

During World War II many farmers found themselves facing a definite shortage of manpower. Sons had been drafted and hired men were in the factories. The Okies and the Arkies had also vanished for other jobs. The ranks of farm laborers had been thinned to a record low while farmers were expected to produce more than ever. It was women who had to fill the gaps. They were needed not only for their traditional occupations of packing and canning, but also for nearly all types of "regular farmwork." Hence in contrast to some 770,000 women over 16 years of age in "agricultural pursuits" in 1900, by April, 1942, more than 1,300,000 women 14 years and over were at work on the nation's farms.[2]

For the 1943 season in the northeastern states, the U.S. Extension Service of the Department of Agriculture sponsored the Women's Land Army, the Women's Volunteer Service, the Y.W.C.A., and other groups in recruiting women through whatever channels they could devise—press, radio, posters, leaflets, and various organizations. A great many women and girls signed up, and the former opposition of farmers to the employment of women was broken down. By the end of the season women had been successfully used on truck or market-garden farms, and on dairy, poultry and seed-growing farms.[3]

According to the United States Women's Bureau there were similar developments on the Pacific coast, where berries, tree fruits, grapes, hops, and certain vegetables grow in pro-

---

[1] Hal Borland, "They Lived the American Dream," New York *Times* Magazine, May 20, 1962; Michael Harrington, *The Other America; Poverty in the United States* (New York, Macmillan, 1962), pp. 43–44; Dale E. Hathaway, "Migration from Agriculture: The Historical Record and its Meaning," *American Economic Review*, May, 1960, p. 386.

[2] Katherine Glover, "Women as Manpower," *Survey Graphic*, March, 1943, pp. 74–75; *MLR*, December, 1942, 1183.

[3] *U.S. WB Bull. 199*, pp. 1, 3, 5.

fusion. Poultry farming was concentrated in some areas. More-over, the food-processing industry was closely allied with farm-ing. Women picked cherries, grapes, berries, vegetables, and citrus fruits. They thinned, picked, and canned peaches, pears, plums, and apples as the harvests came along. Occasionally they sprayed fruit trees. Men were employed for the basic planting and cultivating—Filipinos, Mexicans, Italians. The fields were considered too large and the work too heavy for women, and women were not employed in the dairies.

For the most part the women who did this work had been accustomed to earning their own livings. Among them were a few college students, a good many teachers and other profes-sional women, women from various business occupations, and some homemakers. The attitude of farmers who employed them was like that of those in the Northeast. In general they were reported to be surprised and pleased at the ability of the women to "catch on" and do very good work, and many said they could not have brought their crops in without the women and children.[4] Migratory workers came to the rescue after the war, as we shall see.

The spectacular out-migration of farm workers began on a large scale in the decade of the 1920s, when more than six mil-lion people left agriculture. In each recent decade the number has increased to about nine million, the young people leading the march.[5] Farm people who had taken part in industry's mass effort during the war were reluctant to return to a remote and lonely life. They had learned what it was to illuminate a room by the touch of a button, and farm girls had traded their wood stoves for gas or electric ranges. "I like the city, I like being with other people," said an attractive coed at the State Agri-cultural College in Pullman, Washington (now the Washing-

4 U.S. WB Bull. 204, pp. 1, 2, 11–12, 18–19, 24.
5 Hathaway, "Migration from Agriculture," pp. 379–80, 382.

ton State University), and she listed a doctor, a lawyer, and a scientist ahead of a farmer as her first choice of a husband.[6]

But the family farm has persisted. Centers of poverty and backwardness though many of them are, there appear to be compensating satisfactions from working out of doors with the growing things through the changing seasons—plowing and planting and garnering the ripened crops and garden foods and flowers. Here, family members work together, heroically sharing rewards and hardships. The Department of Agriculture found that, as recently as the mid-forties, 6,500,000 farmhouses—nearly nine in every ten—had no bathrooms or indoor toilets, and nearly as many had no running water. On such farms, aside from "packing" the water from the well and doing all the household cooking and washing, the farmer's wife often cares for the chickens, tends the garden, helps milk the cows, and feed other livestock. She shares the anxiety over mortgage debts and over taxes which threaten loss of the farm. "She knows what it means to have little or no ready cash, to be unable to buy new clothes or go to a movie. Despite all the advertisements in the women's magazines, the majority of farm women in the United States can only dream of such luxuries as electric washing machines, refrigerators, or vacuum cleaners." [7]

It was in the war period that a Minnesota professor of agricultural economics calculated that a good farmer's wife was worth $69,000. In reporting this figure, a New York newspaper editor raised it to "a flat $100,000 without quibbling" for "a lady who runs a house, takes care of children, looks after the chickens, heats the milk and bottle-feeds orphan lambs, helps in the garden, makes pie enough so a man can have a piece for breakfast, bakes beans every Saturday . . . is willing to make home-made biscuits with reasonable frequency . . . and

[6] Richard E. Neuberger, "Why People Are Moving to Town," *The Survey*, March, 1951, pp. 119–22.

[7] Grace Hutchins, *Women Who Work* (New York, International Publishers, 1952), pp. 16–17.

understands that a man wants fried potatoes for supper five nights a week." [8] The editor did not venture a similar analysis of the worth of a nonfarm, working wife.

That the family farm persists along with the trend toward factorylike farm methods was reported in 1962 by President Kennedy's Agricultural Advisory Commission, which declared that the family farm is as strong as ever, if not stronger, and that the proportion of family-type farms is greater than in the previous ten years. The commission added that, during the last decade, while hired hands have been fewer the figures appear to indicate that family farms are producing about 75 percent of the total compared to about two thirds of all 10 or 12 years ago. [9]

In fact, at least up to the present time, technological advances in the field have been considered a boon to farming because they have reduced the toil. There are new corn pickers and hay balers, to name only two; and it is said that it takes a man only six to eight minutes to harvest an acre of wheat. In the midwestern states, so-called push-button farming on the larger 200- or 300-acre farms enables families to do all the work, perhaps with time to spare. [10] One example is that of an Illinois farmer on a 240-acre farm who feeds his cattle by automatic machinery that moves feed from the silo, mixes it, and drops it in front of 400 steers in only a few minutes. [11] On some dairy farms, after udders have been washed and milking machines attached, the cows are given vitamin and hormone nutriments, and milked—all in response to a push button. In North Carolina, Mississippi, and Missouri a recently reported development is that of producing eggs on an assembly-line basis in a 10,000-bird layer house, which enables one per-

[8] New York *Times*, October 8, 1946.
[9] *Ibid.*, July 22, 1962.
[10] I.U.D. *Digest*, "Automation and the Farm," Spring, 1961, p. 100; New York *Times*, February 19, 1961.
[11] New York *Times*, October 9, 1961.

son to care for 30,000 hens.[12] Hence, for their own use many families who are looking cityward don't even bother with a milk cow or a flock of laying hens; and many farmers quickly freeze their home products instead of canning them. All this is freeing many farmers and farmers' wives to work elsewhere while they carry on part-time farming operations. In 1958 a fourth of all farm wives had off-farm jobs.[13] Increasingly they are competing for city work.

It should be added that systematic bookkeeping is becoming a vital part of farm operation. More of the younger generation who have remained on the land realize that their chances of success in this period of rising costs and consolidation of farms depends upon more information. Since the last war all farmers have had to file income-tax reports, and many have found that "its just good business" to be able to compare with others such factors as crop yields, production per man, and investments in machinery. In this way they not only obtain more efficient use of fertilizers, feed, and equipment, but they can plan ahead with more confidence. Many farmers' wives, some of whom have attended college, are keeping these complicated books. And at Michigan State University, electronic devices sort, tabulate, and compute produce quarterly and annually for each of 1,200 farmers in a state program.[14]

A more gloomy side of family farming is that of some million migratory workers (in 1950 almost a third of them women) who were called to fill the yawning local gaps created across the country after the war. The need for temporary workers for short periods of time to meet production peaks has been growing, principally because farms are larger as a result of mechanization, more specialization and seasonality; and the

[12] *Ibid.*, January 2, 1961.
[13] I.U.D. *Digest*, Spring, 1961, p. 102.
[14] New York *Times*, December 31, 1961.

substitution of purchased materials for those formerly produced on the farm.[15] The migrants—poor whites, Negroes, Mexicans, Puerto Ricans, British West Indians—thus travel thousands of miles to meet the labor shortages. Without them many crops would rot in the fields. They must "be ready to go to work when needed; to be gone when not needed," reported the President's Commission on Migratory Labor in 1951.[16] In 1949 male migrants averaged only 116 days of farm and nonfarm work in a year. The women had only 68 days— 50 farm and 18 nonfarm. From a fourth to a fifth of all migrants who worked 75 to 80 days a year in farm and nonfarm employment were between the ages of 14 and 17. For a whole year of effort each individual averaged $514 for both types of work, the men $655 and the women $234. While on the job they lived in barracks, cabins, trailers, tents, rooming houses, or wherever they could. Where two or more families were grouped they were known as "camps" and the women—before and after their work in the fields—did the cooking, perhaps over an open fire or a portable oil stove.[17] The President's Commission was deeply disturbed over health and sanitary conditions.

In John Steinbeck's *Grapes of Wrath*—called the Uncle Tom's Cabin of our depression years of the 1930s—we saw in the personal experience of the Joad family a precedent for migratory farming as they moved out of the Oklahoma dust bowl to the valleys of California. On the Atlantic seaboard a quarter of a century later some 60,000 migrants—men, women, teen-agers, and "'uncounted myriads of children"—settled down for the "pickin' season." They lived in hundreds of camps

[15] U.S. Employment Service, *ESR*, "Adapting Farm Labor to Changing Times," January, 1961, p. 3.

[16] *Migratory Labor in American Agriculture*, Report of the President's Commission on Migratory Labor, 1951, pp. 16, 54, 125–26; U.S. Department of Labor, *They Are America*, 1951, p. 51.

[17] Hutchins, *Women Who Work*, pp. 19–21.

scattered among bean patches, orchards, truck farms, and potato and tobacco fields. Large families were crowded into a
single cubicle to cook, eat, and sleep. In tarpaulin-covered
trucks they had jolted northward from Florida, where they
picked oranges, tangerines, and grapefruit.[18]

But by that time the press reported that these people were
faced with the mechanization of at least some of their work.
"It seems like that iron thing works even cheaper than we do,"
sighed Mrs. Clara Jones, who as in preceding years had brought
a crew of some 80 workers from Florida to a ranshackle camp
in the potato and bean fields of Oneida County, New York,
where picking machines were at work. And in New Jersey the
mechanical potato harvesters that are bringing in half of that
state's white potatoes have displaced more than a thousand
workers in recent years. There is also a well-established cran-
berry picker and a newer blueberry-picking machine.[19]

So it is clear that, just as technological advances helped to
create the migrant pattern, a mechanical revolution has also
been making many of these people unnecessary. Major declines
in their use have been in the "stoop-labor" category which oc-
cupies many women; and practically every crop among the
small grains has become so highly mechanized that on this
lowest skill level the harvesting and storing requires a worker
to be at least a qualified truck driver. Many other crops, including cotton and potatoes, are fast approaching this degree
of mechanization. In 1960, for the first time, half of all cotton
grown in the country was picked mechanically. Harvesting 20
acres a day the two-row mechanical cotton combine can do
the work of 200 experienced manual pickers. In the Lower Rio
Grande Valley of Texas a bale of cotton comes from the cotton

[18] Kenneth Love, "Migrant Labor in the East: 60,000 Jam Farm Camps,"
New York *Times*, August 29, 1960.
[19] Kenneth Love, "Machines Take Jobs, Driving Migrants to Rural Slums,"
Ibid., September 2, 1960; U.S. Employment Service, *ESR*, January, 1961, pp.
9, 11.

combine every 40 minutes. Operated by one man, it picks, gins, and bales the product as it moves through the field. In fact, says Director Goodwin of the U.S. Bureau of Employment Security, "Every day brings a report of some new type of equipment for harvesting some agricultural product which previously we thought could never be mechanized." [20]

But machines have by no means taken over all the work of traveling farm families. Most vegetables and fruit, although sprayed and cultivated and perhaps even planted mechanically, still require human eyes and hands for harvesting. Hence, there continues to be need for many thousands of men and women migrants, and the U.S. Department of Labor, in cooperation with the Secretaries of Agriculture, Interior, Health, Education, and Welfare joined by the Housing and Home Finance Agency, has been making great strides toward ameliorating the plight of "the forgotten people." Since 1956 Social Security benefits have been extended to many American migrants; safety regulations to govern their interstate recruitment have been strengthened and half of the states now have minimum-housing laws or regulations. Public health services for migrants have been expanded; administration of a Mexican Farm Labor Program has been revised to protect Mexicans while in the United States and to prevent adverse effects upon American workers. Moreover, an Annual Worker Plan has been devised to increase employment at the migrants' "home base" and to ensure more continuous employment while they are on the road.[21]

A recent report describes the Annual Worker Plan in Louisiana whereby migrant workers have their entire trip planned, together with living accommodations. When properly regis-

[20] U.S. Employment Service, "Farm Labor Problems—Mechanization," *ESR*, August, 1961, p. 22; *ESR*, January, 1961, pp. 3, 14; see also James H. Street, *The New Revolution in the Cotton Economy, Mechanization and its Consequences* (Chapel Hill, University of North Carolina, 1957).
[21] U.S. Employment Service, *ESR*, January, 1961, pp. 1–2.

tered they travel under U.S. Department of Labor regulations to areas in which the family prefers to work. Usually one or two families are assigned to an area where the farmer provides housing that meets minimum requirements. In brief, the migrant is assured of work before he leaves town, knows what wages he will receive, how much the transportation cost will be, and is certain that his family will have shelter upon their arrival. Here is an example of the way the plan may work, as related by the manager of the Hammond Local Office of the Louisiana State Employment Service:

After the completion of the strawberry harvest, the migrants usually move into Arkansas, Tennessee, Kentucky, or Illinois to pick strawberries there. After the berries are "in" the workers move into Wisconsin and Michigan, where they get into the cherry, apple, and bean crops.

After their tour in these States, the migrants return to Louisiana and Mississippi to work in the cotton harvest, which is followed by the tung nut harvest in both states. Work in the latter generally lasts until the Hammond area strawberry crop is ready again; the migrants move back into the Hammond area berries, thus completing the cycle.[22]

A good start has thus been made toward the solution of a gigantic agricultural problem. Furthermore, there are recent reports from Ohio and Idaho of annual "harvest holiday fiestas" being held for migrants and intrastate agricultural workers where all-day amusements for children and adults are arranged by local and federal agencies in cooperation with growers and processors.[23]

Woman's work on the farm has thus been transformed since the turn of the century. And it continues to change. While there will always be family farms, the Department of Labor

[22] *Ibid.*, pp. 24–25; see also Wisconsin State Employment Service, "The Annual Worker Plan in Wisconsin," in report on *Migratory Labor in Wisconsin Agriculture*, 1960.
[23] U.S. Employment Service, *ESR*, January, 1961, pp. 22–23.

reminds us that there is no better example of American woman's changing role than to recall that "the pioneer had to be as familiar with the plow as with the fireplace. Her modern counterpart is a skilled metallurgist whose responsibilities and knowledge reflect the vastly changed economy of the Nation." [24] Indeed, farmwork is one of only two large, occupational census groups in which women's employment has been declining. Obviously, the other is domestic service.

Women in Domestic Service

Technological change has been far less revolutionizing in the private household than on the farm; and the decline of women's employment in domestic and personal service has been far less than on the farm. In fact, there are somewhat more rather than fewer women employed in these occupations today than at the turn of the century—well over 2,000,000 instead of the little less than 2,000,000 in 1900. (More than 3,000,000 have had work experience as private-household workers.) But with our greatly expanded population this small increase means that many families formerly accustomed to having domestic service do not have it today. We shall see in succeeding chapters the nature of the magnets which drew women away from household work. At this point it is enough to note that, as compared to the almost 40 percent of all gainfully employed women 16 years of age and over who worked in households in 1900, and 18 percent before World War II, today only one in ten is so employed. But that what domestic service remains continues to be woman's work is more than evident in the fact that about 98 out of every 100 such workers are women.[25]

What are these women doing? The Census of Occupations

[24] U.S. Department of Labor, *They Are America*, 1951, p. 11.
[25] *U.S. WB Bull. 285*, pp. 11, 60.

reports for 1960 are revealing. The number of baby-sitters has almost quintupled in a decade. There are about 320,000 of them compared to less than 70,000 in 1950. In round numbers there are 140,000 housekeepers, somewhat less than 40,000 home laundresses, and well over a million women whose jobs are so varied that they cannot be classified. A fact of special interest in comparison with earlier days is that a large proportion of these people live outside the households in which they work. This is true of practically all laundresses. No baby-sitters are reported living in. Perhaps most of them are relatively near neighbors. More than half of all housekeepers are "living out," and less than ten in a hundred of the million unclassified workers are "living in." Moreover, about two thirds of these people work only part time. Less than a fifth are employed the full 50 to 52 weeks of the year.[26] Certainly the nature of household work today compared to yesterday is scarcely recognizable.

It was during World War I that large numbers of women were first drawn out of the kitchens and parlors into factories, where the pay was good and the 64-hour work week was not so long as the one that began at 7A.M. or earlier and lasted until the late dinner dishes were washed and put away. Then when the exodus from the household continued after the war, many families who had been accustomed to servants began to appreciate the privacy of being without them. They found they could get along by having an occasional cleaning woman come in by the hour, and cooks, maids, and white-coated men to take care of special dinners and other parties. During the Great Depression fewer people could afford to have help.

Perhaps it is since World War II that the greatest changes

[26] *U.S. Census of Population, 1960, Summary.* More nonwhite women are employed in households than anywhere else—37 percent of a total of about 2,700,000, all but a small proportion being Negroes. (*U.S. WB Bull. 275,* pp. 10–11, *U.S. WB Bull. 285,* pp. 14–15.)

have developed in the nature of household work. When the men came back from the Army to their brides, many went to school with the aid of the GI Bill of Rights and their wives took jobs to support the family and help pay college tuitions. As one commentator observes, "While Mother was at work, Father was at home studying, taking care of the baby, and doing the dishes. He became, in other words, a part-time wife and part-time Bridget." [27] Before going out together in the evening they installed a baby-sitter who was on the same social level as themselves. They worked and played together as companions. And this has tended to become the pattern of family life among our middle-class people, made easier by the shorter industrial work week. The house has become increasingly mechanized and numerous services reduce the labor that many husbands share. Much of the food is packaged, canned, or frozen and is always ready in the electric refrigerator for a quick meal. There are almost countless other supplies, conveniences, and improvements—and they keep coming. When it can be afforded "help" is brought in when needed.

Our statistics show that many families in the higher income brackets can and do afford to hire people to do their work in the house. At a relatively attractive salary, a housekeeper who lives in has her own room and bath and television, and perhaps air-conditioning and window plants. Recently we hear of women performing the duties of "executive housekeepers" in luxury apartment buildings, performing such services as hiring window washers, preparing breakfasts, and providing maids. It is significant that today's general census classification for all people hired to do some form of domestic service is "household workers," not "domestic service workers."

And now in a summary of the decline of the two traditional

[27] Russell Lynes, "How America 'Solved' the Servant Problem," *Harper's Magazine,* July, 1963, p. 53.

occupations of American women, the census reports serve again. Sixty years ago 58 in every 100 women were doing either farmwork or domestic service. Today the ratio is less than 13 in 100.[28] To follow their exodus, let us look for the concurrent developments in factory, office, and shop.

[28] *U.S. WB Bull. 285,* p. 11.

CHAPTER 9

Women in the Textile Industries

It was the manufacture of cotton, we remember, that brought women out of their homes at the call of Alexander Hamilton in the early nineteenth century. In those days about 90 in each 100 workers were women and girls, whereas by 1900 the proportion had dropped to only 42 in 100. The "speed of machinery," reported the Census Bureau, had caused "a slow but steady displacement of women by men."

Cotton

The revolutionizing innovation of the twentieth century in cotton textiles was the Northrup automatic loom, which came in 1895 to replace the common power loom, making weaving "men's work." Now the bobbins that carried the filler thread no longer had to be replaced by the weaver. They were fed automatically. An empty bobbin was mechanically ejected from the shuttle and a fresh one inserted in the 1/20 of a second in which the shuttle was at rest between trips across the loom. Soon the loom was made to stop automatically when a single warp thread broke.[1]

The new loom made it possible to divide much of the weaver's work into a number of specialized operations for women, such as filling the batteries with bobbins, doffing (removing) the finished cloth, and cleaning the looms. By the end of a decade the weaver was tending as many as 24 looms and making better cloth.[2]

The weave room was now ready to keep up with the output of the spinners even though the spinning department was also to be further mechanized. After World War I warp-tying

[1] Lahne, p. 13; Alderfer and Michl, pp. 341–42.
[2] Clark, III, 178.

machines began tying some 250 threads a minute in a non-stop process—each machine performing the work of about 15 hand operators; and long-draft spinning reduced the number of drawing operations, shortened the process, and made better yarns.[3]

James Northrup's loom was adopted more promptly in the cotton-growing states than in the North. There plants were equipped with new machinery while the cost of reequipping held New England manufacturers back, abetted by organized labor. Loom manufacturers thus found their market in the South, the former slave-owning section of the country where there was an abundant supply of cheap labor. Not only were there women and children who could be summoned, but plenty of men as well who had only arid, hilly ground from which to eke a living. Free from protective labor laws, the cotton mills received whole families who welcomed an opportunity to earn bread. To them half a loaf seemed like a huge meal. Southern workers were said to believe that, rather than greatly improve working conditions, employers would turn to some 10,000 Negroes as a new source of labor.[4] The United Textile Workers Union was able to call several thousand workers out on strikes in the 1920s at the time manufacturers were arriving from the North, but the great multiplant companies of the South have strongly resisted unions.[5]

Soon, inventors widened the use of the automatic loom by adapting it for the manufacture of quality cotton goods, in-

[3] Lahne, p. 153; Alderfer and Michl, p. 345; Harry Jerome, *Mechanization in Industry* (New York, National Bureau of Economic Research, 1934), pp. 84–85.

[4] Broadus Mitchell and G. B. Mitchell, *The Industrial Revolution in the South* (Baltimore, Johns Hopkins Press, 1930), p. 145.

[5] By 1956 the Textile Workers Union of America reported it had organized 15 percent of all southern textile workers—about 70,000. See Solomon Barkin, "Labor Relations in the United States Textile Industry," *International Labour Review*, May, 1957, p. 402; Barkin, "Organization of the Unorganized," Industrial Relations Research Association, *Papers*, December, 1958, pp. 232–37; Barkin, "The Southern Textile Worker," I.U.D. *Digest*, Spring, 1961, pp. 88 ff.

cluding those with patterns; and in 1929 a further advance was a 25 percent faster loom and improvements in plant layout, materials handling, and finishing that reduced the amount of labor needed per unit of output.[6] Within another decade these advances enabled a weaver of plain goods to tend up to 72 or even more automatic looms, and the once sovereign occupation was reduced to one of constant walking on a precise beat, tying broken ends when the looms stopped. The number of skilled weavers was thus sharply reduced—in one mill from 80 to 48 percent of the total weave-shed force, and for the industry as a whole from 27 to 19 percent. Concurrently, in some mills the proportion of semiskilled and unskilled workers—women and young people—rose from 20 to 52 percent.[7]

It should be noted at this point that New England had reached its peak development in cotton-textile manufacture in 1923, and that only four years later the southern states excelled in the number of spindles. It was also in the 1920s that the

[6] Lahne, p. 154; Alderfer and Michl, p. 345. Even by that time only 59 percent of New England's active plain-cotton looms and 33 percent of the fancy looms were automatic, whereas in the South the automatics comprised 80 and 67 percent respectively. (Alderfer and Michl, p. 353.)

Depressed cotton manufacturers had begun to introduce the principles of scientific management in 1923, and embraced them wholly during the general depression of the 1930s. By this system, orderly working methods were established and the weaving job was subdivided so that women and boys and girls were taken on as unskilled and semiskilled "specialists"; and in some mills they comprised as much as 65 percent of the weave-room force. (R. C. Nyman and E. D. Smith, *Union Management Coöperation in the "Stretch-Out"* [New Haven, Yale University Press, 1934], p. 23.) While many mills in North and South accomplished the changeover without serious labor unrest, bitter strikes broke out in some mills, and the system became known as the "stretch-out." (E. D. Smith, "Lessons of the Stretch-Out," in *Mechanical Engineering*, February, 1934, p. 73.) A notable such case was that of the Pequot Mills in Salem, Massachusetts, where the men and women workers were strongly organized. (Nyman and Smith) Since that time the southern mills in particular have made great strides in the application of the principles of scientific management.

[7] *American Economic Review*, a review of *Technology and Labor* by E. F. Baker, June, 1940, pp. 414–15; Jerome, *Mechanization in Industry*, pp. 83–84. Weave-room operations were further quickened by improvements in the preparation of the yarn by a combination of automatic spooler and high-speed warper which could reduce labor requirements by about half, as well as economize on floor space. (Jerome, *Mechanization in Industry*, p. 86.)

passage of immigration laws halted the influx of cheap foreign labor. So, as the Works Projects Administration expressed it, "Since cheap labor no longer came to industry, the industry moved to cheap labor."[8]

Southern cotton manufacture thus expanded rapidly, at first producing only plain cloth without patterns, which the automatic loom could weave.[9] And because of the relatively heavy work on the coarse cotton yarns, and the more common use of the Northrup loom, mill owners tended to employ men as weavers although nearly 40 in 100 were alert women who had learned largely by observation.

On the other hand, mule spinning, which had been a skilled monopoly of the males, became practically extinct before World War II, and on improved ring-frame mechanisms women spun strong, fine yarns at high speeds while performing the simple light work of mending breaks. It seems that mill owners had long preferred women spinners because they found them more tractable, more reliable, more industrious, cheaper, and more likely to stay on the job, while unionized men made trouble.[10]

The industry as a whole was employing around 183,000 women operatives and laborers in 1940—more than 40 in each 100, some 30 percent being evenly divided between skilled and unskilled and 70 percent semiskilled. The skilled women were now weavers as well as manual drawers-in of fibers and smash hands—those who repaired warp yarn after imperfect shuttle operation. Among the skilled males were card grinders, weavers, loom and other fixers, warp-tying machine tenders, and smash hands. Semiskilled males and females were drawing-frame tenders, comber tenders, doffers, frame spinners, warper tenders, winders, spoolers, reelers. Both sexes did the unskilled

[8] Works Projects Administration, National Research Project, *Labor and the Shutdown of the Amoskeag Textile Mills* (Philadelphia, 1939), p. 137; Alderfer and Michl, p. 346.

[9] Clark, III, 178–79; Alderfer and Michl, p. 342.

[10] Lahne, pp. 102–03, 238.

work, including cleaning machinery and sweeping and scrubbing. Both were listed as learners. Only men were reported as laborers and general truckers.[11]

War demands caused the cotton-textile industry to soar beyond its former peak by employing some 520,000 production workers. But by 1954 the number had dropped to 353,000, and by 1960 a further 20 percent decline brought the number to some 277,000, at which time the proportion of women was still about two in five—ring-frame spinners, yarn winders, weavers, battery hands, inspectors, and many others. But there has been no decline in production during these years. Technological changes have accounted for an increased output per worker. Virtually all types of textile machinery and processes have been improved either in speed or in size, or both. For example, even during the war the number of women ring-frame spinners was reduced by a third, and the number of loom fixers and inspectors by a tenth.[12]

Cotton manufacture has been facing trouble from at least three sources: 1. revival of cotton and other textile imports, chiefly from Japan, which has prompted both northern and southern mill owners as well as the Textile Workers Union to plead for an increase in tariffs; 2. the rise in wages in other industries, which has rendered cotton textile mills unable to retain their labor force at peak levels; and 3. the influx of manmade fibers—rayon and acetate, nylon, Orlon, Dacron, and

[11] For jobs by the same name men's wages were higher than women's. For example, men weavers in the North received 56 cents an hour and women 51 cents. In the South they received 45 cents and 43 cents respectively. (*U.S. BLS Bull. 663*, pp. 78–79, 82, 97; *U.S. WB Bull. 218*, p. 106). It is worth noting that in 1940 two out of three of the female operatives were married as compared to few more than one in three 20 years earlier when many children were at paid work. (*U.S. WB Bull. 218*, p. 108.)

[12] *MLR*, September, 1942, p. 456; *MLR*, May, 1961, p. 479, 480; *U.S. BLS Report 184*, pp. 1, 2, 20. This source reported, p. 3, that New England mills having collective bargaining agreements with labor unions employed 15,100 or 93 percent of the workers in that region in August, 1960, as compared to 15 percent of the 36,500 workers in the Southeast.

others, soon to be discussed—which were challenging cotton not only for apparel and household uses but for industrial uses as well.

However, cotton mill owners, especially in the South (which by 1960 had 97 percent of the nation's active spindles and 83 percent of the looms), have applied research that has led to more mechanization and application of the principles of scientific management through time and motion study to find the fabric combination that will yield optimum over-all returns, the human aspects of change in methods being given consideration.[13] The new mills are windowless, generally one-story air-conditioned structures, laid out so that production flows in a straight line, with materials moved mechanically; and electronic devices are being installed to measure quality and control production.[14]

The rise in the minimum wage under the Fair Labor Standards Act—to 40 cents an hour in 1945, 75 cents in 1949, $1.00 in 1956, $1.15 in 1961, and now to $1.25—and partial unionization of the southern mills has tended to reduce North-South competition. But southern mill owners have retained other advantages, such as smaller fringe benefits, heavier work loads, and multiple shifts, as well as economies in the internal handling of goods, which are less applicable in northern mill buildings.

Woolens and Worsteds

While cotton-cloth makers seem to be holding their own fairly well today, particularly in the South, wool manufacture has lagged. It will be recalled that, at the turn of the century,

[13] Clark Publishing Company, *The Southern Spinning and Weaving Industry*, n.d., p. 4; Norbert Lloyd Enrick, ed., *Time Study Manual for the Textile Industry* (New York, 1960).

[14] Textile Workers Union of America, *Report of the Executive Council*, 1960, pp. 31–32.

when children were also employed, women slightly outnumbered men in the worsted branch, but that in the industry as a whole six men were employed to every four women—a situation that prompted the United States Bureau of Labor to conclude that "all that can be said with certainty is that women are not driving out men." [15]

By 1910 the proportion of women operatives and laborers had risen to 46 in 100—some 52,600 of them; but in 1940, although the number of women had grown to approximately 61,000, their proportion had dropped to 44 in 100.[16] In September, 1957, the greatly contracted industry was employing less than 59,000 production workers, nearly 25,000 of whom were women, or 42 in 100 [17]—still a slightly higher percentage than in cotton.

What caused the drop in women's employment in this industry? What of changing technology in the woolens and worsteds? We find that during the depression of the 1930s manufacturers reduced the costs among the woolens by adopting frame spinning for women to replace the man-operated mules.[18] Moreover, while both the woolen and worsted branches installed improved looms that greatly reduced the number of weavers, the automatic box loom for woolens brought a new occupation for women—that of drop-wire girls who hand-serviced the warp-stop motions.[19]

It was in the long and complex process of preparing worsted yarns that changing technology reduced the number of women. Ring-frame spinning was substituted for cap-frame spinning, both of which employed women, but the larger bobbins that could now be used reduced the amount of doffing required. Also the slashing machine which passed the worsted threads

15 U.S. Bureau of Labor, *Woman and Child Wage-Earners*, XVIII, 325.
16 *U.S. WB Bull. 218*, p. 109.
17 *U.S. BLS Report 134*, p. 9.
18 Alderfer and Michl, p. 373.
19 *MLR*, January, 1938, pp. 78–80; *U.S. WB Bull. 232*, p. 33.

through a size solution to strengthen them for weaving, as in cotton manufacture, was equipped with greater drying capacity, which reduced the number of tenders. And there were improvements in preparing the filling yarn for the automatic loom that lowered labor requirements.[20] More recently a method has been developed for processing worsted yarns on simpler cotton-type equipment that again reduces the amount of labor, even though it calls for longer fibers.[21]

Ever since the 1920s, moreover, the woolen industry has been menaced by the coming of rayon, followed by other man-made fiber textiles. Owing to changes in living habits, there was a gradual shift from heavy- to lightweight wool and to synthetic fiber mixtures. Women chose dress goods of rayon and cotton. Men bought fewer suits and more separates—rayon suitings competing with tropical worsteds.[22]

The effect of these style changes has been that although wool manufacture was greatly stimulated by World War II demand, production thereafter declined for the country as a whole while it expanded in the southern states. For just as in the case of cotton, the South has lured the industry because of its new, one-story, air-conditioned mills, its newer machinery, its adoption of modern methods of materials handling, its absence of labor-union strength and protective legislation, and its lower labor costs. Moreover, as blends of wool with synthetic fibers become more popular to give the molding ease and nicety of wool,[23] the South's advantage increases as so many of the new fiber plants are there. By 1957 it was estimated that

[20] *MLR*, January, 1938, pp. 86, 89, 91.

[21] Alderfer and Michl, pp. 383–84.

[22] Moreover, the tariff on raw wool has probably weakened wool's position in relation to the synthetic textiles.

[23] "Wool in a way is its own worst enemy," one writer observed. "It comes from the sheep-lands as 'greese' wool, brown and matted and filled with dirt, grass, burrs and dung," while the synthetics arrive "clean, and ready to be spun." (*Fortune*, May, 1952, pp. 147–48.) The durability of man-made fiber textiles and their immunity to moths are also points in their favor as compared to wool.

the South had 16 percent of the woolen spindles and 28 percent of the worsted spindles.[24]

Some observers have predicted a gloomy future for wool because of fiber competition and foreign imports, but it seems certain that there will continue to be a demand for it, even though far less than for cotton. The United States Department of Agriculture has reported that wool's competitive position has been improving—that in 1959–60 the armed forces used more wool than cotton and man-made fiber textiles.[25]

It is interesting to learn, therefore, that while recent studies report that the total number of workers in the yarn and broadwoven woolen and worsted fabric mills declined precipitately in the 1950s, the number of women dropping from 44,000 to 24,800, the proportion of women remained more than two in every five.[26]

In the woolen mills in 1957, there were more than 2,000 women winders, more than 2,000 women frame spinners, some 1,800 women cloth menders, and more than half as many women weavers as men—1,205 and 2,285 respectively. The men were doing the mule spinning. In the worsted mills, the largest number of women were winders (2,208), then came the cloth menders (1,521), and the 1,342 frame spinners. But the men weavers in this branch outnumbered the women nearly four to one—1,109 compared to 306. In the scouring and combing plants, 705 women comber tenders and pin-drafter operators constituted only 15 in 100 production workers.[27]

In September, 1957, mills employing two fifths of the workers in the industry had collective bargaining agreements, either with the Textile Workers Union of America or the United

[24] Alderfer and Michl, p. 384.
[25] *Ibid.*, p. 385–86; U.S. Agricultural Marketing Service, *The Wool Situation,* August, 1959, p. 12; *The Wool Situation,* October, 1960, p. 11.
[26] *U.S. BLS Report 90, Wage Structure Series 2,* pp. 1, 8–10; *U.S. BLS Report 134,* p. 9.
[27] *U.S. BLS Report 134,* pp. 19–20, 50–53.

Textile Workers, that covered a majority of their production workers. But the amount of unionization ranged from nine tenths on the Pacific coast and about half in New England to a mere tenth in the Southeast.[28] The reports do not reveal the extent to which women were union members.

Silk and Synthetic Textiles

While the woolen industry suffered from the rise of man-made fibers, for the same reason silk manufacture, which was employing some 35,000 women and girls in 1900, was doomed to disappear as a separate industry.

In 1905, about 13,000 women constituted 51 percent of all employees at work on high-quality broad silks in the mills of Paterson, New Jersey—known as the "silk city," where metal workers' families were in need of paid employment. And in Pennsylvania, where there was an abundant supply of wives and children of coal miners, 59 percent of the nearly 27,000 employees producing plain broad silks were women. Only 23.5 percent were men. In the throwing process of preparing the raw silk for weaving the spinners were girls and boys as well as men, and the skilled task of twisting the skeins of silk into tight rolls and bundling them to be sent to the dyers was done by both men and women. Women and girls did the semiskilled work of operating the winding and doubling frames, and only men did the soaking and dyeing.[29]

The displacement of the hand loom by the power loom had opened a new field of paid work for women in the manufacture of broad silk and ribbons. But by no means were they substituted for men on a large scale. This was especially true of the more complicated Jacquard looms, which wove patterns because men could keep the machines "tuned up," employers

[28] *Ibid.*, p. 3.
[29] U.S. Bureau of Labor, *Woman and Child Wage-Earners*, IV, 33, 35, 189–97.

said; and men could make minor repairs, while women depended upon help from the loom fixers. The skilled but unmechanized job of cloth picking, however, was done entirely by women and girls, as was the semiskilled work on the quilling and winding frames.[30]

Changing technology also opened the skilled warping occupation to women. Physically strong men, who had always done the horizontal warping, became so thoroughly organized that mill owners reacted by installing the simpler Swiss warping mill, which women and girls could operate. Then before long the so-called Swiss motion attachment, which made the warp without showing section marks, was applied to the horizontal mill and women were very generally taken on to replace the men.[31] Moreover, it was principally the union's active resistance to an increase in loom assignments after 1910 that prompted Paterson silk manufacturers to begin to leave Paterson.[32]

The nation's silk industry prospered during and after World War I while the "queen of fibers" was supplying cloth for the average woman's dependable dress. In fact, by 1929 the number of woman and girl wage earners had risen to more than 74,500 and constituted 61 percent of all workers.[33]

But there were dark clouds in the silk skies. A high-lustered "artificial silk" made from cellulose had been appearing on the market before World War I, at first especially in the manufacture of knit goods, and by 1924 its texture had been so im-

[30] *Ibid.*, pp. 34–35, 189.
[31] *Ibid.*, pp. 39–40.
[32] Nevertheless, the ability of the Paterson mills, so near New York, to meet rush orders and do specialty work that required considerable skill, kept their collective output increasing until 1927, although production in other localities was rising faster. Automatic looms were not introduced in Paterson until as late as 1935, whereas they had been installed elsewhere during the entire post World War I period. (Works Progress Administration, National Research Project, *Employment Experience of Paterson Broad-Silk Workers, 1926–36,* [Philadelphia, May, 1939], pp. 9, 47, 100–01).
[33] Sophonisba, Breckinridge, *Women in the Twentieth Century* (New York, McGraw-Hill Book Co., 1933), p. 143.

proved that "artificial" was dropped and the name "rayon" adopted.[34]

Established silk manufacturers, particularly those who had remained in Paterson, were telling themselves that for outer-wear luxury-goods rayon could not replace silk. Nevertheless, some of them decided to shift to its use. Also appearing on the scene were producers of fine-cotton fabrics, first in Massachusetts and then in the southeastern states. They were seeking to avoid competition within their own industry, and they could shift to the weaving of rayon by making only minor adjustments on their machines. In addition, new mills sprang up that were especially designed for rayon processing. These and the converted cotton mills could operate at a higher rate of production and the weaver could tend more than double the number of looms than was possible for silk, where few looms were automatic and most of them old. Located outside the former silk cities, these establishments, especially those in the South, also enjoyed the benefits of lower wage rates and the economies of multiple-shift operation.[35]

In 1930 a study of representative rayon-fiber plants found them employing about 13,500 females or about 42 percent of the wage earners, the largest number of women being employed as reelers and lacers; cone, quill, cop, and bobbin winders; skein inspectors, and twisters, and throwers.[36] And where yarn and textile manufacture were combined, 75,700 women operatives and laborers were at work—56 in each 100 wage earners. A decade later the number of workers had declined and the 48,200 women comprised slightly more than half of all employed. The production of silks had apparently

[34] The next year the Census of Manufactures made a separate report on rayon fiber, which had formerly been included with the chemical industries. See Alderfer and Michl, pp. 400, 403, 421.

[35] Paterson, New Jersey, manufacturers were placed at an even greater disadvantage with the increasing use of rayon for dress goods after 1926. (Works Progress Administration, *Employment Experience of Paterson Broad-Silk Workers, 1926–36*, p. 100.)

[36] *MLR*, December, 1930, p. 151.

fallen more rapidly than the output of rayon textiles had risen.[37]

The victory of rayon over woven silk fabrics was virtually complete by 1940, especially for dress goods, and the industry became known as "silk and rayon manufactures." Acetate had soon become a second man-made cellulose fiber, and by 1943 rayon and acetate—known as "cellulosics"—accounted for 10 percent of all textile fibers consumed in the United States.[38]

By this time nylon had also arrived in the man-made fiber production arena—the first of the fully synthetic, "noncellulosic" fibers, soon followed by others. Thus opened a "battle of fibers" in which nylon, Orlon, Dacron, and other chemically produced fibers cut into the market for rayon and acetate for wearing apparel and tires; and since 1950 they have prevented significant expansion of the cellulosics.[39] Altogether, however, by 1957 the man-made fibers had risen to a rank second only to cotton in terms of total fiber consumption in this country—28 percent as compared to 66 percent, cotton having held its own as a style fabric in the apparel field.[40]

Women are employed extensively in only one of three groups or processes in the manufacture of man-made fibers—not in the chemical preparation of the spinning solution, or in the transformation of the spinning solution into solidified filaments, but in the finishing operations that convert the product into the form in which it is to be used—yarn for textiles, for example. Here in the third process, the Bureau of Labor Statistics has found women yarn winders, throwers (twisters), creel tenders, and warper operators in the rayon and acetate

[37] U.S. WB Bull. 218, p. 111.

[38] MLR, June, 1959, p. 653.

[39] But rayon was being applied to a widening range of uses. Gradual technical improvements increased the strength and pliability of the yarn. Also, special, high-tenacity viscose rayon yarn was developed which was suitable for industrial uses, particularly for the rubber-tire industry where it has largely replaced cotton. (Alderfer and Michl, pp. 395, 397, 401.)

[40] MLR, June, 1959, p. 653. Over the 17-year span 1937–53 the end-use consumption of man-made fibers increased by more than 1,200,000,000 pounds or 353 percent as compared to 594,000,000 pounds or 14 percent for all the other fibers. (Textile Organon, June, 1955, Supplement, "Textile Inter-fiber Competition," p. 98.)

establishments, and draw-twist and warper operators in the noncellulosic plants. Women are also laboratory assistants, and many more women than men are physical test operators.[41]

There were nearly 12,000 women in a total of almost 46,500 production workers in these synthetic fiber plants in 1958— about 26 in 100, the many skilled maintenance employees and the chemical operators and spinners being men. In the rayon and acetate plants the proportion of women was only 23 in 100 as compared to 32 in 100 on nylon and other noncellulosics. In both branches of the industry, including specific occupations called by the same name, men's straight-time average hourly earnings were higher than women's; but women were receiving relatively higher wages than in other branches of textile manufacture. Approximately 85 percent of the industry's production-work employment was in the South, yet mills employing three fourths of the production workers had collective bargaining agreements covering a majority of their workers, the major union being the Textile Workers of America.[42]

Many more women are employed in synthetic textile mills that produce yarn and cloth than in the fiber mills. In 1960, of some 73,000 workers employed in regular textile operations through the cloth room (68 percent of them in the Southeast), two in every five were women. They included 8,085 yarn winders, 3,254 weavers—more than half as many as men weavers, 2,283 battery hands, 2,306 ring-frame spinners, 2,137 machine-cloth inspectors, 1,893 ring-frame twister tenders. Men's numerically most important occupations were as weavers, loom fixers, and maintenance machinists. Technological changes have increased productivity so that employment has declined for both men and women.[43]

New synthetic fibers are appearing continuously—some of

[41] *MLR*, June, 1959, pp. 653–54, 656; see also for an earlier account, *U.S. WB Bull. 50*, pp. 22–23.

[42] *MLR*, June, 1959, pp. 654–56; *U.S. WB Bull. 275*, p. 69.

[43] *MLR*, June, 1961, pp. 620, 621, 623. Mills with collective bargaining agreements employed about half of the workers in New England and Middle Atlantic states and less than one tenth in the Southeast. (*Ibid.*, p. 621.)

them quite new and some improved versions of older ones; and they act as a restraining factor in the competitive development of nontextile materials such as paper yarns, flexible and rigid plastics,[44] and fiber glass. In 1960 the Man-Made Fiber Producers Association listed 55 trade-marked fibers which its members were marketing, and Congress passed a Textile Fiber Products Identification Act which required use of the appropriate name along with each trade name, such as Antron nylon, Estron acetate, Avril Rayon, and others.[45]

Knit Goods

The manufacture of knit goods is usually considered part of the textile industry although it differs from cotton, wool, silk, and synthetics in three respects: 1. the mills rarely spin their own yarn; 2. the mills not only knit the fabrics but they make them into garments—outerwear, underwear, and hosiery; and 3. owing to so many technological improvements, the industry employs a much higher proportion of women—more like the women's clothing industry, as we shall see in the following chapter. In 1905, 66 in each 100 operatives were women and girls compared to 57 in silk, and 41 in cotton.[46] At the end of the decade more than 129,000 workers were making knit goods of whom 64 percent were women and 8 percent children. Plants extended all the way from New England to Michigan and Wisconsin with by far the largest number in Pennsylvania, New York, and Indiana. There were only a few mills in the South— in North Carolina and Louisiana.[47]

---

[44] In 1960 some 25,000 women accounted for about 38 percent of all production workers in the plastics-products industry—more than half of them as finishers of molded-plastic products and as injection-molding machine operators. Among others were operators of compression molding machines, inspectors, packers, and janitors, (*U.S. BLS Report 168*, pp. 3, 9.)

[45] New York *Times*, June 15, 1960.

[46] U.S. Bureau of Labor, *Woman and Child Wage-Earners*, IV, 16.

[47] *Ibid.*, XVIII, 194–95, 206–07. By 1930, Massachusetts was still employing 71 women in every 100 workers, Ohio 80, and Virginia 72, all white workers. (*U.S. WB Bull. No. 159*, p. 17.) The industry had expanded throughout the

The settling of knitting mills in the silk towns of Pennsylvania and New Jersey, and the fact that they not only paid better wages but that their work was cleaner and less noisy than silk manufacture, created what the Silk Association called a "veritable famine" in female help. It was also at this time that New York, New Jersey, and Pennsylvania legislatures were increasing the age limit in child labor laws.[48]

There seems to have been little competition for employment between the largely unorganized men and women in knitting mills, at least in the early years of the century. As a matter of course the men, sometimes assisted by boys, usually did the heavy, wet, and dirty work such as dyeing, fleecing, and pressing, as well as the highly skilled jobs of cutting sleeves and legs and shaping bodies of undershirts, operating full-fashioned machinery, and performing duties that required mechanical knowledge. Also, as a matter of course, women, classified as semiskilled and unskilled, operated the sewing machines and some knitting machines, and performed the light hand operations that required their defter touch and keen appreciation of appearance in such work as finishing, folding, pairing, and stamping.[49]

KNIT UNDERWEAR

Underwear factories are said to have developed the highest degree of work subdivision and standardization. Here in the early years both men and women, and some children, wound the yarn on large cone-shaped bobbins, replacing spools and tying broken threads. In the absence of the much more complicated full-fashioned machines used for outerwear and hosiery, women as well as men did the knitting. On circular machines

1920s and much of the growth was in new, nonunionized areas, (Works Projects Administration, *Trade Union Policy and Technical Change* [Philadelphia, 1940], p. 47.)

[48] U.S. Bureau of Labor, *Woman and Child Wage-Earners*, IV, 20–21.

[49] U.S. Bureau of Labor, *Woman and Child Wage-Earners*, XVIII, 199, 213.

they turned out tubes of seamless cloth suitable for men's undershirts. On smaller circular mechanisms they made the cuffs, waistbands, and ankle bands used to finish the legs and arms; and they produced continuous widths of cloth on flat-rib knitting equipment. These women kept their machines in order, threaded them, replaced needles and bobbins, and watched against imperfect knitting. The mechanics who set up the equipment and prepared it for operation were men, and men washed the products and pressed them in mangles.

Among the numerous sewing operations on knitted underwear were the seaming and cuffing on different types of machines in which experienced women were said to become so proficient that they scarcely needed to look as they stitched. Similar operations were those of setting sleeves and inserting gussets in the seats of drawers. The hand-marking, examining, mending, and folding operations were performed on the garments' way to the finishing department where sleeves were stitched up and inserted, drawer legs sewed and fastened together at the top, necks and fronts cut out, bands, buttons, and tape put on, eyelets made, necks, bands, and straps stitched around, and all else.[50]

By 1936–37 some 65,000 workers, from 75 to 80 percent women, were employed in the manufacture of knit underwear —cotton, wool, rayon, and silk. They made women's, misses', and boys' garments as well as men's. The industry was highly concentrated in the Middle Atlantic states, the National Recovery Administration classifying 88 percent of all mills as northern and 12 percent as southern, with New York City housing nearly 90 percent of the cutting and sewing establishments and about 35 percent of all workers in the industry.[51]

A more recent study of a limited number of plants which

[50] *Ibid.*, pp. 200–203.
[51] Underwear Institute, *The Underwear and Allied Products Industry, Business-Building Facts*, 1936–37, pp. 1, 7–9, 16, 39.

represent a cross section of the industry finds that women continue to comprise 80 percent of all workers in knit underwear, and that the majority of them are housewives. Most of the factories have remained in the rural, mining, and heavy-industry areas where employment opportunities for women are limited, and usual working hours—from 7 A.M. to 3:30 P.M., five days a week—are arranged to permit women to meet their homemaking obligations. Training of new workers is usually "on the spot" under the supervision of skilled operatives or foremen and forewomen. In 1951 weekly earnings were only about two thirds of average earnings in all manufacturing industries.[52]

In these plants women are still predominantly employed on the "making" processes—some cutting and practically all of the sewing and finishing. Men as well as women do the knitting, and only men do the bleaching and dyeing. In the medium-size mill the knitting can be done by one machine fixer and a few operators who replace empty cones or warps of yarn, tie knots in broken threads, and unload the roll of finished fabric. The "fixer" who also acts as a working foreman enables the operators to knit more rows at a time. The well-lighted machines stop automatically when needles or yarn break. By power-driven mechanisms the knitted and dyed material is spread on long tables and cut with electric-powered knives—said to be a simple operation.[53]

The sewing department in these mills is usually divided into sections, each making one type of garment, and for women's wear it may be further divided for different colors or styles. Sewing-machine operators trim their own work, using hand scissors. Finishers trim and inspect the garments before they are pressed, folded, and boxed. In some men's undershirt fac-

[52] *U.S. BLS Report 41*, pp. 4, 7, 107, 109. In this study men's undershirt factories were also making "T" shirts and shorts, and panties—from very fancy ones with lace and net edging or inserts, to tailored types. (*Ibid.*, pp. 2, 5.)
[53] *Ibid.*, pp. 1, 5–7, 11, 109.

tories a three-girl team handles the pressing machine on a conveyor belt.[54]

KNIT OUTERWEAR

Making knit outerwear is a far more varied operation than for underwear and employs somewhat fewer women—about 73 in 100. The largest group of products includes polo, tennis, basque, and sweat shirts; sweaters and jackets coming next. There are also, of course, bathing suits, trunks, and athletic shorts, knit headwear, dresses and suits, children's and infants' wear, and kindred articles. Again it has been the Middle Atlantic states that produce the most knit outerwear—nearly two thirds of the value added by manufacture in 1958, including New York's 28 percent. And by this time the southern states were producing 11 percent as compared to little more than 3 percent in 1953.[55]

The increasing use of modern machines such as for cone-bobbin winding, electric-powered knife cutting, high-speed sewing and seaming, pin ticketing, steaming, and automatic button and buttonhole marking, is one of the factors that has tended to increase output and decrease unit man-hours in outerwear knitting mills.[56]

The Department of Labor has found that another leading factor in increasing productivity is the excellent care given to the machinery. In these mills machine fixers devote their entire time to setting up the equipment and keeping it operating, which in turn increases the earnings of workers. Machine breakdowns, other than needle breakage, thus occur less frequently even though the mechanisms may be old. Some sewing machines may have finger guards as a protection against injury

[54] *Ibid.*, pp. 11, 14–15.
[55] *U.S. Census of Manufactures, 1958*, II, Part 1, 22 B–10; *U.S. BLS Report* 40, p. 72.
[56] *U.S. BLC Report 40*, pp. 1, 57. Except in the very large plants the dyeing of wool and synthetics is done by commission dye houses because of the specialized equipment and particular skills required. (*Ibid.*, pp. 34–35.)

and are important when training new employees, but many women remove them as nuisances when they become proficient.[57]

As would be expected, when we come to the sewing, finishing, and examining of knit outerwear we find many women and few men. And the layouts of work and use of equipment may differ in different mills. In some plants, for example, the shoulders of women's cardigan sweaters are seamed to prevent the yarn from unraveling, the collar is looped to the body as is frequently done on full-fashioned garments, the sides are seamed, a backing ribbon is sewed down the front to anchor the buttons, buttons and buttonholes are marked and sewed, sleeves are joined to the body, and the labels stitched on. Likewise, after the collar points are made on a man's slipover the operations may be to seam the shoulders, tape shoulders and back to the neck, and sew on the collar and armhole trim. Finishing garments consists of trimming off excess threads, examining for defects, and repairing damage where possible. Final operations include finish-pressing or steaming, sewing on the labels, folding, and boxing for shipment.[58]

Unionization of knit underwear and outerwear workers varies according to location. Ninety percent of the underwear employees in the New York metropolitan region work under written contracts. Elsewhere, perhaps a great majority are in nonunion plants. The International Ladies' Garment Workers Union and the Textile Workers Union of America are the predominant unions. Typically, union-management contracts provide for equal division of work during slack seasons and for the "right to a job" after a trial period is served. Moreover,

[57] *Ibid.*, p. 26. In some mills the working foreman performs the "fixer" functions and the operators set up their own machines and make their adjustments. The knitting is usually done by men. The cutting of such garments as men's slipover and women's cardigan sweaters requires considerable experience and skill and is usually also a man's job.

[58] *Ibid.*, pp. 4, 7.

they include an allowance of six-months maternity leave for women and an extension of the leave upon a doctor's advice.[59]

A UNION-MANAGEMENT AGREEMENT ON TECHNOLOGICAL CHANGE

Over the past 25 years, with the more rapid growth of labor unions, labor-management adjustments to technological change have often been reached on a case-by-case basis, the experience gained then being applicable elsewhere. An especially interesting example involving women was the introduction of an automatic trimmer to replace hand-trimming of loose threads with scissors in a plant which employed 275 workers in the manufacture of knit juvenile garments. The new mechanism resembled an electric hair clipper in operation, with the added feature of a vacuum suction device which drew in the clipped threads. Before installing the equipment the plant manager discussed his plans with the forewoman for the section and the union chairlady (shop steward). He told them he intended to buy eight machines and select and train eight operators from the 21 existing hand trimmers, and that their selection would be based on dexterity and manual skill. Soon after the machines were installed, four more of the hand workers were appointed to assist the eight operators by buttoning the trimmed garments. This left only nine hand trimmers. Production neither increased nor decreased.

After an eight-week trial period the machine operators asked to be put on a piece rate; and at the request of the union business agent the period was continued for another five weeks. During this time two more hand trimmers were put on the buttoning operations, making six to assist the eight machine trimmers—the final size of the crew. Moreover, the piece rate was somewhat increased for the machine trimmers and button operators with the result—for reasons unexplained—that they began to earn from 30 to 35 percent above the former av-

[59] *U.S. BLS Report 41*, pp. 109–110.

erage, and the manager estimated a cost saving of 30 percent on direct labor in the trimming operation.

What became of the seven surplus hand trimmers? As a result of labor turnover five of them could be placed at once on such hourly jobs as packing and inspection at their former earnings. The other two were too old for this "stand-up" work and were given other jobs. Moreover, all these adjustments were made easier by two fortunate circumstances: 1. style changes called for more buttons per garment, thereby opening two more buttoning jobs; and 2. the volume of orders increased. In fact, more women had to be hired for the work that followed the trimming operations in order to round out production. Both management and the union were satisfied with the outcome and the plant was able to carry out a modest expansion.[60]

HOSIERY

Early in the century the winding process in hosiery manufacture was the same as for underwear, but the next operations depended upon the kind and quality of the product. The ribbed upper portion of cheap grades of children's stockings and men's half hose were often knit first, when, instead of the cloth revolving and the knitting appartus remaining stationary, the knitting machine revolved around the hose. The ribbing was knitted in a long, tubelike web which was then cut to the desired, mechanically indicated lengths by a girl or woman using a machine operated by foot power, or sometimes with a pair of scissors. The separate pieces then went to the "topper," or transferrer, who put them on quills that were used to transfer the tops to the circular knitting machines which made hosiery without a seam. In some factories the topping and knitting were done by the same operator; but where this work was separated, one knitter could keep four girls busy topping.

[60] *Ibid.,* 112–15; *U.S. BLS Report 40,* pp. 63–65.

Sometimes instead of beginning with the ribbing, the foot and lower part of the leg were knitted first, then placed on the needles of the ribbing machine and the top knitted on.

Woman or boy "turners" received the socks or stockings after they were knit. Female "loopers" took them next, having carried the 35- to 50-pound bundles to their machines, where they closed the toe gaps, removed the completed hose, and tied them in bundles. Some hosiery then went to the fleecer, who was almost always a man, for although the work required no particular strength or skill it was very dusty. Women mended damaged spots, turned down the tops of the hose, and hemmed them on a welting machine which was much like an ordinary sewing machine. Men dyed and pressed them in a drier. Women paired, stamped, and stacked the goods in bundles of special sizes and boxed them. Men packed the paper boxes and prepared them for shipping.[61]

Before World War II the Bureau of Labor Statistics studied the full-fashioned hosiery industry, at which time 95 percent of the output was women's all pure-thread silk or pure-thread silk with lisle or cotton tops, heels, and toes. The industry was predominently northern, but a "decided trend" to southern states was noted.[62] The mills in the sample survey employed 28,000 workers, about 15,000 of them women. Of all employees, 64 percent were classified as skilled, 23 percent semiskilled, and 13 percent unskilled. Interestingly enough, more of the skilled workers were women than men, though men did practically all of the highly experienced knitting. Nevertheless, with the exception of forewomen the average hourly earnings of all skilled females were below those of any of the skilled males.

Full-fashioned stockings were knitted flat, being widened or narowed in the process to conform to the leg. The knitting

61 U.S. Bureau of Labor, *Woman and Child Wage-Earners,* XVIII, 203–05.
62 *MLR,* May, 1939, pp. 1148–49.

machines were extremely complicated and the fragile silk had
to be handled with great care. Woman loopers, toppers, and
menders and man knitters were all classed as skilled.[63] Among
the semiskilled workers were male and female, automatic and
nonautomatic, "boarders," who dried and shaped the wet stockings on wooden or metal forms; male dye-machine operators
and packers; female inspectors, pairers, and winders. Women
folders, wrappers, boxers, stampers, and labelers were among
the unskilled. Women accounted for half of all boarders.[64]

The full-fashioned branch of the industry was extensively
unionized, half of all mills studied working under written contracts with the American Federation of Hosiery Workers; but
only one southern mill had such an agreement.[65] In the seamless hosiery mills on the other hand, more than three fourths
of whose employees in 1938 were in southern states, principally North Carolina, there was very little trade unionism.[66]

Seamless hosiery is so named because it is knit in tubular
form, and though it can be shaped a bit in the knitting process
it has approximately the same diameter from top to toe. On
women's seamless hose, and sometimes on men's, it was common practice to make a mock seam up the back to give a full-
fashioned look; and sometimes after the seaming it is said that

[63] *Ibid.*, pp. 1150, 1151, 1157–58.

[64] *Ibid.*, May, 1945, p. 983.

[65] *Ibid.*, May, 1939, p. 1147. In 1937, disputes over multimachine operation
and wage rates for knitters, in the light of nonunionized southern competition,
prompted employees of the Apex Hosiery Company in Philadelphia to call a
sit-down strike which lasted seven weeks with the aim of forcing the company
to accept a closed shop under the National Labor Relations Act. The local
union joined the American Federation of Hosiery Workers (CIO), and litigation under the Sherman Anti-Trust Act ensued. The final outcome was that
the United States Supreme Court denied the union's contention that it was
wholly exempt from prosecution under the Sherman Act, but the court also
refused the company the right to collect $711,952 in damages from the Union.
(Apex Hosiery Company v. Lederer, 310 U.S. 469 [1940].) For the technological changes involved, see Works Projects Administration, *Trade Union Policy
and Technological Change*, pp. 35–36, 45–48, 62–66, 110, 115, 122.

[66] *MLR*, June, 1939, pp. 1388–90.

the stocking could be fairly well shaped by cutting out part of the fabric at the ankle.

In contrast to full-fashioned hosiery, the seamless mills made many different kinds of products. The materials for women's wear in the 1930s were principally all-cotton, all-rayon, all pure-thread silk, and pure-thread silk or rayon with lisle or cotton tops, heels, and toes. All-cotton was most common for young people's and children's wear, and for athletic hose the rayon and cotton mixtures were also used. Much seamless hose was knit in two or more colors, which required previously dyed yarn, or it was cross-dyed after knitting.[67]

But despite the variety of styles and color combinations, this branch of the industry required little skill. In fact only 6 percent of the total labor force in the country was classified as skilled (male working foremen, machine fixers, and indirect employees) as compared to 64 percent in the full-fashioned branch. Seamless-hose workers, who were regarded by employers as semiskilled, constituted 73 percent of all, and the unskilled 21 percent. Women composed 69 percent of all wage earners—53 semiskilled and 16 unskilled.[68]

Both men and women did the semiskilled knitting of seamless hose on highly automatic machines. Their duties were largely those of tying broken yarn, removing completed stockings, and transferring rib tops for certain types of hose. The looping operation was similar to that for full-fashioned hose, although the relatively coarse yarns were less susceptible to damage in handling and more easily placed on the points of the looping machine.[69]

The boarding occupation of shaping the stockings was next to knitting in numerical importance, but only 15 in 100 board-

[67] *Ibid.*, p. 1389.
[68] *Ibid.*, pp. 1388, 1391.
[69] *Ibid.*, pp. 1391, 1397.

ers were women, although they received 1.5 cents more in average hourly earnings than the men. That there were so many fewer women boarders than in full-fashioned hosiery seems to have been a result of inertia on the part of mill owners along with the fact that the product was less dependent on soft hands because it was heavier and less sheer.[70]

During the war women replaced men in important occupations in both the full-fashioned and seamless branches of the industry. It happened that, when the mills were first confronted by a shortage of males, raw materials such as silk and nylon were no longer obtainable, and an attempt was being made to change to the use of rayon and to adjust output to rationed supplies. In fact, the temporary layoffs and fractional work weeks during this transition period contributed to the drift of both men and women away from the industry, with the result that their numbers dropped from about 159,000 in 1939 to 128,500 in 1942. Then by the time a balance between labor and materials had been struck, many of the best male workers were gone, most of them under 38 years of age. Moreover, since hosiery was not considered as essential product the men continued to leave, either to enter the armed forces or to take higher-paying jobs where their mechanical aptitudes were needed. Not only were these men difficult to replace but plant managers hesitated to go to the expense of training new ones for skilled jobs because of the likelihood of losing them under war conditions.[71]

One obvious solution to the problem was to employ women, many of whom had never worked in industry before, probably

[70] Ibid., pp. 1396, 1397. The level of earnings was decidedly lower than in full-fashioned plants. The average hourly wage for men was 42.5 cents, and 31.4 cents for women—the difference being explained mostly by the average of 64.2 cents for the working foremen, machine fixers, and skilled indirect employees. Thus the adjustments to 40 cents under the Fair Labor Standards Act would directly affect the hourly earnings of more than 60 percent of the semiskilled males and 80 percent of the females, and 85 percent of unskilled males and females. (Ibid., pp. 1393, 1399–1400.)

[71] MLR, May, 1945, p. 978.

some of them homemakers. Jobs were thus simplified and other techniques adjusted, and in the five years 1939–44 the proportion of women rose from 57 to 63 percent in the full-fashioned branch and from 67 to 75 percent in the seamless branch.[72]

But could women do the full-fashioned knitting under any circumstances? The answer was yes if the right ones could be found. The most logical recruits were the toppers, who were so familiar with the whole process that they should learn to knit reasonably well within a few weeks. Originally a "man's job," topping called so much for the feminine quick eye and manual dexterity that by 1938 women had replaced all but seven men in a hundred and by 1943 there were no male toppers at all. But by this time there were few women toppers because many had been displaced during the past decade by a process of single-unit knitting, and had left the industry. Others were leaving to enter war work, where their knowledge was particularly useful on precision assembly operations and similar work. For knitter learners, therefore, employers were forced to rely upon women from other jobs in the plants, if not upon those entirely new to hosiery manufacture. The knitting job was adjusted to enable each remaining male knitter to supervise three or four women operators, each attending to one machine. In only a few mills were women given entire responsibility for knitting, largely because it required technical supervision as well as assistance on manual operations too strenuous for most women.[73]

Newer and improved knitting machines in some mills increased women's opportunities, however. For example, an automatic mechanism that turned the welt on all stockings at once eliminated time-consuming manual adjustments on each individual stocking to the extent that at least one mill with a welt turner on each single-unit machine reported satisfactory

[72] *Ibid.*, p. 979.
[73] *Ibid.*, pp. 979, 981, 984.

performance from its all-woman knitting department. In another mill that had employed only men, 11 girls comprised two thirds of all knitters.[74]

Actually, when the efficiency of women in full-fashioned knitting occupations was evaluated as compared to that of men, it seems that the nature of the equipment—whether old or modern—was the principal deciding factor. Types of machines, local conditions, previous experience, and individual aptitudes accounted for large variations in women's performance. It is of interest, therefore, to learn that in 1945, while 7 percent of the knitters in 117 mills in selected areas were women, in southern states where machines were newer 13 percent of all knitters were women. Nevertheless, the fact that men could take complete charge of the mechanisms and make minor repairs, together with the fact that they would probably make the job a lifetime trade whereas women were likely to leave if and when they married, caused most mills to prefer men if they could get them. It is possible, therefore, that the subdivision of duties in full-fashioned hosiery knitting so that women could replace men was only a temporary wartime expedient.[75]

Unlike knitting, the boarding operations on full-fashioned hosiery at the end of the war were said to hold the greatest opportunities for women, provided the unpleasant conditions of excessive heat and humidity which had repelled them could be lessened. Many mills were preferring women boarders largely because of their greater manual dexterity and softer hands, which did less damage in drying and shaping the delicate product, particularly rayon, which was relatively weak when wet. Manicure service and a ban on rings and bracelets further lessened the damage. But even during the war no woman machine fixers were found in the plants surveyed, nor

[74] *Ibid.*, pp. 981–82.
[75] *Ibid.*, pp. 982–83.

did women work under the unpleasant conditions of the dye-house.[76]

In the highly automatic seamless-knitting branch there was little trouble in replacing men knitters by women during the war, the number varying considerably from mill to mill according to the type of knitting and the machine model in use. Women's finger nimbleness made them especially adaptable to "hand-transfer" knitting where they worked on sets of four or five "footer" machines. Something like that for full-fashioned hose, this operation involved the transfer of the knitted rib top (the welt) from one mechanism, link by link, onto the needles of a circular ring to be placed on the footer, which turned out the finished sock. However, between 1938 and 1940, when a less expensive elastic-top knitting machine was introduced, largely as a result of minimum wages under the Fair Labor Standards Act, there was a marked decline in transfer knitting where unit costs were high, and a less marked rise in automatic and converted transfer knitting. Employment of knitters declined 15 percent, therefore, while total employment fell only 3 percent. Then when rubber could not be procured, the mills returned to hand-transfer hosiery. By 1943, 95 of every 100 knitters were women, half of them on automatic machines.[77]

Although the postwar outlook for women seamless-hose knitters looked considerably brighter than in the full-fashioned branch, it was thought likely that they would not be retained on the automatic machines where men were preferred because of their technical knowledge and aptitude for mechanics. This would be true of nylon "bare-leg" hosiery also, in which a boom was expected when nylon became available again for

[76] *Ibid.*, pp. 983–84.

[77] *Ibid.*, pp. 985–86, 987, 988. On a set of four or five hand-transfer machines (footers) one knitter could produce only 14 to 18 dozen pairs of hose in eight hours, while on a set of 20 to 30 automatic or converted machines she could turn out 80 to 95 dozen pairs of similar pattern; and the job required more responsibility.

civilian use. This forecast was not borne out. In 1957 a sample study found about 2,200 women automatic-machine knitters as compared to 406 men! [78]

Since that time new technology has revolutionized women's seamless hosiery manufacture. Woven in tubular form, one stocking at a time, one of the new processes is the bombardment of the stocking with high-frequency ultrasonic waves that change the molecular structure of the nylon and give it properties not before available in seamless hose. Manufacturers say that these hose now fit the leg and are cooler in the summer and warmer in the winter.[79] The end result is that women's seamless hose on which more than four fifths of the workers are women, constituted 86 percent of total production in 1963 as compared to little more than one third in 1957. In fact, fullfashioned hosiery seems to be disappearing from the market.

In the nation's knitting mills as a whole, despite the generalization that women lack technical knowledge and mechanical aptitude, 68 out of every 100 workers were women in 1963—148,200 of them.[80]

Summary

In sum, what can be said of women's employment in the twentieth century textile industry, affected as it has been by two wars, numerous technological advances, and the battle of the fibers in which wool and silk seem to have languished while cotton and knit goods have prospered? In this industry—woman's traditional niche in the world of manufacture—more than 418,000 women constituted 45 percent of all workers in

[78] *Ibid.*, pp. 988–89; *U.S. BLS Report 129*, p. 23.
[79] National Association of Hosiery Manufacturers, Inc., Hosiery Statistics, 1963, pp. 1, 6 and information received directly from representatives of the industry.
[80] U.S. BLS, *Employment and Earnings*, November, 1963 p. 24.

1960 as compared to some 303,000 or a little less than 41 percent in 1900.[81]

The revolutionizing mechanical innovation in cotton textiles was the Northrup automatic loom, introduced at the turn of the century. In fact here was the most important single advance since Cartwright's power loom more than a hundred years earlier. It enabled a weaver to tend many more looms, and as a result of numerous improvements, adjustments, and simplification of processes, which have made it possible to employ more women, this loom weaves both natural and man-made fibers. Fibers are interchangeable for some purposes, but style changes cause shifts from one to another. For example, after rayon had lessened the demand for cotton for dress goods, one writer noted as early as 1930 that "fifty years ago a woman wore nine pounds of cotton and now her clothing, mostly not cotton, weighs nine ounces." [82] By that time, although mill owners tended to employ men to do the weaving, nearly 40 weavers in each 100 were women; and in another decade mule spinning by men had been displaced by ring-frame spinning by women.

World War II brought a great lift to the industry, causing it to employ more than a half-million production workers; but by 1960, when the South had almost taken it over and had improved virtually all machinery, employment had fallen by nearly half with no decline in production, the proportion of women remaining about two in five.

Changing technology had been a strategic factor in the migration of the industry from New England to the South. There mill owners installed the newest machinery and methods of applying power, taxation and labor laws were lenient, the climate genial, and the poor people offered an abundant supply

---

[81] U.S. Census of Population, 1960, Summary; Sumner, p. 251.
[82] Mitchell and Mitchell, Industrial Revolution in the South, p. 132.

of cheap labor. "Paternalism was the order of the day," wrote Professor Mitchell in his *Industrial Revolution in the South*.[83]

But cotton, along with wool and silk, was being challenged by man-made fibers. Rayon made its lasting impression as early as the 1920s, and by 1940 it had virtually displaced silk. By that time, however, nylon and other noncellulosic fibers were appearing, and the interindustry competition became known as the "battle of the fibers." One commentator asked about the future of wool, "Are sheep going the way of the silkworm? Or can wool hold out against the synthetics?" The writer suggested that three industrial revolutions have taken place in the textile industry in the last 150 years; the first by the invention of the cotton gin at a time when wool accounted for 78 percent of the world's textile consumption; the second when rayon was manufactured commercially, forcing wool to relinquish another position among the world's fibers; and the third when chemists found the secret of nylon, which caught wool in "a period of utter confusion." Hence, wool manufacturers have been working on blends of woolen and worsted cloths with nylon to give the fabrics strength and abrasion resistance, and "the whole business is in a state of flux and suspenseful activity." [84]

But the textile industry has a rosy future, according to synthetic fiber manufacturers.

Today's textile industry is dynamic and aggressive, characterized by brisk internal competition and vigorous product promotion. And because of the impact of the new, exciting man-made fibers, textiles

[83] *Ibid.*, p. 123.

[84] *Fortune*, "Wool's Battle with the Synthetics," May, 1952, pp. 128–29, 147. That wool may be winning the battle is indicated in an announcement of a new process that is said to combine many of its best qualities with man-made fibers. It is called "the shape cloth," and tests are reported to have been gratifying. This new fiber, announced the inventor, "permits a more snug-fitting garment which conforms to body movements, with the clothes looking trim and the wearer well dressed." It is also said to absorb less moisture than conventional wool. (New York *Times*, March 14, 1961.)

today is a growth industry. Under construction now and planned for the future are vast expansions of facilities in these fibers.

Mills and dyehouses that process the man-made fibers into finished fabrics are buying new machines, new dyes, new finishing-chemicals and new services to keep up with the changing technology and marketing opportunities offered the new fibers . . . they are bringing new vitality to the established natural fibers, cotton and wool.

Blends are "the overmastering trend of the future," the bulletin continues—blends with cotton, woolen, and worsted, and blends of man-made fibers with one another.[85]

This enthusiasm appears to be fairly well grounded. We have a burgeoning younger generation; and with migration of the population from farm to city reducing outdoor activity, with the more thorough heating of buildings and with heated automobiles, the demand increases for lighter apparel—for fabrics of synthetic fibers and of multiple blends with cotton, wool, and, to some extent, silk. Furthermore, having been given high resistance to acids and fumes, the durable new fibers have been rapidly taking over the market for tire cord and fabric, automobile upholstery and seat covers. It is estimated that about 40 percent of all textile fibers are used in clothing, 35 percent in industry, and 25 percent in the household; and while cotton still constitutes nearly two thirds of all fiber consumption, synthetics amount to 29 percent, wool 6 percent, and silk 0.1 percent.[86]

The industry is not without its problems, however. Cotton is sharing its once important market for window shades with paper and venetian blinds. And glass fabrics that are impervious to moths and mildew, "flameproof, easily washed, won't

[85] *Modern Textiles Magazine,* "Market and Media Data" (New York, Rayon Publishing Corporation, 1958), pp. 1, 2. Among the "new and glamorous" fibers since nylon that are mentioned here are Orlon, Acrilan, Zefran, Arnel, Vycron, Dynel, Dacron, Chromspun, Creslan, Kodel.

[86] U.S. Business and Defense Services Administration, *Cycles and Trends in Textiles,* 1958, p. 6; *Textile Organon,* March, 1961, pp. 40–41.

shrink, stretch, wrinkle, or be affected by climate," are being substituted for various textiles.[87] There is a stronger paper for bags and bagging; plastic table mats are easy to keep clean; and there are plastic book covers. Disposable items such as cleaning tissues and paper napkins are in daily use. We are told that disposable pillow slips, bedsheets, aprons, and other products will be used in institutions, hotels, and railroads, if not in homes, and that they will be made of combinations of textiles and paper, or of modified types of paper with no textiles. Also fiber-glass reinforced plastics are providing new structural materials used in automobiles, boats, trays, counter and table tops, and for other purposes. Nevertheless, the United States Department of Commerce foresees that new textile fibers will continue to appear and that "either along or in combination with nontextile products such as plastics, paper, rubber, etc., will make a greater contribution toward expanding textile comsumption than they have in the past." [88]

It is in the technologically advanced knit-goods industry—underwear, outerwear, and hosiery—that women have predominated in number and continue to do so. They constitute about 70 percent of all workers. In the manufacture of knit underwear—cotton, wool, rayon, and silk—they comprise four fifths of the labor force, most of them being wives of men at work in the mines and heavy industries of the Middle-Atlantic states. Women as well as men do the knitting. In the more complicated knit-outerwear sector, similarly located, the employment of women is about 73 in 100. The mills have been highly mechanized and great care is taken of the machines so

[87] New York *Times*, March 16, 1961; and Special Section on "Miracles of the Times," p. 7 and footnote p. 13 on women in plastics manufacture.

[88] U.S. Business and Defense Services Administration, *Textile Outlook for the Sixties*, 1960, p. 42. Alert officers of the Textile Workers Union also point out that after so much applied research and practical engineering the larger textile companies are beginning to finance research toward the development of new products and new uses for textiles. (*Report of the Executive Council to the Convention*, 1960, p. 34.)

that breakdowns are reduced and production advanced. Here it is not knitting, but the sewing, trimming, finishing, and inspection of the product that provide work for most of the women. Unionization of workers in both outerwear and underwear approaches 100 percent in the New York metropolitan area, but is far less elsewhere.

As for hosiery, more than 80 employees in each 100 in the recently revolutionized seamless branch are women, and more women than men do the knitting. Most of the mills are in the South and are little unionized. Fewer women have been employed in the manufacture of full-fashioned hosiery, which has been extensively organized except in the South, though the number of women increased as equipment was improved. However, in the last two or three years well-shaped seamless nylon hose for women have been replacing the full-fashioned.

In a final word, despite all the optimism for the textile industry, an ever-increasing number and variety of alternative occupations have been opened for women with the arresting result that at the mid-century only 15 in every 100 women at work in the nation's manufacturers were in textiles, in 1960 ten, and in 1962 only nine—a far cry from a century ago, when few employed women were to be found elsewhere.[89]

[89] The International Labour Office has estimated that more than half of the world's textile workers are women: 42 in 100 in the United States, 60 in Great Britain, 64 in Japan, and 78 in Italy. (Alderfer and Michl, p. 343.)

CHAPTER 10
Women at Work on Other
Nondurable Goods

A hundred years ago nearly 60,000 women were in factories making uniforms for Civil War soldiers and suits for civilians on the new sewing machines. By the end of the century more than 200,000 were at factory work on men's, women's and children's clothing; and by 1963 almost four out of five apparel workers were women—more than a million of them, more than twice as many as the textiles were employing.[1]

Clothing

The clothing trades are a complicated group of separate industries which have emerged from home to factory at different stages. For example, although women's suits, lingerie, and shirtwaists were being made in factories in 1910, there were well over 550,000 dressmakers and seamstresses working at home. By 1940, so much of women's clothing was factory-made that nearly 400,000 skilled women had left dressmaking occupations, over which they had held a monopoly, while nearly 350,000 additional women entered apparel and accessories factories where men were also employed—about one man in every five workers. New York City accounted for 73 percent of the total value of all garments produced in the United States.[2]

What occurred in the manufacture of women's apparel was that much of the former custom work of the dressmaker, the

[1] U.S. Bureau of Labor, *Woman and Child Wage-Earners*, II, 485; *U.S. WB Bull. 275*, p. 19; *U.S. Bull. 285*, p. 23; U.S. BLS, *Employment and Earnings*, November, 1963, p. 24.

[2] *U.S. WB Bull. 218*, p. 116; *U.S. WB Bull. 232*, pp. 36–37; Lazare Teper, *The Women's Garment Industry, An Economic Analysis* (Educational Department of the International Ladies' Garment Workers' Union, 1937), p. 3.

tailoress, and the seamstress was split up into special jobs on ready-to-wear garments, men almost exclusively performing the cutting and pressing operations in the larger centers while women pressers and cutters were to be found in smaller towns and on the lighter fabrics.[3] In modern factories scissors have been replaced by electrically-driven devices that cut cloth up to nine inches in thickness, and for hand iron and sponge, steam irons and steam pressing machines have been substituted.[4] There are said to be more than 200 forms of power-driven sewing machines which run at the remarkable speed of 4,000 stitches a minute or faster [5] and perform various tasks that include such specialized operations as sewing on buttons, snap fastening, blind stitching (for basting and felling), hemstitching, scalloping, and spiral braiding.[6] The blind-stitching machine does the work of four hand finishers and the snap-fastening device does the work of two.

Today approximately three fourths of the production workers in the manufacture of women's dresses in New York City are women, four out of five in Boston, Chicago, and Philadelphia, and nine out of ten or more in the remaining centers of the industry, which reach as far west as Los Angeles, where new apparel shops have been established to meet the style demands of the moving-picture industry.[7] Practically all cutters, markers, and pressers are men, and in New York City men continue to operate sewing machines. Women predominate in the sewing

---

[3] Teper, *The Women's Garment Industry*, p. 8.

[4] In fact, the word "automation" seems to be implied in new trade names such as Numatic, Ultramatic, Time-o-matic, Ultra-numatic, and Ultra-Time-o-matic. (*Apparel Engineering and Needle Trades Handbook,* [a Frederick Kogos Publication, January, 1960], p. 281.)

[5] On cotton garments the speed can be as high as 4,500 stitches per minute, and engineers have found from 67 to 85 percent of the operator's time is spent in handling and manipulating the material, while the actual sewing takes only from 15 to 33 percent of the time. (*U.S. BLS Bull. 662*, p. 36.)

[6] Teper, *The Women's Garment Industry*, p. 26.

[7] *MLR,* July, 1961, p. 744; Theresa Wolfson, "The Role of the ILGWU in Stabilizing the Women's Garment Industry," *Industrial and Labor Relations Review,* October, 1950, p. 35.

occupations, however, both in what is known as the "section system," where they perform easily learned, specific tasks, generally on the cheaper dresses, and in the "single-hand [tailor] system" where an experienced operator performs all or nearly all of the sewing-machine work in the manufacture of the complete garment. The tailor system prevails in New York City—the production center for highly styled garments—and 86 percent of the sewing machine operators are women who receive an average of $2.46 an hour as compared to the 14 percent men who receive $3.29.[8]

In the manufacture of women's and misses' coats and suits the Bureau of Labor Statistics reports that most of the hand and section-system machine sewers are women, but that in New York City shops all but 740 of the more than 6,000 tailor-system operators are men. And since coat- and suit-making is heavier work than dress manufacture, we find a somewhat smaller over-all ratio of women to men. In New York City the proportion of women was less than two in five in 1957, in Boston, Chicago, and Philadelphia it was slightly more than half, in Baltimore and the Los Angeles–Long Beach region it was two in three; and only in Kansas City and the San Francisco-Oakland area was it as high as four in five. Virtually all cutters, markers, pressers, and packers are men. As on dresses, women operators predominate in the manufacture of blouses, underwear, and infants' wear.[9]

The division of labor between men and women in the men's clothing industry appears to be somewhat less marked than in the earlier years. Male cutters have always represented the aristocracy of the industry, but the modern electric machines have brought more women into this man's job, especially in the larger shops. Nearly 6,500 men (usually older men)

[8] *MLR*, July, 1961, pp. 744, 745, 747.
[9] *U.S. BLS Report 122*, pp. 2, 8, 9, 26; Teper, *The Women's Garment Industry*, p. 8.

along with some 23,000 women were sewing-machine operators on men's and boy's suits and coats in March, 1957, while
in the same shops, although the pressing operations have usually been men's work, the Bureau of Labor Statistics found
women accounting for more than 13 percent of all hand and
machine pressers,[10] and spokesmen for the industry tell this
writer that the proportion has probably increased since that
time—the number of women differing on different grades of
clothing. On the lighter work of pressing men's and boy's
shirts and nightwear, all but three or four out of a hundred of
the 8,000 hand- and machine-finish pressers were women; and
of all production workers, close to two out of three in the manufacture of suits and coats and nine out of ten on shirts and
nightwear were women.[11]

Since some two fifths of the woven products of textile
workers go into wearing apparel—coats, suits, shirts, trousers,
dresses, skirts, underwear, and children's wear (also some hats,
caps, and gloves), the man-made fiber fabrics and the blends
of synthetic fibers with cotton, wool, and silk have had their
part in changing the nature of our clothes as well as the processes by which materials are handled in making them. Substitution of ready-made for custom-made garments increased
the importance of color and style. Then came the trend toward
suburban living; the growth in recreational activities aided by
shorter hours, Saturday closings, and more holidays; television
entertaining at home; heated buildings, automobiles, and
buses, all of which contributed to the "new look" in men's and
women's clothing.

Particularly since World War II, therefore, men's suits have
tended to give way to less formal separate dress and sports

[10] *U.S. BLS Report 140*, p. 10.
[11] *Ibid.*, p. 8; *U.S. BLS Report 116*, pp. 15, 48. The National Manpower
Council reports that in the South garment factories employ Negro women only
to press garments, and that an Alabama garment factory was said to have an
entire Negro work force, most of them women. (*Womenpower*, p. 100.)

coats and trousers, and to gayer sports and work shirts. And for women, commercially styled "separates," synthetic-fiber sweaters, slacks instead of overalls in factories, and "wash-and-wear" garments are easier to care for, more adaptable, and cheaper than former kinds of apparel. In fact, the clothes of both men and women seem to have become less of a symbol of prestige and well-being in these changing years.

Much of both men's and women's clothing has long been made under a highly competitive contract system in which those who purchase the fabrics and sell the product put out the work of making the garment to any one of numerous highly specialized contract shops that vie with one another. In earlier days New York City contract and subcontract shops were nothing more than "sweatshops" where thousands of immigrants—predominantly Jewish and Italian—who toiled in overcrowded and unsanitary tenement houses were required to purchase or rent the machines on which they worked and to pay for thread and needles, and even for the "privilege" of working. And to eke out a living many of them took work home, where the entire family toiled from morning to night. Then the Tenement House Act of 1892 began to force contractors out of tenements into loft buildings. And it was in one of these lofts that the terrible Triangle Waist Company fire of March 25, 1911, took 146 lives, most of them young immigrant women, and marked a turning point in the evolution of working conditions—prompted by social workers and progressive lawmakers, and by alert trade union leaders, who may have been more responsible than any other single force in finally bringing the majority of contract shops under control.[12]

[12] Teper, *The Women's Garment Industry*, pp. 15–16; Louis Levine, *The Women's Garment Workers, a History of the International Ladies' Garment Workers' Union* (New York, B. W. Huebsch, 1924), pp. 12–17, 40, 218, 387; New York State *Industrial Bulletin*, March, 1961, "Improved Labor Laws Result From Tragedy Fifty Years Ago," pp. 2–7; Leon Stein, *The Triangle Fire* (Philadelphia and New York, 1962).

First organized in 1900, the International Ladies' Garment Workers Union (ILGWU) took form ten years later during a nine-week strike in New York City which led to a "Protocol of Peace" with the Cloak, Suit and Shirt Manufacturers Association—an agreement that outlawed subcontracting within a shop, prohibited employers from sending out homework, and stated a preference for the employment of union members. A Joint Board of Sanitation Control was established which included a public representative. A Board of Arbitration and a Committee on Grievances were set up to make strikes and lockouts unnecessary. Soon similar agreements were concluded in the manufacture of women's and children's dresses, waists, kimonos, and underwear, also in the Boston cloak and dress industries. And to protect the workers from ruthless and unscrupulous employers, minimum-wage rates for pieceworkers were generally recognized.[13]

But then there was the persistent and almost insuperable problem of enforcement in the vicious competition—contractor against contractor, worker against worker; and in the depression of the 1930s girls toiled 60 to 70 hours a week for the sum of $2.00 or $3.00. In fact, Secretary of Labor Frances Perkins reproduced in a *Survey Graphic* article a two-week-plus-overtime paycheck of an experienced garment worker which amounted to one dollar! [14] Then under the National Industrial Recovery Act a unionization drive swept the country and this shocking state of affairs began to crumble. There were wage increases, shorter hours, and many improvements in working conditions; and before World War II the union had 240,000 members.[15]

Competition in the men's clothing industry has been as re-

[13] Teper, *The Women's Garment Industry*, pp. 18–19; Levine, *The Women's Garment Workers*, pp. 146–47, 178–94, 542–45; New York *Times*, May 17, 1959, Section 10, "Picture of a Union . . . the ILGWU."
[14] Teper, *The Women's Garment Industry*, p. 15.
[15] *Ibid.*, pp. 16, 29.

lentless as in the women's, and the "sweatshop" and "contract shop" were almost synonymous terms in the early days of the century.[16] In 1914 the Amalgamated Clothing Workers of America (ACWA) took form when its leaders walked out of a convention of the United Garment Workers of America after a series of paralyzing strikes in Chicago.[17] Settlement of the dispute in the Hart, Schaffner and Marx plant for better working conditions and an equitable division of work in slack seasons, machinery for the orderly adjustment of grievances, a minimum wage, and a 54-hour week promised an improvement in the status of the workers and also gave the union a foothold for developing greater production efficiency. For example, in the 1920s the ACWA assisted this firm in a reorganization of operations in order to shift to a lower-priced line of garments that would enable the company to meet nonunion competitors. The change brought a minute division of labor and the employment of more unskilled workers. At that time the union had some 177,000 members, reduced to fewer than 70,000 during the depression; and at the beginning of World War II the number had soared to 275,000.[18]

Many unions have decided from time to time not to "bother" with organizing women workers. Apparel manufacture was so predominantly female, however, that the socially minded leaders of the ILGWU and ACWA recognized the importance of drawing women into their ranks "eternally and continuously." The problems of organizing them were as difficult as in any

[16] Robert J. Myers and J. W. Bloch, "Men's Clothing," Chapter 8 of *How Collective Bargaining Works* (New York, Twentieth Century Fund, 1942), pp. 391–92.

[17] *Business Week*, August 31, 1957, "Labor Violence and Corruption," Special Report, p. 81; Amalgamated Clothing Workers of America, *Profile of a Union* (New York, 1958), p. 8. Since the growth of the ACWA, most of the occupation of United Garment Workers has been on work clothing and about 28,000 of their members are women. (Myers and Bloch, "Men's Clothing," p. 395; *U.S. WB Bull. 275*, p. 55.

[18] Works Projects Administration, *Trade Union Policy and Technological Change* (Philadelphia, 1940), pp. 112–14; Myers and Bloch, "Men's Clothing," pp. 396–97.

other industry, however. In the beginning, Italian women were restrained by religious and social considerations. Americanized and native-born women had notions about "foreigners." Jewish women, who had come from politically revolutionary environments in Europe, wanted the union to have "soul" as well as "body"—to provide for "intellectual" and "emotional" life of members. Union offices were not neatly kept, and some of them were over saloons, so women stayed away from them. Moreover, workers on women's garments had gained a sense of union "responsibility" during the long New York strike of 1909 when men and women of wealth, the clergy, newspapers, and prominent public persons rallied to their protest against their working conditions.[19]

To organize apparel working women, therefore, union officials took a fresh course of action by mingling idealism with persistent organizing policies. They appointed women organizers who spoke foreign languages, planned social activities, dramatic clubs, sewing circles, picnics where union ideas could be put forward, issued special leaflets, organized campaigns and mass meetings—all to appeal especially to the great army of unskilled women workers, remembering that "the woman trade unionist is first a woman, and then a trade unionist." The ACWA created a Women's Bureau with the primary object of bringing women into the union, and it began its educational work in 1917. The ILGWU had pioneered in educational programs in 1914–15 after which Unity Centers were organized for holding classes.[20]

By 1924, women accounted for almost two in five of the 80,-500 members of the ILGWU and more than two in five of the 125,000 ACWA members.[21] Today 75 to 80 percent of the

[19] Wolfson, pp. 120, 130, 167, 176, 194; Levine, *The Women's Garment Workers*, p. 485.

[20] Wolfson, pp. 121, 198, 201; Levine, *The Women's Garment Workers*, pp. 486 ff., 496.

[21] Levine, *The Women's Garment Workers*, p. 431; Wolfson, pp. 120–21.

nearly 400,000 ACWA members are women; and women constitute about 80 percent of the 455,000 ILGWU membership. The ILGWU has many women serving on local executive boards and on joint boards of the International Union. It also has one woman on its General Executive Board, and the ACWU has three. Union leaders tell this writer that both organizations have made some progress in organizing workers in the cotton-growing states.

These proportions of women in the clothing unions as reported by their officers appear in neat accord with a census report for 1960 in which the 975,000 women employed in the manufacture of apparel were 80 percent of all apparel workers, their number having increased 7 percent over 1950. Furthermore, the apparel and finished textile products industry employs 23 out of every 100 women in all manufactures, more than twice as many as in textiles.[22]

Footwear and other Leather Products

Shoemaking was no longer a skilled craft when the twentieth century opened. To achieve style and finish as well as comfort and durability at relatively low cost, the modern shoe was made of some 40 separate pieces by 50 woman and girl operatives involving from 100 to 150 different processes.[23] Men as well as women also became workers in specialized jobs for which apprenticeship was unnecessary.[24] In their numerous operations the nearly 47,000 women of 1900 had risen to about 70,400 in 1911—a third of all the nation's shoeworkers scattered among more than 13 states, with Massachusetts still in the lead.[25]

22 U.S. WB Bull. 275, p. 19.

23 U.S. BLS Bull. 180, p. 32.

24 Augusta Emile Galster, The Labor Movement in the Shoe Industry (New York, The Ronald Press, 1924) p. 102.

25 U.S. BLS Bull. 178, p. 22; Marguerite Coughlin, Outlook for New England's Shoe Industry to 1970 (Federal Reserve Bank of Boston, December, 1959), p. 6.

There continued to be little competition between men and women in shoemaking, despite the minute division of labor. By long custom men invariably did the heavy, clumsy, but exacting work of cutting the leather, linings, and trimmings, and women performed the intricate stitching operations on the dozens of cut pieces—each process on its own group of machines, each operator doing one sort of stitching and no other. The stitching department—termed the "women's room"—employed almost a third of all workers in the shop.[26]

Among the many stitching operations, women sewed the toe piece or "tip" to the vamp, stitched the ornamental tip, joined the vamp at the back, seamed up the quarters (tops), pressed open the top seam and smoothed it by machine, stitched on the back stay, stitched up and down the eyelet row, or sewed on the button fly, and stitched vamp and top together. At other machines the linings went through generally similar processes. Then lining and leather were skillfully sewed together to make the "uppers" ready, after tying threads, buttoning, and lacing, to be stitched to the soles and heels which the men had made with heavy machinery in a suffocating odor of hides and glue.[27]

Attaching the upper to the sole was done by three different methods—the Mackay processes, the Goodyear welt process, or the hand-turned shoe process—according to the grade of the shoe and perhaps the sex of the future wearer. But, declared investigators in 1915, except for many of the operations on the turned shoe and the nimble-fingered assembling of the various shoe parts in the lasting room where the shoe was made, "there is no question of its unfitness for women. Most of the operations must be done standing." It was explained that "the foot

---

[26] U.S. BLS Bull. 180, pp. 34–35; Galster, The Labor Movement . . . , p. 204.

[27] U.S. BLS Bull. 180, p. 36. The Bureau found that some of the best-paid stitching operations were being done by foreign Jews or youths from southern Europe, that employers said they held out longer than women on heavy work, and that the state law permitted them to work longer than women during rush seasons. (Ibid., p. 41.)

is frequently used in the manipulation of the machine; muscles of arms and back are subjected to constant strain. Even men of slender build dislike lasting-room work." "Assembling, as in the case of skiving, is unsuitable for girls only because of its being done in the 'men's room.' " [28] Boys and girls were frequently employed in the finishing department, and although packing-room work had formerly been done by men it had come almost completely into the hands of women.[29]

Following the second draft of men into war service, women were not only employed as upper skivers but they skived insoles, and were even substituted for men in the cutting of uppers, linings, and trimmings—almost entirely by machine except for the tongues, eyelet facings, and other small parts. But as soon as men were available most of the women cutters left voluntarily or were transferred to the women's fitting and stitching departments. On the other hand, one shoe firm, which retained about a third of the women who substituted for men as sorters, inspectors, machine tenders, and on other minor operations after the skins had been tanned, explained that these departments "had always been 100 percent men and the introduction of one or two girls into a room of 100 to 150 men would have had an undesirable effect upon discipline. . . . During the last two years, however, this prejudice has been broken down, and we are able to use a few girls in a large department of men without causing any comment or being considered an unusual thing." [30]

In the 1920s more than 300 different machines were in use in shoe manufacture, although frequent style changes, particularly in high-grade shoes, prevented their full use because of the small quantity of any one style.[31] More recently, while the

---

[28] Skiving is the cutting-room machine work of shaving down edges of the uppers so they may be turned over smoothly. (*Ibid.*, pp. 34, 39.)

[29] *Ibid.*, p. 41.

[30] *U.S. WB Bull. 12*, pp. 130–31.

[31] Galster, *The Labor Movement* . . . , p. 201; Harry Jerome, *Mechanization in Industry* (New York, National Bureau of Economic Research, 1934), p. 116.

output of footwear has substantially increased, changes in shoemaking techniques have required less than a corresponding increase in the number of workers, especially men. A relatively simple new process of cementing instead of stitching soles to uppers has been making shoes lighter, more flexible, trimmer, and more easily styled than the sturdier footwear; and since World War II, along with changes in clothing, synthetic materials have been used for some shoes in place of leather, thus reducing handling and preparation time.[32] Moreover, because of style changes, production of the lighter-weight women's shoes has consistently gained over shoes for men. Frequently as many as 200 distinct operations are performed in a single establishment. Hence, by 1957, women production workers outnumbered men by a ratio of nearly three to two, employed largely on sewing operations. Here are fancy stitchers who sew decorative designs on shoe uppers, top stitchers who sew the lining to the upper, and vampers who sew together the forepart of the upper and the two quarters of the shoe. Substantial numbers of women are also at work as pasters, or fitters, and as floor girls. Men are largely employed on the cutting and lasting operations and in plant maintenance.[33]

In sum, the numerical effect of technological change upon all women connected with the manufacture of footwear has been that, whereas in 1910 the more than 70,000 of them were a third of all employees, by 1960 the more than 142,000 were 57 percent of all.[34]

The Boot and Shoe Workers' Union had not succeeded in enlisting all men and women employed in the industry as we recall it set out to do when it was organized at the end of the nineteenth century. Many of its members, especially the cutters and lasters, resented the strong central control which the leaders exercised, and in 1909 they seceded along with others

[32] Marguerite Coughlin, *Outlook for New England's Shoe Industry to 1970*, p. 11; New York *Times*, March 1, 1961.

[33] *U.S. BLS Report 133*, pp. 2, 5, 8.

[34] U.S. BLS, *Employment and Earnings*, May, 1961, p. 19.

and formed the United Shoe Workers of America.[35] By 1959, this organization reported a membership of 58,000 of whom one half were women, while the Boot and Shoe Workers' Union claimed 40,000 members without reporting the number of women.[36]

In other sectors of leather-products manufacture in 1960, 67 in each 100 people making handbags and small leather goods were women, 60 women in each 100 were making gloves and miscellaneous leather products, and 45 in 100 were turning out luggage. While men outnumbered women about eight to one in the preparation of the leather—in the tanning, currying, and finishing operations—the leather and leather-products industry as a whole was employing 52 in each 100 workers— more than 193,000; and as an employer of women it ranked fifth among all nondurable goods industries.[37]

Tobacco

The tobacco industry, which includes chewing and smoking tobacco and snuff as well as cigars and cigarettes, employed more than 66,000 women in 1905—more than two fifths of all its workers.[38] By 1920, the 98,800 women accounted for more than half of all, and in 1940, while the proportion of women had risen to almost 63 percent of all operatives and laborers, their numbers—owing largely to mechanization and large-scale production—had fallen roughly to 61,000. After further mechanization, women operatives numbered only 43,000, but by 1950 they comprised seven out of ten of all—probably the highest proportion on record. Of all employees in 1960, including office workers, the 44,400 women represented one half, their number having fallen 17 percent in a decade. Two years

[35] Galster, *The Labor Movement* . . . , chapters V to IX.
[36] *U.S. BLS Bull. 1267*, pp. 45, 58.
[37] U.S. BLS, *Employment and Earnings*, May, 1961, p. 19.
[38] Sumner, p. 250.

later the number had fallen again.[39] Let us look to progress in the preparation of tobacco leaves for a partial explanation.

For whatever purpose tobacco is to be used, the leaf must first be processed—until recently perhaps the most disagreeable and certainly the poorest paid of all occupations in the industry. In the first decade after the turn of the century, a report on stripping the leaf from its mid-vein in a large and otherwise well-equipped factory ran as follows:

The stripping here is done by women, some of them very old, others crippled. They carry their tobacco, in amounts varying from 30 to 60 pounds, in aprons or sacks tied around their waists, from a central point to their benches, and after it has been stripped, to the scales to have it weighed. The strippers' benches are very low, without backs or rests of any kind; the floors are very dirty, the light is poor, and the women have to lean over their work. Twice a day they get new supplies of tobacco.[40]

Although this account did not specify the race of these women, it has long been the custom to employ Negroes in the low-skilled leaf processing occupations. In 1940 another government survey found that Negroes accounted for no less than four fifths of the working force, more than six out of ten being women; and in a total of more than 38,000 workers in the manufacture of cigarettes, smoking and chewing tobacco, and snuff close to 44 percent were Negroes.[41] But in recent years the work of hand-stemming the leaf and breaking the woody matter away from the leafy materials has been accomplished by a "tipping and thrashing" machine which substitutes thrash-

[39] U.S. WB Bull. 218, pp. 101–03; U.S. WB Bull. 253, p. 42, 49–50; U.S. WB Bull. 275, p. 19; U.S. WB Bull. 285, p. 23.

[40] U.S. Bureau of Labor, Woman and Child Wage-Earners, XVIII, 79. This source noted that other stripping rooms were found which were clean, well lighted, and sanitary, and that leaf stems were sometimes removed by machine.

[41] MLR, January, 1942, pp. 189–90, 195–97. In cigarette plants 42 percent were Negroes, 40 percent in chewing-tobacco manufacture, 27 percent in the smoking tobacco branch, and slightly more than 13 percent in the manufacture of snuff. The cigarette industry employed about an equal number of men and women, but men slightly outnumbered women in chewing- and smoking-tobacco plants, and in snuff manufacture only 38 percent were women. (Ibid.)

ing for stemming and which has resulted in the reduction of four out of five workers, mostly colored women in the South.[42]

CIGARS

We left the cigar industry in 1900 when the Cigar Makers' International Union was actively opposing both machines and women in their trade. But the battle was lost even then. Already cigar manufactures were meeting the competition of the cheaper cigarette smoke by introducing tools for stripping the leaf from the stem, bunching, rolling, and other operations, with the result that only five years after the turn of the century almost 54,500 women were making cigars—their number in cigar and cigarette manufacture combined having increased more than 50 percent.[43]

At that time the industry was in all stages of development, from tiny family establishments in the proprietor's cellar, attic, or living room to large plants in each of which machinery was used in nearly every process and the labor force numbered well into the hundreds. Here the employment of women may have been as high as 90 in 100 or as low as 14 or 15 in 100, according to the preference of employers. In some factories women and girls did only the least skilled work such as stripping, machine bunching, and labeling or stamping. In others they were skilled "out-and-out cigar makers"; or they were "shaders," whose exacting occupation was that of assorting the finished cigars by precise shades and subshades of color. Handmade cigars were likely to be rolled and packed by men, though women were employed here as well.[44]

The rapidly growing popularity of cigarettes, especially during World War I, again forced cigar manufactures to act if they were to survive. The result was that in 1917–18 an "almost

[42] Information given to this writer in an interview with a representative of the industry who asked not to be named.

[43] U.S. Bureau of Labor, *Woman and Child Wage-Earners*, XVIII, 88.

[44] *Ibid.*, pp. 90, 91, 99, 100, 102.

human" electrically driven automatic machine which performed all processes except the packing caused a shift from hand labor in small plants to machine work in large factories, a shift from men to women, from inexperienced women to young girls, and in all a reduction of the working force by one half to obtain the same output.

Here was the first successful machine for making a completely headed, long-filler five-cent cigar at the rate of 500 a day. The acute labor shortage after the war prevented its rapid production, but by 1929 more than 4,400 of these machines had been installed or ordered—a lively response to Vice-President Marshall's exhortation that, "What this country needs is a really good five-cent cigar." [45] Meanwhile, in their apparent preference for women, partly because they accepted lower wages and were not easily influenced by labor agitation, manufacturers made a special effort to locate their factories where there were heavy man-employing industries which left wives available for work. Some companies even arranged working hours so the women could be at home to get the family meals and start the children off to school.[46]

Operated by four unskilled women, the large and complicated new machine performed all the necessary processes.[47] The first operator—the "filler feeder"—fed the long-filler leaf into the mechanism; the second—the "binder layer"—placed the binder leaf on the binder die where it was held down by suction and cut to the form desired; the third was the "wrapper layer"; and the fourth was the "inspector" of the cigar as it came from the machine. After the cigar had been formed it

[45] U.S. WB Bull. 73, p. 50; U.S. WB Bull. 100, pp. 2, 3; Jerome, *Mechanization in Industry*, pp. 118–19; Robert K. Heimann, *Tobacco and Americans* (New York, McGraw-Hill, 1960), p. 235.

[46] Lucy Winsor Killough, *The Tobacco Products Industry in New York and Its Environs*, Regional Plan of New York and Its Environs, 1924, pp. 21, 26, 30.

[47] At about this time, a short-filler machine was also introduced which required two operators instead of four and reduced labor costs considerably. (*U.S. BLS Bull. 660*, pp. 1–2.)

was usually wrapped in cellophane and banded, and the larger machine factories soon began operating cellophane-wrapping and banding mechanisms as a unit.[48]

The efficiency of the new machine was striking. For example, one manufacturer reported that the output of his hand department of about 300 women turned out from 350,000 to 400,000 cigars a week while 230 women in the machine department averaged 1,120,000 a week.[49] Actually, the required amount of labor was cut in half for the same output.

At least eight out of ten of the employees in most of these mechanized plants were women, the engineers and mechanics, who did not touch the cigars, being men. And just as experienced foreign women gave way to adaptable young American girls "who get the rhythm quicker," so the experienced, male cigar makers, who were neither machinists nor physically able to do heavy work but who quite consistently refused to operate the machines, were left with little to do except to be maintenancemen, or packers and selectors, who were very expert in judging the quality of a cigar by feeling its weight and noting its general appearance. But the "good old days" were over, the days when the packer was the aristocrat of the trade who demonstrated his superiority by arriving at the factory in a silk hat and carrying a cane. Now, said one manufacturer in a mechanized factory, "We haven't a cigar maker in the place." Each machine had displaced ten skilled individuals, chiefly men, and given four or five new jobs to unskilled women machine tenders. And now the packers who grade, sort, inspect, and pack the cigars are almost all women and girls.[50]

Looking back upon developments, of the 111,400 hand cigar makers in 1920, only 50,375 or 45 percent were men, according

[48] *MLR*, December, 1931, pp. 11–15; *U.S. WB Bull. 100*, p. 128.
[49] *U.S. WB Bull. 100*, p. 32.
[50] *Ibid.*, pp. 7, 24, 25; Alderfer and Michl, pp. 641–42; Killough, *Tobacco Products in New York*, p. 26.

to the Cigar Makers' International Union. It was the small shops that were employing skilled and experienced men who regarded it as a permanent occupation; but even if women had attained perfection, the small New York shops were not equipped with separate dressing rooms for women, which the law required. In the large factories, however, men did not touch the cigars at all. Only women were employed to tend the cigar machine, and in one large Manhattan factory where no machine work was done the managers "never hire a man if they can get a woman." This was partly explained, doubtless, by the necessity to lower unit costs in competition with the mechanized factories where women received lower rates of pay.[51] By 1933, a special census report thus revealed that of a total of almost 27,000 hand pieceworkers (mostly hand cigar makers) only 31 percent were men compared to the estimated 45 percent in 1920; and union membership had dropped from more than 50,000 to about 15,000, a number of local branches having been abandoned.[52]

But 1920 had been the peak production year for high-priced cigars. The demand for them sagged as mechanization made cheap cigars possible. Hence, whereas in 1921 only 30 percent of all manufactured cigars retailed at 5 cents or less apiece [53] by 1936 the proportion had risen to 88 percent, and the number of workers had been reduced by one half—from 112,000 to 56,000. As a direct result of the use of the long-filler cigar machine alone, for instance, an estimated 44,000 highly skilled men and women hand workers had lost their employment, while jobs had been provided for some 17,000 new workers, mostly young unskilled women.[54]

But handmade cigars had not disappeared from the market.

[51] Killough, *Tobacco Products in New York*, p. 26.
[52] *U.S. BLS Bull. 660*, pp. 61–62, 65.
[53] Many 15 cent cigars were also being made by machine, and the leaders of the Cigar Makers' Union had decided they could no longer afford to ignore the machine. (Killough, *Tobacco Products in New York*, p. 29.)
[54] *U.S. BLS Bull. 660*, pp. 2–4.

Indeed, the official estimate was that in 1936 some 15 percent of all cigars were the long-filler handmade ones, some of them being of lower grades. The two-fold explanation was that the term "handmade" continued to have a selling appeal, and that the oversupply of skilled, hand cigar makers had caused many of them to accept work at very low wages, "in many cases at levels below those prevailing for machine operators in mechanized plants." [55]

Meanwhile both long-filler and short-filler cigars had become at least three fourths mechanized, and the U.S. Department of Labor considered mechanization had not much farther to go.[56]

But mechanization had by no means come to an end. In a new determination to meet rising prices and cigarette competition, cigar manufacturers in the last few years have been using machines that turn out 3,500 to 6,000 cigars a day, and fewer than five in a hundred are now handmade. A major advance is a new binder sheet of ground or crushed tobacco that is fashioned into ribbons and wound on reels. A reel of tobacco ribbon is then placed in an attachment to a cigar machine which automatically feeds it to the binder die, eliminating one of the four female operators on the long-filler machines and one of the two on the short-filler machines. Developed by several companies, the tobacco ribbons have trade names such as Homogenized Tobacco Leaf, Reconstructed Cigar Binder, and Unified Tobacco Binder. These binder sheets have been increasingly substituted for the natural-leaf binders on many leading brands of cigars, and especially on cigarillos—little cigars—which have become increasingly popular, constituting more than an eighth of the total consumption in 1958.[57]

[55] *Ibid.*, pp. 64–65.
[56] *Ibid.*, pp. 65–66.
[57] Alderfer and Michl, p. 638; U.S. Agricultural Marketing Service, *The Tobacco Situation*, September, 1955, p. 46; *The Tobacco Situation*, June, 1958, p. 9; *The Tobacco Situation*, December, 1958, pp. 10–11.

An even more recent step toward fully mechanizing cigar making, still in the testing stage, is the manufacture of the wrappers from tobacco sheets "which will look, feel, and taste like the natural whole leaf." While a few "technological bugs" remain, experts are said to believe that the new wrappers may eventually eliminate the final hand operation in making cigars.[58]

Along with the new technology, the number of cigar factories has dropped from more than 1,800 to 527 in the past ten years, and the industry has plunged into "saturation" advertising which includes a publicity campaign aimed to win younger men to "wear" a cigar and look smart just as they wear shoes, hats, and sports ensembles.[59] The gains in cigar sales have been largely among those selling at 8 cents or less and the cigarillos at 4 cents to 6 cents.[60] The industry employed some 38,500 persons in 1954, and in a survey of representative plants in the Southeast two years later women were found to account for almost four fifths of 12,000 nonsupervisory workers.[61]

As for the Cigar Makers' International Union, whose story is one of the rise and decline of an organization of handicraftsmen in a world of growing mechanization, membership plummeted from a peak of more than 51,000 in 1910 to less than 6,300 in 1959 with 4,700 or 75 percent of them women. On the other hand the more inclusive Tobacco Workers' International Union, which was organized in 1897 with 4,100 members, had by 1920 accumulated a membership of 15,200, of whom 6,500 or 43 percent were women, and by 1959 its number had

[58] U.S. Agricultural Marketing Service, *The Tobacco Situation*, June, 1960, p. 48; and September, 1960, p. 15; *Barron's Weekly*, "The Mellow Cigar," September 5, 1960, pp. 3, 18.

[59] *Barron's Weekly*, "The Mellow Cigar," pp. 3, 15.

[60] U.S. Agricultural Marketing Service, *The Tobacco Situation*, June, 1960, p. 12.

[61] U.S. *BLS Report 117*, p. 3; U.S. *Census of Manufactures, 1954*, II, Part I, 21 A-3.

reached close to 34,900, 55 in each 100 being women.[62] In January, 1961, 75 in each 100 of the nation's cigar workers were women.[63]

CIGARETTES

Twenty years after cigarettes came on the market it was an act of daring for a lady to smoke them, even in New York City. Thirty years later a personal *tour de force* made it proper for city women to smoke them in public. It was in the early thirties that Albert D. Lasker's wife was forbidden to smoke in the public dining room of a Chicago restaurant. Determined to overcome the taboo, Lasker appealed for cooperation from popular foreign actresses and opera stars who smoked, and they were joined by almost the entire roster of the Metropolitan Opera. Soon movie stars were shown enjoying their cigarettes, and women began to smoke all over the country. It became smart; and those who reached for a cigarette were more likely to keep slender than those who reached for a sweet.[64] In New York City today, despite the alleged relation between cigarette smoking and cancer and heart disease, one sees about as many old and young women as men smoking on the sidewalk as well as in the restaurant; and 507 billion cigarettes were manufactured in 1960, more than half of them filter tips, as compared to some three billion in 1900.[65]

Do women make cigarettes as well as smoke them? Yes, almost as many as men. We have seen that modern cigarette manufacture was largely mechanized long before 1900 and that women operated the lighter machines. In 1930, 8,000

[62] Leo Wolman, *Growth of American Trade Unions, 1880–1923* (New York, National Bureau of Economics Research, 1924), pp. 114–15, 136; *MLR*, December, 1941, p. 1518; *U.S. BLS Bull. 1267*, pp. 33, 46, 58.

[63] U.S. BLS, *Employment and Earnings*, May, 1961, p. 19.

[64] John Gunther, *Taken at the Flood, The Story of Albert D. Lasker* (New York, Harper & Brothers, 1960), pp. 167–69.

[65] *U.S. WB Bull. 100*, p. 11; U.S. Agricultural Marketing Service, *The Tobacco Situation*, September, 1960, pp. 8, 9; *The Tobacco Situation*, March, 1961, front cover; *U.S. BLS Report 167*, pp. 1, 16.

women accounted for nearly six out of ten production workers in representative factories in North Carolina, Virginia, and Kentucky. Most of them were engaged in processing the tobacco leaves and in inspecting and packing the finished product. But 600 of them worked at the foot of the making machines as "catchers," who gathered up handfuls of cigarettes as they dropped on a moving belt and placed them on a tray. This was not heavy work but it required strict attention, including examination of the cigarettes to see whether they were being properly made. All catchers were women, and about one in ten of the machine operators was a woman. Even then the capacity of the machine was from 700 to 1,000 cigarettes a minute.[66]

Today, after continuous mechanical improvements, the cigarette machine turns out from 1,200 to 1,600 cigarettes a minute —filter and nonfilter tips—and it seems that no women are operating it, although 76 out of every 100 women workers are "catchers." Others inspect the product as it comes from the machines as well as during the packing process, and some are janitors.[67] We have seen that the majority of women in the leaf-processing departments have been displaced.

Packing cigarettes by machine is now the second largest of the women's occupations—more than 1,500 of them as compared to scarcely 1,200 men, according to a recent survey of representative plants. In a complicated series of processes the packer fills the hopper from a sliding tray, fills other hoppers with labels and paste, places spools of paper or aluminum foil on spindles and threads them through rollers. The machine automatically groups and wraps the cigarettes into packages and affixes the labels to each. The packer also inspects the packages as they come from the machine and makes minor mechanical adjustments such as setting guides and adjusting

[66] U.S. BLS Bull. 532, pp. 2, 12.
[67] MLR, November, 1960, p. 1195.

tension on rollers.[68] From this survey in 1960 it was estimated that approximately 11,500 women constituted less than half of the cigarette production workers as compared to three out of five in 1930 before leaf processing was mechanized. Moreover, women received somewhat lower wage rates than men for what seemed to be the same kind of job.[69]

In May, 1960, about seven out of ten of the cigarette production employees—still largely in North Carolina, Kentucky, and Virginia—were in establishments with collective bargaining agreements covering a majority of workers.[70]

In sum, while cigar sales now tend to show an upturn, and cigarette production has been soaring, the manufacture of chewing tobacco has greatly declined. And sales of smoking tobacco have risen somewhat—it is cheaper than cigarettes. Strangely enough, snuff consumption hangs on at a relatively even rate, usually not for sniffing as of old, but lodged in the cheek to be sucked or tasted.[71]

Printing and Publishing

Women have a scanty place in the oldest of our cultural manufactures. More than a century ago, it will be recalled, Harriet Martineau found typesetting and bookbinding two of seven occupations open to women. And the Philadelphia *Ban-*

[68] *U.S. BLS Report 167*, p. 18.

[69] *Ibid.*, pp. 6, 18; *MLR*, November, 1960, pp. 1194–95. Mechanization has not been the cause of the precipitous drop in the number of cigarette factories from 381 in 1914 to 19 in 1954, for apparently there is no important technical advantage for large producers. The principal causes of large-scale production are said to be advertising expenditures, heavy daily cost outlays for revenue stamps, and the fact that two- to three-year supplies of tobacco are customarily carried because of the necessity of at least 18 months for aging it. (*Census of Manufactures, 1954*, II, Part I, 21 A-3; Alderfer and Michl, pp. 632–33; Richard B. Tennant, *The American Cigarette Industry* [New Haven, Yale University Press, 1950], p. 237.)

[70] *MLR*, November, 1960, p. 1194.

[71] U.S. Agricultural Marketing Service, *The Tobacco Situation*, September, 1955, p. 15; and March, 1961, pp. 17–18; Heimann, *Tobacco and Americans*, pp. 237–38.

ner of the Constitution was saying there was no reason why printing should not be turned over to them. But we have seen that women have more enemies than friends in this industry, the most influential being technological change, physical strength, and prejudice based in part upon the questionable belief that women have an inborn lack of facility with machinery. Printing techniques continue to require highly skilled craftsmanship and extended experience; much of the work is too heavy for women; and for the most part strongly organized unions have turned thumbs down on women, especially when jobs are scarce.[72] Moreover, some state laws against nightwork for women have doubtless reinforced the prejudice against their employment.[73]

Nevertheless, the total number of women employed in printing and publishing industries today tallies more than eight times the 29,000 in 1900, and the proportion of women to men has also risen slightly. Let us see what these women have been doing.

THE COMPOSING ROOM

With few exceptions the composing room is the only mechanical division of printing in which men and women have competed for work. We have seen that in the first decade of

---

[72] During the period of World War II one woman compositor on a New York daily newspaper and a member of the ITU explained in writing why men resent women in their trade. She said they have been brought up to feel that a woman does not belong on a man's job, and that this gospel is brought home to them practically every day when a woman requires a man's help on some task that is too heavy for her. She emphasized that this is particularly true when there are not enough jobs to go around. (Constance Roe, "Can the Girls Hold Their Jobs in Peacetime?" *Saturday Evening Post*, March 4, 1944, p. 28.)

[73] For example, since newspapers are factories, a New York State law in 1913, which ruled a nine-hour day, 54-hour week, and no nightwork for factory women, included women printers—proofreaders, linotypists, and hand compositors. And not until 1921, as a result of the complaints of the women so employed against what they deemed discrimination against them in their competition with men, was the law amended to free those of them who were over 21 years of age. (Baker, *Protective Labor Legislation*, pp. 242–44, 362–66, 432.)

this century women constituted 10 percent of all composing-room employees, but that few more than 700 out of 12,000 were operators of typesetting machines, and only three in a hundred unionized compositors were women. By 1940 the 8,000 women hand and machine compositors and typesetters amounted to less than five in a hundred, most of their displacement probably having been in newspaper offices where on all shifts swift and certain output is always of paramount importance.[74] Moreover, we recall that both union and non-union employers agreed with the organized typographers that only men possessed the requisite stamina to operate the Lino-type over long periods of time. Thus, since the union required that if women were to be employed they must be paid at the same rate as men, union shops preferred men; and when women did find employment it was more likely to be in non-union shops at much lower wages. Wives and daughters ran small "bedroom shops" in remote places, many of which were probably missed by census takers.

After World War II the composing room began to undergo a mechanical transformation which was hastened, it seems, by a 21-month strike against all Chicago newspapers. "We have to let the Chicago papers know that if they are going to print papers, we're going to have to get more money," announced International Typographical Union (ITU) President Randolph.[75]

Printers and publishers had never availed themselves whole-heartedly of technological advances that would have meant large capital investments. But in their dilemma in November, 1947, Chicago newspapers turned to an inexpensive "glorified typewriter" which they had theretofore ignored owing partly, doubtless, to its shortcomings as compared to traditionally set type. The Varityper could be operated by any stenographer,

[74] Jacob Loft, *Labor in The Twentieth Century—The Printing Trades* (New York, Farrar & Rhinehart, 1944), p. 68.
[75] G. Lester Walker, "Look At This, Mr. Gutenberg" *Harper's Magazine,* July, 1948, p. 57.

and many girl typists were taken on. The machine had interchangeable typefaces of 600 sizes and styles in 50 different languages. Also it could justify the lines—make them even on the right-hand margin as typesetters do. The typed columns were then pasted up on a newspaper-size cardboard, headlines pasted above, and pictures alongside; a photograph was taken, the picture photoengraved, and plates put on the press and printed. But while typesetting had been bypassed, it was a strange-looking newspaper, and late stories could not get in.[76]

Meanwhile, a more automated system of typesetting which made use of the Linotype had been introduced in some of the nation's large plants. On the Teletypesetter, which had first appeared in the late 1920s, the operator touched the keyboard and punched a tape which in turn automatically operated the Linotype machine; and by means of telegraph the same impulses could be sent to distant points.[77] As early as 1933, for example, the Newburgh, New York, Beacon *News* had replaced seven manually operated composing machines with four Teletypesetters. The change caused five out of seven machine compositors to be displaced. Five girls were employed to run the perforating devices at less than journeymen's wages, and the daily amount of set matter rose more than 10 percent. In another newspaper office the average type production per hour on the Teletypesetter is said to have been more than a third greater than on the manually operated Linotype with an average of half the number of errors per galley of type.[78]

But the unionized Chicago publishers refrained from using the Teletypesetter during the strike because, they explained, it would require hiring nonunion operators, which would enable the strikers to charge that they were seeking to "break the union." Hence they preferred to bypass the composing

[76] *Ibid.*, p. 58.
[77] Florence Clark, *The Printing Trades and Their Workers* (Scranton, Pennsylvania, 1939), p. 19.
[78] Loft, *Labor in the Twentieth Century*, p. 51.

room entirely, and the ITU president commented that "the Varitype process wouldn't be competitive if the operators were paid journeymen's wages." [79]

This observation proved to be one cue to the agreement that ended that long strike while the Linotype machines had been in "moth balls." During the life of the new contract Chicago publishers agreed to abandon the substitute varitype-photoengraving process and to resume regular printing methods within something like 21 days. About 350 varitypists and 100 proofreaders on five Chicago papers were thus dismissed with severance pay,[80] and the contract permitted use of the Teletypesetter on six-months notice.

New York Typographical Union No. 6 also came to an agreement with ten metropolitan daily papers in March, 1955. Here, after several months of deadlock on the question of jurisdiction over new processes, the union won jurisdiction over the various phototypesetting machines, and the publishers agreed not to install Teletypesetters or related equipment without union sanction on the terms of their operation which would not be subject to arbitration.[81] In the following year, a referendum vote of the members of the International Union authorized the executive council to "establish jurisdiction over all new processes of work in the industry," that is, in union shops.[82]

This referendum vote of course included the book and job or commercial branch as well as newspapers. Book and commercial printing plants in Chicago, Philadelphia, and New York had also been struck by the compositors in the late 1940s,

[79] New York *Times,* April 22, 28, 1948. The manager of the *Antioch Press* observed that "the best all-around judgment seems to be that daily papers can be put out without printers but that the result is awkward, messy, wasteful of newsprint, and plays havoc with speedy news coverage." (Freman Champney, "Taft-Hartley and the Printers," *The Antioch Review,* Spring, 1948, p. 59.)

[80] New York *Times,* September 9, 1949.

[81] *Ibid.,* March 14, 1955. The ITU was avoiding any relations with the National Labor Relations Board for the very reason that it intended to keep the matter of jurisdiction over new processes in its own hands.

[82] New York *Times,* December 5, 1956.

and they, too, had investigated new printing techniques. In 1951 the Government Printing Office, after five years of testing, had used a photographic machine called the Fotosetter to set the first hard-bound book by photographic means, *Typography and Design*. And the first hard-bound, commercially produced books by the new method came on the market early in 1952 from the Blakiston Company in Philadelphia.[83] Soon the Fotosetter was joined by two more photographic typesetting machines—the Monophoto and the Photon, designed to produce about the same product;[84] and these were to be followed by the Linofilm and a whole new group of machines for the photographic composition of type.

The International Typographical Union thus turned its attention to the impact of these innovations on their book and commercial printing members. The protective reasoning was that paying stenographers or typists two thirds as much as journeymen operators would save only a small percentage of the total cost of what they produced. Moreover, it had been "conclusively proven that the economical operation of photographic keyboard machines requires the most skillful and competent personnel that the industry can supply," especially since the cost of making film corrections places a high premium on setting the work correctly the first time. And aside from clarity and sharpness of film type characters, union spokesmen pointed out, text matter must be spaced properly, must be free of objectionable word divisions, must be assembled to meet the high standards which have been established by many years of experience. "The better the operator the lower the cost of production."[85]

At least on paper, these arguments seem to have been ef-

---

[83] *Bookbinding and Book Production*, December, 1951, a reprint; Intertype Corporation, *Facts You Should Know About Photographic Typesetting* (no date).

[84] Frank Sherman, "The Impact of Photographic Type Composition on the Graphic Arts," in *The American Pressman*, February, 1954, p. 34.

[85] *Ibid.*, 36.

fective in union shops as indicated by recent union-management agreements such as that in 1959 between New York Local No. 6 and the New York employing printers in which for the first time provision was made for the operation of Teletypesetters in New York City commercial printing plants.[86] Since that time some Teletypesetters have been installed in some New York unionized newspaper composing rooms,[87] and some of those who operate them are women who cut the tape in a process much like that of operating a typewriter keyboard. A few women are also at work on the Monotype, the Linotype, and other photographic typesetting machines. But, according to union officials, 90 percent of the 500 women members of New York Typographical Union No. 6, whose membership is some 10,000, are proofreaders. A good many women are proofreaders in large newspaper, book, and periodical plants where journeymen typesetters and advanced apprentices are less likely to read proof than in smaller shops.[88] It seems that women acquire their journeyman status in the union not as apprentices, who are required to be helpers and may do dirty and often heavy work, but by learning the trade in nonunion shops.

In sum, it is clear that women have been playing a very inconspicuous role in the nation's composing rooms. According to the 1960 census few more than 15,000, or 8 percent, of about

[86] New York *Times*, October 19, 1959.

[87] One of the major factors in the 114-day blackout of eight daily newspapers in New York City from December 8, 1962, to April 1, 1963, was the publishers' insistence upon the right to have all their Stock Exchange and other financial tables set by Teletypesetter tape supplied by the Associated Press or the United Press International. They offered a contractual guarantee that no regular employees would lose their jobs as a result. But the Typographical Union, fearing that this would be a first step toward the use of computers to displace Linotype operators, asked that a share of the savings go into a special fund for retraining, early retirement payments, or supplemental unemployment benefits. In the final agreement, the use of the Teletypesetter tape was limited to about two thirds of the materials the publishers had hoped to include and a joint committee was appointed to study savings and their allotment, with an arbitrator to take over if no agreement can be reached. (A. H. Raskin, New York *Times*, April 1, 1963.)

[88] Baker, *Printers and Technology*, p. 61n.

179,500 compositors and typesetters were women. It is possible, however, that the coming of the Teletypesetter may prove to be an example of technological advance that brings an important occupational opening for women as tape cutters on tape-punching machines. "Women should be doing this work," says an employers' representative.

THE PRESSROOM

The work of the twentieth century pressroom is heavy—so much so that no women are to be found near the giant newspaper presses, and relatively few among the large and small machines in the commercial branch. When women and girls are employed, it is usually as hand feeders of small platen presses as before. Even these jobs have been limited, owing to technological advances; and the work of man and boy hand-feeder assistants to the pressmen has included carrying piles of paper to the presses as well as making ready the forms while they learned to operate the machines, more than a few hoping to be promoted.

The small platen, or job, presses—the Ford cars of the pressroom—continued to constitute a large proportion of all machines sold up to the decade of the 1930s, many of course to hundreds of "one-man" or "bed-room" shops such as were set up, perhaps in cramped living quarters, to bid for neighborhood patronage. And although automatic feeding attachments were available at the turn of the century, most of the platens were hand-fed in 1912, and possibly two thirds of them as late as 1928. The International Printing Pressmen and Assistants' Union (IPP&AU) estimates that at the end of World War I about 40 percent of its press assistants and feeder members were women—some 10,000 of them.[89]

Girls were also at work on the platens in nonunion shops at

[89] From Secretary-Treasurer George L. Googe in a letter to this writer, September 15, 1961; Baker, *Displacement of Men By Machines*, pp. 9, 20.

wages far below those of the unionized feeder assistants. And in Chicago when the men precipitated a revolt against union rules that restricted promotion of their competent men chaos ensued, contracts with employing printers were broken, and there was widespread employment of girl feeders.[90]

But pressroom technology was also not at a standstill. A new, highly competitive, automatically fed small press which appeared in the first year of World War I made a spectacular sally upon the job pressroom, crowding back platens and some of the larger presses because they were faster, cheaper, and simpler to operate and maintain. Known as "job-automatics" they saved the labor of hand-feeding, eliminated the adjustments which automatic feeding attachments required, and made it practical for pressmen to operate them as one-man machines.[91] Hence, they gave work to pressmen and took work away from feeders and assistants.

It thus became clear that the hand-feeding of presses was a blind-alley job for young men, or at best only a threshold occupation. Many such feeders were displaced by the new automatics, and those who remained continued to feed and to assist the pressmen, the more mechanically minded of them being chosen to begin a two- to four-year apprentice training period leading to journeyman status. Nevertheless, as we have seen, a great deal of hand-feeding continued at least up to the depression of the 1930s, including the work of a surprising number of New York City union shops which comprised 85 percent of all the city's book and commercial printing. By this time, however, there was only one woman among the 2,400 members of the New York Press Assistants' Union! [92]

This fact seems to reflect the well-ingrained masculine attitude toward women in the printing trades. However, the Press-

[90] Baker, *Displacement of Men by Machines*, pp. 118, 119, 128.
[91] *Ibid.*, pp. 12, 13.
[92] *Ibid.*, pp. 66, 86.

men's Union reports that it still has approximately 1,000 women press feeders and assistants who are at work in some of the older unionized plants which have continued to use hand-fed presses. And the union has 76 women 60 years of age and over on its pension payrolls after 20 years or more of continuous good standing in the union.[93]

Who, then, is employing the 11,000 women whom the IPP&AU reports in its membership of 110,500? [94] Here is an interesting story of the adaptation of this craftsmen's organization to technological change by recognition of industrial unionism in the manufacture of so-called specialties where printing is supplementary to the semiskilled production of the product—all sorts of converted paper goods such as commercial envelopes, corrugated and folding boxes, bags, bread wrappers, greeting cards, and numerous other items.[95]

In entering this field, which has grown out of the mass production of paper and cardboard for packaging in which printing enters, the Pressmen's Union would have been willing to disregard those who made the products if they could take jurisdiction over the men who did the printing. But it was not possible to "carve out" these "forgotten pressmen." Hence, if they wanted the pressmen in a specialty plant they would have to take the whole family—a compositor or two, a paper cutter or two, and "a whole flock of girls," each of whom might otherwise have been in any one of several other unions, including the bookbinders. A move into industrial unionism was thus the only solution, and the first charter to a specialty union

[93] In his letter to this writer, Secretary-Treasurer Googe added that about 2 percent of the female press feeders and assistants became journeymen platen pressmen, and that the wife of IPP&AU past President J. H. de la Rosa is a retired platen pressmen.

[94] *U.S. BLS Bull. 1267*, pp. 42, 58.

[95] The Pressmen's Union says it has only scratched the surface in organizing these people and that the vast majority of them remain unorganized by any union. And we have no way of knowing how many women are employed here. The Bureau of the Census does not include specialty printing with "Printing and Publishing," nor does it report specialty workers by sex.

was issued during the depression of the 1930s. Since that time many Printing Specialties and Paper Products locals have been organized within the IPP&AU to the present extent of about 50,000 members, about one in four of whom are women.

But technological advances during the past five years or so have reduced the proportion of women in specialty printing to about two in five. For example, commercial envelope manufacture grew up with women operating the plunger, or folding machine, which requires finger dexterity. They then put on the glue and men did the printing. For such products as greeting cards and announcement envelopes the plunger is still in use. But for many other envelopes a more complicated, wide-range mechanism prints as the paper is being folded, and few women are employed to operate it. A male adjuster can tend four machines. Also, the manufacture of paper bags calls for about the same processes as for envelopes—light work for women until the heavier machines were introduced. Both men and women are waxers and slitters in the manufacture of bread wrappers, but it takes a strong man to load the machine with 1,000-pound rolls of paper.

A great many women are at work on greeting cards; and on those for which they do such things as make bow ties and hand-paste a beard on a Santa Claus they outnumber men. In 1960, the Bureau of Labor Statistics reported 14,000 women engaged in making greeting cards—nearly two out of three, an unknown number of whom were in specialty shops.[96]

Paper-box manufacture is another example of the recent displacement of women. At the mid-century there were about as many women as men employed in turning out corrugated boxes. Many were stitcher operators who inserted staples that were fed down through a cylinder, four to each corner. Now, new automatic machines both feed and stitch, and the work is too heavy for women. Again, in at least one folding-box factory, a machine now does all that a half hundred girls did

[96] U.S. BLS, *Employment and Earnings,* November, 1960, p. 19.

earlier. On the other hand, after three- to six-months training, women still make candy boxes, all but setting up the machines.

In concluding these notes on specialty printing, it should be mentioned that, according to union officials, many women impair their opportunities for employment by their insistence on putting femininity before performance. It seems that during working hours many keep on their rings, which may be hazardous, many will not wear overalls, and they do not like uniforms, although loose clothing may be caught in the machinery.

THE BINDERY

By far the largest number of women production workers in printing and publishing are still to be found in the binderies. In fact, except for journeymen binders who operate complicated machines, most of the workers are women. In this service branch of the industry in which folding and sewing machines have long been in use, more than 17,000 women comprised 59 percent of all bookbinders in 1950, and at the end of the decade the International Brotherhood of Bookbinders reported that six in ten of its members were bindery women, 35,400 of them.[97]

Bindery workers are employed by independent binders, in bindery departments of big printing plants, in libraries, and in government agencies; and their numbers have risen considerably since the war. The training period for inexperienced men and women is one or two years, and a four- or five-year apprenticeship is usually required for the skilled male bookbinder.[98]

Women are always found where there is sewing to do. But in the binderies they do much more than sew, and the increase in their numbers is said to be largely due to the elaborate

[97] U.S. WB Bull. 232, p. 41; U.S. Census of Population, 1950, pp. 1C–32–33; U.S. BLS Bull. 1267, pp. 32, 58.
[98] U.S. BLS Bull. 1126, pp. 328–29; U.S. BLS Bull. 1255, p. 350.

mechanization of large-edition book and magazine binding where the work closely resembles the factory assembly line.[99]

In the most complicated branch of bindery work—edition binding—this may be the sequence of women's major operations: first, by machine they fold the printed sheets into sections of 16 to 32 pages called "signatures," so that the sheets will be in the right order; next, any separately printed illustrations are inserted; then at a gathering machine girls assemble the signatures, and stitchers at automatic machines sew them together.[100] Extreme nimbleness of fingers as well as dexterity and high speed are needed in this work. Accuracy is essential, of course, also neatness and patience. But all these occupations are only semiskilled and the wage rates are among the lowest in the printing industry.[101]

In unionized binderies no women are permitted to work at the skilled book-covering operations—the exclusive province of men apprenticed to the trade. Here, to get the books ready for covers, men shape them with great power presses that force the air from between the signatures; and with trimming machines they cut the signatures so the pages can be turned. They paste fabric strips on the book backs to reinforce them, then glue on the covers, and perform a variety of finishing operations.[102]

[99] *U.S. BLS Bull. 1255*, p. 350.

[100] *Ibid.*, pp. 349–50. One large-edition magazine pictures women in the bindery, where the magazine "is born," tending an automatic gathering machine on which "as many as 30 mechanical 'hands' grip signatures . . . and add them for assembly on a moving belt, which carries . . . double magazines down the line for binding and cutting in two." (*National Geographic Magazine*, December, 1961, p. 880.)

[101] Loft, *Labor in the Twentieth Century*, p. 68; Florence Clark, *The Printing Trades and Their Workers* (Scranton, Pennsylvania, 1939), pp. 41–54; *U.S. BLS Bull. 1255*, pp. 349–50. It has long been a firm policy of the International Brotherhood of Bookbinders to organize the semiskilled "bindery women," and in larger cities they are grouped by themselves in women's locals that manage their own affairs.

[102] *U.S. BLS Bull. 1126*, p. 328; *U.S. BLS Bull. 1255*, pp. 349–50; Florence Clark, *The Printing Trades and Their Workers*, pp. 43, 47; *U.S. WB Bull. 232*, p. 41.

But the bindery is less strongly organized than the other major divisions of printing and publishing, and a very large number of binderies are nonunion. In fact, one must infer from the census report that 59 percent of all bindery "craftsmen, foremen, and kindred workers" are women, that the majority of the binderies do not recognize the union. Thus, while all book-covering occupations in union shops "belong" to men, elsewhere it appears that men have competition from women for any skilled work that is not too heavy for them. Moreover, it seems that demand for the fine hand-binding of books, with its artistic designing and decorating of leather covers, has been declining in importance, and that where large quantities of books are bound on a mass-production, edition basis, emphasis is on the most modern machine methods. Hence, little increase in the numbers of jobs for skilled bookbinders is expected during the 1960s, while there continue to be openings for the less skilled bindery workers, most of whom are women.[103]

OTHER PRINTING OCCUPATIONS

Very few women are employed in the other major printing occupations. For instance, compared with 8,550 well-organized stereotypers and electrotypers, who make duplicate plates from type forms that come from the composing room, there were only 60 women in 1950; and no women were reported among the 14,000 members of their International Union in 1959. This work is highly skilled, involves lifting heavy plates and type forms, and is frequently done in the midst of fumes, dust, high temperature, and humidity.[104]

Also photoengravers, who supply the composing room with any needed plates of illustrations and other material that can-

[103] U.S. BLS Bull. 1255, p. 350.
[104] Ibid., pp. 343–44; U.S. BLS Bull. 1126, pp. 315–17; U.S. BLS Bull. 1267, pp. 45, 58; U.S. Census of Population, 1950, pp. 1C–32–33.

not be set in type, often work with acids and other chemicals that give off fumes. They are among the highest paid of all printing craftsmen, and are almost completely unionized. In a membership of nearly 17,000 they report 200 women members most of whom are retouchers.[105]

Lithographic workers include cameramen, artists and letterers, strippers, platemakers, and pressmen. In 1958 an estimated 45,000 to 50,000 journeymen lithographic workers were at work, and in a membership of 35,087 in 1959 the Amalgamated Lithographers of America reported 400 women.[106]

SUMMARY

In July, 1960, 244,700 women were employed in the nation's printing and publishing industry—28 in each 100 persons, a slight increase over the some 237,000 of a decade before, but the proportion had remained the same.[107] After what has been said of the scarcity of women in the mechanical departments, we return to the question with which we began: What are all these women doing?

A major answer may be gleaned from the mid-century census. In that report, close to 25,000 or a little more than 11 percent of all women were professional and technical people more than half of whom were editors and reporters; and about 105,000 or 48 percent were stenographers, typists, secretaries, bookkeepers, cashiers, telephone operators, and others. There were almost 9,000 women managers, officials, and proprietors. In other words about six out of ten women in printing and publishing were in the white-collar categories. Among these, it may be added, more and more women are said to be doing a good job on the layout and design of in-plant publications

---

[105] U.S. BLS Bull. 1126, pp. 318–19; U.S. BLS Bull. 1255, pp. 341–42; U.S. BLS Bull. 1267, pp. 40–41.

[106] U.S. BLS Bull. 1255, pp. 347–48; U.S. BLS Bull. 1267, pp. 37–38, 58.

[107] U.S. BLS, Employment and Earnings, November, 1960, p. 19.

in many industries, in advertising agencies, and art departments.[108]

As for the production departments, we have seen that the feminine sex is numerically unimportant in union shops, that women constitute a fluid group upon which nonunion shops can draw for some kinds of work, and that from these shops a few become journeymen in union composing rooms, with the possibility of more of them in the future as Teletypesetters accumulate. There are few if any women in the highly skilled and often disagreeable work of stereotyping, electrotyping, photoengraving, and while some women are still feeding small obsolescent presses, the heavy work of the highly mechanized pressroom rules them out. Increasing technological advances have reduced their numbers in specialty printing. Only in the bindery branch of the industry is there a preponderance of women that continues, one which may possibly even increase with the growth of mass-production and paperback books. All in all, therefore, we find that women's place in printing and publishing is noticeably below their status in the manufacture of textiles, clothing, footwear, and tobacco products.

Food

Probably no industry has altered our ways of living more than that which has taken food production from home garden and family kitchen into factory; so that now we can buy whole meals, such as packaged turkey dinners, that require only warming, with frozen strawberries that need only thawing, and fresh chocolate cake for desert. The ever-increasing employment of women outside the home was of course an important factor in this development. Young women at work in

[108] In the paper mills, thousands of women are employed to inspect sheet and roll stock.

offices and factories before marriage have had less experience than their mothers in the selection and preparation of food, and the rise of the standard of living has increased the desire for greater variety and more convenience in serving.

Processors of foods have thus become the third largest employers of women among the nondurable-goods industries, following apparel and textiles, and here was an average of some 350,000 women in 1960 compared to 65,000 in 1900. The fact, however, that men are taking a much greater part in cooking than in the old days largely explains why in these 60 years the proportion of women has risen only from 21 to 24 or 25 in each 100 employees. In 1962 the proportion was 22 in each 100.[109]

CANNING AND PRESERVING

Whether or not the tin can promoted the woman suffrage movement by releasing women for activties outside the home, it certainly brought women into factories to fill the can. The gradual breaking down of prejudice against canned goods and their greater variety, more knowledge of nutrition, the growing concern over obesity that has tended to reduce the amount and alter the kinds of food we eat (just as new ways of living have changed the kinds of clothes we wear)—all these developments have caused a drop in the production of food high in calories and starch and a rapid growth in the production of fruits and vegetables. Hence, while for many years canned food consisted largely of peas, corn, stringed beans, tomatoes, peaches, pears, pineapple, and some sea foods, now well over 200 different products are canned, with juices, baby foods, and meats among the fastest growing.[110] And quick freezing has become an integral part of the canning industry.

In the canning and preserving division of the industry, "men's jobs" have been largely those of cooking, material han-

[109] U.S. WB Bull. 275, p. 19; U.S. WB Bull. 285, p. 23; U.S. BLS, Employment and Earnings, November, 1960, p. 18.
[110] Alderfer and Michl, pp. 570–71.

dling, and tending and adjusting machines, and "women's jobs" those of preparing the fruits and vegetables in the relatively simple tasks of washing, grading, sorting, trimming, peeling, pulping, and blanching. At higher rates of pay women have been separating citrus fruit sections from the membrane and core and filling the containers, all by hand, while others added sugar, water, brine, sauce, sugar, syrup, or other fillers. Although some plants altered their operations after the $1.00 minimum wage became effective in 1956, mechanical "sectionizing" has not become economical not only because the fruit cannot be arranged as attractively where done by machine, but because of the wastage resulting from failure of the machine to remove all fruit from the core and membrane.[111] Today from 1,000 to 1,400 women are still hand-sectionizing the fruit in the Kraft Lakeland, Florida, factory, a representative tells us. Standing all the time—sometimes mother and daughter side by side—these women use a very sharp double-bladed triangular knife like a spatula with a point at the end so both sides can be used. During the height of the season they toil in two or two and a half 8-hour shifts. It takes about half as many women to do the peeling, as the sectionizing, and it is all very fast work.

Some technological advances in canning and preserving are noteworthy, however. They include machines for picking and shelling peas, for husking, cutting, and silking corn, for grading fruit and vegetables for size. The sterilized can and the conveyor belt also speed the process. Five women instead of ten are thus able to turn out, say, 1,000 cans of peas or corn, peaches or plums, but the industry has grown so rapidly that many more rather than fewer women are at work.[112] And now in the current march of "automation" has come a machine that fills cans with four ounces of semisolid baby food "untouched

[111] U.S. BLS Report 117, pp. 32, 35–36, 38, 53, 104–05.
[112] U.S. WB Bull. 232, pp. 25–26; U.S. WB Bull. 218, p. 98.

by human hands" at a rate of 800 per minute. Here the human function is limited to manual push-button starting and stopping, observing and adjusting the performance to correct malfunctioning, and repair and maintenance of the mechanism. Routine decisions such as determining when a can is filled are made by highly accurate, specially designed devices built into the machine.[113] And in Florida, whence 90 percent of our frozen juices come—60 million gallons a year—some women have been feeding the empty containers into a chute or putting them on a conveyor that leads to the filling and capping operation.[114]

Since canning, freezing, and preserving are largely seasonal operations, they are generally located in rural areas so the food can be processed at its proper level of maturity. Thus the majority of workers are temporary—casual laborers, local housewives, and whole families. All in all, this division of the food industry was employing 103,900 women at the seasonal peak in July, 1960, and women accounted for about two in every five workers.[115]

MEAT PROCESSING

Pork trimming is said to be one of the principal job openings for women in the meat-packing industry. These workers trim lean from fat and separate fat from lean according to specifications for use in sausage, canning, and other processed meat products. Women usually work on small pieces of meat, and retrimming trimmings is almost always their job. In some plants women also trim loins, shoulder hams, and steaks, and trim and roll small roasts. They must be skilled in handling knives which are usually kept honed by men.[116]

[113] U.S. BLS Bull. 1287, p. 4.
[114] U.S. BLS Report 117, pp. 35, 104.
[115] Alderfer and Michl, p. 579; U.S. BLS Report 117, p. 32; U.S. BLS, Employment and Earnings, November, 1960, p. 18.
[116] U.S. WB Bull. 251, pp. 3–4.

Extensive employment of women in meat processing has also come with the development of by-products and specialties such as sausage, sliced and packaged bacon, canned meats, and baby foods that meet high standards of purity. Women stuff, tie, and link sausage, weigh and pack products, package lard, prepare raw materials, weigh and mix spices. As yet meat packing has not been highly mechanized and two thirds of the jobs are said to be repetitive.[117]

Between 73,000 and 76,000 women were at work on meat products in 1960—about one in four, and a reported 28,400 and 48,800—18 and 15 percent respectively—were members of the United Packinghouse Workers and the Algamated Meat Cutters and Butcher Workmen, who have recently signed a forward-looking contract with Armour and Company for "technological adjustment pay" and the upgrading of workers in the firm's modernizing program.[118]

CONFECTIONS

Little mechanized, candymaking employs a higher percentage of women than any of the food industries—half of all employees, 36,500 of them in 1960. Apparently there is little competition between the sexes here. The men and their male helpers actually make most of the candy, and women do the hand- and machine-dipping, filling, inspecting, bulk and fancy packing, and wrapping.[119]

Women are especially adept at hand-dipping expensive chocolates. They work with candy centers and a small vat of melted chocolate or other icing material which must be kept

117 U.S. WB Bull. 88, pp. 17, 24–25; U.S. WB Bull. 218, p. 99; Alderfer and Michl, pp. 558–59.
118 U.S. BLS, Employment and Earnings, November, 1960, p. 18; Ibid., May, 1961, p. 18; U.S. BLS Bull. 1267, pp. 39, 40, 58; MLR, October, 1959, pp. 1109–10; Ibid., November, 1961, pp. 1246–47; New York Times, September 8, 1959; May 5, 1961; September 11, 1961.
119 U.S. BLS, Employment and Earnings, May, 1961, p. 18; U.S. BLS Bull. 1275, p. 5; MLR, July, 1961, pp. 737–39.

at exactly the right degree of fluidity. They drop the candy center into the vat, then with great finger deftness lift it swiftly out of the chocolate, twist or twirl it to give a smooth, uniform coating, stroke on a decorative, identifying mark that tells what the center is made of, and perhaps put a nut, a cherry, or other garnish on the top. Some dippers do their work with forks. Less expensive candies are coated in a moving wire conveyor or enrobing machine, and as they emerge on a conveyor belt, a corder or hand decorator finger-strokes a mark of melted chocolate or other coating material so the candies can be identified and will look as though hand-dipped. Sometimes the decorator uses a bag with a small nozzle from which she squeezes the "ornament." [120]

BAKERY PRODUCTS

The shift from household to commercial baking is said to have converted this industry from art to science; and as usual men have taken over the skilled jobs to the extent that 1960 from 58,000 to 61,000 women constituted little more than a fifth of all workers on bakery products, half of them in semi-skilled occupations.[121]

Unlike meat and confectionary establishments, bakeries are well mechanized and scientifically controlled, with materials-handling devices and high-speed mixers; and a traveling-hearth oven has been rapidly replacing all other types of ovens. Fewer women participate in pie, bread- and cakemaking, perhaps because much of the work is heavy, and much of it is done at night to be fresh the next day. Cookies, biscuits, and crackers, on the other hand, are less perishable, and their large-scale production has brought specialization of operations and opened new jobs for women who pack, wrap, and label. In one large, mechanized bakery in the early fifties nine out of

[120] *U.S. WB Bull. 232*, pp. 26–27.
[121] U.S. BLS, *Employment and Earnings*, November, 1960, p. 18; *Ibid.*, May, 1961, p. 18.

ten of the production workers in the doughnut-finishing department were women and three out of four in the finishing of cake and pastry. The Bakery and Confectionary Workers' International Union has a membership of more than 88,000 of whom nearly a fourth are women.[122]

BEVERAGES AND DAIRY PRODUCTS

Women play a relatively minor role in the production of beverages and dairy products. In 1920, when the Prohibition Act became effective, the number of women beverage workers fell to 900 from 2,300 the decade before. By 1940, following the repeal of the act, almost 7,600 women were at work; and by 1960, while their number exceeded 20,000, they comprised only a tenth of all employees, and of these nearly half were clerical workers. In that year dairy products employed well toward 22,000 women, who accounted for more than a fifth of all workers, but here also nearly half of all were clerical workers.[123] No longer do we hear of the dairymaid.

Thus, while the food industries stand third from the top as employers of women in the manufacture of soft goods, they fall far below apparel and textiles.

Other Nondurable Products

The manufacture of chemicals and allied products engaged more than 155,000 women in 1960 and 153,000 in 1962—18 in each 100 employees. Nearly 40,000 of these were in factories making drugs and medicines where they filled containers, labeled, and packaged, while men usually processed the materials. Of those at work making soap, cleaning and polishing preparations, 24 in each 100 were women—12,500 of them.

122 *U.S. WB Bull. 218*, pp. 99–100; *U.S. WB Bull. 232*, p. 27; *U.S. BLS Report 109*, p. 13.
123 *U.S. WB Bull. 232*, p. 28; *U.S. Census of Population, 1950*, IV, Part I, 1C–28.

And among other manufactures, including paints, fertilizers, and miscellaneous chemicals, the proportion of women ranged from 6 to 30 percent.[124]

Traditionally, petroleum refineries have employed very few women, but they were substituted for men to some extent in both world wars; and while some worked in the refining departments the largest proportion were in the offices. During World War II more refinery operations were made possible for women by job dilution, reorganization of functions, and other adjustments. Women's limited strength and state laws against their lifting of heavy weights had to be taken into consideration. In some instances, therefore, counterbalances, rollers, and conveyor belts were belatedly installed, which enabled women to do more work than men had formerly done. Moreover, since refinery operations required a sense of timing and ability to keep track of several continuous duties, some company officials deemed women particularly suitable for the work because of their household experience in cooking and cleaning. Nevertheless, it would seem that few women were retained when the servicemen returned, for by 1960 of some 237,000 workers in the manufacture of petroleum and coal products only 7 percent were women, 8 percent in 1962. Most company executives find women responding better when directly supervised by men than by women.[125]

In the paper and allied products industry the fast-growing custom of packing manufactured articles in individual boxes has led to widespread mechanization in boxmaking in which women and girls have become an important part of the labor force because of the light weight of the product and the required dexterity in machine operations. In 1900 more than 27,000 women had been so employed, and by 1962 the number

[124] U.S. BLS, *Employment and Earnings*, May, 1961, p. 19; *U.S. WB Bull. 275*, p. 19; *U.S. WB Bull. 285*, p. 23; *U.S. WB Bull. 218*, p. 123.

[125] *MLR*, August, 1943, pp. 1–4, 7; U.S. BLS, *Employment and Earnings*, May, 1961, p. 19; *U.S. WB Bull. 275*, p. 19; *U.S. WB Bull. 285*, p. 23.

had reached 123,000—more than one fifth of the labor force.[126]

During World War I a considerable number of women took men's places in tiremaking factories, where their success was attributed to "their deftness, quickness, and neatness," although the necessary lifting was deemed too severe for them. In 1960, 14,500 women were 14 percent of all employees in tire and inner-tube factories; and in the manufacture of rubber footwear where mechanized conveyor systems were in use, one in every four workers was a woman—67,600 in number.[127] By 1962, with miscellaneous plastics added, the number of women rose to 108,500 or 29 percent of all workers.[128]

To sum up our findings on women's work in the major woman-employing, nondurable-goods industries: apparel, textiles, food, printing and publishing, leather products, chemicals, paper, rubber, tobacco, and derivatives of petroleum and coal, in order of numerical importance, we find 2,551,000 women and girls at work in 1960, and 2,590,000 in 1962. And while in those years the number of women ranged from less than 10 percent of all workers in petroleum and coal products to 78 or 80 percent in apparel and related products, the average was 36 or 37 in each 100 employees 14 years of age and over.[129]

What, now, of women in the durable-goods industries?

[126] *U.S. WB Bull. 218*, p. 119; *U.S. WB Bull. 285*, p. 23; U.S. BLS, *Employment and Earnings*, May, 1962, p. 24.
[127] *U.S. WB Bull. 12*, p. 130; *U.S. WB Bull. 275*, p. 19, U.S. BLS, *Employment and Earnings*, May, 1961, p. 19.
[128] *U.S. WB Bull. 285*, p. 23.
[129] *U.S. WB Bull. 275*, p. 19; *U.S. WB Bull. 285*, p. 23.

CHAPTER 11

Durable Goods and the Advent of Electronics

Technological progress and the exigencies of the two world wars appear to have loosened forever the clinging grip of the textile and sewing trades upon the American working woman and to have drawn her into a new world that manufactures electrical equipment, airplane parts, and numerous other durable goods. Basic technical propellants were Eli Whitney's system of interchangeable parts of 150 years ago, which made mass production and division of labor possible, and Thomas Edison's Pearl Street station of the 1880s, that led to the way of making electricity so cheap and so readily distributed that sooner or later it would be applied to anything from opening a tin can in the family kitchen to controlling and navigating planes in the air and nuclear missiles in outer space.

The Twelfth Census emphasized the marked advances which had been made in machine tools and machine-shop practice in the decade before 1900. Automatic and semiautomatic principles had been extended to new and larger classes of work. The electric motor had come into general use despite the charge by mechanical men that it was an electrician's fad. Electricity supplied the modern method of driving cranes for lifting and maneuvering heavy weights. Electricity supplied the power for countless other purposes such as electric fans, irons, heaters, washers, on which more than 12,000 women operatives were at work as early as 1910—about 36 in every 100 workers.[1]

And technological advance combined with skill and patience enabled women practically to take over electric lamp manu-

[1] U.S. Twelfth Census, 1900, Manufactures, Part 4, p. 386; U.S. WB Bull. 218, p. 133.

facture. When Edison established his first factory at Menlo Park in 1880 only men were employed to make lamps—specialists who knew both the method of manipulating glass and wire and the basic theory upon which the lamp was constructed. It was largely handwork, and costly. Then, by a series of steps, the work was so greatly simplified, minutely divided, and consolidated that it could be performed by machines tended by women. Thus, also before 1910, according to an investigation by the United States Department of Labor, a surprising 80 out of every 100 makers of electric lamps were women and girls, and in occupations in which females were employed at all—that is excluding such work as stoking, freight handling, and tending dynamos—they constituted 97 percent of the labor force.[2]

Women continued to outnumber men in this industry. In one large lamp factory in the 1920s, the socket alone—from molding the porcelain base to its final parts assembly—required 237 operations, almost all of which were performed by women. They wound and mounted the fine filaments, made stems, tubulated the bulb, assembled the parts, tested the lamp, cemented the base. They also made fuse plugs, lever switches, and push buttons.[3] Thus by 1960 almost 20,000 women accounted for two out of three of all classes of employees in electric lamp manufacture; and 14,600 others were 29 percent of all involved in making lighting fixtures.[4] Women have indeed become as essential for giving us light today as they were in candlelight days.

In the fabrication of metal products, we have seen that standardization of performance, the minute division of labor, and nimble fingers took farmers' daughters to work on watches and clocks even before the Civil War, and that this skilled men's trade was pronounced "admirably adapted" to women.

[2] U.S. Bureau of Labor, *Woman and Child Wage-Earners*, III, 438, 459–60; *Ibid.*, II, 12.

[3] *U.S. WB Bull. 50*, pp. 35, 36.

[4] U.S. BLS, *Employment and Earnings*, May, 1961, p. 18.

In support of that early judgment we find that, during World War I, among 19 branches of woman-employing metal trades, more than 4,000 women were at work on clocks, watches, and watch cases; that just before World War II more than 11,000 were so employed, and that by 1963 their number had risen to 17,400 or 58 in each 100 persons.[5]

More thousands of women were at work on fabricating brass, bronze, copper, and jewelry during World War I. Others were making hardware pieces and turning out parts for typewriters, calculating and sewing machines. In fact women had begun to handle machines they had never known before, and to take part in many tasks in heavy industry. For example, they operated high-speed cutting tools to reduce metal castings or forgings to desired shapes and sizes. In cages they rode high above the floor steering cranes in steelworks, rolling mills, and machine shops, those who were successful being reported better judges of distance, quicker, and more careful of the lives of workers below than were men. And they were so successful at making cores in foundries that had never employed women [6] that one foundryman observed that, "Women have come to stay in the core room. . . . Only by elevating core-making to an attractive occupation can foundrymen hope to hold the services of efficient women workers." Women also inspected heavy shells that moved past them on rollers. They scrutinized all parts of gun sights. They gauged numerous parts of machine guns, pistols, and revolvers for inaccuracies; and many plants depended heavily upon them to catch faulty castings or machinings.[7]

[5] *U.S. WB Bull. 12*, pp. 58, 59; *U.S. WB Bull. 193*, p. 1; U.S. BLS, *Employment and Earnings*, November, 1963, p. 23.

[6] This was true either because the molder's union considered coremaking a part of a molder's apprenticeship with which the employment of women interfered, or because the work was so often done in poorly ventilated baking rooms, which was the basis of New York State's prohibition against this occupation for women.

[7] *U.S. WB Bull. 12*, pp. 95–111.

By this time the muscular strain involved in hand and machine work on smaller electrical apparatus had been so reduced that women were said to do this work also as well as if not better than men. Thus, many were employed in generator, transformer, and dynamo departments. They tested motors and adroitly avoided the dangers of severe-electrical shocks. Few but women did the simple work of cutting mica insulation in different shapes on punch presses. Others wound and insulated armature and transformer coils, and with the required deftness and some muscular strength they assembled and connected armatures. By hand and machine they shaped molded sockets, buttons, keys, plates, and plugs. These and other tasks on the numerous parts that went into the manufacture of electric power-producing and utilizing apparatus became regular occupations of women. Little skill was required for much of the work, but the ability to follow written specifications was essential.[8]

When the war was over only two out of 20 investigated electrical firms expressed dissatisfaction with women's work. One charged that woman machine workers were "less reliable and more inclined to floating than men and the discipline in the departments where men and women work suffered considerably." The second company said that the output of 114 women on assembly and inspection work was 10 to 15 percent lower than men's. On the other hand, 18 plants in which the work of men and women was comparable reported that women had proved a decided success. And in 1919, before the great spurt in the manufacture of radio parts had begun, the Census Bureau reported approximately 63,000 women and girls at work on electrical machinery, apparatus, and supplies. Hence, traditional woman-employing manufactures were sighing that, "We can't get women back at the old wages" because they "are sticking to their war jobs." And the *Textile World Journal*

[8] *Ibid.*, pp. 113–116; *U.S. WB Bull. 50*, pp. 36–37.

noted ruefully that "women may be regarded as fixtures in the machine shops and foundries." [9]

Moreover, with the presidential election campaign of 1920 came the debut of the radio, and with it a host of new employment opportunities for women in electronics manufacture in which electricity is used not only as power but is applied to the rapid and accurate *control* of electric power and machines. Girls made vacuum tubes for assembling, wiring, soldering, inserting and fastening, and testing for individual ratio units—much like what they were doing in the manufacture of telephone apparatus.[10] By the end of the decade women and girls were not infrequently 85 to 90 percent of all employees in the electronic-tube factory, and in one plant which bought many parts and accessories they composed three fourths of the labor force. While few women assembled consoles and cabinets, more than 6,000 as compared to some 400 men were assembling receivers, speakers, condensers, transmitters, and sets, and more women than men were employed as receiver inspectors.[11] The broadcast receiver had become a standard household fixture.

Thus before World War II some 100,000 women operatives were at work producing the nation's electrical machinery, many of them highly skilled. And at the height of war production the number rose to nearly 379,000.[12] In government arsenals women turned out small-arms ammunition and loaded shells and bags in artillery ammunition plants. They made gas masks, balloons, rubber life rafts, and parachutes. They made blankets, uniforms, tenting fabrics, aircraft instruments, and wire for the Signal Corps. They worked as overhaul and repair

[9] *U.S. WB Bull. 50*, pp. 35, 54; *U.S. WB Bull. 12*, pp. 24, 116.

[10] *U.S. WB Bull. 50*, p. 36; New York State *Commercial Review*, "New York's Electronic Industry," March, 1957, p. 7.

[11] *U.S. WB Bull. 83*, pp. 27–28.

[12] *U.S. WB Bull. 232*, p. 48; *U.S. WB Bull. 218*, p. 133; *MLR*, December, 1947, p. 667.

mechanics, assembling and disassembling machine guns for testing, and disassembling wrecked airplanes. They cleaned spark plugs and painted luminous dials.[13] In one highly mechanized ordnance plant, turning machines were monitored by girls who presided over large consoles of signal lights and switches controlled by electrical relays, and when something went wrong the girls altered the sequence of operation or stopped the machine.[14]

The most dramatic war use of women was in the aircraft industry. They were not wanted there, and just a week before Pearl Harbor fewer than 4,000 women were so employed. Then when the draft created a shortage of men the barriers against women were dropped and by June, 1943, well over 300,000 were at work in factories making airframes, engines, and propellers. More than another 100,000 were in the offices and other nonfactory jobs, and an additional indefinite number were helping to make airplane parts in plants working on a contract or subcontract basis. Women were employed on all kinds of planes from Lightnings and Thunderbolts to Flying Fortresses and Liberators; and on autogyros, helicopters, gliders, and sky "locomotives." [15] The Curtiss-Wright Corporation reported that one in four of the workers in its Buffalo airplane division in January, 1943, was a woman, and in the Boeing Aircraft Company of Seattle the proportion was approximately one half, with plans to increase the ratio to about three fourths by the end of the year.[16]

In aircraft plants women operated hand drills, hand screw machines, turret lathes, and light rivet guns. At the drill press they changed and sharpened their own drills. In the wood-

[13] U.S. WB Bull. 194, p. 1.
[14] Diebold, Automation: The Advent of the Automated Factory, p. 78.
[15] MLR, April, 1943, p. 662; Ibid., October, 1943, p. 658.
[16] Katherine Glover, Women at Work in Wartime, Public Affairs Pamphlet 77, 1943, p. 7. At this time Curtiss-Wright was said to be giving 800 young women recruited from 100 colleges a ten-months intensive training in aircraft engineering with all tuition and expenses paid. (Ibid., p. 9.)

working department they operated band saws, sanding belts, and did the nailing and gluing of small wooden parts. They did wiring, light grinding, profiling, sheet-metal cutting, spot and arc welding, spray painting, and many types of bench-work. On power sewing machines they did the upholstering of aircraft, stuffing the cushions with pig's hair and cotton and punching holes in hammocks to be attached to the cushions. They made rugs for the floor of the plane, cutting and shaping them to pattern. And those who sewed airplane covers had to keep eyes alert for flaws that might cost the pilot his life. Any sharp edges or corners that could cut or wear a hole in the finished cover had to be discovered and smoothed. Several large aircraft companies had women on production jobs throughout the plant. Over a third of women's jobs could be learned in less than two months and the other two thirds in six months.[17] Their special assets as aircraft assemblers were their ability to work in cramped places, owing to their small stature, and their understanding of how to plan a sequence of operations. Moreover, in this industry, perhaps above all others, woman's light touch was needed because of the fineness of the delicate balances of the airplane parts.[18]

The skill and ease with which women adjusted themselves to drill operations in these plants were often commented upon by personnel administrators or supervisors. Foremen could point with pride to a young girl who as a spot welder had more than doubled the previous records of boys, or to a woman operating a sensitive drill who maintained daily output double that of the man for whom she substituted. Women were said often to be more careful than men of the tools and materials, and there were instances of notable decreases in

[17] *U.S. WB Bull. 194*, p. 1; Laura N. Baker, *Wanted: Women in War Industry* (New York, E. P. Dutton & Co., 1943), pp. 20, 151, 158, 177.
[18] Laura N. Baker, *Wanted: Women in War Industry*, pp. 174, 176.

both accidents and labor turnover after the introduction of women.[19]

In the great majority of cases the entrance rates of pay for men and women were reported to be the same. As the Women's Bureau put it, "The job and the work done, rather than the sex of the worker, is the standard for rate fixing as advocated by the War Production Board, the Army, the Navy, and the Department of Labor." However, ten states found it necessary to pass new laws or to modify existing laws affecting women's employment, 33 states established exemption procedures, and all of the major industrial states made provisions for emergencies.[20]

All employment in airframe, engine, and propeller plants declined sharply after November, 1943, but the proportion of women—more than 36 in each 100—remained about the same, at least until June, 1944.[21] But after the virtual collapse of the industry the drop of women's employment was as spectacular as the rise had been. The Census of 1950 reported a total of 32,970 women (about 13 percent of all employees) of whom only 8,310 were operatives and about 20,000 were clerical workers. Then with the Korean conflict and the great surge of airplane production in the decade of the fifties, as international tensions continued, women's employment rose to more than 106,000. But they were only 15 percent of all employees, which may be partly explained by the fact that the Selective Service Act had assured drafted men the right to return to their peacetime jobs.[22]

What about electric machinery manufacture after the war? Television had made its formal appearance at the opening

[19] *U.S. WB Bull. 194*, p. 6.
[20] *Ibid.*, pp. 6–7.
[21] *MLR*, September, 1944, pp. 475, 478.
[22] U.S. *Census of Population, 1950*, IV, Part I, 1C–24–27; U.S. BLS, *Employment and Earnings*, May, 1961, p. 18.

ceremonies of New York's World's Fair in April, 1939, but production had ceased until the fighting was over. Then thousands of television sets, as well as radios, were made, and more women found employment in this new world of electronics. On the many component parts, production workers comprised about three fourths of the labor force, most of whom were semiskilled and unskilled, women comprising more than half of all; and almost two thirds of those in electronic-tube manufacture were women.[23]

Nearly a third of the television workers were in assembly occupations in which they handled several hundred component parts with considerable specialization. In a large "Y" plant, which the Bureau of Labor Statistics studied in the early 1950s, these assemblers—nearly all women—sat on each side of a 300-foot table using hand tools on one or more repetitive operations; wiring, soldering, or lacing on each set, or inserting the parts in a required sequence. By conveyors the wired chassis were moved to another line where the tubes were inserted, and after being tested electrically, those approved were bolted into cabinets. After the entire set had been tested, it was packed for shipping. This company purchased its standard parts from suppliers.[24]

Then in 1954 the "Y" company promoted further mechanization which somewhat altered women's work, but, it seems, did not reduce it. Photoetched circuit boards laminated with copper film (printed circuits) were substituted for many of the hand-wiring operations. This lowered the need for hand wirers, lacers, and routine assemblers, but hand labor remained imperative in tasks that required delicate movements where fragile materials were involved. Moreover, the new technology—"automation"—created some new machine-tending jobs

[23] MLR, October, 1953, p. 1053.
[24] U.S. BLS Bull. 1287, p. 80.

for which only two weeks' training was given; and since printed circuits usually make lighter TV sets, women were assigned to some of the packing occupations. Thus, according to company officials, no employees were laid off as a result of the new techniques because they were introduced during a model changeover and employment expansion.[25]

By 1960 the nation's soaring electrical machinery, equipment, and supplies industry—which included firms making telephones, electric lamps, electric measuring instruments, and household appliances as well as radio and television sets—had distinguished itself by employing well over half a million women who comprised almost two fifths of all employees. This great division of manufacturing had thus become the second largest employer of factory women—more than textiles, and topped only by wearing apparel. And in the recession year 1958 women numbered more than 380,000 or 32 percent of the combined membership of the three electrical workers' unions.[26]

Among nonelectrical machinery manufactures in which 230,-600 women were employed in 1960, some 35,000 were helping to make office and store machines and devices—more than a fourth of all so employed; 31,000 were in general industrial-machine factories; 30,600 were making metalworking machines; 26,800 were working on service industry and household machines; and 49,000 were in plants making miscellaneous machinery parts.[27]

In the production of transportation equipment, more than 19,000 women were in ship- and boatbuilding and repairing, in railroad and other equipment; and aside from the 106,000 in the manufacture of aircraft and parts, 83,000 women were

25 *Ibid.*, pp. 79–81.
26 U.S. BLS, *Employment and Earnings*, May, 1961, p. 18; *U.S. WB Bull. 275*, pp. 19–20; *U.S. WB Bull. 285*, pp. 23–24., *U.S. BLS Bull. 1267*, pp. 34, 58.
27 U.S. BLS, *Employment and Earnings*, May, 1961, p. 18.

engaged in turning out motor vehicles—one in every ten employees. This was also the ratio of women to men in the United Automobile, Aircraft and Agricultural Implement Workers' Union in 1958 when their reported number was more than 102,000.[28]

The fabricated-metal products industry was employing approximately 192,000 women in 1960. They comprised 29 percent of all workers making cutlery, hand tools, and hardware; 29 percent of those making lighting fixtures; a fourth of all engaged in fabricating wire products, 18 percent of those turning out tin cans and other tinware; a fifth of all miscellaneous products workers; and somewhat smaller percentages in the manufacture of nonelectrical heating apparatus, structural metal products, and in metal stamping, coating, and engraving.

More than 119,000 women, ranging from 23 to 54 percent of all employees, were at work on instruments: optical, surgical, medical, dental, mechanical, measuring, and controlling; on laboratory, scientific, and engineering equipment; on photographic apparatus; and on watches and clocks. Nearly 200,000 other women were engaged in the manufacture of stone, clay, and glass products; primary metal industries; furniture and fixtures and other lumber and wood products; and ordnance and accessories. About 181,000 were helping to produce numerous miscellaneous goods, including: jewelry and silverware; musical instruments and parts; toys and sporting goods; pens, pencils, and other office supplies; and fabricated plastic products. In the International Union of Doll and Toy Workers of the United States and Canada (AFL-CIO) six out of ten members were women.[29]

In all, almost 1,700,000 factory women—18 in each 100 employees—are now at work in the "heavy" industries—those outside the soft-goods manufactures which had held them

[28] U.S. BLS Bull. 1267, pp. 32, 58.
[29] Ibid., pp. 46, 58; U.S. BLS, Employment and Earnings, May, 1961, p. 18.

throughout the nineteenth century. In fact, two fifths of all of them are now in the durable-goods industries where advanced technological change—automation—has entered more intensely. There are almost a half million more than in 1950, when women were 16 percent of all such employees. In 1900 there were practically no women.[30]

[30] *U.S. WB Bull. 285*, pp. 19–20.

CHAPTER 12

Twentieth Century Manufactures—
the Advance of Automation

In 1960, 4,284,000 women were at work in the nation's factories—26 in each 100 of all such workers and four times as
many as in 1900, when they were less than a fifth of all. And
within the manufacturing groups of industries notable changes
in women's work have occurred. For, whereas practically all
factory women were in nondurable or "soft goods" industries
at the turn of the century, two out of five are now employed in
the durable-goods or "heavy" industries.

What has caused this remarkable shift? The answer lies once
again in technological change, the early developments of which
took women into factories in the first place. "Automation" has
been said to be as hard to define as sin, and countless pages
have been written about it. To some observers it is nothing
more than a continuation of technical advance that began in
the age of the steam engine when Arkwright perfected an
automatic carding engine to provide thread for fast spinning
machinery; when Oliver Evans built an automatic loom the
movements of which were controlled by punched paper cards
that could be rearranged to weave various patterns; when Eli
Whitney introduced the principle of interchangeable parts.

Today these commentators point to "Detroit automation,"
where machines are integrated with one another, where hydraulic or electrical controls permit loading and unloading of
special-purpose machine tools, where automatic movements of
work pieces transfer parts from one operation to another—a
development which has spread to some divisions of metalworking, electrical and electronic, meat-packing, and food-
processing industries. In other words, wherever repetitive
operations produce large quantities of a standardized product

Detroit automation—advanced mechanization—is likely to be applied.

Other observers say that in true automation the master key is not only advanced mechanization but the "feedback" or correcting servomechanism made possible largely during World War II by electronic devices hooked up to machines that feed, control, handle, and adjust automatically according to need, and with even greater precision than by the most skillful human workers. Briefly stated, there is feedback control when information about the output at one stage in the process is fed back to an earlier stage to influence the process and change the output itself. In short, the "feedback" enables a machine to correct its own errors with almost no human labor. The control of room temperature by use of the thermostat is a simple example. Here a change in temperature which expands or contracts sensitive metals transmits a signal to the starting switch of the furnace which operates until the desired temperature is reached, then stops.[1] Today the term automation is being used when advanced technological change is meant, whether or not it is true automation. In the pages that follow, therefore, we shall at times use this term in the more popular sense.

This innovation, which is still in its infancy, is so full of potentialities for industry, society, and men and women workers that before the century ends it is likely to have gone down in history as the Second Industrial Revolution. The forecasts are that true automation will be introduced only gradually in the manufacturing industries because of the high cost of new types of equipment, the long time required for designing and custom-building the complex machinery, and the necessary long-range planning and complex decisions in the field of corporation finance, marketing, administration, manufacturing methods, personnel selection and training, and bargaining collectively when the workers are organized. It is quite possible,

[1] *MLR*, June, 1955, p. 640.

however, that revised federal tax depreciation schedules will tend to hasten replacement of obsolescent machinery by automated equipment.

We have witnessed effects of technological change upon woman's work throughout the first six decades of the present century, punctuated as they have been by two world wars and a deep depression. In the manifold and widespread textile industry, continued improvements of the automatic loom have revolutionized weaving, and new mechanisms for other processes have taken some jobs away from women and brought some former men's work to them despite the supposition that they are mechanically inept. Meanwhile, the reluctance of New England mills to modernize their operations was an important factor in the migration of the industry to the South, where mill owners installed the newest machinery and are now introducing electronic devices to measure quality and control production. But this has always been a relatively low-paying industry and many women have been lured away into other occupations, often new to them, to the extent that textile mills have lost their first place as employers of women.

In the largest woman-employing industry—wearing apparel —where women predominate in the numerous sewing operations, more than 200 forms of power-driven machines run as high as 4,500 stitches a minute or faster. As a result of technological changes, women greatly outnumber men in footwear and other leather products, and they have almost taken over the manufacture of cigars. Cigarette manufacture has been mechanized almost from the beginning, and a recent mechanism for preparing tobacco leaves has reduced women's employment, especially Negroes. But today half of all employees in the tobacco industry are women.

On the other hand, the highly mechanized and highly unionized printing and publishing industry has almost eliminated women in the production departments; although it looks as though the coming of the Teletypesetter in the composing room may in time bring in a good many women to cut tape on tape-punching machines. Advancing technology in specialty printing, where women have prospered, has also reduced their numbers. But it may be that the preponderance of women in the bindery will increase with technological change and the demand for paperback books.

In at least one recently automated bakery, nine out of ten of the doughnut finishers are now women, as are three in every four of those who finish cake and pastry. In the production of meat products about one in four people are women, and those who are union members will benefit by a recent contract with one of the major firms for "technological adjustment pay" and upgrading of status as a result of a modernization plan.

But advanced mechanization has made greater strides in the production of durable goods. As machines took over the heavier work during World War I women performed many "men's jobs" on electrical apparatus and fabricated metal products. And after radio had made its formal debut in the new electronics industry the numbers of women in electrical machinery and equipment manufacture soared between the two world wars and rose to just under 380,000 at the peak of employment in 1943–44. At the same time almost 487,000 women were at work in aircraft plants, where they displayed special skills and received good wages.

By 1960, and since then, while there has been a sharp decline in the number of women in the manufacture of aircraft and parts, the increasing demand for television sets along with the radios has brought well over half a million to work in electrical machinery and equipment plants which now top textiles as employers of women. Moreover, in at least one establishment in the television division which had been inactive during the war, women assemblers did not lose work as a result of automation because new machine-tending jobs opened and they could now pack the lighter TV sets.

Aside from electrical machinery, aircraft and other transportation equipment, more than a million women are employed in the manufacture of nonelectrical machinery for offices, stores, metalworking and general industrial machinery, and service household machines; fabricated metal products, including cutlery, hand tools, hardware, and metal stamping; coating and engraving, and the manufacture of various and numerous instruments, including watches and clocks. On these, as well as many other durable products, women employees in 1960 comprised 18 in every 100 workers and two in five of all factory women. It seems significant, moreover, that women appear to be less inclined than formerly to leave their work, and that consistently they quit their jobs less frequently in the durable- than in the soft-goods industries,[2] stimulated possibly by the higher pay they receive.

What will be the effect upon women factory workers as automation advances? Much remains for the future to tell, but some points in favor of their increased employment seem to be the promised relief from dangerous, dirty, heavy, and backbreaking jobs, the reduction of some skilled operations to tasks that require only a few days or weeks of training, the probable decentralization of plants into rural areas where local workers, whom union organizers largely fail to reach, will be employed. All observers seem to agree that automation will reduce the number of repetitive, monotonous, and highly specialized tasks on the assembly line and increase the need for better education in order to carry greater responsibility. Have we reason to believe that women will shrink from this advance? Some authorities believe that construction, installation, maintenance and repair service, together with the operational and super-

[2] *MLR*, August, 1955, pp. 893–94.

visory care of automated machinery that is necessary for all equipment, will attract more women. Moreover, the supply of women in the prime working age will grow more than that of men, while economists in and out of the federal government consider ways of hurrying up automation to help solve our serious unemployment problems.

Finally, only a fifth of all working women today are in the manufacturing industries, including the office work involved. Hence, to find more of them we must enter the widening field of white-collar work where automation, particularly in the office and at the telephone switchboard, is revolutionizing woman's work.

CHAPTER 13

Women in the Office and
the Electronic Computer

Factory mechanization had a hundred-year start over offices, and now, in the new era of electronics, offices are more than catching up. When the great-grandfather of office machinery—the typewriter—began to click in the 1870s, American business routine was still in its primitive stage and office work was largely a man's occupation. By 1900, despite male traditions, some 96,000 young women—most of them single and living at home—were employed as stenographers, typists, and secretaries—seven out of every ten. In clerical positions, which numbered nearly a million, women were holding close to one in four. Six decades later two thirds of the 9,600,000 clerical workers were women, and they constituted almost a third of all working women as compared to 1/25 in 1900. Their number has increased faster than the labor force. Half of these women are 35 to 64 years of age, and more than half are married and living with their husbands. Women stenographers, typists, and secretaries, who are found wherever there are offices—and offices are everywhere—hold all but 3 percent of those positions while "help-wanted" newspaper columns bulge with offers for more and more of them.[1]

Manually operated typewriters and other office machines met the needs of business at the turn of the century as countless thousands of them do today. But the Bureau of the Census had discovered that it took nine years to compute the returns for 1880, and that with increasing population the data for 1890 would not be processed until after the 1900 census had been

[1] David L. Kaplan and M. Claire Casey, *Occupational Trends in the U.S., 1900–1950*, U.S. Bureau of the Census, Working Paper No. 5, Department of Commerce, 1958, pp. 7, 17, 23; *U.S. WB Bull. 275*, pp. 7, 32, 38.

taken. It was in this predicament that Herman Hollerith of the Census Bureau developed an electro-mechanical system by applying the punched-hole principle to cards for sorting them mechanically. Holes punched in various places on a card represented specific items of information. The cards were fed into a machine that made electrical contacts through the punched holes. With this innovation the Census returns for 62 million people were tabulated in two years.[2] Here was a forerunner of today's electronic computer system.

The electromechanical principle, variously applied, came into extensive use. It was capable of turning out data at the approximate rate of 400 cards per minute, or more than six per second. In 1906, World's Work reported that, "There has been placed on the market a remarkable calculator which adds, subtracts, multiplies, and divides by electricity. It so completely does the work of a human being that it is almost uncanny in its efficiency and speed." And in 1913 a bank-statement machine was said to enable "one clerk to do the work of two bookkeepers"; and there were improved electric calculators which "literally devour figures." [3]

But before machines were introduced on any scale the office was enlarged to accommodate a systematic arrangement of business facts. A numerical file with alphabetical index came into wide use. The clerk managed complicated "systems" alongside the bookkeeper and stenographer. And as the army of clerks grew, they were divided into departments, specialized in function and "socially rationalized," as one authority puts it.[4]

Both business and government were thus ready for the office machinery that came during World War I along with Frederick Taylor's principles of scientific management and study

2 U.S. Employment Service, Occupations in Electronic Data-Processing Systems, 1959, pp. 1–2.

3 Georgina M. Smith, Office Automation and White Collar Employment, Institute of Management and Labor Relations, Rutgers University, Bull. 6, 1959, p. 5.

4 C. Wright Mills, White Collar: The American Middle Classes (New York, Oxford University Press, 1961), pp. 192–93.

of "the one best way." In the 1920s machines invaded every corner of the office, and some hundred new ones made their appearance each year. To the accounting department there came new machines for bookkeeping, billing, money handling, and for various kinds of statistical work. There were adding and calculating machines, cash and credit registers. In the correspondence and circularizing division there were varieties of typewriters, addressing, duplicating, dictating machines, envelope feeding, folding, and sealing, stamping and franking devices. All these and other mechanisms and systems were in use on the mounting work of advertising and sales promotion, small hand-to-mouth orders, and installment selling . . . and new models kept coming.[5]

Economic use of the new machines began to require office centralization that brought more specialization and division of labor among some 45 different occupations exclusive of executive and professional. For example, in the office of a large electrical company typists who had been turning out only 31 letters a day produced 92 a day after installation of dicta-phones in a separate stenographic bureau removed from de-partmental offices. And Commonwealth Edison Company con-centrated 80 girls in one room, including stenographers, typists, and dictaphone operators. Even as early as this the office of one large firm was reported to resemble a factory.

Orders are passed along by means of a belt and lights from a chief clerk to a series of checkers and typists, each of whom does one operation. The girl at the head of the line interprets the order, puts down the number and indicates the trade discount; the second girl prices the order, takes off the discount, adds carriage charges and totals; the third girl gives the order a number and makes a daily record; the fourth girl puts this information on an alphabetical index; the fifth girl time-stamps it; it next goes along the belt to one

[5] Grace L. Coyle, *Present Trends in Clerical Occupations* (New York, The Women's Press, 1928), pp. 8, 17.

of several typists, who makes a copy in septuplicate and puts on address labels; the seventh girl checks it and sends it to the store-room.[6]

It seemed apparent that young women were particularly suited to office occupations. They were less expensive than men. Their more or less temporary attachment to the job made most of them less interested in advancement, which office positions usually lacked. Thousands of girls were pouring out of high schools in a rising wave that came with a higher standard of living. In the 34 years up to 1924 the public school population increased 20 times more than the total population of the country. And while machines made high school education less necessary for occupations such as receiving and shipping clerks, junior high school was usual for filers, multigraph operators, and billing, stock, payroll, and mail clerks. For stenographers, dictating-machine operators, bookkeepers, and bookkeeping-machine operators, office managers required senior high school education; and college for the secretarial stenographer.[7] By this time woman suffrage had been won, and the movement to improve the status of women was alive in all spheres of activity from manual to professional. Moreover, the number of married women in offices was increasing, and without Lucy Stone exhortation many of them thwarted prejudice against their employment by retaining their maiden names.

By 1930 the number of office women was approaching 2,000,000—more now than in the manufacture of products; and for the first time women outnumbered men. The largest number among those studied by the Women's Bureau were 20 to 25 years of age. Three fourths of them had attended high school, although more than half had not remained to be graduated. Median salaries were higher for those who had gone

[6] *Ibid.*, pp. 19–20.
[7] *Ibid.*, pp. 11, 14, 33.

beyond grammar school. The number at work on bookkeeping and letter writing was often overshadowed by those engaged in new but unstandardized activities in connection with advertising, sales campaigns, market and credit analysis and collections, statistical reports on costs, and a variety of other recording operations. The duties of the secretaries, stenographers, typists, and machine operators thus varied with the nature of the enterprise. Insurance companies, for example, needed numerous clerks to check rates, risks, elaborate records of policies and expiration dates, and to send out notices. In banks, the women computed interest, counted and checked money and securities, made routine entries, and checked customers' accounts. Public utilities furnishing light and fuel required much work on meter records and customers' bills.[8]

Upon the introduction of bookkeeping and billing machines, the Women's Bureau reported, women had taken the place of men in some instances while in others where women had been employed fewer were needed. Automatic typewriters, which were turning out from three to ten times as much work as could be done on an ordinary machine, were used in competing with commercial letter-writing bureaus instead of reducing the number of women employed in the office. Nevertheless, the rapid rise in the relative number of office workers had slackened.[9]

In the decade of World War II, however, the influx of office machines was so great that the number of operators increased 138 percent, and 3,000 machines were exhibited annually as the mid-century approached. The "craftsman" clerk of the early 1900s thus became "as rare as a rolltop desk," and "help-wanted" columns summoned girl high school graduates with "no experience necessary." They could be trained in a few weeks to do a single job such as routine billing, cardpunching,

[8] U.S. WB Bull. 120, pp. 1, 5, 10–12.
[9] Ibid., pp. 16–17; Coyle, Present Trends in Clerical Occupations, pp. 17–20.

calculating, or filing. By 1956, some 8,770,000 clerical workers comprised about a third of all salaried employees, and more than two out of three of them were women and girls. Moreover, for the first time in the nation's history the count of white-collar people exceeded that of the blue-collar workers.[10]

Indeed offices had become "full of women" between the two world wars, and the woman secretary had come into her own. "For women only," Katherine Gibbs had opened her first secretarial—not stenographic—school in 1911, and the career girl had become the head of the office. The editors of *Fortune* drew this verbal picture of the office.

The male is the name on the door, the hat on the coat rack, and the smoke in the corner room. But the male is not the office. The office is the competent woman at the other end of the buzzer, the two young ladies chanting his name monotonously into the mouthpieces of a kind of gutta-percha halter, the four girls in the glass coop pecking out his initials with pink fingernails on keyboards of four voluble machines, the half dozen assorted skirts whisking through the filing cases of his correspondence, and the elegant miss [sic] in the reception room recognizing his friends and disposing of his antipathies with the pleased voice and the impersonal eye of a presidential consort.[11]

Today, in fact, secretarial jobs go begging. One reason given is that the expansion of metropolitan-area headquarters' activities requires considerable traveling, if not actual moving one's home. Another is that most employers want secretaries not more than 35 years of age while more girls are continuing their education, and as college graduates they look at once for better jobs or they accept secretarial work to gain experience in a particular industry or business and later work up to a professional or administrative position. Thus we have reports of the importation of British secretaries on contracts. And a London employment agency thinks secretaries may become a new Brit-

[10] Smith, *Office Automation*, pp. 5, 6, 9.
[11] *Fortune*, "Women in Business," August, 1935, p. 50.

ish "export" to the United States. "I have 500 applicants already interested in the possibilities," said the woman proprietor of this agency. "All of the girls . . . are presently employed in top secretarial positions . . . thoroughly trained. . . . None is more than thirty, and each is ready to pay her own way . . . and sign a two-year contract with an American employer." [12]

The Electronic Computer

Electronic computers—lightning speed data-processing systems—had appeared in the war decade as aids in solving intricate scientific and engineering problems such as gunfire control. But these would not serve business and government where general and special-purpose mechanisms were required to process masses of repetitive data, record, and store information, and perform mathematical operations. Hence, like Eli Whitney's system of interchangeable parts for the manufacture of muskets, the new electronic machines that make automation possible proved useful in turning out weapons then were adapted to the needs of civilian enterprises for which clerical work is so essential on the countless time-consuming office chores such as those we have noted.[13]

Again the Bureau of the Census put new life into its vast decennial undertaking by installing in 1951 the first UNIVAC (Universal Automatic Computer) to add, subtract, and divide at speeds ranging from 250 to 5,000 calculations per second. In the same year the Bank of America installed a specially designed ERMA (Electronic Recording Machine Accounting) to handle the daily bookkeeping operations for 50,000 checking accounts. The great IBM-700 series became popular with insurance companies, utilities, and banks. And those first com-

[12] New York *Times,* February 22, 1960; May 5, 1961.
[13] *U.S. BLS Bull. 1241,* p. 3; Jack Stieber, "Automation and the White Collar Worker," in *Personnel,* November–December, 1957, pp. 8–17.

puter systems have been followed by a flood of successors—some to perform special tasks, others for general-purpose work. Some are no bigger than an office desk, others are large enough to fill a whole room.[14]

By early 1959 an estimated 2,000 computers of all sizes—each with various pieces of auxiliary equipment—were in use for a variety of business, scientific, and engineering purposes of private companies and government agencies—at prices ranging from $25,000 to $1,000,000 or more, and monthly rentals from $7,500 to $25,000.[15] Today federal government agencies are operating more than 600 computers which are especially useful in digesting the masses of data collected by the Census Bureau, in keeping records of millions of persons covered by Social Security, and in many other bureaus and departments. The Bureau of the Census is also using an electronic machine called FOSDIC (Film Optical Sensing Device for Input to Computers) for translating data on record sheets of census enumerators made by an ordinary pencil or pen into a form that can be fed directly into the computing machines and perform work which otherwise would require employment of 2,000 clerical workers.[16] In 1960, 50 statisticians were able to do tabulations that required 4,100 in 1950.[17] And the mountainous paper work attending the sharp slump in the stock market on May 28, 1962, and after was handled far more easily that in 1929 because of automation.

It was the broad stream of scientific research that produced the radio and television, on which so many women are employed today, that contributed basically to the development of these remarkable electronic computer systems. The principal feature

[14] Hoos, "When the Computer Takes Over the Office," p. 28; Smith, *Office Automation*, pp. 6, 7; *U.S. BLS Bull. 1300*, p. 287.

[15] Smith, *Office Automation*, p. 7; *U.S. BLS Bull. 1241*, p. 4; *U.S. BLS Bull. 1276*, pp. 1, 7; *U.S. BLS Bull. 1287*, p. 109.

[16] *U.S. BLS Bull. 1287*, pp. 22, 100; U.S. Congress, Joint Economic Committee, Hearings, "Automation and Technological Change," 1955, p. 577.

[17] Michael, p. 15.

of the innovation is high speed—millionths of a second movement (and tomorrow even billionths of a second) and control of the sequence of their operations automatically according to built-in and alterable instructions known as "taping" or "programming." By electronic circuitry—through so-called printed circuit cards—the system can do more than add and subtract. It compares, collates, and makes logical choices between alternatives according to instructions. When a digital computer is attached to the control of automatic processing equipment in a manufacturing plant, it can monitor the operation of the entire factory.[18] Likewise, in an office the computer equipment reduces paper work by processing a mass of punch-card data in the preparation of useful statistics. It achieves not only a larger clerical output in routine activities with the same or fewer employees—a major objective—but also economies in processing time, space, and equipment with greater accuracy.[19]

Observers seem to agree that the displacement of workers will go farthest and fastest in the office, and that since office automation aims principally to replace routine, repetitive jobs, women clerical workers may be the largest affected group. For example, a vice-president of the San Francisco Bank of America recently told the Joint Economic Committee of Congress that the single largest area of common interest in mechanizing both large and small banks is check handling and checking-account bookkeeping—both repetitive clerical tasks generally performed by "young women employed during the transitory period between graduation from high school and their perma-

[18] *U.S. BLS Bull. 1287*, p. 7; Diebold, *Automation: The Advent of the Automatic Factory*, pp. 26, 29.

[19] A fascinating example is that of American Airlines, which in 1957 was handling plane reservations with a "Reservisor" that held a record of all seats available on 1,000 flights for a ten-day period and, at the push of a button, showed what flights had vacancies for a given destination on a given date. (Diebold, *Automation: Its Impact on Business and Labor*, p. 15; and see *U.S. BLS Report 137*.)

nent occupation as housewives and mothers." He said that 90 percent of his bank's 2,300 bookkeepers were young women for whom the turnover in 1956 was some 78 percent "most of which was caused by marriage and other family reasons." Hence, with the growth in the volume of checking-account activity, which was increasing faster than the number of people available to handle it manually, automation was the only alternative.[20]

By 1962, therefore, vice-president Zipf continued, customer accounts would be handled on a centralized basis with the electronic computer ERMA; and the bank was planning 17 ERMA centers throughout California. If this caused displacement of bookkeepers, the bank would still need tellers. And since 2,000 or 50 percent of the woman tellers resigned every year, 2,000 more would be needed each year for replacements alone, exclusive of the growth of business. Moreover, ERMA transition would extend over a period of several years, and available personnel would be promoted to tellers' positions— two salary grades higher than bookkeeping. Also new positions would be created by introduction of the computer system, and more than half of these positions would be at least four salary grades above the bookkeeping level, and those who held them would come from within the bank through training and promotion.[21] Although the vice-president did not say so, we shall see that employers were inclined to appoint men rather than women to the new positions of preparing programs for the computer.

The most recent major development in banking operations which may take a heavy toll in women's employment is magnetic ink character recognition (MICR), which was adopted

[20] U.S. Congress, Joint Economic Committee, Hearings, "Automation and Technological Change," 1955, p. 213; U.S. Congress, Hearings, "Automation and Recent Trends," 1957, p. 83, by A. R. Zipf.
[21] "Automation and Recent Trends," by A. R. Zipf, pp. 85–86.

in 1956 by the nation's bankers as the common machine language most suitable for mechanical check handling.[22] Instead of the manual sorting of checks, first at the bank where they are deposited, then at the regional Federal Reserve Bank, and again at the bank on which they are drawn, MICR and related equipment reduces the number of steps and, what is more important, it processes the checks automatically and at much higher speed. Many of us are now finding a long line of code numbers and signs at the bottom edge of the checks we write. So far the process is in the early throes of conversion and no prediction is ventured on its ultimate employment effects. However, the volume of checks increases every year, and bankers expect that in the next few years it will rise from the current 14 million per annum to some 20 million. It is possible, therefore, that more rather than fewer women will be needed, and it seems certain that it will be a long time before a machine can read a signature on a check and say that it is genuine.

A more explicit account of the impact of office automation upon women's employment comes from an investigation by the Bureau of Labor Statistics of the experience of a large insurance company which had been plagued for many years by a shortage of clerical workers while business was expanding. In the early postwar years this company was using punched-card machinery with a high proportion of unskilled high school girl graduates whose brief stay on the job, owing to marriage or to accepting other employment, caused a complete turnover every five years. To get the work done, many of the firm's operating divisions were hiring a considerable number of part-time high school students. Women comprised 66 percent of total employment in the home offices, where all large computer

22 U.S. Congress, Joint Economic Committee, "New Views on Automation," *Papers*, 1960, pp. 349, 375.

installations were made. Hence they were among those most affected by the conversion to automation.[23]

In this company's X Division about 850,000 policy transactions a month (death claims, policy changes, and the like) had been processed on 125 modern punched-card machines and some key-punch machines which handled about 3 ¼ million cards. The work involved sorting, classifying, and calculating. After installation of the computer equipment in 1954 it was found that the information contained on 850,000 punched cards could be recorded on 71 reels of magnetic tape. As a result, 21 punched-card machines and 85 employees (71 or four fifths of whom were women and girls), at an average salary of about $4,200, managed the work that had required 125 machines and 198 employees at an average salary of $3,700. Nevertheless, the investigator noted that "the net upgrading effect on the 198 persons in the original section could not have been more than a transfer of five persons to more skilled jobs." [24]

The employees concerned had been advised in advance of the impending change and assured that there would be no job loss or downgrading because of the new techniques. There was meticulous concern for individual job preferences for other operations in the company. Hence, 78 women were transferred to other jobs within the same or other company divisions and 19 resigned—14 to be married, two to accept jobs elsewhere, two to move to other areas, and one to retire.[25]

Of the 85 persons retained in the X Division, eight women and 12 men were selected to operate the computer, although

[23] U.S. BLS Bull. 1287, p. 81; U.S. BLS, Studies in Automatic Technology, No. 2, pp. iii, 15.
[24] U.S. BLS, Studies in Automatic Technology, No. 2, pp. 3–4, 7, 11; K. G. Van Auken, Jr., "A Case Study of the Impact of Automation on Skills and Employment," in Man and Automation (Technology Project, Yale University, 1956), p. 31.
[25] U.S. BLS, Studies in Automatic Technology, No. 2, pp. 1, 6, 8.

except for five men (the only ones given more skilled jobs) their work was on a skill level roughly comparable to that of former operations performed on modern punched-card equipment.[26] One of these women became a tape librarian, who classifies, catalogues, and cross-indexes reels of magnetic tape according to data content, and prepares the record for file references. Two were put to work on auxiliary equipment converting to machine language current transaction data and new insurance policies from punched cards to magnetic tape—one a converter-team head and one a converter clerk. One woman became a routine key-punch operator, who punches holes on cards that represent coded instructions for the computer, and four were assigned to the control of the central unit or console —one control captain, one assistant, and two control clerks. Criteria for the selection of these people were experience, proficiency in mathematics, and perhaps a college degree, which was considered desirable but not essential.[27]

In addition to the 20 were nine more highly skilled programmers and analysts who had been part of the small nucleus around which planning for the computer installation had centered—three women and six men. Fifty-six women and girls out of the total of 71 were given noncomputer duties similar to the jobs they had held before—converting information on punched cards to magnetic tape, storing and distributing tape and cards, and similar duties. The new staff with its more than 80 percent women worked a regular 37-hour week with overtime as needed. Two persons worked on a late shift.[28]

According to the investigator, at least three factors had contributed to this company's success and ease of adjustment in automating its home-office X Division: 1. an expanding vol-

26 Van Auken, in *Man and Automation*, pp. 30–31.
27 U.S. BLS, *Studies in Automatic Technology*, No. 2, pp. 8, 9; *U.S. BLS Bull. 1241*, p. 5.
28 Van Auken, in *Man and Automation*, pp. 30–31; U.S. BLS, *Studies in Automatic Technology*, No. 2, pp. 10, 11.

ume of business; 2. a shortage and relatively high turnover of female clerks; and 3. the basic similarity of job requirements among many of the company's divisions, which permitted easy transfer of workers. (The report might have added the fact that the workers were not unionized). Nevertheless, the combination of normal personnel turnover together with increasing business left the X Division 10 percent understaffed at the time of the study.[29]

In contrast to the above report of little upgrading of personnel as a result of computer installation, the automation of the commercial department of the home office of another large and expanding insurance company, also during the early fifties, brought considerable upgrading of job content and skill, as well as the average salaries of clerical workers. But in this case the change was from a largely manual to an automatic system, bypassing the intermediate electromechanical methods.

Within the different sections of this department before automation, the company had organized the clerks into groups, most of whose leaders and all senior clerks were women. In fact, women comprised 95 percent of the 539 persons employed in the department, many of them at manual work of a detailed, repetitive nature. For instance, clerks manually sorted and recorded 150,000 dividend notices each week—an average of 30,000 forms each working day. For processing the transactions there were numerous tape adding machines, 30 bookkeeping machines, and 200 typewriters on many of which "rewrite" girls made new listings for the agents.[30]

In this conversion to electronic accounting, according to the

[29] U.S. BLS, *Studies in Automatic Technology,* No. 2, pp. 1, 9. This informative report, together with Van Auken's article in *Man and Automation* has also been reviewed in *U.S. BLS Bull. 1287,* pp. 81–83; Stieber, "Automation and the White Collar Worker," pp. 5–6; Smith, *Office Automation,* pp. 12–13.

[30] Harold Farlow Craig, *Administering a Conversion to Electronic Accounting—a Case Study* (Boston, Harvard University Press, 1955), pp. 26, 32; Craig, "Administering Technological Change in a Large Insurance Office," Industrial Relations Research Association (IRRA), *Papers,* December, 1954, p. 130.

Harvard man who made the intensive study, the labor force was reduced to 406 people with an average weekly salary of $49 as compared to the previous average of $37; for now only 63 percent were in job grades 1, 2, and 3 as compared to 87 percent before. Although some operations were still manual, the detailed, repetitive work had been mechanized and the job of many of the clerks was either to control the accuracy of machine work or to operate the machines themselves. No one had been laid off, perhaps because of the relatively high turnover of the personnel. During the last six months of the conversion period, for example, there were 71 terminations—45 percent because of marriage and pregnancy, 27 percent because of accepting positions elsewhere, 10 percent to return to school, and others for reasons such as health and moving to another state.[31]

Very few negative or hostile sentiments were expressed to the investigator, who testified that a part of the success of the installation was "a feedback of enthusiasm" for the new system. He found that the girls who were operating the machines were proud of their speed and efficiency; and those employed in preparing information and controlling the accuracy of machine work referred to the old manual system as "tiresome, tedious, and dull." [32]

An interesting and perhaps prophetic effect upon the women clerical workers in this office was that it made them more independent in choosing employers. The specialized nature of their work before automation had made it difficult to find desirable work elsewhere after they had been with the company for two years or more. But the new IBM machines caused greater standardization of procedure so that a trained

[31] Craig, IRRA *Papers*, pp. 133–134; Craig, *Administering a Conversion to Electronic Accounting*, pp. 70–71.
[32] Craig, IRRA *Papers*, pp. 137, 138.

operator could work almost as well in one establishment as in another. In truth, this meant that the company whose work force was not organized for collective bargaining now had to compete in salary payment with other concerns in the area where IBM equipment was in use.[33]

Still another empirical study of the impact of office automation upon clerical workers (and more studies keep coming) is that of the Bureau of Labor Statistics of 20 metropolitan-area manufacturing and business firms. Seven of these were insurance companies,[34] where over a span of three years computers were first installed in the home offices, with more to follow.

For many years all but one of these firms had processed their data by electromechanical tabulating and related punch-card equipment. The introduction of electronic computers was thus only the latest step in the sequence of technological improvements. In preparation for the change, hiring was curtailed so that vacancies created by quitting, deaths, retirement, and leaves of absence could be filled by those directly affected.[35] A year after the installations approximately 2,800 employees had been affected, 53 percent being women. About a third of the 2,800 had been reassigned to other positions in the same unit or elsewhere in the office. Many young women had left, presumably to become housewives.[36]

In these offices it was found that the new technology had lessened the proportion of employees on routine jobs—from about 85 percent to 80 percent of the group affected. Three percent of the tabulators were transferred to electronic data-processing occupations, probably men, though we are not told

[33] *Ibid.*, pp. 133–34.
[34] The others were public utilities, air transportation, aircraft, chemicals, electrical machinery, petroleum refining, steel manufacture, and railroads. Seven of these had collective bargaining relations with unions.
[35] *U.S. BLS Bull. 1276*, pp. 3, 7, 17; *U.S. BLS Bull. 1287*, p. 97.
[36] *U.S. BLS Bull. 1276*, pp. 3, 31, 53.

their sex, or the sex of the 52 who were transferred to these jobs. There was a total reduction in employment of about 25 percent.[37]

In making these reassignments the objective was to minimize the extent of transfer, especially among the permanent employees. One insurance company stressed the need to avoid placing employees where they might be subject to displacement a second time. Another firm, anticipating further applications of the computer system, selected for reassignment women employees and potential draftees who were likely to be among the less permanent workers. Avoidance of double displacement had been set down as the first of several principles, some others being that, when a complete unit (division or section) was to be abolished, all employees should be considered as surplus workers to be assigned to special projects and absorbed by promotion without undue delay; also that "whenever practical" female employees should be assigned to higher level positions traditionally occupied by males.[38]

A negligible number of some 2,400 employees of the 20 companies had been downgraded, and close to a third were promoted to a higher grade—most of them under the age of 45. Because of general policies assuring job security—seniority provisions in two union contracts, and other protective provisions —the job status of older employees was affected somewhat less than that of the younger ones.[39]

And now what about the programmers—those who operate, program, and manage electronic data processing? Although computers are often described as machines that can "think," this is of course not so. Like little children, they have to be told what to do and exactly how to do it. Therefore, where great quantites of information are to be processed in the same

[37] Ibid., pp. 3, 4, 35; U.S. BLS Bull. 1287, pp. 97–98.
[38] U.S. BLS Bull. 1276, pp. 27, 72–73.
[39] Ibid., pp. 34, 58.

way so that a large number of repetitive steps are involved in the solution of a problem, the computer's operations are carefully planned and programmed. The function of the professional programmer is to reduce each problem to a series of very simple steps of instructions by which the computer system can act. The "program" is converted into holes on punched cards and paper tapes or magnetic indications on magnetic tape, so that at each stage of the computations the machine "asks" a question that can be answered by "yes" or "no" respectively represented by 1 or 0—in computer "language." Finally, the programmer must make several trial runs of the cards or tapes in order to "debug" the program—check its accuracy. The entire programming process may take a few months or a year or longer, and the instructions may fill several bulky volumes. (But it should be noted that one forward-looking observer says that "much successful work has been done on computers that can program themselves.") [40]

The average number of programmers employed by the 20 offices studied by the Bureau of Labor Statistics was 29, though there were as few as 2 or 3 for a medium-size system, or as many as 30 or more for a large computer. One large insurance company employed as many as 200. In all, 915 of these new positions were created, only 103 or 11 percent of which were given to women, and of these women only 17 were among the 173 newly hired people.[41]

[40] Diebold, *Automation: The Advent of the Automatic Factory*, p. 28; *U.S. BLS Bull. 1241*, pp. 3, 9; New York *Times*, April 4, 1961, Section 11, "The Information Explosion"; Michael, p. 8.

[41] *U.S. BLS Bull. 1276*, pp. 38, 53.

All but 5 percent of the 915 were at least high school graduates, and 78 percent of all were at least college graduates. More than 99 percent of the newly hired persons had completed high school. The median age of both men and women was about 32, and there were relatively few 45 years and over. The median age of newly hired persons was 26, and there were none over 45. It seems that important factors retarding the advancement of older workers are educational qualifications and their own lack of confidence in their learning capacity, which makes them reticent about applying for training, as well as employers' opinions and preexisting hiring practices. Nevertheless, many per-

The typical persons these firms selected for programming and planning, according to the report, were men between the ages of 25 and 34 who had some college education, and who had been engaged in accounting, procedure analysis, or related work. Men outnumbered women at least eight to one in electronic data-processing positions, whereas in the units affected by the change women outnumbered men eight to seven. There was no charge that women lacked the ability to be programmers. The differences were said partly to reflect the preference for men explicitly voiced by management officials; their reluctance to pay for women's training in view of the large proportion who leave when they marry or when children come; and because computers presently cost so much that they are used on the shift basis, sometimes around the clock. Another significant reason for not employing women is that in many states women's hours and nightwork are restricted by law, which makes them ineligible for such work solely because of sex. Moreover, electronic data processing seems to reduce the amount of part-time work which many women prefer.[42]

On the other hand the New York State Department of Labor tells us that women's knack for detail puts them in a favored position among programmer candidates. "The successful programmer for automation," says the official journal, "is one with a chess player's facility to keep each thing in its separate place, a mathematician's ability with figures, the persistence of a re-

---

sonnel administrators cited the "reliability" of these people, their "care of details," their "mature judgment," and their low rate of absenteeism. Hence, in view of the variability in learning capacity at all ages, and the emphasis placed upon adaptability and flexibility, the investigators urged the need for giving more study to the abilities of middle-aged and older persons. The importance of this view is underscored by the estimate that 5.5 million of the 13.5 million increase in the labor force in the present decade will come from persons 45 years and over with especially sharp increases among women. (*Ibid.*, pp. 2, 6, 52, 53, 55, 61; *U.S. BLS Bull. 1287*, pp. 99–100; see also *MLR*, January, 1960, pp. 39–43.)

[42] *U.S. BLS Bull. 1276*, pp. 5, 52; *U.S. BLS Bull. 1241*, pp. 8, 11; Floyd C. Mann and Lawrence K. Williams, "Organizational Impact of White Collar Automation," in IRRA *Papers*, 1958, pp. 67–68.

searcher, the zeal of a gambler, and the single-mindedness of a crusader." [43] In other words, the programmer must have a special kind of intelligence. The important ingredient to success in programming, an employee of the United States Census Bureau states, "is not learning how to program for the equipment, but knowing and understanding the problem." [44] Here are the remarkably contrasting backgrounds of some of the members of a programming team at a government base: an ex-farmer, a cellist, a former tabulating-machine operator, an ex-key-punch operator, a girl from the secretarial ranks, and a mathamatics major with a master's degree who was considered the least competent of the lot.[45]

When a team is set to work on a problem, a senior programmer may have the responsibility for the entire undertaking and direct the others. Beginning or junior members are usually assigned to write specific parts of broad programs; and methods, systems, or procedure analysts sometimes may do most of the analytical work and recommend whether a particular operation can be handled efficiently by a computer.[46]

The field of programming is so new that few exact personnel qualifications have been established, but training in accounting and mathematics seems to be considered desirable preparation.[47] In the federal government a college degree or equivalent experience is required, but in private employment college education is less likely although courses in business administration and statistics are considered very helpful. Many employers no longer stress a strong mathematical background provided the candidates show aptitude for the work.[48]

[43] Frank E. Hewens, " 'Automation Gap' Presents Two-phased Problem for Labor, Industry, Schools," in New York State *Industrial Bulletin*, August, 1961, p. 7.

[44] Diebold, *Automation: Its Impact on Business and Labor*, pp. 36–37.

[45] Hoos, "When the Computer Takes Over the Office," p. 104.

[46] *U.S. BLS Bull. 1241*, pp. 9–10.

[47] Hoos, *Automation in the Office*, p. 122.

[48] *U.S. BLS Bull. 1241*, p. 11.

At present the training of programmers is expensive and is usually provided by the company. Trainees generally spend a few weeks in lecture courses accompanied by practical demonstrations of the computer system used by the company. They then practice writing and coding instructions which they test on the machine. Those who satisfactorily complete the basic work are usually given several weeks of additional preparation on the job before starting their first regular assignments. Selection of people to be trained for the 20 companies discussed above was usually based upon various aptitude tests and personal interviews, as well as upon recommendations from supervisors.[49]

More than a dozen colleges and universities have now introduced basic courses in computer training such as the mechanics of computers and the general logic of programming and coding. At the IBM Watson Scientific Laboratory affiliated with Columbia University about one in four of the students is a woman. (The New York *Times* of March 12, 1964, reported that the IBM Corporation was employing 1,200 young women, almost all college graduates, as programmers and systems engineers.) Speaking on mathematics and other areas relevant to highly technical work, former Secretary of Labor Mitchell has been quoted in this way:

I would predict that with the shortages anticipated in the labor force over the next decade, business and industry will discover that some of their quaint inhibitions about hiring women must be set aside. Adjustments were made quickly during World War II, and some of the gains made by women during that period have been held. Business will be equally pragmatic in the future and this time it may be hoped that an even larger proportion of the changes will become permanent.[50]

At least a few women have already found high places. Bar-

[49] *Ibid., U.S. BLS Bull. 1276*, pp. 42–43.
[50] *U.S. WB Bull. 276*, p. 24.

bara E. Harris, computer programmer for the IBM Corporation, teaches computer programming at the New School for Social Research in New York City. Dr. Grace L. Hopper, a well-known mathematician who while a lieutenant in the WAVES during the last war was assigned to the computation project of the Navy Bureau of Ordnance at Harvard University and who has been associated with Remington Rand's UNIVAC division since 1950, has been made responsible for broad-scale systems and programming research for all of that company's divisions. In 1952 she published a paper on "The Education for a Computer," said to be the first work on automatic programming.[51] Dr. Mina S. Rees—mathematician, statistician, and teacher—distinguished herself in government service during the war by developing mathematical research programs for the design and engineering of high-speed computers, hydrofoil craft, and logistic data. In 1962 the Mathematical Association of America honored her with its first Award for Distinguished Service to Mathematics.[52] Moreover, according to the Women's Bureau, "many industrial laboratories employ only women for their computing groups; others employ a high percentage of women. In one instance, for example, 67 percent of the programming staff are women—many of them with only a bachelor's degree." [53]

An important factor affecting clerical personnel in the 1960s, the U.S. Bureau of Labor Statistics notes, will be the more widespread use of less expensive office equipment such as improved bookkeeping machines, calculators, adding machines, and photographic and other duplicating devices.[54] Two routine occupations closely associated with computer activity are tabulating-machine operation and key punching. The former is usually a man's job because it is heavy work that requires the

[51] New York *Times,* August 18, 1961.
[52] *Ibid.;* New York *Times,* January 26, 1962.
[53] *U.S. WB Bull. 262,* p. 6.
[54] *U.S. BLS Bull. 1255,* p. 227.

lifting of cumbrous trays of cards and frequently calls for over-time on swing or graveyard shifts. Women and girls do the key punching.

Key-punch operators transcribe information from records onto tabulating cards on machines equipped with a keyboard similar to a typewriter or with a numerical keyboard. This work involves little, if any, upgrading and may even represent demotion.[55] It is said to be a dead-end occupation with few or no promotional opportunities. The work is simple, monotonous, and repetitive, but requires a high degree of accuracy and speed, which create much tension. In fact, one key puncher describes the girls as "nervous wrecks" who stay at home often and keep supplies of tranquilizers and aspirin in their desks at which they are "frozen" as though it were a spot on an assembly line. "Card-choppers are floaters," a government department manager comments. "With 500 people, there is a 65% turnover." [56]

It seems that the key-punching job is threatened by a recent inovation that makes it possible to transfer data directly from tape to cards without punching the cards. A converter is said to do it automatically and often more economically. A government personnel officer has stated that, "Right now, key-punch operators are in demand, but when we begin to use tapes exclusively, their jobs will disappear and there will be nothing for them to do. Many of these and our other low-grade clerical jobs are done by Negroes, some of whom have been here for a long time. When they lose their jobs, I wonder where they will ever find others. It is altogether likely that they will become public charges." [57]

But again it must be emphasized that the whole system of

[55] Hoos, *Automation in the Office,* p. 52; Hoos, "When the Computer Takes Over the Office," p. 105.

[56] Hoos, "When the Computer Takes Over the Office," pp. 104–05; Hoos, *Automation in the Office,* pp. 53, 67–68.

[57] Hoos, *Automation in the Office,* pp. 55, 57.

electronic data processing is so new, so underdeveloped and unstandardized, that there is no firm basis for a forecast of what its ultimate impact will be. Some believe the demand for workers will continue to expand as and if our economy grows, and with proper training and retraining of workers automation will bring benefits and new opportunities. Others forecast a downgrading of skills and "no-help-wanted" advertisements as output per man increases, clerical workers feeling the greatest effects as automation spreads. Some suggest that office automation may have less serious repercussions than factory automation for the reason that large companies such as insurance and public utilities can take more time for the change because they are not in the day-to-day competitive economic position which manufacturers face. Some rely upon normal labor turnover to absorb a considerable portion of displaced clerical workers because they include so many young unmarried girls just out of high school who are working for only a few years before marriage.

But when we recall that half of all female clerical workers are 35 to 64 years of age, and that more than half of them are married and living with their husbands, we can be certain that many thousands of those office girls return to work as heads of family, to help pay living expenses, or for self-support. Moreover, day care of children is being provided for working mothers by our social agencies to a greater extent than ever before. Provided no severe depression develops, an estimated 26 million new young workers under 25 are expected to enter the labor force during the 1960s, one in two of whom will be a girl. Also the numbers of older women are expected to increase more than those of men. We can only hope, therefore, that while office automation may not bring an upgrading of many skills, the optimists are right when they say that an expanding economy will supply clerical jobs for all who seek them. "There is no expectation that clerks will vanish from the business scene," writes one observer. "Even in the most automatic office situations people will play an important role." He notes that

computers and common-language machines have definite limitations. They will serve as receptionists only in a very limited way and run errands not at all. Although automatic telephone answering devices exist and it is possible for machines to analyse speech and select the information content, we are some distance from the application of such principles to business systems. Meeting the public, tracing exceptions, and preparing input for an office work system are jobs which people will continue to do. While the preparation of input is capable of considerable mechanization, there are practical limits to replacement of human endeavor.

The writer concludes, "We can expect people at the clerical level to have a continuing role in office operations. There is little doubt, however, that the duties of clerical employees will change greatly. In many senses the level of clerical work will be raised [and] be more challenging and the responsibilities heavy." [58]

The forecast of other observers is that "the office employee of the future will be more the programmer and operator of complex equipment than a simple bookkeeper of the past," that "jobs relating to the computer and its programming . . . will create a blending between the clerk and the professional which may make them indistinguishable in practice," and will call for college education.[59]

Among the numerous other office workers it looks as though there will continue to be a slower growth in employment, but with exceptions. The introduction of electric typewriters, du-

[58] Howard S. Levin, *Office Work and Automation* (New York, John Wiley & Sons, 1956), p. 192.
[59] George S. Odiorne and Arthur S. Hann, *Effective College Recruiting*, Bureau of Industrial Relations, University of Michigan Report 13, 1961, pp. 9, 11.

plicating equipment, machines to take dictation, and kindred improvements in the methods of writing and copying letters and reports seems not to halt an insatiable demand for secretaries, stenographers, and typists.[60]

[60] Even here, Office Employees International Union President Howard Coughlin told a United States House Subcommittee in 1961 that a phonetic typewriter being developed by the Radio Corporation of America could when perfected "eliminate the jobs of 1,500,000 secretaries, stenographers and typists." But a high RCA authority tells this writer that Mr. Coughlin is "fabulously mistaken," that the phonetic typewriter is only in a rudimentary stage and may be decades away; and even then secretaries will still be needed.

CHAPTER 14
Women at the Switchboard

Automation and "one best way" methods have also transformed our telephone system and have increased rather than decreased employment because of the expansion of services. In six decades the number of female switchboard operators has soared from 37,000 to nearly 354,000—a number which includes operators employed by the Bell Telephone System and the independent companies but does not include the estimated million or more at private branch exchanges (PBX) who take care of switchboards in apartment houses, hotels, office buildings, and factories.[1] Girls had replaced unruly boys before 1900 and now 98 in every 100 Bell System operators are women—from a little younger than 18 years to as old as 65 or more. Some sister-mother-daughter and grandmother-granddaughter teams are now working at the boards. The average age is 35 years and the average length of service 11.7 years. A man is almost never found at the switchboard in a central office nowadays, except at night, perhaps, or in a lonely unprotected spot.

In the early years of the century, girls in long dark skirts and white waists sat on high chairs at telephone switchboards pushing plugs into low and high rows of "answering jacks" in response to subscribers' rings at a rate of from 250 to 350 calls in a busy hour.[2] A number of service improvements were then introduced which boosted this rate. One was a simple device known as "restricted repetition" by which the operator repeated the called number back to the caller only if uncertain of it. This increased by 10 percent the number of local calls she could handle. There was also "straightforward trunking," a

[1] *U.S. WB Bull. 285*, p. 16; *U.S. BLS Bull. 1300*, p. 740; U.S. Bureau of the Census, *Census of Population*, "Occupational Characteristics," PC(2)7A, Subject Reports, p. 4.
[2] Elizabeth Beardsley Butler, *Women and the Trades* (New York, Russell Sage Foundation, 1909), pp. 282–83, 286.

method of improving the speed and accuracy of trunked calls in multioffice exchanges which during busy hours increased the number of calls of this type that the operator could manage by about 7 percent.

Probably the most important of these service improvements was in the handling of toll calls. For example, in the eight years before 1930 the average time required to establish a toll connection was reduced from about 12 to two minutes, and 82 percent of the toll calls were made without the caller having to hang up his receiver. But long-distance calls remained complicated and time-consuming, in some cases requiring six or more operators for their completion.[3] A beginning had been made for later advances, however, as we shall see.

For local calls, the revolutionizing dial system—the cutover from the manual to automatic switching—was in operation on nearly a third of the telephones in the United States by the end of 1930. In small, unattended rural exchanges as well as in the great multioffice exchanges of the metropolitan centers, the new system was in use.[4] No longer did telephone operators at these switchboards have to say "number please?" and "thank you," unless customers had dialed incorrectly or needed other help.

One of the early effects of the dial system, aside from rapid expansion of telephone usage, was that the number of calls per operator at the Bell Telephone Operating Companies was now 15,771 a month as compared to 10,641 in 1921. These companies, which owned 92 percent of all dial telephones and 86 percent of all manual telephones, were employing close to 144,000 operators to do the work it would have taken 213,400 to do eight years before. The hypothetical reduction of well over 69,000 jobs was greatly lessened, however, by the growth of the business. Similar advances were made by the independ-

---

[3] *MLR*, February, 1932, pp. 242–43; Jacobson and Roucek, pp. 175–76.
[4] *MLR*, February, 1932, p. 235.

ent companies, and the Bureau of Labor Statistics estimated that, without the increase in telephones and telephone calls, complete conversion to the dial system would have meant a loss of about two thirds of the employment opportunities afforded by the manual system, not including effects in the private branch exchanges.[5]

Nevertheless, anxiety over what to do with surplus operators became acute after the beginning of the business depression in 1929. During the preceding years of economic expansion displacement problems had been met through careful planning in connection with a large normal turnover—about 40 in each 100 per year—by transferring operators from one central office to another, and by the absorption of displaced workers in other industries.[6]

In an attempt to learn the nature of the displacement problem and what was being done about it, the Women's Bureau studied the employment effects of one cutover to the dial system which took place at midnight on July 14, 1930. It was a small New England man-employing manufacturing town of about 200,000 inhabitants, and the event had been planned two years in advance. Indeed, the director of the bureau reported that "the success of the industry in so planning its employment program for 2 or more years ahead that practically the only operators laid off at the final cut-over were temporary workers engaged only for the last few months, makes this a notable example of the possibilities of long-view planning in cases of technological change."[7]

Employment conditions had been very good in this com-

[5] *Ibid.*, pp. 235, 240, 243, 246.

[6] In her book on *People at Work* in 1934, p. 209, Secretary Frances Perkins recalled that "the human problem of the displaced worker when the cutover was made from the manual to the dial system telephone exchanges is an almost perfect example of technological change made with a minimum of disaster. It was accomplished through human as well as technical planning."

[7] *U.S. WB Bull. 110*, pp. ii, 3, 4.

munity during the 1920s, and the familiar plan for the conversion was to let normal resignations of operators gradually reduce the regular, or permanent, force while the total force was kept at full strength by hiring temporary workers. To recruit new girls a representative had visited the homes of accepted applicants, but when he explained to parents and guardians that the work would probably not be permanent, some withdrew their daughters' names from the list. In search of experienced operators who would be classed as "occasional" workers, the company drew upon an available group of former employees, mostly married women who had come to help from time to time when extras were needed, and who did not desire permanent status. But only half of those who had resigned in the last five years could work full time because of duties at home; and to meet the shortage, sharpened by the need of a two- to four-week retraining period for most of the operators and of four to six weeks for a small selected group, the company borrowed 91 women from other cities.[8]

A major result of this cutover was a reduction in the number of operators from 534 to 249, all regular operators being retained. After the borrowed girls were returned, the "occasional" women released, and the usual number had resigned, probably to be married, the company canvassed employers in the community to find jobs for the temporary people who had been laid off. Some 38 openings in various concerns were found, including jobs as saleswomen in stores, clerical employees in offices, as private, branch-exchange operators, and as factory and beauty-parlor workers. Only 11 of the girls accepted these positions as permanent, however, the others not being interested. Many of them chose to find their own jobs or wanted to rest before taking new work. Many mothers were unwilling to have their daughters leave home for positions in

[8] *Ibid.*, pp. 4, 5.

other cities where wages were too low to pay for board and room, or because their services were needed at home.[9]

After interviews with these young women, the Women's Bureau reported that, even though they understood they were only temporarily employed, they regretted leaving the company. They liked the work because of the better pay and better hours, or only because they had become accustomed to it. "Telephone work is the only thing I'll ever like," said one. Another complained that she had "walked and walked" looking for a job. "I've even thought of trying housework," she said, "but that only pays room and board. I may have to take it, but I don't want to." A third summed it up in this way: "I liked the bosses, I liked the girls; oh, gee, I even liked the building." [10] The time of the cutover, just before the depression, had of course been unfortunate for these women, but many were brought back to work later.

Heavy wartime communications needs caused a general expansion in the demand for operators, and company requirements were reduced in respect to age and schooling. Nevertheless, the vital nature of the work meant that normal intelligence, good health, and a friendly personality continued to be criteria for hiring, and the "voice with a smile" remained a necessity. The job continued to be exacting, each operator being connected to her board with an individual headset.

She must have a fingertip mastery of the ringing, listening, dial, and other keys on her key shelf; of the row or rows of cords for making connections; of the location and meaning of all parts of the honeycombed formation of jacks and trunks for recording, for switching, for toll circuits, for tandem, for information, etc.[11]

Today, telephone operators are "service specialists" who have contacts with more than 25 million customers every work-

[9] *Ibid.*, pp. 5–6, 7, 9.
[10] *Ibid.*, pp. 8, 9.
[11] *U.S. WB Bull. 207*, pp. 2, 4.

ing day, and the company considers that in their helpful, understanding way they promote the company image. A professor of sociology glowingly describes work at the switchboard in this way:

Here is a job with considerable demand for some highly select and all too rare personal qualities . . . Integrity, Responsibility, Reasonableness, Patience in a situation in which one is dealing with people who seldom manifest these same qualities or seem to have no appreciation of them when demonstrated by the operator. Efficiency, Accuracy, and Swiftness. Respect for the privacy of the customer or a capacity to keep things confidential. Concern for others and a skill in helping them. Calmness and self-control, so that emergency calls can be handled expediently and without panic . . . Great capacity for comprehension and retention so that the complexities of an elaborate world-wide communications system can be manipulated by the girl. Personal physical stamina and energy—a "healthy mind and a healthy body."

The professor adds that

fortunes are made and lost on phone calls! An operator can make the difference. . . . Lives are saved and property is protected through her loyal performance of her task. Our elaborate economic system as well as other complex aspects of our society operate on the scale they do, and as well as they do, because of her.[12]

In air-conditioned rooms the Bell telephone operator has a normal work week of five days, but her hours may fall on any of the seven days of the week; for evenings, Sundays, and holidays she receives additional pay. She has a comfortable lounge in which to "take it easy" during rest periods, and appetizing, well-balanced meals are served at minimum cost. We shall consider her less rosy union activities in Chapter 20.

The operator who possesses supervisory qualifications has opportunities for advancement: first, perhaps, as a service assistant while she continues to operate part of the time, then

[12] Peter B. Howell, quoting Dr. Walter M. North of Knox College, "The Modern Telephone Operator," *Bell Telephone Magazine*, Autumn, 1960, pp. 22–23.

as assistant chief operator, who shares the management of the office under the direction of the chief operator. And she may become chief operator with four or five assistants directing the entire central office and responsible for the efficient operation of 50 to 150 girls. Finally, in the position of traffic superintendent she would be in charge of a group of central offices.[13]

Numerous improvements have been made in dial switching and in services to subscribers in recent years. Among them, customer dialing of long-distance calls throughout the nation is outstanding. We are told that by 1965 it will be general practice for nearly all telephone users to dial long-distance station-to-station calls directly, without the intervention or aid of an operator, although operators will continue to be needed for other types of calls. In 1958, more than 95 percent of the operator-tended long-distance calls over the Bell Telephone System were connected while the customer remained on the line, as compared to less than 10 percent in 1920; and the time needed to establish the connection had been reduced from an average of ten minutes to a little more than one minute, with some going through directly in 15 seconds. By that time subscribers' "trouble reports" had been reduced by 70 percent.[14]

More frequent use of the telephone instead of the telegram seems to be one explanation for the marked decline in the number of telegraph operators. But the increased relative importance of women telegraphers should not be overlooked.

Although women found limited employment at the telegraph key in the nineteenth century, by 1920 their numbers approached 17,000, or more than a fifth of all operators. Their substitution for men began with the introduction of the printer telegraph (teletypewriter) during World War I. Here was a device that required only the ability to operate a typewriter

[13] The New York Telephone Company, *Telephone Careers for Girls*, n.d., p. 5–6.
[14] Jacobson and Roucek, p. 176.

keyboard adapted for telegraphy on which women, at lower pay, could be advantageously employed. Hence, by 1931, women constituted 77 out of every 100 operators on the printer equipment, and almost two thirds of all when Morse manual operators were included. By 1959, somewhat more than 7,000 women were 80 percent of all Western Union operators.[15]

Returning to women at the switchboard, we find that technological advances and expanded service caused an increase in their number from about 178,000 in 1920, when the dial system began to be introduced, to almost 342,000 at the midcentury. Further improvements then reduced their number to less than a quarter of a million when, in 1960, the proportion of operators among all employees was somewhat less than a third as compared to 46 in 100 after World War II. For while only 30 men were reported as operators, the wider use of telephones, which calls for construction, installation, and maintenance of dial equipment, has increased the proportion of men among all employees from a third to more than two fifths. The total employment of 360,000 women on Class A telephone carriers,[16] however, is double that of 1920, including many clerks and supervising clerks to say nothing of the multitude of secretaries, typists, stenographers, and service representatives. Nearly a quarter of a million are operators—still the largest group in the industry.[17]

In sum, it is possible that the decline in the relative importance of telephone operators may be nearing an end. It seems that in the foreseeable future no machines will be devised that can completely handle person-to-person calls, credit-card calls, emergency calls, information calls, transient calls, messenger

[15] Joseph A. Hill, *Women in Gainful Occupations, 1870–1920* (G.P.O. 1929), p. 65; *MLR*, March, 1932, pp. 501, 514; *U.S. BLS Report 171*, p. 10.
[16] Those with annual operating revenue of more than $250,000 and subject to full jurisdiction of the Federal Communications Commission.
[17] *U.S. BLS Bull. 1300*, p. 748; *U.S. BLS Bull. 1306*, pp. 4, 10, 11; *U.S. Census of Population, 1950*, IV, Part I, 1C–45.

calls, marine and mobile calls, civilian defense calls, conference calls, and coin-box, long-distance calls. Indeed, although an executive vice-president of the American Telephone and Telegraph Company has said that the number of dial telephones will reach almost 100 percent in the next few years and that there will be an increasing amount of customer dialing of long-distance calls, "Yet we will still need about the same number of operators we need now, perhaps more." Automation will undoubtedly continue to change the nature of some telephone jobs, he concludes, but "we expect these changes will be of an evolutionary nature." [18] The Bell System employs about 184,000 operators, but to maintain a full force the company hires 50,000 each year and it has difficulty finding enough of the right quality. And now the revolutionary event of the launching of satellite Telstar on July 10, 1962, will tend to increase the volume of overseas communication, which for many years will be operator-handled.

[18] U.S. Congress, Joint Economic Committee, "New Views on Automation," *Papers*, 1960, statement by Paul A. Gorman, pp. 266–67; Jacobson and Roucek, pp. 179, 181–82; see also *U.S. WB Bull. 286.*

CHAPTER 15
Women Behind the Counter

Up to now the twentieth-century trend in selling in stores where the personal equation is so important is one not of "automation" as in the case for work in the office and at the switchboard, but of new techniques that modernize the work, and of some women's rise to high positions. A hundred years ago a working woman's great ambition was to be a sales clerk to relieve men for more "manly pursuits" than "handing down tapes and ribbons, and cramping their genius over chintzes and delaines," as their abettors put it. Today, about a million and a half women, accounting for 59 percent of all retail sales workers, are to be found in almost any position in the retail store—from stock girl to president. In 1950 the Women's Bureau found that some women's specialty shops were largely staffed by women, that almost all specialized shopping-service positions were held by women, that women held 85 percent of the higher-level jobs in personnel and employee-welfare departments, nearly two thirds of the higher-level jobs in publicity work, as well as more than half of those in the merchandizing division, which has been called the "hub" of department-store activities, most of whom were buyers or assistant buyers. Moreover, well toward half of the floor managers in stores were women, nearly 5,000 of them, as compared to less than a third in 1940.[1]

Noteworthy also is the fact that the median age of saleswomen jumped from 28 to 37 years in the war decade, that nearly a third were 45 years and over in 1950 as compared to about two in ten before the war, and that by 1959 almost two out of three were married and living with their husbands.[2]

[1] U.S. WB Bull. 236, pp. 12–13; U.S. WB Bull. 253, p. 67; U.S. WB Bull. 271, pp. 8, 13; U.S. WB Bull. 285, p. 11.
[2] U.S. WB Bull. 253, pp. 62, 63, 82–83; U.S. WB Bull. 275, p. 38.

The classic ailments of women behind the counter have been aching feet and aching backs. At the turn of the century customers were provided with stools screwed to the floor, but clerks were not permitted even to bring up boxes from the basement to sit on when not busy. If they pulled out a drawer at the back of the counter and sat on its edge they were rebuked by the floorwalker. If they leaned on the counter, they were told it looked unbusinesslike. Straight posture was required. When girls fainted they were laid out on the concrete floor in the retiring room, and if they did not recover promptly they were sent home with reduced paychecks. To greet customers, a smiling face and a pleasant remark were expected no matter what the physical discomforts might be. There was a reprimand if the customer was permitted to leave without making a purchase. Six days a week most girls worked from 8 A.M. to 6 P.M.[3]

In those days saleswomen usually started work as cash girls, who carried customers' money to the cashier and brought back the change. Their first contact with merchandise was when they were promoted to be stock girls, or package wrappers. Then they were given selling jobs in the basement, and eventually on one of the upper floors, perhaps in departments that carried low-priced items or where women's clothing and accessories were sold. A girl's size was a factor in the speed of her advancement. For early promotion the cash girl had to be well built, usually tall for her age, and quick to learn. If she showed aptitude for clerical work she may have been transferred to the office where then the paper-tape recorder was begining to play a steadily growing role in the field of record keeping. The social position of shopgirls was higher than that of girls in the factory, and competition for jobs was one cause of their low pay. They were usually untrained and untaught. While some were very young, the average age of those who

[3] Nathan, pp. 5–6.

lived at home was 22.5 years, and of those "adrift" (keeping house, living with private families, or in boarding and lodging houses) was 28.2 years.[4]

Managers of department stores were well aware that they did not pay women enough to live on honestly, and some gave preference to applicants who lived at home—subsidized by their families. According to an investigation by the U.S. Bureau of Labor, however, it was "current in every city" for the superintendent to ask a girl who complained of her low wage, "But haven't you a man friend to help support you?"[5]

By 1908 the New York Mercantile Inspection Act of 1896, which the Consumers' League had sponsored, had been amended to provide for a chief mercantile inspector and a small staff to enforce the law. For women under 21 years of age and boys under 16, the act limited the week to 60 hours and the day to ten hours between 7 A.M. and 10 P.M., *except* for the holiday season, December 15 to January 1. Children under 14 were prohibited from work, and a certificate of age, health, and school attendance was required of children under 16.[6]

By the decade of the twenties, when a record number of women entered the selling field, the pneumatic tube had replaced the cash girl, and "the little shopgirl" had been largely superseded by the "saleslady," who was likely to be a mature woman holding her job by competence rather than by charm. For instead of the casual approval of a department manager, a girl now got her job and held it on the basis of psychological and intelligence tests. "She is, for the most part, selected by a woman and bossed by a woman—her sex appeal doesn't count,"

[4] Elizabeth Beardsley Butler, *Women and the Trades* (New York, Russell Sage Foundation, 1909), pp. 296, 298, 307; U.S. Bureau of Labor, *Woman and Child Wage-Earners*, V, 10–12; Jacobson and Roucek, p. 141; Smuts, pp. 21–22, 84, 95.
[5] U.S. Bureau of Labor, *Woman and Child Wage-Earners*, V, 22, 29–30.
[6] Nathan, pp. 50–54.

an investigator reported. "She must be neatly dressed, it is true, but she need not be pretty and appealing. Any reasonably intelligent girl can get a job in a city store and earn enough so that she can live comfortably. . . . There is a fine comradeship among these girls." [7]

Here is a first hand view of the employment department of a large New York department store in 1928 from one of some 200 girls who had come in response to an advertisement in a Sunday newspaper and who became a successful seller of women's dresses.

[The woman's section, managed by a woman about 35 years of age] is crowded with "girls"—for in a department store every woman is a girl—girls of every type and of every age: girls who are under seventeen, with and without working certificates; girls who are graduates of high schools or grammar schools of Manhattan and its environs; girls who have worked many seasons in department stores; girls who have never held any kind of job; girls who have tried out every occupation offered in the want-ad columns of the city newspapers; girls who are brides seeking employment so that their wages may help out until husbands are given promotions or to provide a reserve fund for the time when the first baby will arrive; girls who are mothers with children whom they wish to keep in school well dressed and with money in their pockets to pay for school entertainments, to buy the school annual, or to meet the expenses of the graduation outfit; girls who are grandmothers left without means of support; girls who are widows by grass or by sod whose husbands have died without leaving insurance or from whom alimony cannot be collected; but girls, all girls who if they are successful applicants will become Miss Moore, Miss Smith, Miss Kuntz, Miss Levinsky, Miss Du Costa, or Miss O'Brien in the departments to which they are assigned.

In this store the new girl attended hour-long classes on each of several days to learn how to make sales checks, how to fill

[7] Frances Donovan, *The Saleslady* (Chicago, University of Chicago Press, 1929), pp. ix, 189.

in "cash takens," "cash sents," "charge takens," and "charge
sents," "C.O.D.s," "tallies," and other items. She was then
turned over to a fellow clerk who initiated her into the work of
the department and looked after her until she was familiar
enough with detail to go it alone.[8]

By this time there were fixed seats behind the counters, and
the honorary president of the New York Consumers' League
reported that in the leading department stores "the firms show
with pride their fine rest rooms (often on the top floor, with
open-air loggia on the roof) including rooms where their employees' teeth can be attended to by a good dentist, their feet
cared for by a pedicure, a physician's office where they can
consult a good physician, and a trained nurse to care for them
if they feel tired or slightly ill." In some stores, she added,
there was basketball, a piano, magazines, papers, "and every
luxury." The girls were allowed 45 minutes to an hour for
lunch in "a well-appointed restaurant." A "store mother" was
not unusual. Saleswomen were given a week's vacation, sometimes two, with pay, and the 48-hour week was "gradually becoming the standard." This was indeed a big step toward the
five-day, 40-hour week in department stores today, together
with paid sick leave and other benefits which many stores
provide.[9]

The logical promotion for the expert saleswoman of the
1920s was to the position of head of stock in her department,
then to assistant buyer, and finally to the coveted post of buyer
at a salary anywhere from $2,500 to $50,000 a year. In some
stores the majority of buyers were women, since the majority
of customers were women. Other positions open to women,
sometimes as stepping stones to buyership, were assistant in
the office of a store official, where they did research work, com-

[8] *Ibid.*, 4–6, 21, 28, 66–67, 190.
[9] Nathan, pp. 106, 109–10, 121; *U.S. WB Bull. 271*, pp. 10–11.

parison shopping, director of training, and employment manager.[10]

Labor turnover in the department store was high, but many girls returned to work after marriage, at least for a time. In fact, even then a large proportion of saleswomen were married and living with their husbands, or widowed.[11] "Can Mother Come Back?" was the title of a current magazine article in which Lord & Taylor was reported to consider that the social experience of the married woman seemed to help her meet customers pleasantly, and that almost all part-time salesclerks who came to relieve peaks of trade were married, since the hours fitted into the domestic schedule: 11 A.M. to 4:30 P.M. for one group and three days a week for another.[12]

Yes, large numbers of mothers can and do come back to selling behind the counter, but authorities seem to agree that, more than anything else, it is women's lack of permanency because of marriage and family responsibilities that explains the nature of their work as compared to that of men. For example, according to the mid-century census of retail trade, women and girls comprised 95 percent of the five- and ten-cent store salespeople and 79 percent of those selling general merchandise. At the other extreme, it was usually men who fitted and sold shoes to both men and women; and only two women in 100 were selling automobiles and accessories.[13]

It is possible that men's and women's educational backgrounds also partly explain the division of labor among salespersons. It appears that, while about two thirds of the women and girls will have attended high school as compared to a few more than half of the men and boys, the proportion of men who will have had one to four years of college education is

[10] Donovan, *The Saleslady*, pp. 83, 193–94, 196.
[11] *Ibid.*, pp. 202–04, 216.
[12] Mary Ross, "Can Mother Come Back?" *Survey Graphic*, April 1, 1927, pp. 38–39.
[13] *U.S. Census of Population, 1950*, IV, Part I, 1C–53, 57.

almost three times greater than the proportion of women.[14] Moreover, the fact that college women are less likely than men to stay at the work is the reported experience of one department store which had recruited 12 women and eight men for special junior-executive training. A year later all of the men but only four of the women remained in the store. This management considered that it was compensated for the effort and expense of training only if recruits remained four years—a judgment which has led some stores to give longer training to men than to women, with the result that men are more likely to hold the top positions.[15]

But so-called career women do not fit into this category. One instance is that of a college graduate who had spent a year in an advertising agency, had then become a salesgirl in a department store, after four months was transferred to the personnel department as an interviewer, and in less than another year was promoted to employment manager. The Women's Bureau comments, however, that women in higher-level positions formerly held by men must face a twofold challenge. "Not only must they prove themselves capable of holding a 'man's job,'" but because of the tendency of management to generalize about women, their performance on the job will be an important influence in changing management's attitudes toward women.[16] The bureau also notes that in 1959 women held the presidencies of at least five major stores, and that Dorothy Shaver, deceased president of Lord & Taylor in New York City, had been in retailing for 35 years.[17] Today women are in charge of the New York divisions of large department stores; they head public relations departments and personnel departments. And according to Mrs. Gertrude G. Michelson of Macy's, New York, "forty-five percent of our executives are

[14] *MLR*, February, 1961, p. 145.
[15] *U.S. WB Bull. 236*, pp. 33, 35.
[16] *Ibid.*, pp. 41, 58.
[17] *U.S. WB Bull. 271*, p. 37.

women with the same responsibilities and the same salaries as men in like jobs." [18]

To what extent has technology changed the nature of the work behind the counter? The new terms are "self-service" or "simplified selling," which the standardization of numerous products has made possible. At the drop of a coin, ubiquitous automatic vending machines emit thousands of items such as cold soft drinks, cigarettes, chewing gum, snacks, and candy. In some industrial plants, schools, and hospitals these machines dispense courses of food from soup to nuts. Like a supermarket, tooth paste and standard drugs with price and size labels are put into bins in stores for self-selection. And mass-produced women's ready-to-wear clothing in many sizes and styles is often arranged on racks so that without assistance customers can examine them and make tentative selections. Only then is a saleswoman needed, to give advice perhaps and attend to having the garment fitted, then to complete the sale. However, for many kinds of merchandise that require explanation, demonstration, or matching, saleswomen continue to be needed.[19]

Recently the R. H. Macy Company experimented with an "electronic salesgirl." "This machine," said a report on *New Views on Automation*, "is smart enough to dispense 36 different items in 10 separate styles and sizes. It accepts one- and five-dollar bills in addition to coins and returns the correct change plus rejecting counterfeit currency." [20]

In commenting on this innovation, a writer on *Cybernation* —a term he prefers to automation—suggests that people may learn to like this type of salesmanship, as in the case of the

---

[18] New York *Times*, January 11, 1960.

[19] *U.S. WB Bull. 271*, pp. 4, 5.

[20] U.S. Congress, Joint Economic Committee, "New Views on Automation," *Papers*, 1960, statement by Howard Coughlin, p. 513; Harold F. Clark, Harold S. Sloan, and Charles A. Hebert, *Classrooms in the Stores* (Sweet Springs, Missouri, Roxbury Press, Inc., 1962), p. 90.

supermarket. He holds that the salesclerk rarely knows the "real" differences between functionally similar items, so that the customer must do much of his own selecting. Hence, "as automation increases, the utility of the salesclerk will further diminish." The author believes that with some products automation will permit extensive variation in design and utility, and in others an "endless proliferation" of only slightly different items about which the salesclerk will be no more knowledgeable than she is today.[21]

It is illuminating, however, to hear from Macy's New York Division manager that the "electronic salesgirl," which the store called an automatic vending machine, was a failure. The machine dispensed men's undershirts and shorts in a variety of styles and sizes, and received cash payments, but it took up so much room—an important item in a department store—that it was discarded after a three-month trial.

Moreover, the comment of merchants who consider store-customer relationships vital to success is that you cannot teach a machine to smile. And one New York department store executive reports that his salespersons are taught that each of them is a personal representative of the store and that what customers think of the store depends upon what they think of the salespeople.[22] The United States Department of Labor puts it this way: "Courteous and efficient service from behind the counter or on the sales floor does much to satisfy a customer—and satisfied customers build a store's good reputation."[23]

But this does not mean that some of the work of saleswomen will not be "automated." In fact we are told of demonstrations of a Uni-Tote, which is said to replace sales books and pencils as well as other manual operations. "In eliminating handwrit-

[21] Michael, p. 17; Clark, Sloan, and Hebert, *Classrooms in the Stores*, pp. 90–91.

[22] Wilmer E. Bresee, *A Practical Retail Training Program*, New York (State) Department of Commerce, Small Business Bulletin No. 8, p. 7.

[23] *U.S. BLS Bull. 1300*, p. 292.

ten sales slips," runs the report, "the device issues a printed, extended and totaled sales check, taking note of charge sales and a warning on blocked credit. It also produces a standard punch card for every item sold. A demonstration seemed to corroborate the concern's assertion that very little training was required to run the device." [24]

Moreover, it appears that the training of saleswomen may be automated by a device in the field of programmed education, more popularly known as teaching machines. Here, we are told, are self-teaching courses that use a simulated cash register, sales pad, and other tools of the trade which can be adapted to the needs of individual stores. The president of TOR Education, Inc., which has developed the system, is reported to hold that the procedures can cut out a store's training time for new personnel from 20 to eight hours, and that the method enables the trainee to move at her or his own speed without an instructor.[25] We shall have more to say of teaching machines in Chapter 17.

But these developments are on the fringes of women's work behind the counter, and leaders in the field believe that as long as fashion is a vital factor in sales appeal the place of women in the industry is assured.[26] In the office, meanwhile, electronic data-processing machines may be doing bookkeeping chores such as handling customer records and billing, accounts payable, check writing, payroll computation, processing of mail orders, sales-check accounting, departmental reports, inventory control, and the final profit and loss statement.[27] In fact, one writer observes that technology has been converting white-collar salesclerks into blue-collar employees.[28]

[24] New York *Times*, September 20, 1960; January 10, 1961.
[25] *Ibid.*, June 12, 1962; Clark, Sloan, and Hebert, *Classrooms in the Store*, pp. 13–14 and Chapter VII.
[26] *U.S. WB Bull.* 271, p. 1.
[27] Clark, Sloan, and Hebert, *Classrooms in the Store*, pp. 86–87.
[28] Michael Harrington, *The Retail Clerks* (New York, John Wiley & Sons, 1962).

PART III
Change in Women's Professions

CHAPTER 16
Broadening Opportunities

If by 1970 we can have laid a firm foundation for a society in which *education* has become the "major industry," we shall have gone a long way toward building a truly civilized country—one in which the whole citizenry can *actively* participate in cultural, artistic, and recreational programs, not a citizenry which can merely *sit* and passively view a TV show. Unskilled labor is rapidly disappearing under the impact of automation. Technical skills, science, crafts, and the arts will of necessity place education at the center of all activity, the pivot around which all else revolves. Education will encompass the whole gamut of life from childhood to old age. Leisure without education can be a curse. . . . Education and leadership—that is the answer. Without these the people perish.[1]

In Chapter 13 we noted the emergence of talented women programmers for electronic computers—one significant example of the present trend toward their specialization as a result of rapid advance in technology. In the following pages we shall consider a few of the many other occupations of professional women which require special education and training. What sort of difficulties have they faced in their struggle for status?

We recall that public school teaching was women's first successful invasion into the professions, and it meant permitting girls to go to school although such a step had been looked upon as "inconsistent with the design thereof." Led by Oberlin, where four women were admitted as early as 1837, colleges for women and other institutions of higher learning were enrolling some 85,000 women in 1900—more than one in four of all students.

But while the battle had been won for women to teach in the elementary and secondary schools, the question of the proper nature of women's education on the higher level that would enable them to join college and university faculties, and

[1] Alvin H. Hansen, *Economic Issues in the 1960s* (New York, McGraw-Hill, 1960), pp. viii–ix, 77.

to enter other professions, seems not to have been entirely settled even today. Founders of the seven women's colleges before the turn of the century—Mount Holyoke, Vassar, Smith, Wellesley, Bryn Mawr, Radcliffe, and Barnard—set their various objectives to give women an education equal to that for men, and perhaps they tended to undervalue housekeeping. For despite the fact that women lost neither health nor beauty when they succeeded academically, there was stormy reaction to the educational programs.

Taught as they had been from the beginning of time that woman's real place was at home, women began to call for college studies in nutrition, home economics, and child care. But to this the future president of Bryn Mawr College, M. Carey Thomas, replied in 1908, "Nothing more disastrous for women, or for men, can be conceived of than this specialized education for women as a sex . . . which . . . will tend to unfit women . . . to teach their own boys at home, as well as, of course, other boys in the classroom. . . . Sanitary and domestic science are not among the great disciplinary race studies." Moreover, it was not shown that the family was actually impoverished by women's activities outside the home. Nor was it shown, except in analytic theory, that the modern woman can devote her full energies to her family and home to the exclusion of other activities, ranging from playing bridge and being on committees to becoming a college president. And many believed women's education should no more follow a single pattern than did education for men.[2]

But the psychologists and psychoanalysts demurred. "Her whole soul, conscious and unconscious," wrote G. S. Hall in 1905, "is best conceived as a magnificent organ of heredity, and to its laws all her psychic activities, if unperverted, are

[2] Katherine Elizabeth McBride, "What is Women's Education," *Annals of the American Academy of Political and Social Science*, May, 1947, pp. 144–45, 147–48, 152.

true." Later, Jung held that, "Nature has *first claim* . . . only long afterwards does the luxury of intellect come." And as late as the 1940s Deutsch talked of the more masculine woman who developed a feeling of inferiority because "the feminine components of the personality hinder achievement of the desired aims," and so the mother who achieves success professionally "instead of feeling satisfaction, is tormented by guilt feelings with regard to her children." By Deutsch and the "neo-antifeminists" the "active" woman was identified with the neurotic one. She was schizophrenic.[3]

The male president of one women's college, Mills, urged a "truly feminine higher education" for daughters. He counseled deans and teachers to steer away from the abstract sciences in which men (presumably) delight, and stress child care and home planning—"the studies dealing with the institution of the family and all that contributes to its well-being through food, beauty and warmth, shelter and security—which will be developed to supplement the traditional curriculum in proportion as women lose their sense of inferiority in the realm of higher education." President White included in the women's college curriculum such arts as textile design, handicrafts, and flower arrangement.[4]

Psychological tests have been showing much greater differences within each sex than between them, however—that men and women are complementary rather than wholly equal or wholly opposite. Hence, one well-known sociologist has noted that the harm of forcing women into the masculine pattern of education might be no greater than the harm of forcing all women into the so-called feminine pattern. Men should have a course on "the family" quite as much as women, says Dr. Mirra

[3] *Ibid.*, pp. 145–46; Mirra Komarovsky, *Women in the Modern World* (Boston, Little, Brown & Co., 1953), pp. 4 ff., 40.

[4] Lynn White, Jr., *Educating Our Daughters; A Challenge to the College* (New York, Harper, 1950), pp. 86–87 and Chapter V; White, "Do Women's Colleges Turn Out Spinsters?" *Harper's Magazine*, October, 1952, pp. 44–48.

Komarovsky, for "we need to extend the insightful participation of the father into the lives of children." Family life reflects the life of the country.[5] "We are still living in an era of stereotypes about women," wrote former president Mildred McAfee Norton of Wellesley College and chief of the WAVES during the war. And the president of Vassar urged that "what we are concerned with is not . . . either physics or child psychology, but the creating of understanding which enables the student to develop her own philosophy and values." [6]

Meanwhile, under the massive pressure of technological advances, the search for brain power during the last war and its aftermath cast searchlights upon women's inclinations and abilities. In the blue-collar field we recall that hundreds of thousands of women, including many housewives, took jobs in industry to meet the scarcity of labor as the demand for goods and services mounted—some to support dependents while husbands and fathers and brothers were at the front, some to support themselves. And there were talented women who saw opportunities for study and employment where they had not been accepted before. A history-making example was the acceptance of a limited number of women students and instructors at America's oldest engineering college—Rensselaer Polytechnic Institute at Troy, New York—which broke a 116-year tradition. Other institutions, including Columbia University, opened their doors "to prepare women for the increasingly important place they will occupy in the engineering sciences." [7]

Indeed there had developed an extraordinary demand for scientifically trained women. We are told that every woman whose college major was mathematics had her choice of 25 jobs in industry, government, or research; and in many respects

[5] Mirra Komarovsky, "What Should College Teach Women?" *Harper's Magazine,* November, 1949, p. 35; Komarovsky, "Measuring the Yardsticks," *Journal of the American Association of University Women,* Summer, 1948, p. 210.

[6] New York *Times,* February 5, 1950; November 18, 1950.

[7] *Ibid.,* September 12, 1942.

the armed forces seemed more venturesome than civilian industry in utilizing them. A small group of WACs (Women's Army Corps) who had a mathematics background were given such titles as mathematician, computer, geodetic computer, and cryptographer. They worked in Ordnance, Signal Corps, and the Engineering Corps of the War Department, where special courses in mathematics were given. They were also to be found in the Naval Research Laboratory and in the National Advisory Committee for Aeronautics, with the Federal Bureau of Investigation as cryptographers, with the National Bureau of Standards, and the Coast and Geodetic Survey. As more men were drafted into military service, women were taken on to relieve the shortage of high-talent teachers of mathematics and statistics where the doctoral degree was important; and opportunities for women mathematics teachers in secondary schools as well as in colleges and universities continued after hostilities had ceased. Of women actuaries, one prominent man noted that, "a woman can succeed in this field, but she has to be 50 percent better than her nearest male competitor to do it."[8] Here, indeed, is an example of "sex-typing" within an occupation.

A recent notice of women's skill in teaching mathematics is that paid to Verona A. Spicer, formerly of Newton High School in Queens Borough, New York City, by the two O'Neill brothers, now in their early forties. One is director of Telstar at the Bell Telephone Laboratories and the other is director of basic research in the ballistic-missile defense program at Columbia University. For a 1962 citation which Columbia University awarded to Miss Spicer, Eugene Frank and Lawrence H. O'Neill wrote that she is "a perfect example of the influence a secondary school teacher can exert in creating the spirit of intellectual and scientific inquiry in a youthful and pliable mind." Miss Spicer had introduced both boys to algebra and

[8] U.S. WB Bull. 223-1, p. 1; U.S. WB Bull. 223-4, pp. 3, 4, 5–6, 9–10, 17.

trigonometry in their sophomore years, and they give her the major credit for launching them on their careers.[9]

Modern mathematician Dr. Mina Spiegal Rees, whom we met in connection with her important work on electronic computers, played a significant role in mobilizing the resources of today's mathematics for national defense during World War II as technical aid and executive assistant to the chief of the Applied Mathematics Panel, Office of Scientific Research and Development. "The whole driving force of the office was to do something now to get scientific results into the field of battle," she recalls. Her success in making a place for herself in a man's world led to her assignment in 1946 as head of the mathematics branch of the Office of Naval Research, and in 1949 as head of the Mathematical Sciences Division—a post she held until she returned to Hunter College in 1953 as Professor of Mathematics and Dean of the Faculty. She now holds the position of Dean of Graduate Studies in the City University of New York. In tribute to her administrative ability a colleague describes her as that rare type of woman for whom men are willing to work.[10]

Engineering has the lowest proportion of women of all the professions—less than 1 percent of all engineers. But even here women were actively recruited as the war progressed and the need for engineers skyrocketed. Nearly two thirds of more than 56,000 women completed the courses in engineering subjects under the Engineering, Science and Management War Training Program; and the associate dean of the Columbia University School of Engineering recalls that specially selected housewives were trained for one year to the level of proficiency that enabled them to replace male engineering graduates. Both the profession and American industry are "profoundly at fault" in failing to recruit women, he is reported to have declared.[11]

[9] New York *Times*, July 26, 1962.
[10] *Ibid.*, July 10, 1961, and courtesy of Hunter College.
[11] Robert Amon, "Engineering Talent in Short Supply," New York State *Industrial Bulletin*, June, 1962, pp. 2–3; *U.S. WB Bull. 254*, p. 4.

Women had rarely found opportunities to obtain the rounded experience necessary for normal promotion in this field, but a few broke through the bounds and became graduate engineers. For example, we recall that when electronic computers were installed in business offices a good many employers set aside "quaint inhibitions" and opened a door to women programmers and other technicians whose numbers have been increasing each year. And as some electronic devices are reduced in size, the need will be for more delicate hand skills on the smaller units.[12]

During the war some 1,500 college graduates, most of them mathematics or science majors, became WAVES (Women Appointed for Voluntary Emergency Service). They were trained for technical work in communication, air navigation, aerology, often by other WAVES whose earlier science and teaching experience had resulted in their selection as instructors. Most of the celestial link-trainer instruction was given by WAVES, and some authorities said they proved to be superior to men in this field. Moreover, we have seen that accomplished mathematician Dr. Grace Hopper, who was a lieutenant in the WAVES, was assigned to work on a computer project at Harvard University, and then became an executive in programming research. In 1959 a WAVES commander was made assistant officer in charge of a fleet weather facility at a naval air station. As an aerologist she was charting the best route, weatherwise, for ships at sea and providing meteorological services for planes departing from her area.[13]

More than a year after V-J Day at least 34 women were still employed by the federal government as civil engineers;

[12] U.S. WB Bull. 223-5, pp. 12, 17, 18–19, 21; Mary B. Meyer, "Jobs and Training for Women Technicians," U.S. BLS, Occupational Outlook Quarterly, December, 1961, p. 10.

[13] U.S. WB Bull. 223-4, p. 4; U.S. WB Bull. 270, p. 56. On July 20, 1962, the WAVES celebrated their twentieth anniversary. Headed by Captain Viola B. Sanders and 500 officers, they have an enlisted personnel of 5,000 to 6,000. Eight of them were sworn in as seamen recruits at the Navy Recruiting Station in New York. (New York Times, July 21, 1962.)

and the Tennessee Valley Authority had two civil and two hydraulic engineers. In fact, only a few of the estimated 2,000 women who had taken engineering-aide training during the war lost their jobs because of plant shutdowns, mainly in the aircraft industry—and they are said to have easily found positions elsewhere. Women with engineering degrees were usually absorbed more promptly than the aides, and all the industrial firms interviewed by the Women's Bureau said they would consider their applications at any time.[14]

There are other examples of rising pressure upon women to enter the field of engineering. During the Korean War, in the early fifties, the American Society for Engineering Education urged girls to take college courses that would fit them for sub-professional work such as drafting and computing as assistants to professional engineers. The official journal remarked that

women have certain inherent characteristics which stand them in good stead. For instance they are conscientious, they know how to use their hands, they are careful about detail, and quite important, they are not averse to trying something new.[15]

It was at this time that the Society of Women Engineers, whose president was an aeronautical engineer, was incorporated "to foster a favorable attitude in industry toward women engineers; and to contribute to their professional advancement" whether they were interested in the field of mechanized consumer products, building bridges, aircraft design, or highway construction. "Our high school youngsters and their parents must revamp their old impression of the term 'engineer,'" declared the society's national representative. "They must be given a chance to realize that many of the most exciting jobs in the coming years can be filled only by persons who, whether

[14] *U.S. WB Bull.* 223-5, pp. 29, 30, 59, 61.
[15] Fred C. Morris, "A Plan for Training Women in Engineering," *The Journal of Engineering Education,* November, 1952, p. 175; *U.S. WB Bull.* 254, p. 5.

they are men or women, are first of all engineers with experience and advanced training in mathematics, physics, chemistry, meteorology, astronomy and other aspects of science. We women are going to do our share in the new world of science." [16] The median age of women classified as engineers in the mid-century census was 31 years—five years younger than the median age of all women workers. Men's median age was 38.[17]

The U.S. Women's Bureau believes that without doubt more women will consider an engineering career if and when traditional attitudes against them are relaxed. It explains that except for military service under combat conditions many of the jobs require no more physical exertion than wielding the compass or slide rule. In fact, Arthur S. Flemming, director of the Office of Defense Mobilization, encouraged the enrollment of women engineers before the Association of Land Grant Colleges and Universities in 1953, noting that

it is true that, in many instances, women graduates of engineering schools would work a while and then marry and raise their own families. . . . But later on in life they would be available. And in the event of an emergency a large number of them would be willing to return to work even though it called for real sacrifice on their part to do so.

Moreover, a large electrical equipment manufacturer reported that his company has maintained a nondiscriminatory policy toward women for many years, and that the company would continue to train women professional engineers to do the same work as men, despite the fact that some of them may leave for marriage and family responsibility.[18] We even read of the hiring of a "pregnant engineer" who was flown to California for work in vital defense projects. Now a mother of four small

[16] U.S. WB Bull. 254, pp. 26–27.
[17] Ibid., p. 19.
[18] Ibid., pp. 7, 11.

children, a candidate for the doctorate, and national vice-president of the Society of Women Engineers, Maryly Van Leer recommends engineering to high school girls, telling them that "women are the untapped source of brainpower in the country today." "At the places I've worked," she urges, "they wanted an engineer, and whether I was a woman or not made not one iota of difference to them." [19]

That encouragements such as these had some effect seems apparent in the fact that women's enrollments in engineering courses rose steadily from 1952 to 1957, when President Eisenhower's Committee on Scientists and Engineers declared that "long established prejudices against women in engineering and science need to be broken down not only among employers, supervisors, and co-workers, but among women themselves." [20] In 1960 more than 7,000 girls and women received technical training in courses established under the provisions of the Vocational Education Act of 1946, and, after the Soviet launching of the first Sputnik, under the National Defense Education Act of 1958. Women constituted 20 to 30 percent of all students enrolled in data-processing and computer programming, laboratory technology, and design technology. They were told that opportunities do exist for the qualified worker to advance in her job—that while "there should be three to five technicians for every engineer . . . it is probable that the average ratio is one to one in the United States at present." [21] And the Bureau of Labor Statistics forecasts favorable employment for women in the engineering field in the sixties, and notes indications that employers are eliminating salary and other differences between men and women of comparable education and experience doing similar work.[22]

[19] *Life*, September 14, 1962, pp. 102, 106.
[20] *U.S. WB Bull. 270*, p. 1.
[21] Diebold, *Automation: Its Impact on Business and Labor*, p. 21, quoting the Dean of the College of Engineering of Rutgers University.
[22] *U.S. WB Bull. 270*, pp. 4, 9–11; *U.S. BLS Bull. 1300*, p. 104.

A few women are receiving doctor's degrees in engineering. In 1961 there were six in aeronautical, civil, electrical, engineering mechanics, engineering science, and sanitary engineering as compared to three in the previous year in only the first three fields. Master's degrees were conferred upon 27 women, and bachelor's or first professional engineering degrees upon 135. But it must be noted that men continue to account for more than 99 percent of the total number of engineering students, and the Office of Education comments that "the scarcity of women in this field suggests a source of much needed talent." [23]

In science as a whole nearly 6,000 women received college degrees in 1959–60, more than 800 MA's, and the number of doctorates approached 200. This was a small number to be sure, but significant because women's pioneering in men's fields makes degrees beyond the bachelor level especially important.[24]

Among our professional women today, a principal research engineer with the Republic Aviation's Space Research Center in Farmingdale, New York, is engaged in an orbital satellite testing program. A 23-year-old electronics engineer with a degree in physics from the University of Michigan is involved in the company's studies of reentry communications, microwaves, and plasma. And a 22-year-old technician in the company's life sciences laboratory with training in biology and biochemistry works on studies such as sensory deprivation and other areas leading to America's attempts to put a man on the moon.[25]

Indeed, one daring soul has asked, "Why not 'Astronauttes' also?" It was eight months before textile-factory spinner Valentina Tereshkova became the first heroine of the Space Age by

[23] U.S. Office of Education, *Engineering Enrollments and Degrees*, 1960, p. 23; *Ibid.*, 1961, pp. 6, 23–24.
[24] *Ibid.*, *Earned Degrees Conferred*, 1959–60, pp. 35, 37.
[25] Amon, "Engineering Talent in Short Supply," p. 4.

hurtling around the earth more than 48 times in 70 hours and 50 minutes in June, 1963, that Dr. Louis Lasagna of the Johns Hopkins Medical School was saying that "it appears inevitable that women will eventually be space travellers. If man is to colonize the planets, if celestial housekeeping is ever to be instituted . . . the story of outer space cannot discard the traditional boy-meets-girl plot." He declared that the physical differences between men and women do not rule out women despite the menstrual cycle, and that the very size and muscularity of men may be a disadvantage. Color and night blindness and eye defects are far more usual in men than in women, he has found, and women are less prone to accidents. Moreover, "if experience with stereotyped boredom is any recommendation, the average housewife would win, with reddened hands down."

Dr. Lasagna concludes that two motives urge the "rapid adoption" of selecting and preparing women for space travel. Scientifically, their exposure to the rigors will yield important data complementary to that obtained from men. Politically, "The propaganda value of putting a woman into orbit would be tremendous," although failure might perhaps seem even more tragic than for a male pilot. Both of these motives relate to the problem of extracting greater use of women's talents as a part of the fulfillment and self-realization of all individuals in society. "It is not only unjust but shortsighted for Adam to continue to view Eve through the astigmatic spectacles of culture lag. . . . It is too wasteful to diminish a culture's contribution by one-half. . . . The evaluation of female capacities is conditioned by cultural bias and habit rather than biological fact." [26]

Anthropologist Margaret Mead would seem to approve of this reasoning. "Sex-typing" of occupations, she is reported as

[26] Louis Lasagna, "Why Not 'Astronauttes' Also?" New York *Times,* October 21, 1962.

saying, loses "not only the brightest members of the other sex, but 50 percent of the top talent. It loses also the balancing and complementary values gained by the differing approaches of the two sexes to the same problems." Corrective measures, she adds, must start with changes in home attitudes and in the early primary school grades. The time lag in recognizing the changing social patterns by the schools, industry, the public, and the family is the accepted main obstacle to the greater utilization of female brainpower.[27]

A special problem faced by many women in technical work where changes are constant and rapid is that of keeping up with new developments and retaining their skills while away from the job to meet family responsibilities. Some of them are effectively bridging the ten-year "tunnel of love" by doing part-time free-lance work, as consultants for example.[28] At any rate, as one writer puts it, they have not followed our affluent society's advice: "Don't take the high road to a career. It's long. It's tough. It's lonely. Take the low road. It's easy, It's short. It's more fun." [29]

That the cultural lag in education for all professional women is being overcome seems clear when we note more of the recent advances. "Harvard Goes Co-Ed, But Incognito." headed a New York *Times* Magazine piece more than a decade ago. Radcliffe women now go to Harvard instead of Harvard professors going to them, and beginning in 1963 they received Harvard rather than Radcliffe diplomas. Moreover, with the recent appointment as the first woman full professor of education at Harvard, Anne Roe joins five others of her sex on that faculty.[30] New York University opened to women its College

[27] Amon, "Engineering Talent in Short Supply," pp. 2, 3, 5.
[28] *Ibid.*, p. 3.
[29] John B. Parrish, "Professional Womanpower as a National Resource," *Quarterly Review of Economics and Business*, February, 1961, p. 60.
[30] New York *Times*, May 1, 1949; June 10, 1962; August 10, 1962; March 20, 1963.

of Arts and Science and College of Engineering on the Bronx campus for the first time in 1958. "What could constitute a better education for women," queried the director of the Fund for the Advancement of Education, "than one which provides them with the necessary skills and work habits to think at constantly higher levels of maturity about essential ideas?" [31] At Cornell University, still predominantely male with its 8,000 men and 2,000 women, a woman has been named Dean of Students.[32] Rensselaer Polytechnic Institute now receives women in open competition with men for training in engineering science. Princeton University began its 215th year in September, 1961, with a woman student enrolled for the first time. And a special faculty committee of Yale University reported to President Griswold that "Yale has a national duty, as well as a duty to itself, to provide the vigorous training for women that we supply for men." [33] The committee allowed that "ultimately" a woman's place may be at Yale.

At Rutgers University a project for salvaging the talent of women mathematicians was started in February, 1961, under the direction of Mrs. Helen M. Marston, mathematics lecturer at the Women's Douglass College, with a grant from the Ford Foundation. A previous study had discovered that some 300 women in a ten-county New Jersey area who had studied mathematics in college wished to take courses in order to qualify for scientific or teaching positions. "It is an experiment in salvaging the now wasted talents of women college graduates whose professional knowledge has grown obsolete while they have raised their families," Mrs. Marston explained. By 1962 the project had led ten women into teaching and nine into industrial research, including computer programming and

[31] *Ibid.*, April 30, 1959.
[32] *Ibid.*, April 21, 1960.
[33] *Ibid.*, October 18, 1960; September 17, 1961; April 17, 1962; May 7, 1962; *Barnard Alumnae Magazine*, Summer, 1961, p. 7.

statistics. And the project continues with the express purpose of fitting women for today's hundreds of job openings. "Women with Ability in Mathematics: Industry, Research, Teaching—Need You," ran the advertisement.[34]

Moreover, despite Benjamin Franklin's advice to "first thrive, then wive," more and more colleges are providing living quarters for married students, some even including day-care facilities for the children. And a professor of economics suggests that "advanced training centers for students should include classrooms, laboratories, libraries, living quarters, nurseries, kindergartens, and perhaps minimal shopping, medical, and recreational facilities, all in coordinated units." [35]

The women's colleges have also been moving in various ways to check the waste of women's talent by initiating plans for further study and advancement. In November, 1960, Radcliffe's President Bunting announced a new Institute for Independent Study to help "intellectually displaced women." Set to start on September, 1961, with the moral support of Harvard's President Pusey, the nucleus of the institute was a group of 20 highly educated women from the Boston area who would each receive a $3,000 stipend to pay for a babysitter and other expenses to enable her "to take advantage of all the facilities of a great university . . . without abandoning her domestic responsibilities." Among these, Mrs. Bunting suggested there might be "a female Toynbee" who otherwise might have been merely an educated woman "interested" in philosophy and history. Included also was a smaller group of distinguished women who had already done notable scholarly or other creative work, known as resident fellows who would come from any part of the world for one to five years with an annual stipend of $10,000. Mrs. Bunting called the program so "worth-while and imperative" that she had no doubts that

[34] New York *Times*, October 30, 1960; August 26, 1962.
[35] Parrish, "Professional Womanpower as a National Resource," p. 62.

the means could be found. She considered it a pilot program which she hoped in some form or other would become nation-wide.[36]

With a grant from the Carnegie Corporation, Barnard College established the Seven College Vocational Workshops to guide alumnae who want to reenter the labor market, enter it for the first time, or do voluntary work in their communities. Here, registration is limited to approximately 50 college-trained women for a fee of $40 for eight-week periods of two hours each. They come from many colleges, and range in age from 30 to 60, the majority being 35 to 45 years. "There is now a large reserve of college-educated women in whom society has already made considerable investment," President McIntosh noted. "The assumption that a woman will either marry or have a career cannot be made. She is more apt to do both. . . . Three of every four college women now working are married." "The era of the intellectual bluestocking is dead and buried; the period of 'women's rights' has merged into the period of women's opportunities." [37]

In this vein Sarah Lawrence College opened a Center for Continuing Education of Women in the fall of 1962, largely financed by the Carnegie Corporation. With it Dean Esther Raushenbush has offered to all American educators a new and imaginative proposal for women's undergraduate study that would make it possible for many of the more ambitious ones to enter professional life instead of the relatively few, who either postpone or give up marriage.[38] Half of the girls who enter college remain only one, two, or three years—not four, Mrs. Raushenbush notes, but if they could count on having a

[36] New York *Times*, November 20, 1960; November 27, 1960; May 7, 1961; June 4, 1961; August 13, 1961.

[37] *Barnard Alumnae Magazine,* Fall, 1960, p. 4; *Barnardiana,* February 5, 1962; New York *Times,* January 11, 1962; February 7, 1962; *President's Report,* Barnard College, 1961–62, p. 4.

[38] Esther Raushenbush, "Second Chance: New Education for Women," *Harper's Magazine,* October, 1962, pp. 147–52.

second chance later they would probably take college more seriously. Dropouts might be reduced.

At present the roadblocks are often forbidding. In our ambivalence about the education of women, doubts persist along with increasing interest in extending women's education. Some psychoanalysts insist that the educated woman is a split personality, and some educators consider women expendable because they don't make contributions worthy of the time invested in them. In addition to such prejudices, the Sarah Lawrence dean records that a woman who attempts to return to college after an absence may be told that her credits are "too old," that she has not met the freshman and sophomore requirements, that she has not had a college preparatory course, that she can't swim fast enough. And while some colleges are making exceptions to an age limit, "change is very slow."

To salvage the brainpower of women who want a productive professional life along with husband and children, the take-it-or-leave-it educational climate must be replaced by a "sensible program" that will meet the needs "realistically." Women in their forties who find themselves no longer useful at home and who want to professionalize their talents rather than continue work with the PTA, Cub Scouts, town libraries, political parties, and other voluntary groups, are in more of a hurry than those in their thirties, although they have an average of another thirty years of active life. But what Mrs. Raushenbush calls the "wave of the future" are the women in their early thirties with no feminist cause to fight—women who cherish their homes and children. They want more education, perhaps to become teachers, but they don't want to interrupt the economy of their households. They don't want to go to school at night when their husbands are at home. They don't want an intensive program that would take them away from home many hours a day or many days a week. In brief, they are in no great hurry, but they want to start in a continuing intellectual experience. They cannot work by the conventional male schedule, but they want college training.

What, then, is the Raushenbush proposal of a "sensible program" for these undergraduates? First of all, colleges must accept the idea that their education is "a continuing long-range enterprise." They should encourage part-time students who perhaps would take only one course at a time. Class periods should be longer and less frequent. The mature woman can study alone. Also it might be educationally sound to give credit for some of the work women have done in relevant experience outside of college. Solutions to money problems range all the way from provisions for baby-sitters to awarding fellowships, which should be covered by special financial support. Most women are not free to move, so there should be something like a common market to which qualified people may repair. In communities where there are enough older students, the classes might be organized in convenient places and at acceptable hours. Even for ordinary undergraduates, boys as well as girls, education could stand decentralization to bring colleges nearer to where they live. And colleges should reconsider the requirement that students who have had three years of study with them must spend the final year physically present on their campuses.

Above all, flexibility is needed in college administration and teaching so that women who are still bringing up their children can study seriously—a little at a time—toward a goal they will reach in later years. Dean Raushenbush urges women's colleges to take leadership in devising such creative experiments that would make it more possible, as President McIntosh suggested, for women to have both marriage and a career.[39]

For, directly or indirectly, the gigantic thrust of technology, which now gives us world-wide television through Telstar, has

[39] *Ibid.*

heightened the demand for men's and women's brainpower, and has laid open to women, married and single, the whole range of professions and semiprofessions. Doubtless all of these women are not yet free of a sense of inferiority, but just as certainly they cannot all be given the Deutsch and neo-antifeminist label of neurotic. One of the numerous examples is that recorded by a woman surgeon about the first woman interne in a New York Hospital in 1931. "At first the men internes wouldn't speak to her, said she looked frail and hoped she wouldn't last. She showed them, and in a few weeks had the men standing up for her like so many Sir Galahads." During World War II, Dr. Charlotte Hughes, who related this story, sought inclusion of women in the defense program for doctors. She told of a young surgeon who said, "I suppose most people think surgery is like being a butcher, but there is very little blood; there should not be any. You may not know it, but your insides are really beautiful. I think surgery is nearer dressmaking; you clip with scissors and you sew with a needle. It is a very delicate business, and small quick hands are an asset." [40] It was at this time that President Roosevelt signed a bill providing for the appointment of women physicians and surgeons in the Army and Navy medical corps.

A mid-century census recorded 11,500 women physicians and surgeons (among whom was Dr. Janet Travell, Senator Kennedy's physician, who remained with him when he became President), some 2,000 dentists, 7,000 chemists, 62,000 medical, dental, and testing technicians, 50,500 librarians (90 percent of all), 28,500 editors and reporters, 1,740 lawyers, about 25,500 social workers, and numerous others. By 1954 the number of women mathematicians and statisticians in the federal service had risen more than tenfold in 15 years until they accounted for more than a fourth of all, and women's representa-

[40] Charlotte Hughes, "The Woman M.D.," New York *Times* Magazine, February 16, 1941.

tion among professional scientists ranged from 4 percent of the physicists to 27 percent of the bacteriologists. Government agencies have been instructed to do their hiring strictly on merit, and the President's Commission on the Status of Women, headed by Mrs. Eleanor Roosevelt until her recent death, has been studying "all barriers to the full partnership of women in our democracy." In 1960 the number of professional and technical women exceeded 2,800,000—more than a 50 percent increase in a decade.[41]

The impressively wide diversity of women's professional occupations may be largely the result of the entrance into the labor force of a greater number of educated women rather than a large-scale desertion of teaching, their oldest profession. For if engineering ranks lowest in the number of women, teaching ranks by far the highest, although it now absorbs a smaller percentage of all of them.

[41] *U.S. Census of Population,* 1950, IV, Part I, 1C–11–12; U.S. WB Pamphlet No. 4, *Women in the Federal Service,* 1954, pp. 13, 14; *U.S. WB Bull. 275,* p. 8; New York *Times,* December 19, 1961.

CHAPTER 17
Teachers and the Technology of Education

That the teaching profession in America has been in the grip of rapid and far-reaching change in this atomic age should surprise no one who has been aware of some of its weaknesses: low salaries, insufficient training, lack of social prestige, inadequate educational standards, scarcity of teachers, and classrooms uneconomically utilized. Thus, until recently at least, less than the best college graduates have been attracted to the profession.

Teachers

Yet everyone knows teaching is the major occupation of professional women, and their number has risen almost 50 percent since the mid-century. In April, 1960, nearly 1,300,000 women were at work in the elementary and secondary schools—75 percent of all so employed and 45 percent of all professional women. Since then more men have enlisted as teachers so the proportion of women has fallen to 70 percent. In the colleges and universities women constituted about a fifth of about 105,500 instructors and professors in 1959–60.[1] It is expected that a total of some 200,000 new men and women teachers will be needed in the colleges and universities in the present decade. For as the postwar babies grow into the 18–21 age group and more high school graduates continue their educations, a 5,000,000 increase in enrollment is projected. Teaching innovations and technological developments may affect the demand for teachers at all levels from kindergarten to university, but the number of well-qualified persons available for teaching posi-

[1] *MLR*, February, 1961, p. 139; *U.S. WB Bull. 275*, pp. 12–13, 14, 76; *U.S. WB Bull. 285*, pp. 11, 17.
[2] *U.S. WB Bull. 275*, pp. 14, 76; *U.S. BLS Bull. 1300*, pp. 39, 40, 42–45.

tions in many subject fields throughout the decade is expected to continue to be insufficient.[2]

In the early years of the century when there seem to have been few if any academic requirements of teachers, women's positions were largely confined to the elementary and secondary schools. It was not until 1907 that Indiana became the first state to require licensed teachers to be high school graduates. And as late as 1910, 80 percent of the nation's school buildings had but one room and one teacher. Books and even paper were often scarce, and the rural schoolroom was in constant war between teacher and adolescent boys.[3]

At that time President Harper of the University of Chicago displayed concern over the prevailing prejudice against the appointment of educated women on college and university faculties. He urged that "the women now being graduated, with the Doctor's degree, from our strongest institutions, are, in almost every particular, as able and as strong as the men. If the opportunity were offered, these women would show that they possess the qualifications demanded." But he added that even in some of the women's colleges "second-rate and third-rate men are preferred to women of first-rate ability." "Is this progress?" he queried, or were prejudices growing stronger instead of weaker? [4]

Following World War I, however, the Association of University Professors noted a weakening of the masculine tradition owing to: a. the introduction of women into higher teaching positions in war emergencies; b. the scarcity of men because of the competition of better-paying occupations; c. the development of schools of education where women could be properly prepared for teaching; and d. the success of the woman suffrage movement and a new realization of women's rights and capacities. Indeed, in the academic year 1921–22 about a fourth of the faculty of American colleges and universities

3 Smuts, pp. 20, 81.
4 Woody, II, 327–28.

were women, while women were approaching a nine-tenths percentage of all teachers in the public and private elementary schools and two thirds of all in secondary and high schools.[5]

But there was a critical shortage of teachers. "What is the Matter with Teaching?" asked a popular magazine; and the answers reflected various complaints. One was that, under the annual-election system, the teacher "is not accorded the tenure of position given to street or steam-railway employees, general business employees, policemen, firemen, or government clerks." Some states had enacted permanent tenure laws, but there were staunch opponents who believed that the resulting sense of security would quench teachers' thirst for professional growth.[6]

Aside from lack of tenure and low salaries, another serious drawback was that teachers had no share in determining the conditions under which they worked. They had no voice in the selection of textbooks, or in the framing of policies, organization of the curriculum, selection of administrators and of fellow teachers. This was reported to be largely true also of higher education. Hence, the appeal of the teaching profession was diminishing especially as other occupations became available during the prosperous twenties. In fact, college professors told of the laughter of some of their ablest students at the idea of preparing to teach. Those who did become teachers, from the elementary school to the university, were joining trade unions that revealed "a new initiative and a new group consciousness that are bound to give teachers a better professional standing."[7]

Social restrictions upon women teachers in the first decades

[5] *Ibid.*, pp. 329, 330; *Ibid.*, I, 499–500.

[6] Charl Williams, "The Position of Women in the Public Schools," *The Annals of the American Academy of Political and Social Science,* May, 1929, pp. 163–64, quoting from *The Delineator,* October, 1925.

[7] Elizabeth Kemper Adams, *Women Professional Workers* (New York, Macmillan, 1921), pp. 373–79. The American Federation of Teachers had been formed in 1916, and as everyone knows it is still struggling for a better status for teachers, a subject to be discussed in Chapter 20.

of the century were almost unbelievably strict. For example, 11 of them were dropped by a Kansas board of education because they had attended a local country club dance. Smoking and drinking were cardinal sins. Some contracts stipulated that teachers should not "keep company" with "young men" or "go with" other teachers, on penalty of dismissal. In some communities, teachers were afraid to "go out" on school nights, and in others they could preserve their good reputations only by being in by ten or eleven o'clock. Marriage was a frequent ground for dismissal. They should make room for their "more needy" sisters who were graduating from normal schools. Teachers were not permitted to campaign actively for a political cause, or to run for a political office; and the new view of science and religion which they were bringing to the classroom from their college and university experience was opposed.[8]

Conditions such as these prompted many young girls to take up stenography instead of teaching when they graduated from high school; and it is not surprising that more than 100,000 women—a sixth of the teachers—were reported to have left the profession every year. The situation was graphically pictured by a distinguished Columbia University Teachers College educator who envisioned the nation's teachers filing along in an imaginery line of more than 300 miles in which not before the 150,000th teacher was reached was there one who had taught more than two years. And not until the middle of the line was there an individual who had had four years experience.[9]

The question "What is the matter with teaching?" was asked again after World War II. One survey found that the profession no longer attracted the nation's best-qualified young men and women—that the teacher shortage was "tremendous." Young people could get more money, easier working condi-

[8] Elsbree, pp. 535–42.
[9] Williams, "The Position of Women in the Public Schools," pp. 155, 163.

tions, greater community respect, and more freedom working for the government, for private industry, or for the neighborhood druggist. "Everywhere teachers are regarded with pity or scorn; too often they are treated as second-class citizens." Only 7 percent of all college students were training to be teachers as compared to 22 percent a quarter of a century earlier, and "although we are living in an atomic age, our children are receiving a horse-and-buggy education." [10]

In this survey's list of twenty findings, these stand out:

1. The teachers who have left the American public schools since 1940 number 350,000;

2. After 1940, 50,000 men left the teaching profession and are not coming back. Only 15 percent of all elementary and high school teachers are men;

3. Fifty-six percent of the teachers of the country do not have tenure protection;

4. One in every seven teachers—125,000 of them—are serving on emergency sub-standard certificates;

5. Twenty percent of all teachers (175,000) are new to their jobs each year—twice the turnover that existed before the war;

6. The morale of teachers has dropped to a new low;

7. Twelve major school strikes have taken place since September 1948, and many more are being threatened.[11]

The alarming postwar state of affairs in the nation's teaching world prompted several productive moves. A striking and imaginative project to tap the reservoirs of teaching talent by stimulating ranking liberal arts graduates to enter the profession, made possible by the Ford Fund, was begun in 1952 by Harvard's Graduate School of Education, which joined forces with seven eastern women's colleges and others to form the

[10] New York *Times*, February 10, 1947.
[11] *Ibid.*

Twenty-Nine College Cooperative Plan. "Nothing of a permanent character can be accomplished for improvement of the schools," declared Dean Keppel of the Faculty of Education, "without giving first attention to the quality of the staff." The plan included a one-semester internship under which liberal arts graduates taught elementary, junior and senior high school classes in the morning under the supervision of master teachers and Harvard faculty, then conferred with their supervisors. The trainees spent the second semester taking courses under the faculty of arts and sciences, as well as courses basic to education such as educational psychology and measurement, the philosophy and sociology of education. They received $1,800 for their teaching, which in many cases made their graduate training possible. Of those who were teaching after a period of nine or ten years, the average salary for men was $6,300 and for women $5,500. However, a considerable number of both men and women found it necessary to supplement their incomes with part-time or summer employment. Four fifths of them declared they were satisfied with their positions.[12]

Doubtless this project was one of the forces which have brought more men into the teaching field. In a recent investigation, the National Education Association has found that more than a fourth of all classroom teachers were men in 1959–60 and that men comprised over half of the secondary school teachers. However, more than one in eight of all public school teachers, whose average age was 41 years, were without a four-year college degree, five in eight had a bachelor's degree, and two in eight a master's or higher degree.[13]

Improvements in academic qualifications have been made, nevertheless. Licensed teachers are required to take more hours of work in specialized education courses, almost univer-

[12] Arthur D. Morse, *Schools of Tomorrow—Today* (New York, Doubleday & Co., 1960), pp. 162–65, 168, 169.
[13] National Education Association, *Financing the Public Schools, 1960–1970*, p. 18.

sally a bachelor's degree for high school teaching is exacted, and beginning in 1953 this degree has been required for an elementary certificate in 31 states.[14] Salaries have also been lifted. For urban public school teachers in the decade 1945–55 salaries rose at an annual rate of 6 percent as compared to 3 percent in the previous five years, and less than 1 percent before 1939. As a result, in the 1950s more than four fifths of the men and women in city school systems of the largest population centers were employed where salaries averaged at least $4,800, and in communities of less than 100,000 about half of the teachers averaged from $4,400 to $4,800 or more. In 1961–62, according to the National Education Association, the average annual salary of all classroom teachers was $5,527.[15]

Nevertheless, the supply of qualified teachers in 1955 was only 79 percent of the demand for them—partly because of the higher certificate requirements and the availability of other better-paying jobs for well-educated people and partly because of the increase in childbearing. The number of women under 35 years of age who chose teaching had declined; the total number of college graduates prepared to teach in high schools had dropped 41 percent in five years. Hence, according to the U.S. Office of Education, almost 79,000 elementary and secondary school teachers were holding emergency licenses because they had not met the established requirements for certificates; and from 20 to 25 percent of all those newly hired held substandard certification in their states.[16] Thus, despite improvements, a crisis in American education was at hand.

[14] National Manpower Council, *Womanpower*, pp. 266–67.

[15] *MLR*, April, 1956, pp. 427–28; National Education Association Research *Report 1962–R 7, Economic Status of Teachers, 1961–62*, p. 8. There seem to be no factual data on the proportion of women who held administrative positions such as superintendent and principal, but it is generally conceded that they are much fewer than men. The NEA reports that 92 percent of the personnel administrators (who are responsible for professional personnel) are men. (NEA Research Monograph 1962–M1, *The Public School Administrator*, pp. 48–49.)

[16] *MLR*, April, 1956, p. 404; National Manpower Council, *Womanpower*, pp. 269, 270, 272. And see Dr. James B. Conant's revolutionizing new book on *The Education of American Teachers* (New York, McGraw-Hill, 1963) in

The crisis appears to have been immeasurably sharpened by the Soviet Union's successful launching of two Sputniks. For it was the very next year that forward-looking educators throughout the country received the support of the National Defense Education Act of 1958. Here was stressed the growing conviction that graduate study must be vigorously supported to produce trained professional men and women, especially to meet the critical shortage of teachers in science, mathematics, and the foreign languages. Research Director Sam M. Lambert of the National Education Association wrote in these strong words:

The American people must begin to plan for public education with greater vision and more boldness than ever before. In the years that lie ahead, this country must outproduce, outthink and outplan the Communist bloc countries which are also depending on universal education as a way to outdistance the Western Democracies. The public schools of the United States must progress to dramatically new levels of quality while providing for an increasing number of children and youth every year. . . . We are moving into the most demanding era in our history.[17]

This director noted that we tend to identify the classroom teacher as a young girl just out of college who is looking for two or three years of work before marriage, with the married woman who turns to temporary teaching to supplement the family income, with the young man who uses teaching as a stepping stone to another career, with the older man retired from other employment. These concepts of teaching must

which he declares the teaching of teachers "pathetic," and the existing certification system "bankrupt." Professor Conant confirms the two assumptions which guided the Barnard Education Program: 1. "that teaching candidates should be carefully selected on the basis of substantial academic and personal qualifications"; and 2. "that practice teaching should precede or accompany study of educational theory and method." (*The Barnard College Education Program, 1956–1962*, 1963, p. 17.)

[17] National Education Association, *Financing the Public Schools, 1960–70*, 1962, Preface, p. 8.

change, he urged. We need professional persons who will devote a lifetime to teaching, who will increase their knowledge
by attending summer school every second or third year. "The
people of the United States are rapidly . . . becoming a nation
of high-school graduates. . . . No occupational group, including
teaching, is immune to the demands of automation for higher
and more versatile skills. . . . We can no longer afford to let a
high proportion of youth leave school because the program
does not meet their needs. We have many top quality career
teachers, both men and women, in our schools and we need
many more." They must be paid adequate salaries commensurate with their professional training and experience.[18]

After extensive research to develop a "goal salary schedule"
for a "quality education program" with federal and local
grants, these are the recommendations of the Representative
Assembly of the National Education Association for classroom
teachers, presented—it should be noted—with no sex distinctions whatsoever.

Average salary:

Bachelor's degree	$ 7,992 to be given in steps from	$6,000–$9,773
Master's degree	10,148	6,615–13,097
Master's degree plus 1 year	12,037	6,946–13,752
Doctor's degree	13,251	7,658–15,162
All teachers	9,710	[19]

Along with these impressive comments and proposals for the
1960s came pressure from the Ford Fund for the Advancement
of Education for greater utilization of our talented teachers.
Teaching "is the only profession in American society that has
been untouched by the revolution that has transformed agriculture, industry and all other professions during the last fifty
years," noted Dr. Alvin C. Eurich, vice-president of the fund.
And now the outlook for the future makes it "imperative" that

[18] *Ibid.*, pp. 8, 9, 11, 12.
[19] *Ibid.*, pp. 20, 116–118. In its *Report 1962–R 7*, p. 16, the NEA shows a
difference in earnings between men and women owing to the relatively fewer
women at each successively higher level of responsibility.

educational institutions utilize "every new idea and technique which might improve the quality of education and at the same time put into practice the most efficient and economically intelligent methods." Dr. Eurich suggested among other things that the number of hours a week the college student spends in class could be reduced from 15 to perhaps 12, accompanied by more independent work; and that more use should be made of teaching devices "such as television, language laboratories, films, tape recordings and teaching machines." [20]

The Technology of Teaching

Some of the developments in teaching techniques have been in the offing for two or three decades, and beginning in the 1950s our areas of experiment have been making headlines—each aimed to increase educational efficiency in American schools and colleges. Two of the innovations—team teaching and a new kind of textbook—are nonmechanical. Two are very much so. It would seem that they all affect men and women teachers alike, for, in the maze of reports, technical descriptions, analysis, discussions, and criticisms, this writer has yet to see any treatment by sex.

TEAM TEACHING

Perhaps it was none other than the distinguished leader of the progressive school movement—Professor John Dewey—who initiated the idea of team teaching when in his effort to raise the standard of learning he began the fight against the "self-contained" classroom with one teacher in charge throughout the day.

Team teaching breaks radically with the tradition of the "self-contained," one-teacher classroom, and its supporters be-

[20] Alvin C. Eurich, "Increasing Productivity in Higher Education," in Seymour E. Harris, ed., *Higher Education in the United States; The Economic Problems* (Cambridge, Harvard University Press, 1960), pp. 185–88.

lieve it will contribute to a better utilization of qualified teachers. It is explained, for example, that instead of 18 teachers and 18 classes in a six-grade school with 500 or 600 pupils, there may be three to six teaching teams of varying size, each responsible as a whole for from 90 to 250 students. The team is usually led by a master teacher with over-all responsibilities, one or more senior teachers with special talents, and several regular teachers. The children are grouped according to the nature of the instruction. The teachers perform various roles; and aside from presenting a lesson to a large group they give special attention to children who are either ahead or behind the others. It has been noted that part-time specialist teachers are more easily integrated into a team program.[21]

Under Dean Francis Keppel, the founder of team teaching, Harvard was one of the early experimental laboratories under a grant from the Fund for the Advancement of Education. Conviction that our schools cannot be permanently improved until the quality of the teaching staff has been heightened led to a program for team teaching on the premise that people will not consider a teaching career until the schools are organized to recognize and reward quality work with prestige, responsibility, and salary.

The Harvard experiment that began in the latter half of the last decade went under the name of SUPRAD (School and University Program for Research and Development), and its laboratory was the Franklin School in Lexington, Massachusetts, which built a new elementary school for team teaching with large and small rooms as well as standard classrooms. Because it was an experiment, however, the architect planned for its inexpensive convertibility back to ordinary use. A general pattern for team teaching was thus developed which has been variously adopted elsewhere, and to a rather spectacular ex-

[21] P. Martin Mayer, *The Schools* (New York, Harper & Brothers, 1961), pp. 387–90.

tent. Indeed, whereas in 1956 team teaching was in use in only 4 percent of the large American high schools, by 1961 30 percent had installed it.[22]

Another pilot project in team teaching under the supervision of Mrs. Helene M. Lloyd was being introduced in six New York City elementary schools in the autumn of 1962 to enable the children to benefit from the special abilities of individual teachers (probably all women) in such subjects as creative writing, science, music, and art. Each teacher on the team has primary responsibility for taking attendance of members of her own class, submitting report cards and records, and seeing the parents. All teachers on the team have the joint responsibility for the educational program of all the children in the group. And according to the associate superintendent in charge of elementary education, a further aim of the project is to explore ways in which teachers can benefit from participation in team teaching. Among the questions to which answers will be sought are: How does working as a team affect their interest in teaching? Does the beginning teacher learn more rapidly by team participation? How does team teaching affect teacher creativity and leadership.[23]

Psychologists have been critical of team teaching for young children on the ground that they need the security of having one teacher and a single class group. SUPRAD has insisted, however, that children would work just as effectively and securely under the more fluid conditions of team teaching; although it has not suggested that in the early stages they would learn more. For elementary pupils, moreover, SUPRAD has said in its literature that each teacher should continue to teach all subjects rather than to concentrate exclusively on the areas in which she felt best equipped.[24] Dean Keppel, who is now

[22] *Ibid.;* Morse, *Schools of Tomorrow—Today,* pp. 11–25; Fred M. Hechinger in New York *Times,* May 20, 1962.

[23] New York *Times,* April 30, 1962.

[24] Mayer, *The Schools,* pp. 388–89.

United States Commissioner of Education, has warned that there is no promise of instant education reform, whatever its nature. As for team teaching, however, he remains "one of its prophets." [25]

TELEVISION

Team teaching and television instruction have at least one premise in common: that the average child at school is not likely to have instruction from more than one or two highly talented teachers, and that his education would be better if he came in contact with more of them. In favor of the camera, New York University's Thomas Clark Pollock is quoted as saying in 1957 that "it now seems clear . . . that television offers the greatest opportunity for the advancement of education since the invention of printing by movable type." [26] To report on the use of television in teaching, however, past president Arthur S. Adams of the American Council on Education warns, "is like trying to catch a galloping horse." [27] And so it seems, for in the crisis in which American education finds itself—the prospect of an enrollment of 46,700,000 public school children by 1970 [28] and an alarming shortage of competent men and women teachers—some of the basic criticisms of educational television appear to be in the process of being met by continuous improvement.

The pioneer closed-circuit television center—the Hagerstown community of Washington County, Maryland—where thousands of elementary and secondary school children are being taught, has found ways of better utilization of good teachers in a system of teamwork between television teacher and classroom teacher. This community, like many others throughout the nation, was suffering from a lack of competent faculty to

[25] Fred M. Hechinger in New York *Times,* February 12, 1961.
[26] Mayer, *The Schools,* p. 392.
[27] *The California Monthly,* section on "The College of Tomorrow," April, 1962, p. 32.

meet an ever-growing enrollment. In the elementary schools, 97 of the 352 teachers had no college degree and 75 had only emergency teaching certificates. Instruction in arithmetic, science, music, art, and foreign languages was particularly neglected. Hence, Hagerstown was chosen in 1956 by the Fund for the Advancement of Education for its most ambitious project in educational television. And it has received widespread attention.[29]

In a carefully prepared plan of procedure, strongly accepted by parents and citizens, most of the men and women television teachers were selected from the regular staff, and the close association between them and the classroom teachers was significant as both a teaching and a teacher-training device, for television was used sparingly in these schools. Elementary pupils averaged little more than a half hour a day, and only junior high school boys and girls received as much as 80 minutes a day, the rest of the time being spent in the classrooms where the work benefitted from the fact that the teachers themselves probably learned something in front of the screen. In all subject areas there was a division of labor between studio and classroom teachers.[30]

An outstanding example of teamwork between studio and classroom teacher in these Maryland schools was that of gifted Mrs. Pearl C. Snively's seventh-grade "core" classes which combined social science with geography, language, and the customs of different countries. The class was held once a day in eight of the schools. During the telecast, after extensive preparation, Mrs. Snively asked questions and paused for students to write answers to be checked later by classroom teachers who, a month earlier, had received detailed guide sheets outlining the lesson together with suggestions for follow-through

[29] Henry R. Cassirer, *Television Teaching Today* (New York, Kings Crown Press, 1961), p. 29; Morse, *Schools of Tomorrow—Today*, p. 89.

[30] Morse, *Schools of Tomorrow—Today*, p. 87.

work during a subsequent 55-minute class period. The students had been assigned textbook study. One effect noted was a marked increase in student use of school libraries and cultural resources throughout the community.[31]

In this experiment television proved to be particularly effective in teaching art and music, for which the schools had relied entirely upon outside personalities. Instead of 34 music and art teachers who would have been required to serve the elementary schools, two gifted music teachers and two artists gave televised lessons of exceptional quality. And instead of passivity on the part of the pupils, for which television procedure is often criticized, the result was just the opposite. Here is a description of a lively music class:

The music teacher will address the children, ask them to sing along with her, to beat the rhythm, play simple instruments or even dance or march to music. Under the supervision and encouragement of the classroom teacher, children respond enthusiastically and the classroom is transformed into a group of singing, drumming and dancing children without the need for a piano or other musical instrument.[32]

The elementary school teacher is said to have welcomed the television presentation of subjects she had neglected because she felt poorly qualified. She preferred, rather, to lead the class in the following exercises and discussions after she had learned more about her subject and ways or presenting it by watching the telecast with her pupils.[33]

The over-all results after four years of the Hagerstown experiment were reported to have been decidedly favorable. One was that after carefully conducted interim studies those groups which had received televised instruction were found to have outperformed the nontelevision students at every grade level. For instance, during a nine-month period sixth-grade, tele-

---

[31] *Ibid.*, pp. 82–85.
[32] *Ibid.*, pp. 89–90; Cassirer, *Television Teaching Today*, p. 32.
[33] Mayer, *The Schools*, pp. 391, 393.

vision-taught pupils in arithmetic with an average IQ of 99 advanced 11 months in growth compared to five months for the other group. And in some subjects such as science and American history larger classes could be taught effectively by television, which of course relieved the acute shortage of teachers by reducing the number needed. A special danger which required constant checking had been that of covering too much territory too quickly. Superintendent of Schools Dr. William Brish concluded that "as we worked on television it became apparent that we were really working on education." [34]

An important economy of the program was that Washington County schools required 32 fewer teachers because of large-class viewing, with an annual saving of $180,000 in salaries, which covered the entire annual cost of television including the telephone company's cable charges. Moreover, it is estimated that more than $400,000 would have been required to give the lessons in French, reading skills, special education, advanced mathematics, music, and art had they not been taught by television. The economics are said not to have been at the expense of qualified teachers, and even more instructors will be needed as enrollments increase. What it did mean was that the administration was not forced, as in the past, to hire incompetent teachers to fill vacancies owing to retirement, marriage, and resignations.[35] The program has continued, being modified and enlarged in keeping with research that goes on continually. It is considered a potent tool both for teaching and teacher training. But Superintendent Brish warns that it "is no universal panacea." [36]

Television is being increasingly acclaimed in many other

[34] Cassirer, *Television Teaching Today*, pp. 35, 37; Morse, *Schools of Tomorrow—Today*, pp. 87–88.

[35] Morse, *Schools of Tomorrow—Today*, p. 98.

[36] Cassirer, *Television Teaching Today*, p 37; letter to this author from T. Wilson Cahall, administrative assistant, under date of September 20, 1962; the New York *Times* of April 19, 1964, reports that the project has become an integral part of the instructional program.

schools as a teacher-training device. At Hunter College in New York City large groups of prospective teachers under the direction of a trained supervisor watch the unstaged progress of ordinary classes by way of closed-circuit live television rather than to "sit in" on small class groups which tends to turn them into demonstration projects that make either children or teachers or both self-conscious, and where there can be no running comment and questions. Thus, for the first time all teachers are given an opportunity to watch colleagues in action—a way of weaving teaching "methods" courses into regular classroom lectures. Also, use of a kinescope (the television equivalent of film) permits particularly able teachers to guide those in practice without the limitations of scheduling observation time.[37]

Also in the New York City schools, with Mary McKee as instructor, elementary science teachers have been sitting before screens in a 29-week television series known as "Science for Teachers" which is required for all new elementary teachers. "We have discovered that children do better in math and science than was ever thought possible," said Dr. Samuel Schenberg, head of the Board of Education's Science Division.[38] In its third successful year, 1962, there were 280 workshops of two hours each, which included a half hour a week before a television screen combined with a home viewing program.

Another application of television for teaching was in use in Cortland, New York, from 1958–62, where an experiment was conducted by the New York State Department of Education, the local school board, and the New York Telephone Company. Here, the studio teacher was not only seen and heard by the students but the students could ask questions and receive

[37] Fred M. Hechinger in New York *Times*, December 25, 1960; Cassirer, *Television Teaching Today*, pp. 127–29.
[38] New York *Times*, October 5, 1960, and a more recent interview by this author with Dr. Schenberg.

answers during the tele-classes. The "talk-back" was discontinued in June, 1962, however, because the device was imperfect and the cost excessive. The Cortland Board of Education then became the exclusive administrator of the project.[39] Everywhere that closed-circuit television mechanisms are used in classroom instruction, the teacher must of course have learned enough about their technique to know how to operate them.

Something should also be said of the venture known as "Continental Classroom" in the training of teachers by commercial television. Here was a nationwide science course begun in the winter of 1958–59 by the National Broadcasting Company in cooperation with a committee of the American Association of Colleges for Teacher Education with financial support from several foundations and industrial organizations. The project was conceived in response to a report on *Education in the Age of Science* by the Science Advisory Committee of the President of the United States which urged that the gap must be closed between scientists on the frontier of discovery and those who teach science in the schools. A series of studies had revealed that a fairly large proportion of high school teachers of physics had done no formal work in the subject since the opening of the Atomic Age, and that some had never had college physics.[40]

The two-semester lecture demonstration in "Atomic Age Physics" was presented by Professor Harvey E. White of the University of California at Berkeley, and broadcast by 149 television stations throughout the country from the early morning hour of 6:30 to 7:00 five days a week. Roughly half of the several thousand viewers were teachers for whom the course

---

[39] The New York Telephone Company, advertisement, "A New Way of Talking to Teacher," December, 1961; letter to this author under date of September 26, 1962, from Raymond W. Graf, supervisor of the State Aid Program for Classroom Television.

[40] Cassirer, *Television Teaching Today*, pp. 107, 132.

was primarily designed. They were registered at some 250 colleges and universities where questions were asked and discussed. Most of the colleges offered the course for three hours of credit, combining it with seminars which the students were required to attend. The course dealt with theory and findings rather than with pedagogical problems, and during its last stages outstanding physicists gave lectures, many of them Nobel prize winners. In 1959–60 a similar course in "Modern Chemistry" was added.

Two of the limitations of the program were that the same lessons were viewed by students with entirely different preparation, and that they took the course for very different reasons. The lecturer was thus constantly faced with the problem of what to teach and how, and at what pace to present what he had to say. However, accompanied by textbooks and lesson synopses for sale to students, "Continental Classroom" is said to have revitalized the teaching of science by television even though about half of the teachers dropped out of the course in the second semester because it required too exacting work for which they could not spend time along with their daily work in the classroom.[41] Recently, television channel 13, with no advertisements, has been introduced for educational purposes in New York, New Jersey, and Connecticut.

That television has become an accepted teaching device in higher education seems apparent in the recent move of organized professors in formulating a policy for its use in regular college courses. The report of an American Association of University Professors' committee of nine from the faculties of education, history, mathematics, psychology, physics, sociology, and anthropology, declares it "imperative" that the faculty have the basic responsibility for the content and objectives of televised courses, as well as of student eligibility and the credit to be awarded. It is held, moreover, that while professors pre-

41 *Ibid.*, pp. 107–09, 112, 131, 133–34.

pare television courses, and at least during their first experience in teaching them, their other duties should be "dras-
tically" reduced. They should also have rights to the profits
from sales or rentals of audio-visual tapes and films as they
have for printed materials.[42]

Today, thousands of communities throughout the nation are
experimenting with television in various ways and degrees, and
foreign-language teaching, with its laboratories, has been revolutionized. But it seems to be generally agreed that the prospects are incalculable because the enduring effects cannot be
known for a generation. Thus far the criticisms persist that television is in danger of standardized rather than individual instruction, that it presupposes a class with all members moving
at the same rate, whether they are fast or slow learners, that
the lockstep of large-scale "air-born" television necessitates
that schools in a number of states give their classes in particular subjects at the same time. A further major objection is
that, whatever the response pupils may give orally or on paper
after a television lesson, the television teacher has no way of
judging the *quality* of the response, and that it offers no accurate guide which can be used to improve teaching methods.[43]

TEACHING MACHINES

It is on these points that teaching machines—programmed
instruction—appear to have a distinct advantage over team
teaching and television, to say nothing of the conventional
textbook, for they include what is known as a corrective "feedback." This feedback is not the purely mechanical, electronic
correcting servomechanism which we have seen to be the key
to factory automation. The teaching-machine feedback serves
both student and teacher. The individual student works at his

[42] American Association of University Professors *Bulletin,* September, 1962,
p. 290.
[43] *The California Monthly,* April, 1962, p. 33; Mayer, *The Schools,* pp. 393–
94.

own pace without interference. The machine tells him at once when he has responded correctly to a question and this reinforces his confidence, increases his retention, and encourages him to continue. An incorrect answer, in turn, enables the teacher to discover why it is wrong and what to do about it. The program will thus be promoted. In fact, distinguished teaching-machine inventor B. F. Skinner acts upon the educational truth that "there are no wrong answers, only wrong questions." [44]

Psychologists have always given attention to the learning process, and as early as the 1920s, pioneer Sidney L. Pressy at Ohio State University envisioned an "industrial revolution in education." He designed several machines for automatically testing students' intelligence and information by multiple-choice questions. If the student selected the right answer by pressing a button, the machine moved to the next question. If he was wrong, the error was recorded and he had to keep choosing until he hit upon the correct answer. Each student could proceed at his own pace, and he learned while he was being tested. [45]

But Pressy found that the world of education was not ready for machines. Indeed, Professor Skinner agrees with the vice-president of the Ford Foundation for the Advancement of Education when he urges that "scarcely any area of human activity has been more resistant to scientific analysis and technological change than education." [46] Even today, moreover, the thought of educational teaching machines conjures up so many horrors for some people that thoughtful inquiry into their

[44] Mayer, *The Schools,* p. 400; B. F. Skinner, "Teaching Machines," in *Scientific American,* November, 1961, p. 97; Skinner, "Teaching Machines," in Seymour E. Harris, ed., *Higher Education in the United States: The Economic Problems* (Cambridge, Harvard University Press, 1950), p. 189; Donald A. Cook and Francis Mechner, "Fundamentals of Programmed Instruction," *Columbia Engineering Quarterly,* March, 1962, p. 19.

[45] Skinner, "Teaching Machines," in *Scientific American,* p. 95; and Skinner, "Teaching Machines," *Science,* October 24, 1958, p. 969.

[46] Skinner, "Teaching Machines," in *Scientific American,* p. 91.

merits has been blocked. This despite the report of the National Education Association in 1961 of a total of more than 97,000 uncertified teachers and a shortage of public school classrooms in excess of 127,000 [47]—a situation which perhaps more than anything else induced resort to technological assistance.

The teaching machines of today got their start in the 1950s (as did team teaching and educational television) when Professor Skinner turned his attention to the basic question of why children don't learn. Too many people come out of school without a satisfactory command of reading, spelling, and arithmetic, he notes in a recent article in the *Scientific American.* Too many cannot use the English language. Too many become discouraged and leave school as soon as the law allows. He reminds us that one remedy frequently suggested is to return to greater "discipline" in the schools. "The discipline of the birch rod may facilitate learning, but we must remember that it also breeds followers of dictators and revolutionists"; and it "can be replaced with far more powerful techniques." [48]

Professor Skinner had taught pigeons, rats, and other animals various tricks in which satisfactory results won them rewards that encouraged repetition. Professor Edward Thorndike had formulated this process years earlier as the Law of Effect. In the contemporary terminology of Skinner, the immediate "reinforcements" of the feedback, which correct answers supply, "shape" the child's learning behavior and increase effectiveness in teaching. More interested in having the pupil learn than be tested, he abandoned the multiple-choice device in favor of the Socratic method by which the machine requires the student actively to compose answers and receive rewards

[47] Fred M. Hechinger in New York *Times,* September 2, 1962.
[48] Skinner, "Teaching Machines," *Scientific American,* p. 91; Skinner, "Teaching Machines," *Science,* p. 977.

when they are correct. By contrast, the average classroom student has infrequent occasions for responses and such reinforcements as he receives on examinations are delayed for many hours or days and are not specific.[49]

Perhaps today's most widely used Skinner machine is that described as a "box-like device with three windows in its top. When the student turns a crank, an item of information, along with a question about it, appears in the lefthand window (A). The student writes his answer to the question on a paper strip exposed in another window (B). The student turns the crank again—and the correct answer appears at window A." Simultaneously the student's answer has been moved under a transparent shield covering window C, so he can see but not change what he has written. When his answer is correct he turns another crank which notches the tape. The machine will then bypass this frame when the student again goes through the series of questions. The questions have been carefully arranged, or programmed, so that each frame builds on previous information that the machine has given.[50] "In studying by machine something is happening all the time," Professor Skinner points out. "The student continues to participate in contrast with watching television, for example, where he may just sit and stare. He is active, and he gets something positive out of it which keeps him going." [51]

[49] Mayer, *The Schools*, pp. 395–96; John W. Blyth, "Teaching Machines and Human Beings," *The Educational Record*, April, 1960, p. 117; Kenneth W. Spence, "The Relation of Learning Theory to the Technology of Education," *Harvard Business Review*, Spring, 1959, p. 94.

[50] *The California Monthly*, April, 1962, p. 32.

[51] Harris, *Higher Education in the United States: The Economic Problems*, p. 189. Professor Skinner has been using another kind of machine to teach part of a course on human behavior to a selected group of Radcliffe and Harvard undergraduates. During a one-semester course each student spends an average of 15 hours at one of the machines, advancing through the equivalent of a 200-page textbook. Here they always know where they stand without

But no more than the electronic computer in the office—the data-processing machine—can the teaching machine do anything but what it is told to do. It is qualified human teachers—men and women—who present the program which must proceed in infinitely small steps that lead in the direction the teacher wants the student to go, starting with a question to which he already knows the answer or which contains such clear clues that he almost inevitably makes the correct response. For example, the child in beginning arithmetic may be given the equation $1 + 1 = 2$ and be asked to fill in the blank in $2 - 1 =$. Then the next step, and the next, and the next. Gradually the obvious clues are "faded" and the pupil performs without help. When the teacher analyzes the responses of perhaps 50 pupils to a set of questions, she can spot the troublesome ones and improve the program by breaking the items down into smaller pieces, or by moving them to other places in the sequence. Nothing like such a feedback had ever been used in a textbook or instructional film.[52]

The teaching machine is thus considered an indispensable asset to teacher training, for nothing handicaps a beginning teacher more than the notion that her words mean to the children what she wants them to mean. After she has programmed a day's work and tried it out on children, however, she learns something of the process of education and can never again brush aside a child's question as irrelevant or stupid.[53]

Interesting use of the teaching machine in combination with classroom instruction is being made at Hamilton College. With the aid of the Fund for the Advancement of Education two

waiting for a test or final examination, and they report that they learn more in less time than in the conventional ways. The machine does not examine them on material studied before using the machine. No appreciable differences by sex were found. (*Ibid.*, p. 190; Skinner, "Teaching Machines," *Scientific American*, pp. 95–96, 100; Jacobson and Roucek, p. 128n.

[52] Mayer, *The Schools*, p. 397; Harris, *Higher Education in the United States: The Economic Problems*, pp. 189–90.

[53] Mayer, *The Schools*, p. 403.

psychology professors have been experimenting with the teaching of logic by presenting a program with a machine using microfilmed questions designed for individual student use in preparation for the classroom work that follows. Professor John W. Blyth reports that they have found no disadvantages in the project, and many advantages. The fact that the students come to class prepared has made it possible to reduce classroom time from three to two hours, and the morale of students has greatly increased. "Students who discover the pleasure of success in school," runs the comment, "are unlikely to feel compelled to develop skill in throwing rocks through school windows." It is suggested that in the long run it might be economical to place a teaching machine in every home rather than double the size of school buildings.[54]

Professors Blyth and Jacobson point out that, although their teaching machine is merely an instrument for presenting instructional materials, it provides superior private tutoring for every individual—superior because the programs are the product of experts who have tested them on many students and revised them until they do the job intended. The use of these machines will surely not hamper an inspiring teacher, they urge, but they should reduce the number of student comments such as, "I would have been able to learn physics if I had only had a good teacher when I started mathematics."[55]

With a new grant from the fund these professors have been experimenting further with courses in mathematics, psychology, French, and German. They believe that, since the teaching machine has equal patience with the slow and the quick, does not discriminate between rich and poor, makes no distinctions because of race, color, or creed, "thoroughly tested programs will make it possible for us to come closer to realiz-

[54] John W. Blyth, "Teaching Machines and Human Beings," *The Educational Record*, April, 1960, pp. 118–19, 123–24; New York *Times*, March 3, 1959.

[55] Blyth, "Teaching Machines and Human Beings," p. 124.

ing the democratic ideal of equal educational opportunity for all." [56]

Industry is also using the teaching machine for training employees. A thoughtful representative of the American Management Association reports that it not only saves time and cuts costs but it enables the night-shift workers to receive the same instruction as the day shift "even though the best human instructor is home with his family." Programmed instruction thus gives the training director a new role in industry by relieving him of getting a class together with himself as instructor, attendance checker, and test administrator; and he can spend more time refining his courses to meet actual company needs. The representative sees the possibility that the teaching program in industry may in time be presented in a complete unit that includes its own "machinery" in something that looks like a textbook on the outside. But he notes that the "look of a book" seems not to motivate the learner as do some of the machines. [57]

But with all its accepted advantages, automation authority John Diebold reminds us that the teaching machine is still but an infant. He notes, however, that with skillful programming some professors have already reduced university courses to a third and a fourth of the time formerly needed, and that machine-taught students exhibit a higher average retention level a year or two after completing their courses than has been achieved with conventional methods of instruction. [58]

Nevertheless there is a sobering fact about today's genus teaching machine. National authority P. Kenneth Komoski, who is president of the Center for Programmed Instruction, which was established by a grant from the Carnegie Corpora-

[56] *Ibid.*, pp. 119, 125.
[57] Theodore B. Dolmatch, "Programmed Instruction—The Managerial Perspective," *Personnel*, January–February, 1962, pp. 45–52.
[58] Diebold, "The Application of Information Technology," p. 40.

tion, agrees that the device is very young and that it needs serious attention to assure healthy survival. He is severely critical of the current output of these machines by more than 100 companies. They are faulty, he charges, because they are not flexible enough to adapt themselves to programs other than those for which they were designed. They may, therefore, be using obsolete material. They do not keep pace with educational progress. These are his words:

It is my belief that existing teaching machines can severely limit the very thing on which their future depends—that is, the art of programming. Many programmers are beginning to realize that by accepting the limitations of the current machines the art of programming becomes the art of compromising what you would like to do for what one of these devices will allow you to do.

Any large-scale adoption of the rather immature machines which are now on the market may well mean that schools will inadvertently place restrictions on many teachers who at present are just beginning to understand what programming is.

Mr. Komoski believes the machines will eventually become a valuable adjunct to teaching, but "they must first be adaptable enough to meet the requirements of any program which teachers can create." He advises school boards against installing them until they overcome present limitations.[59] If and when they do, it would seem that they, along with team teaching and television, may prove to be a strategic tool for the better utilization of men and women teachers and classrooms.

PROGRAMMED TEXTBOOKS

A new type of textbook appears to be a fourth innovation in the technology of education. Already we find some impatient teachers using them to replace the "hardware" of the teaching machine. At the University of Pittsburgh two psychology professors have been developing what they classify as a minor

[59] Gene Currivan in New York *Times*, March 4, 1961.

variation on the machine-teaching theme that can be known either as a "paper teaching machine" or a programmed textbook.

The programmed textbook will not differ in external appearance from the conventional book, say professors Homme and Glaser, but the interior is very different. In their version each page usually consists of four or five panels, the sequence of which is not from the top of the page to the bottom as in the conventional book. The student "reads" or responds only to one panel before he turns the page. He begins with the item on the top panel of page one, responds to it, turns to the top panel on page two to have his answer confirmed, goes to the item on the top panel of page three, responds to it, confirms his answer by turning to page four, and so on to the end of the unit, where he is instructed to return to page one and repond to the second panel on each page. In this way he finally works through all the panels to the end of the chapter. Since each panel is numbered, the results are not confused.[60]

The programmed textbook is clearly capable of performing the main functions of the teaching machine, say these experimenters. It causes the student to compose each response, and it leads him through many simple steps designed to minimize the probability of incorrect answers. In fact they see nothing to preclude making a program available both as a programmed text and in the form of disks, cards, or tape for machine use. An important deficiency in the programmed textbook, they say, may be that it is not equipped to control "cheating." As compared to Professor Skinner's machine, where once the disk is locked there is no way the student can discover the correct answer before he has composed his own, in the programmed textbook he needs only turn the page.[61]

But the Pittsburgh professors suggest that, before condemn-

[60] Eugene Galanter, ed., *Automatic Teaching: The State of the Art* (New York, John Wiley & Sons, 1959), pp. 103–04; see also Donald A. Cook and Francis Mechner, "Fundamentals of Programmed Instruction," pp. 20–21.
[61] Galanter, *Automatic Teaching*, pp. 104–05.

ing the programmed textbook on these grounds, at least three points should be considered.

1. It is not yet known whether hardware is essential, whether other means of controlling behavior cannot be found.

2. It is not really known how damaging to the learning process this kind of cheating is. It is possible that it is not damaging at all.

3. Cheating will occur infrequently when adequate programming techniques are developed to make the steps simple and small enough. There will then be no problem of any magnitude. "It is quite conceivable that the tendency to 'cheat,' as well as the current widespread insistence upon a 'foolproof' hardware machine, represents nothing more than a vestige of traditional modes of educational control which will soon be displaced by other techniques."

The verdict is, therefore, that cheating is not a problem of vital concern in the programmed textbook, and that extensive methods of circumventing it are not required—at least with college students.[62]

The Pittsburgh programs were constructed on topics in elementary number theory, statistics, and fundamentals of music. The results showed that for elementary number theory, as with teaching machines, smaller steps in the program were associated with better immediate test performance, better retention, and fewer errors. In the teaching of statistics and music reading the new method brought higher achievement scores and less variability of performance than did the same materials presented in the conventional way. It is believed, moreover, that adequate programming which maximizes the reinforced responses will largely eliminate the necessity of the automatic dropping out of frames to which correct responses have been given on the machine. In fine, professors Homme and Glaser

[62] *Ibid.*, pp. 105–06.

explain that the programmed textbook is a simple means for presenting learning sequences, such as by machine, without hardware.[63]

Textbook publishers are being told that the book of the future must create an active "dialogue" between reader and book. According to a Harvard psychologist the trend will be toward a combination of books, teaching machines, and all kinds of experimental equipment which a child can use to test what he has read while giving him all possible opportunity for independent study and experience. In such a development, Professor Jerome S. Bruner forecasts that the textbook of the future "may have to come as a package along with simple laboratory equipment, records and such other tools of learning." [64]

Today, therefore, publishers are reported to be competing not only with one another, but with the new technological teaching aids. Most of them are said to agree that the textbooks of the future must implement the various reform trends —satisfy the experimental "far-out" teachers as well as the most conservative—and at the same time offer materials for students of varying abilities. A compromise seems to be the use of basic textbooks accompanied by "clusters" of books, usually specially prepared paperbacks such as one publisher has provided to supplement a new science curriculum.[65]

The comment of mathematician Robert E. K. Rourke, according to report, is that any development of new books and methods must make sure that the men and women teachers understand what they are doing. "It's very easy to say," he remarks, " 'Let them study calculus in high school,' but the fact is that many high school mathematics teachers have never studied calculus." Speaking as both writer and user of textbooks, Rourke points to a vast new body of knowledge "waiting

[63] *Ibid.*, pp. 106–07.

[64] Fred M. Hechinger, "Tools for Study," New York *Times,* May 13, 1962.

[65] Fred M. Hechinger, "Textbook Market Faces Revolution," New York *Times,* February 19, 1962.

for the final polish to turn it into textbooks suited for our times." But he adds the warning that "traditional texts do not need revision; they need replacement. The most important aspect of contemporary courses is a new spirit that must pervade the whole content, and such a spirit cannot be achieved by scissors and paste and an old text." [66] One publisher suggests that much of what is wrong with textbooks could be avoided if the writers programmed the contents and tried them out before the type is set.[67] That the textbook arena is alive with experimentation appears evident from the report that there are today more programmed books than teaching machines.[68]

In fact the Center for Programmed Instruction has decided that up to the present time programmed textbooks are probably more useful than teaching machines. In a research survey of seven studies comparing their relative advantages, Goldstein and Gotkin discovered no "significant differences in mastery of subject material between machine and programmed text presentation of the same programmed sequence," but that the machines had these disadvantages:

a. they tend to be expensive;
b. they are difficult to store and transport;
c. they often break down and require the services of a trained technician;
d. detailed instruction may be necessary before the machine can be used;
e. shifting from one program to another requires either several machines or removing one program and inserting a new one;
f. in some situations, a machine advantage which prevents the learner from going back in a program may actually be a disadvantage to the learning process.

[66] *Ibid.*
[67] Mayer, *The Schools,* p. 403.
[68] David Lloyd Morrisett of the Carnegie Corporation of America, radio program, "What Can Teaching Machines Teach?" June 6, 1962.

By contrast, programmed textbooks

a. do not keep the learner to a rigid sequence of presentation, since he may turn back in the program or go ahead as desired;

b. therefore they are not as "cheatproof" as machines, but this feature may even be desirable where the program is used for review purposes;

c. they are relatively inexpensive;

d. storage and transportation problems are usually minor;

e. they are easy to use in that they simulate the familiar medium of books;

f. the shift from one programmed textbook to another is easy;

g. in the situation where required, all students can easily turn to the same place in the program.

An ultimate criterion for determining the relative merits of the two devices *at this stage in their development,* these men conclude, "is mastery of the program subject matter" and here "there are no significant differences" The general finding was that there is a time-saving feature connected with the use of programmed textbooks.

Goldstein and Gotkin warn against the generalization that all programmed textbooks are equal or superior to all teaching machines, however. They remind us that improvements are continually being made in the teaching-machine hardware, and that the observed time differential that favors programmed textbooks "may very well be overcome." [69]

THE IMPORTANCE OF TEACHERS

There appears to be general agreement that, whether the technology of education is in the form of team teaching, tele-

[69] Leo S. Goldstein and Lassar G. Gotkin, *A Review of Research: Teaching Machines* vs. *Programmed Textbooks as Presentation Modes* (The Center for Programmed Instruction, Inc., New York, 1962), 10 pp.

vision, teaching machines, programmed textbooks or any other foreseeable device, good men and women teachers will continue to be indispensable. For is not education both the root of technological progress and the means of its successful adaptation to the situations it presents? Educational technology, accompanied by better schools and enough good teachers, will increase the adaptability of American people to an era in which jobs for the untaught become increasingly scarce. The teacher will thus be as necessary as the engineer in directing the way to tomorrow. Is it, then, possible if not probable that Pressy's vision of an "industrial revolution" in education may be at hand, as was the revolution in industry 150 years ago?

CHAPTER 18
Nurses

Although nursing was established as a profession in England a hundred years ago in honor of "The Lady with a Lamp," it is still in the throes of attaining the "usefulness and honor" which the American Nurses' Association resolved to promote when it was organized in 1896. As the second largest occupation of professional women in this country, now providing jobs for more than a half-million persons, nursing has many points in common with teaching. It is in constant shortage. It is dedicated to personal service in search of quality as well as quantity of personnel. It is beset by substandard working conditions. It is traditionally underpaid and talents are underutilized. It has developed a form of collective bargaining. It is affected by changing technology. But while we hear of an "electronic nurse" that can serve ten patients at once for some purposes, automation in the sickroom is a very tiny infant indeed compared to the burgeoning if still infant television and teaching machine in and out of the classroom.

Nursing began to achieve professional status in America when the Census of 1900 distinguished "trained nurses" from the numerous "nurses and midwives," but it had much in common with domestic service in the early decades of the century. At least until the period of the Great Depression of the 1930s trained nurses took care of private patients in their homes and did whatever was needed, while students provided practically all the nursing services in hospitals. But as the depression deepened and private patients became scarce, hospitals permitted the graduates to remain at work, often with little more pay than they had received as students. By 1937, therefore, the number of graduate nurses in hospitals had risen 700 percent—from 4,000 to 28,000. And by that time their value to the medical service was so apparent that the new system prevailed. Before World War II, for the first time, the majority of trained nurses—more than 100,000—were at work in hospitals.[1]

And just as the demand for more educational service called for more teachers and classrooms, so the demand for more health service increased the need for more doctors, nurses, and hospital facilities. But the number of physicians has grown only slowly—far less than the number of registered nurses, and although the ratio of active graduate nurses kept pace with the rising population, the supply fell far short of the rising demand for a wider variety of nursing services. The number of nonprofessional people who provide some form of nursing service has greatly grown, however, along with the development of several new professional and semiprofessional occupations, including the trained women in medical offices and in drug-company laboratories. Thus as new diagnostic and therapeutic techniques have broadened the range and improved the results of medical care, professional nurses, technicians, and related groups have taken over functions formerly performed by doctors. And this in turn has led to widespread research into the proper functions of nurses, especially since World War II, in an effort to make the best use of their skills.[2]

There have been other developments which have increased the demand for nurses. Although modern medical practice encourages home convalescence so that patients are kept in hospitals a shorter time than before, a larger proportion of patients who enter hospitals are acutely ill or are undergoing diagnostic or therapeutic treatments which require more nursing care. Moreover, widespread subscription to hospital and medical prepayment plans together with people's rising economic status brings more patients to hospitals. Hospital facili-

[1] Smuts, pp. 74, 103–04.
[2] National Manpower Council, *Womanpower*, pp. 274–75; *U.S. WB Bull.* 203-5, p. 5.

ties and public health services have thus been extended to include greater attention to the prevention of illness and to the rehabilitation of the handicapped.[3]

The critical shortage of doctors and nurses during World War II seems to have marked the beginning of a serious quest for more economical allocation of their skills, as well as to respond to nurses' dissatisfaction with assignments that make too little demand upon their specialized knowledge and training. It is said, for example, that nearly a third of the time of registered nurses was usurped by housekeeping and clerical duties —"extraneous hotel-service type of functions"—and that many students were dropping out because they resented the numerous tasks included in nurses' duties. Thus, in 1946 the federal government reclassified its registered nurses from subprofessional to professional status; and despite objections from some medical officers the Army made the professional nurse an important member of the medical team—a notable step toward raising her prestige, her pay, and other emoluments. Practical men and women nurses and other supplementary personnel were given the less skilled duties.[4]

In fact the practical nurse came to the rescue of the registered nurse during the war, with the result that her status has also undergone notable changes. She may now receive a license after at least a year of training and classroom study in a vocational or hospital school; and when properly trained and supervised she performs many former tasks of general-duty nurses with whom she works in a nursing team.[5] Indeed, the increasing presence of licensed practical nurses has

[3] National Manpower Council, *Womanpower*, pp. 275–76; U.S. WB Pamphlet Six, *Nurses and Other Hospital Personnel*, 1958, p. 1.

[4] Eli Ginsberg, "Perspectives on Nursing," *American Journal of Nursing*, July, 1947, p. 1; Ginsberg, *Program for the Nursing Profession* (Committee on the Education of Nursing, New York, 1948), pp. 30–32; *U.S. WB Bull. 203-5*, pp. 12, 26; U.S. WB Pamphlet Four, *Women in the Federal Service*, 1954, p. 11.

[5] *U.S. WB Bull. 203–5*, p. 3; *U.S. WB Bull. 256*, p. 36; *U.S. WB Bull. 274*, pp. 43–44.

prompted R.N.s to refer to themselves as registered professional nurses. And the status of the R.N.s was also further advanced by the exigencies of the war, as it had been by those of the depression decade. In the Army's search for efficiency, emphasis was now placed upon teamwork between the nurse and the doctor, which seemed to point to the surmounting of the hurdle in civilian life that required the nurse to come to attention when the doctor entered, and with hands behind back to speak only when spoken to.[6]

With the ever-rising demand for nurses after the war an almost countless number of different classifications and specialties were developed. For example, since 1950 nearly half of the nursing personnel in hospitals has been nonprofessional attendants, practical nurses and nurses' aides; about 35 percent has been professional, while 15 percent are student nurses. Among the registered nurses are those with a degree and those with a diploma—those with four or five years of college training which lead to a bachelor's degree, those who receive a diploma after a three-year training program offered by hospitals, and those who take training for a two-year associate degree at some junior and community colleges. About 82 percent of the new nurses in the academic year 1960–61 were admitted under the shorter programs, most of them by diploma.[7] The American Nurses' Association says careers in nursing are open to men as well as women. All nursing schools require high school graduation, a minimum age of 17 years, and usually a maximum of 35 years.[8]

In light of the estimate that there are two inactive professional nurses to every three who are active, however, special refresher courses are being offered to lure these women back and to teach them about the new drugs, treatments, equip-

6 Ginsberg, "Perspectives on Nursing," p. 3.

7 National Manpower Council, *Womanpower*, pp. 276–77; National League for Nursing, *Fact Sheet*, May, 1962, pp. 3–4; *U.S. BLS Bull. 1300*, pp. 50–51.

8 *U.S. WB Bull. 274*, pp. 41–42.

ment, and current practice. Some hospitals favor a formal course at a relatively low cost to the nurses, while others give in-service training on an individual basis where special help is needed. It is found that such special attention is profitable because it encourages the nurses to stay on the job—for part-time if not for full-time work. Some hospitals have even made arrangements for child-care centers and special transportation facilities.[9] Today an estimated sixth of all professional nurses in the country are employed part time.[10]

Moreover, with the increased enrollment of students and the expansion of health services, the shortage of nurses has stimulated measures to train more leaders. In 1956 a federal law established a three-year program of traineeships for advanced education in nursing administration, supervision, and teaching, as well as for public health work, and in the first year more than 550 trainees received scholarships that covered tuition, fees, certain allowances, and a stipend. This is a continuing program. Other scholarships and fellowships for both basic training and graduate work are also being offered by public and private agencies as well as by hospitals and schools of nursing.[11]

The scarcity problem has been attacked from still other angles. During the past decade the Committee on Careers of the National League for Nursing, aided by state and local committees, hospitals, and schools of nursing, made a nation-wide effort to recruit more trainees. Organized to promote both education and recruitment, the league distributed leaflets, articles, newsletters, and other materials intended to stimulate interest in nursing as a career. Other media used to inform the public of the great need included exhibits, films, radio and television announcements, and outdoor posters. It

[9] U.S. WB Pamphlet Six, pp. 6–7.
[10] MLR, July, 1961, p. 704.
[11] U.S. WB Pamphlet Six, pp. 3–4.

was at this time, 1952, that Teachers College of Columbia University sponsored the above-mentioned two-year program of training with a minimum of repetitive practice. The National League thus ventured the suggestion in its *Nursing Outlook* of December, 1957, that "a significant new source for the education of bedside nurses may be taking form to ease the problem and help provide an adequate number of nurses for our growing nation." [12]

A major effort has also been made to encourage more efficient use of the skills of professional nurses. The nursing research unit of the Public Health Service made studies in hospitals, and techniques were developed to determine whether professional nurses were performing clerical, housekeeping, or other routine duties that could be assigned to others. And we shall amplify below the revelations of an ambitious five-year study sponsored by the American Nurses' Association, the early findings of which were promptly used as a basis for revising both education and administration in an attempt to strike a reasonable balance between current practice and emerging patterns.[13]

Better utilization of practical nurses has also been a problem under study. While these women are wanted in hospitals to help meet the shortage of registered nurses, many authorities cite an unprecedented need for them in private households, especially for less acute and chronically ill and invalid patients. Other leaders insist that such work can be done by families instructed in home nursing, by women trained to perform housekeeping duties along with some elementary nursing care, and by a wide extension of public health and visiting nurse services. In any case the demand for licensed practical nurses continues to rise, and in recent years Dorothy Weddige, director of nursing service in New York City municipal hos-

[12] *Ibid.*
[13] *Ibid.,* pp. 5–6.

pitals, has told of their being used with satisfactory results in administering almost all medication.[14] At the mid-century there were more than 144,000 practical nurses (95 percent of them women), which was a 35 percent increase over 1940. In 1953 they were being graduated from approved training programs at the rate of some 6,000 a year, and the Office of Education said the rate should be stepped up to 15,000.[15]

That there has been some improvement in the economic status of nurses was revealed in a study of 15 metropolitan area hospitals by the U.S. Bureau of Labor Statistics in the summer of 1960. Salaries in private hospitals had risen an average of 20 percent in three years. The majority of general-duty nurses now received from $70 to $90 a week not including overtime, and the salaries of directors of nursing ranged from $118 to $158.50 a week. As in 1956–57, most nurses had a 40-hour week schedule beyond which they received either straight-time pay or compensatory time off duty. Most nurses in private hospitals assigned to late-shift duty received a differential of from $2.50 to $10.00 a week. Also as in the earlier period, nearly all private hospitals granted from five to 13½ paid holidays a year and at least a two-week vacation after one year of service. Sick leave and retirement benefits were usually provided and many received hospitalization, surgical, medical, and accident benefits, as well as life insurance. All or part of these costs was paid by the employer. But the practice of providing rooms, meals, free uniforms and/or the laundering of uniforms was reported less prevalent than in 1956–57. Nurses in Veterans' Administration hospitals and members of the commissioned corps of the U.S. Public Health Service were receiving 30 calendar days of leave a year.[16]

But of course more vacation time and the shorter work week

14 New York *Times,* September 27, 1959.
15 *Ibid.; U.S. WB Bull. 203–5,* pp. 6–7, 10, 12.
16 U.S. WB Pamphlet Six, pp. 28–29, 32–34; see also *U.S. BLS Bull. 1294.*

further increased the scarcity of nurses, and while the nation's
nursing force is the largest in its history, thousands more are
needed, according to the U.S. Women's Bureau. A New York
Times editorial of September 6, 1961, thus echoed that the
country needs three nurses for every two it now has. In 1952
the President's Commission on the Health Needs of the Nation had included a special recommendation for the encouragement of Negroes in the profession; and at its convention of
May, 1962, the American Nurses' Association, under its presi-
dent-elect, Mrs. Margaret B. Dolan, emphasized its Intergroup
Relations Program of 1946 by resolving to "encourage all members, unrestricted by considerations of nationality, race, creed
or color, to participate fully in association activities and to
work for full access to employment and educational opportunities for all nurses." [17] President Kennedy also authorized the
Public Health Service to establish a consultant group to seek
ways of meeting the acute shortage. Some have concluded that
the federal government will have to step in to help expand
training facilities, raise nurses' earnings, and lift the prestige
of their profession "to a level more nearly commensurate with
its true worth." [18]

That the American Nurses' Association is alive to the need
of attention to their profession was demonstrated at their 1962
convention. There had been a wave of mass resignations in
several states, but the delegates made it clear that such "orderly" action as was being taken did not violate their no-strike
pledge—all resignations having been submitted systematically
to allow hospital administrators time to provide for patient
care.[19] Hence, the convention paid official tribute "to the cou-

[17] New York *Times*, May 19, 1962.

[18] *Ibid.*, editorial, April 8, 1962; and see Ginsberg, "What Nurses Need is
a Chance to Grow," in *The Modern Hospital*, April, 1962, pp. 103–06, 186.

[19] New York *Times*, May 17, 1962. It is of interest to note in the library of
the American Nurses' Association that although 98 percent of the nation's registered nurses are women, at least two presidents of State Nurses' Associations
(Michigan and Louisiana) are men, who joined in paying tribute following the

rageous nurses who now and in the past have implemented the basic principle of the economic security program . . . for the democratic participation of nurses in establishing conditions of employment and conditions for practice [which] permeates all aspects of our professional life—the giving of service, relationships with patients, with colleagues, and employers." [20] In Chapter 20 we shall consider the special form of collective bargaining by organized nurses and teachers as compared to that of some other white-collar unions.

We come now to the five-year investigation of the 1950s which the American Nurses' Association sponsored. It was planned to find out what was going on within the profession—how nurses spend their time, the organization of work assignments, the methods of supervision, interpersonal relations among nurses, between nurses and patients, between nurses and doctors.[21] The studies were made in and out of hospitals from coast to coast, and the results have been published under the title, *Twenty Thousand Nurses Tell Their Story*. And what a story it is! For perhaps, above all else, the lack of standardization of the profession and the constant flux through which it is passing are the most spectacular. "To generalize very broadly from the reports today," writes author Hughes and his collaborators,

the professional nurse is chiefly an administrator, organizer and teacher, and the practical nurse is the bedside tender. More accurately, this is a statement of trends. What is a fait accompli in some hospitals is the coming thing in others; the frontiers between the

---

mass resignation as an "effective tool" in bringing about changes, and as a "fine line of demarcation" between this form of action and the strike. Moreover, one authority suggests that there is a large number of potentially competent men whose induction into the profession would probably tend to raise the income of nurses. Much of the bedside care during World War II, as well as work in the dispensaries, was performed by men—"practical nurses" in civilian terms. (Ginsberg, *Program for the Nursing Profession*, pp. 24–25.)

[20] Release from the American Nurses' Association 1962 Convention, May 14, 1962.

[21] U.S. WB Pamphlet Six, p. 5.

work of the various ranks of nurse are shifting lines and the sifting and sorting of tasks is still going on in hospitals all over the country; but it was not planned or foreseen and it proceeds at an uneven pace, differing from one hospital to another, uncontrolled and un- predictable.

It happens piecemeal. One must imagine that in a given institu- tion certain tasks always performed by professional nurses are, now one, now another, pressed upon a reliable practical nurse. . . . Conse- quently, the nursing career consists of both movement among posi- tions and changes in the positions themselves.[22]

The work of the licensed practical nurse in the hospitals was found to be the most erratic and unstandardized of all, and jurisdictional disputes were bound to occur. For example, most of the general-duty and head nurses in Minnesota hospitals thought penicillin should be given intramuscularly only by professional nurses, yet 46 percent of the practical nurses and 4 percent of the nurses' aides had given it in this way. The checking of narcotics was another such example. In effect, the practical nurse is repeating the history of the registered nurse, who inherited tasks from the physician. She builds up her career by the piecemeal accretion of activities which someone higher up has no time for; and once she has undertaken a task she is likely to think it is hers, while the professional nurse continues to claim it as her own. "The practical nurse is cer- tainly right in asserting that the professional nurse no longer monopolizes the highly responsible jobs, though the latter thinks she does," says Hughes. And this has led to his tentative hypothesis "that as the morale of the professional nurse goes down, the esprit de corps of the practical nurse goes up." [23]

Ironically, moreover, in contemplating the nurse's aide the licensed practical nurse "talks just like a regular nurse!" She has fairly complete command of bedside nursing, but she be-

[22] Everett C. Hughes, Helen MacGill Hughes, and Irwin Deutcher, *Twenty Thousand Nurses Tell Their Story* (Philadelphia, J. B. Lippincott, 1958), pp. 135, 251.
[23] *Ibid.*, pp. 137, 145, 147–49.

queathes the cleaning and housekeeping jobs to the aides and others. She builds up her own status just as her betters built up theirs, and so the work overlaps. Some aides undertake responsibility and highly technical tasks, as in New Hampshire, where the testimony was that "the longer the aides are here, the more they do what the practicals do." The chief point was corroborated in study after study, says Hughes, "that today not one but several categories of nurse attend the sick and run the hospitals and that the frontiers of each one's work are all changing at once." It is a "large and heterogeneous company of women who are all called nurses." And the shortages of course make the confusion worse. With it all, however, the professional nurse is the teacher, and she must know *all* the techniques whether she performs them or not.[24]

Finally we come to the question of automation in the nursing profession. It comes as a surprise to the layman to learn that hospitals found their lesson in the program which transmitted vital information from spacemen to a central station receiver in the process of gathering physiological data under zero gravity conditions. The news of how the lesson was applied was heard at a regional meeting of the medical-care section of the American Public Health Association held at Columbia University in September, 1961. There, an electronics expert told of the successful use at the National Institute of Health in Bethesda, Maryland, of a monitoring system that keeps track of at least five body variables of patients—respiration, temperature, blood pressure, blood oxygen level, and pulse or heart rate. Meanwhile, the nurse sits at a machine and cares for as many as ten patients at once. Speaker Edward A. Hebditch told the delegates that the process provides a permanent record of physiological data gathered; also that it had been estimated that an electronic unit serving ten patients in

[24] *Ibid.*, pp. 124, 136, 143, 149, 150.

a postoperative recovery room could replace four nurses a shift at an annual saving of $110,000 in salaries.

Another speaker charged that hospitals had not kept up with medical science, but that with 70 cents of every dollar of hospital expenditure going for labor, they would have to look to more automated means of providing scientific care for patients. For example, he noted that half of the nurse's time is spent rushing from one place to another to collect supplies that could be brought to her by conveyor belt. Too much emphasis is placed on hospital architecture, a consultant charged. "Let's develop the organization first, and then put a roof over it." [25]

At the American Nurses' Association convention, in 1962 Dr. Hildegard E. Peplau, professor of nursing at the Rutgers College of Nursing in Newark, told the delegates that "automation will change nursing practice, but it should not change its central mission"—that of warm personal relationship with patients. She said that "initially it [automation] will provide bedside nurses with more time for the human relations aspect of nursing, but in the long run there may be fewer nurses employed." For, "while the 'nurse shortage' may be solved, the 'nursing shortage' may be greater unless the larger interpersonal mission of nursing is taken into account." Dr. Peplau pointed out that while automation may give more constant surveillance of body functions, make the processing and storing of information more efficient, and allow for more comparison of data, nurses must enlarge their skills and knowledge, and nursing educators must strengthen nurses' resistance to the use of technical advances "in a way that negates the human mission of nursing." She urged nurses not to fear or fight automation, but to help mold it to the proper use—to guard against a tendency to treat patients as "things." She predicted

[25] New York *Times*, September 13, 1961.

that within two or three decades the nursing shortage might subside through use of new procedures in a "cybernated culture." [26]

Nevertheless, the National League for Nursing has estimated that the need for professional nurses in 1970 may be as much as 700,000 as compared to the 504,000 in 1960, 99 percent of whom were women. And should the 1960 ratio of about two to one professional to practical nurses remain the same there may be as many as 350,000 practical nurses in 1970. Some 25,250 men and women entered practical nursing courses in 1961 as compared to 23,700 in the previous year. Moreover, the need for nursing leadership—teaching, supervision, administration—is prompting more graduate study, the 2,263 enrollments of professional nurses in masters' degree programs in 1961 being almost twice as many as there had been ten years earlier. In medical and health services as a whole, there were 775,000 women in 1960—27 percent of all women in professional positions.[27]

[26] *Ibid.*, May 18, 1962.
[27] National League for Nursing, *Fact Sheet,* May, 1962, pp. 2, 3; *U.S. WB Bull. 275,* p. 14; U.S. WB Leaflet 29, *Memo to Communities Re the Nurse Shortage,* 1958; New York *Times,* August 2, 1961. Closely associated with the ANA is the National Federation of Licensed Practical Nurses, established in 1949 and incorporated in New York State.

CHAPTER 19
Professional Women Since 1900

Despite the disagreements over what college women should be taught in the twentieth century—whether courses in home-making or the regular courses offered to men—the period of World War II seemed to bring the practical if not the theoretical answer. There was an urgent call for talented women, especially those versed in mathematics and engineering, and many rose to the occasion, some of whom we have named who especially distinguished themselves and continue to do so. Rensselaer Polytechnic Institute broke a 116-year tradition by accepting women students and instructors. The Columbia University engineering school opened its doors to women. Both the engineering profession and American industry had been "profoundly at fault" in failing to recruit women, said its dean. The WACs and the WAVES were installed in many highly responsible positions in the War, Navy, and Air departments. The Korean War then prompted new calls for women engineers, and President Eisenhower's Committee of Scientists and Engineers declared that prejudices must be broken down among women themselves as well as among employers and co-workers.

Several thousand women and girls received technical training under the National Defense Education Act of 1958 after launching of the Sputniks, and the Bureau of Labor Statistics noted that employers were beginning to eliminate salary differences between men and women doing similar work. A number of eastern university and college departments welcomed women for the first time and we have seen that at Cornell a woman was made Dean of Students. The women's colleges have been giving special attention to salvaging the talent of women by giving them a second chance for education during or after the care of their children. By 1960 the number of professional women in the nation approached 3,000,000, teachers leading the list.

But as everyone knows, the American teacher's twentieth century path has not been one of roses, although they have traveled far. Inadequate salaries have persisted, and it was not until the National Education Association drew up its "goal salary schedule" for 1960–70 that no difference was made by sex. In the early years of the century women teachers' social engagements—even marriage—were sharply restricted. Teachers were not consulted in the choice of textbooks or in the planning and administration of courses of study. Able college students were not entering the profession. Teachers began to form unions to enhance their professional standing—a subject to which we shall return in the following chapter. It was after World War II that the Twenty-Nine College Cooperative Plan initiated by Harvard brought more men into the profession—doubtless one factor in the gradual rise in academic qualifications and salaries.

Nevertheless, the supply of qualified teachers has remained alarmingly inadequate. In our public schools the average continuous teaching career is still said to be only five years. The number of women under 35 years of age who choose teaching has declined, the total number of college graduates prepared to teach in high schools dropped some 40 percent in five years, and many thousands of elementary and secondary substitutes teachers have been holding emergency licenses. Then the whiplash of Soviet Sputniks and the National Defense Education Act that prompted attention to women's education also inspired forward-looking educators to take a fresh look at the problems of teachers. We have noted Dr. James B. Conant's new book on the grave necessity of better training of teachers, and the Ford Foundation has joined in seeking their better utilization by the adoption of new ideas and teaching techniques that may eventually make it possible to dispense with incompetent teachers.

Perhaps we have overextended the discussion of the technology of education—team teaching, television, teaching machines, and programmed textbooks—but these new devices as they are improved seem to hold so much promise for advancing the education of our children and college students that this writer could not resist looking into their development and use in some detail.

Our medical and health services in which women are so prominent are also in a state of transition. For just as the demand for more and better education has called for more talented teachers and more classrooms, so the demand for more health services, including prevention of illness and rehabilitation of the handicapped, has increased the need for more doctors, nurses, and hospitals. But with the lagging rise in the number of doctors, professional nurses have been taking over many former functions of doctors; and in turn, licensed practical nurses, and even aides, have been taking over work formerly performed only by registered professional nurses. Indeed, practical nurses—all but a few of whom are women—are now largely depended upon for bedside care and administration of medication. And a recent analysis of the stories of 20,000 nurses reveals an "uncontrolled and unpredictable" shifting and sorting of nurses' tasks—a "movement among positions and changes in the positions themselves."

Moreover, although the country's nursing force is the largest in its history, we are told that three of them are needed for every two we now have. The President's Commission on the Health Needs of the Nation encourages Negroes to enter the profession, and at its 1962 convention the American Nurses' Association urged all members regardless of nationality, race, creed, color (or sex) to work for "full access to employment and educational opportunities for all nurses." Although 98 percent of all registered nurses are women, at least two presidents of State Nurses' Associations are men.

The "electronic nurse" has also begun to enter the sickroom by the route found to test body changes in spacemen under conditions of weightlessness. This device can give constant surveillance of body functions and store information. "Automation" will thus change nursing practice and may in the long run reduce the number of nurses employed, says a professor of nursing, but not "in a way that negates the human mission of nursing." The estimate is that by 1970 there may be more than a million professional and practical nurses as compared to something over 700,000 in 1960.

Some of our more robust and idealistic professional women —including teachers, nurses, home economists, and social workers—have chosen challenging two-year vacations from whatever they were doing to join the Peace Corps to help less developed countries catch up on education, health, agriculture, and general welfare. Established by presidential order in March, 1961, on a "temporary pilot basis" as a branch of the State Department, with congressional approval, 5,000 young and older volunteers were accepted during the first year after rigorous tests and training—the average age being 24 years, with some over 60. By the fall of 1963 there were 6,700 volunteers. Mr. Sargent Shriver is the able and enthusiastic director. The ratio of women to men is about one to two, but of the 13 persons who returned in less than the designated two years, only two were women. The first Peace Corps baby was born in May, 1962, to a young volunteer couple in Nigeria. There have been 121 weddings, 55 between members and 11 with natives.[1]

Teaching is said to be the biggest Peace Corps specialty. Fifty young men and women who studied at the University of

[1] New York *Times,* June 25, 1962; August 17, 1963; November 13, 1963.

Pennsylvania were scheduled to teach mathematics, science, physical education, and other subjects for two years in Ceylon. Forty-seven graduates from New York University (34 men and 13 women) flew to be teachers in the New East African Republic of Somalia after having done some practice teaching in the New York City schools. They have reported satisfaction in "really teaching" because the youngsters were so eager to learn. And New York City's Mayor Wagner speaks approvingly of the dozens of his public school teachers who have joined the Peace Corps, believing that they will learn as well as teach and do better work when they return. The experience is also expected to recruit teachers, as many of the volunteers have said they intend to enter the profession when they return.[2]

Peace Corps nurses are staffing rural clinics in the backwoods of Malay—the "ulu"—and 36 men and women in the team have already made improvements in a 2,500-patient leper colony there. In Chile, 45 men and women nurses, home economists, social workers, and home builders who were trained at the University of Notre Dame went to work with the Institute of Rural Education; and other home economists are in Brazil. On October, 1962, under the supervision of the New York School of Social Work, 45 women and 27 men—including four married couples—began work in Manhattan's "gray areas" to prepare for service in the slums of Colombia.[3]

In August, 1962, after an Asian tour, Mr. Shriver said Peace Corps operations were "going almost too well to be believed," that the "Yankee Go Home" slogan had been replaced by "send us more Peace Corps Volunteers," and that in his view the corps' greatest strength is that the volunteers are making friends for the United States. They live as the natives do, as in Ghana for example, where 51 teachers ride to work in packed "mummy lorries" along dusty country roads in sweltering heat.

2 *Ibid.*, June 17 (editorial), 19, 21, 25, 1962.
3 *Ibid.*, June 25, 1962; September 4, 1962; October 11, 1962.

Health was found to be "incredibly good," nevertheless, except for minor intestinal upsets from unfamiliar diets. All living expenses of the volunteers are paid for them, and $75 a month for two years of service is being banked for each to claim upon his or her return. Before the end of 1962, corps headquarters was reported to have received some 27,000 applications for duty, and in November, 1963, the House of Representatives approved a new budget of $102,000,000 for continuation of the project. A 27-year-old nurse who served the two years in Pakistan has reenlisted for another year.[4]

Probably the adventurous Peace Corps project has enrolled few if any college students, but its reflection of general restlessness of undergraduates, which New York *Times* education editor Fred M. Hechinger reports, seems unquestionable. For while numerous students have thought of college as "an experience to be lived," many are now feeling they will make better use of college resources after they are a little more mature, that they are not quite ready to take advantage of what higher education has to offer. Able students are often plagued by serious doubts that make them want to prove themselves in a nonacademic setting. Hence, we have the relatively new phenomenon of the "leave of absence" for reasons other than financial or health deficiences. A student takes a year off "just to read." Another goes to a foreign country to work and study. Radcliffe's dean of students estimates that 25 to 30 girls take the equivalent of leaves every year, and its president, Mary Bunting, says, "The lockstep isn't good for everybody." Harvard's Dean Monro adds that, "The important thing is breaking stride. After fourteen straight years of education, a lot of students get restless." They want to get away from the academic competition. Coeducational Stanford University in California has built traveling into its curriculum by

[4] *Ibid.*, June 25, 1962; August 31, 1962; September 12, 1963; November 13, 1963.

operating permanent campuses in Germany, France, Italy, and Japan where about a third of all students spend at least half a year. A number of other colleges have similar plans.[5]

Campus restlessness among women is said also to be a result of the trend toward serious dating and early marriage which has caused girls to transfer to a college closer to their husbands and their fiancés, one of the reasons that colleges are trying to build escape hatches to reduce the dropouts. For some time, for example, six of the Big Seven women's colleges (Bryn Mawr, Barnard, Mount Holyoke, Smith, Vassar, and Wellesley, but not Radcliffe) have been permitting students who have a good reason to take their senior year at one of the other five colleges and come "home" for commencement.

The ferment among college students is the more notable of course when we realize that, as compared to 1900 when only 4 percent of our high school graduates went to college, in the spring of 1962 out of the high school class of 910,000 boys and 980,000 girls, nearly 59 out of every 100 of them—about 643,000 men and 464,400 women—would probably enroll as college freshmen.[6] By 1970 the National Education Association estimates that the number of high school graduates will have risen 111 percent in a decade.[7] Many college students are now working part time—earning while learning to help meet the mounting cost of their educations.

Part-time work is extensive among professional women who are taking advanced college work without worrying about credits, many of them far past college age. Here the enrollment of women is reported to be dramatic. Indeed, in 1958 more than 600,000 women in various professional and technical positions—about one fifth of all—were working only part time. Approximately 165,000 of these were teachers outside of colleges

[5] *Ibid.*, November 4, 1962.
[6] *Ibid.*, September 16, 1962.
[7] National Education Association, *Financing the Public Schools,* p. 17.

and universities, many being substitute teachers in daytime classrooms and some in evening schools. More than a fourth of our librarians were at work part time according to the mid-century census. And in 1958 two fifths of all general-duty hospital nurses were on part time, and their number is rising to meet the extreme shortage of nurses.[8]

What seems to be important to stress in concluding these chapters on professional women is that, in the search for brain-power in our fast-moving technological age, more women are not only receiving the needed education, but as never before are finding ways to have both a marriage and career. While by no means have all their problems been solved, they and their employers and associates are learning that women are not wholly like or wholly unlike men, but that they are comple-mentary, that in many respects women have far more in common with men than our culture has admitted, that "sex-typing" spells waste of talent.

[8] *U.S. WB Bull. 273*, pp. 25, 29; New York *Times*, September 16, 1962.

PART IV
White-Collar Unionism

CHAPTER 20
Can White-Collar Workers be Organized?

One of the far-reaching effects of technological change, as automation has taken over so much of the direction of machines by other machines, has been the rise of white-collar workers. In fact in 1956 for the first time in the nation's history men and women in white-collar occupations outnumbered those at blue-collar work, and by 1960 the proportions employed in non-farm occupations were just under 47 and 40 percent respectively—28,507,000 white and 24,780,000 blue.[1] Since the turn of the century the white-collar group—nonfarm proprietors, managers, and officials; professional, technical, and kindred employees; clerical and salespeople—have grown three and a half times faster than the entire labor force, clerical occupations having expanded most rapidly. This, as we have seen, meant more employed women—now one in every three of the total as compared to less than one in five in 1900.

Representing two thirds of all union membership in the United States, both the craft unions of the American Federation of Labor and the industrial unions of the Congress of Industrial Organization had given little attention to the unionization of white-collar workers. However, after their merger in 1955 they became seriously concerned over the fact that the organized portion of the labor force was declining. They attributed the cause partly to automation, and partly to what President McDonald of the United Steelworkers of America termed "a well-conceived plot" by the National Association of Manufacturers and the Chamber of Commerce just after World War II to cripple the unions by passage of the Taft-Hartley Act of 1947. Other causes were the fostering of an antiunion climate by congressional committees, and the "right-to-work"

[1] *MLR*, January, 1961, pp. 11, 13.

laws enacted in more than a few states.[2] Furthermore, the aversion of white-collar people to unionism was heightened by McClellan Committee revelations of the seamy side of labor-management relations and the inability of the American Federation of Labor and Congress of Industrial Organizations (AFL-CIO) and the government to clean up in the enormous Teamsters Union.

In an attempt to attack what they doubtless considered the major angle of their problem, the Industrial Union Department (IUD) of the AFL-CIO held a conference in 1958 on the impact of automation and technological change upon union size, structure, and function. Here, Counsel of the United Papermakers and Paperworkers drew the conclusion that the structure of labor organizations must change. "We must either take into them in positions of influence . . . the non-production, professional and technical employees, the office clerical workers and other types of white-collar workers, or we must see to it that strong unions are created to organize those persons and that we throw behind the present weak unions in those fields the full force of our cooperation and our strength." The IUD research director added that "unless the labor movement does measure up to this challenge it will enter a period in which it will decline in importance in American society." [3]

What special problems have the leaders faced in their attempts to organize white-collar people? One is that they do not always agree on whether a craft union or an industrial union should do the job, as we shall see for example in the organization of office and clerical workers. Another is that 51 percent of all white-collar workers are women, and that as re-

[2] J. M. Budish, *The Changing Structure of the Working Class* (New York, International Publishers, 1962), p. 53.

[3] AFL-CIO Industrial Union Department (I.U.D.) Conference, *Automation and Major Technological Change, Impact on Union Size, Structure and Function*, 1958, pp. 21, 25; see also Albert Rees, *The Economics of Trade Unions* (Chicago, University of Chicago Press, 1962).

cently as 1958 scarcely three and a third million women were in unions—about one in seven of all employed women and about one in six of all union members.[4] The number of white-collar women workers who were in unions at that time seems not to have been reported, but that there were relatively few seems indicated by the fact that all white-collar employees constituted only 12 percent of the membership in the national and international unions. One commentator suggests that "we know nothing about the comparative propensity of men and women to join unions," and that the difference in the membership rate is largely explained by the fact that most women work in occupations into which unions have not deeply penetrated—offices, sales, and services, especially the thousands of small units where the expenditure of time and money to organize them has not seemed justified.[5]

A major hurdle is that white-collar workers on the whole are salaried, middle-class people who by tradition feel a sense of superiority if not of superciliousness toward wage-earning manual workers, and an indifference toward their unions. They have a desire for status and approval. They look for promotion on the basis of merit instead of seniority. It was the typewriter, it will be recalled, that brought middle-class women and girls into the employment world for the first time nearly a hundred years ago, and they were held and held themselves in higher esteem than women who had been sweating in the factories from the beginning of the century. They had received more education and they knew something of the rewards of leisure. "I have been chairman of the Board of Directors of the Summer School for Office Workers for a good many years," said Professor Theresa Wolfson in1949, "and I have been impressed with the change in attitude of white-collar workers toward

[4] U.S. Department of Labor, *The American Workers' Fact Book* (G.P.O. 1960), p. 128; *MLR*, January, 1960, pp. 5–6; *MLR*, February, 1961, p. 140.
[5] Irving Bernstein, "Don't Count the Unions Out," in *Challenge*, November, 1961, pp. 17–19.

unionism. The proportion of organized white-collar workers attending the school has increased tremendously in recent years, but the desire for status and approbation, the conflict of loyalties, are still a number one problem." [6]

The Women's Trade Union League, under the direction of women of leisure, among whom Margaret Drier Robbins was prominent, had done its share in introducing factory women into trade unions from the time it was organized in 1903 to its closing in 1950. And in 1933 the American Labor Education Service (then known as the Affiliated Schools for Workers), under the able direction of Eleanor Coit, established the Summer School for Office Workers, which later admitted teachers, social workers, telephone operators, and others under the name of the White Collar Workshops, which several hundred men and women attended. The chief purpose of these workshops was to make white-collar people more aware of their position in the labor force and of their economic and social problems, to probe their peculiar psychology, and to acquaint them with the uses of trade unions. Some of the students later became active in organizing new white-collar trade unions.[7]

But it was the terrible depression of the 1930s and the passage of the National Labor Relations (Wagner) Act in 1935, declared constitutional by the United States Supreme Court two years later, that made unionism seem respectable to many white-collar people throughout the nation and gave them their first sense of entity with the labor movement. Collective bargaining had become a national policy. Here was labor's Magna Charta. And during World War II, with the help of the maintenance-of-membership clause of the War Labor Board, which required all employees who joined a union to remain members

[6] Theresa, Wolfson, "The Difference: Fascism or Democracy," *Labor and Nation*, May–June, 1949, p. 21.

[7] *MLR*, May, 1952, pp. 508–10; Clara A. Kaiser, "Learning to Make History," *Social Work Today*, May, 1938.

during the life of the contract, the industrial unions of the CIO gathered in thousands of white-collar workers. They organized them in separate locals in deference to their feeling of "not belonging," or to the "differentness" which they professed—differences which are surely being overcome as mechanization advances.[8]

In the following pages we shall attempt to trace the development of unionism or the lack of it among our teachers, nurses, social workers, and librarians; and among office workers, telephone operators, and saleswomen—groups in which women abound. Some of the groups not included in the discussion are actresses and airline stewardesses. Officers of the Associated Actors and Artists of America say that they have no way of reporting on either the number or the activities of women members of their component unions. In the International Air Line Pilots Association about 6,000 women constitute more than a third of the membership, but lack of space in what must at best be an overlong chapter seems to rule out this relatively small group. And although we have seen that women are making headway in engineering, this calling cannot yet be treated as a woman's occupation.

Teachers

The newspapers have brought vibrant tidings of the activities of American teachers and their unions in recent years. Does this mean that the men and women instructors of our children have all become union members despite the National Education Association, which presumes to represent them and their professional interests in matters of general welfare? Let us examine the record.

It was as far back as the turn of the century that the Teach-

[8] Theresa Wolfson, "White Collar Workers and Organized Labor," *Journal of Educational Sociology*, February, 1952, p. 367.

ers' Federation of Chicago—almost wholly a women's organization—affiliated with the Chicago Federation of Labor and
with the American Federation of Labor. And as early as 1916,
2,800 teachers in eight local unions founded the American
Federation of Teachers (AFT-AFL) which in three short years
had attracted more members than the study group known as
the National Education Association (NEA). Promptly the
association transformed itself into a professional organization
with the aim of representing all teachers in matters of employment and of making the young union unnecessary.[9] Nevertheless, by 1938 the AFT had gathered in a membership of 30,000,
despite opposition from their school administrators and many
local and state associations as well as the NEA. The federation
held firm, however, with its no-strike policy and its slogan:
"Democracy in Education; Education for Democracy." [10]

But as inflation advanced in the 1940s, many elementary
and high school teachers—outside of unions as well as union
members—who did not leave the profession for better pay during the war period joined in the postwar strike wave that
swept the country. The pace seems to have been set by the
Norwalk (Connecticut) Teachers Association when in August,
1946, it caused school doors to be closed for a week and won
the greater part of its wage demands in a signed collective
agreement that included all members. Even the State Commissioner of Education supported the contract but warned all
teachers against affiliating with "any outside organization." [11]

[9] Myron Lieberman, "Teachers Choose a Union," *The Nation*, December 2,
1961, p. 444.
[10] Elsbree, pp. 510, 512.
[11] Vera Shlakman, "White Collar Workers and Professional Organizations,"
Science and Society, Summer, 1950, pp. 232–33. The Norwalk case report
quotes Franklin D. Roosevelt as having said, "A strike of public employees
manifests nothing less than an intent on their part to prevent or obstruct the
operation of government and such action is unthinkable and intolerable."
(Reynolds C. Seitz, "Rights of School Teacers to Engage in Labor Organizational Activities," *The Marquette Law Review*, Summer, 1960, p. 42.)

Because of its aftereffects, a more disturbing strike was that in Buffalo, New York, in 1947 when, under the leadership of the local federation of teachers, 2,400 strikers closed the schools for a week in protest against their low salaries. They said the people had to be shocked out of their complacency before the city fathers would do anything about their plight. The public treated them sympathetically, and the flare-up served to call attention to the deteriorating effects of teachers' economic status upon the public school system.[12] But the revolt so incensed the state legislature that it promptly enacted the punitive Condon-Wadlin law which, with some reductions in penalties by the 1963 legislature, stands on the statute books today. The edict forbade strikes by all state and city employees, and penalized strikers by automatic dismissal. And dismissed strikers who were rehired would receive the same pay as before the walkout for a period of three years (now six months), and rehired persons were to be placed on probation for five years (now one year). In addition, twice the employee's daily earnings may now be deducted for each day he was on strike, up to 30 days. The Condon-Wadlin law has been so drastic that it has never yet been enforced against teachers, unionized or not, for the many strikes they have declared since it was passed.[13]

In fact, the combination of the Condon-Wadlin law and unbearably low salaries has continued to keep New York teachers in a turmoil. In New York City in 1951 there was a 15 month "strike" by teachers against extracurricular activities which ended when the Board of Estimate approved pay rises recom-

[12] Herbert Northrup, Chapter 8, in Richard Lester, *Insights Into Labor Issues* (New York, Macmillan, 1948), pp. 141–42; Eliot H. Kaplan, "Concepts of Public Employee Relations," *Industrial and Labor Relations Review*, January, 1948, pp. 225–26.

[13] In many ways Condon-Wadlin served as a model for the more effective Taft-Hartley Act passed by Congress in the same year which forbids strikes by federal employees and demands permanent dismissal of those who disobey.

mended by the Board of Education and the United Parents'
Association.[14] In 1959, more than 700 of the 800 teachers in
New York City's 16 evening high schools, organized in the High
School Teachers Association, "resigned" en masse on the opening day of the spring semester because their pay for a three-
hour session had increased only from $10.00 to $12.50 since
1932. After the schools had been closed for more than two
weeks they received slight salary increases and a two-night
instead of a three-night schedule—with no reprisals. The association had received the support of the Teachers' Guild (AFL-
CIO) and the independent Teachers' Union.[15]

In April, 1960, the Teachers' Guild became the United Federation of Teachers (UFT) of the AFL-CIO, with a vigorous
president, Charles Cogen, who promptly threatened a city
walkout, which he called off after promises from Superintendent John J. Theobold of salary improvement and other emoluments, including duty-free lunch periods, sick pay for substitutes, and consideration for holding an election to determine
what one of the more than a score of groups of New York City
teachers should represent them. The superintendent said he
would recommend a collective bargaining election if the school
employees wanted one. He reminded the new federation, however, that the Board of Education had never sanctioned contract dealings between the city and a teachers' union.[16] Nevertheless, in June UFT members voted three to one in favor
of collective bargaining.[17]

Soon the UFT charged Superintendent Theobold with
breaking promises, and its members—now about 10,000—voted
to strike the public schools on November 7 to test the constitutionality of the Condon-Wadlin law. The superintendent
countered with a threat to invoke that law if they did. And

[14] New York *Times*, August 16, 1951.
[15] *Ibid.*, February 7, 8, 23, 25, 1959.
[16] *Ibid.*, May 17, 1960.
[17] Lieberman, *The Nation*, December 2, 1961, p. 460.

the federation found little public support on the strike issue. Eight groups, including the Secondary School Teachers' Association and the Teachers' Union, as well as affiliates of the NEA, opposed it.[18] For beneath the surface was serious disagreement among these men and women and their organizations over aims and policies, heightened by the impression that the UFT wanted to be spokesman for all city teachers, which in fact it did. NEA conventions openly opposed this procedure while the AFT staunchly supported it, charging the NEA with company unionism because it admitted school administrators along with teachers.[19]

The teachers' strike of November 7, 1960—the first in New York City—began and ended in one day. AFL-CIO President George Meany and local labor lieutenants intervened, and Mayor Wagner appointed a three-man board of arbitration. The strikers were docked a day's pay, but received no other penalty. Superintendent Theobold assured them that there would be no blacklist, and he advised school principals to destroy any such lists which they might have prepared.[20]

It took a year to clear away state-city political entanglements in the New York school system, and to stifle indecisive bickering by some of the teachers' organizations before the collective bargaining election could be held. Inasmuch as almost 10 percent of all teachers in the nation live in the New York metropolitan area, where there are more teachers than in the ten smallest states combined, the outcome of the election was bound to have major repercussions on other organizations of teachers throughout the nation. UFT victory would thus invigorate the entire American Federation of Teachers, and the

[18] New York *Times*, October 21, 26, 1960; November 2, 1960.

[19] Lieberman, *The Nation*, December 2, 1961, p. 446, tells us that in 1960–61, 85 percent of NEA members were classroom teachers but that it was so administrator dominated that only three of the 11 members of the Executive Committee were teachers.

[20] New York *Times*, November 8, 10, 11, 1960.

locals in other urban centers would probably press for similar elections. Hence, it seemed that no event in many years had so great a potential for creating a teachers' organization capable of dealing with major problems of education.[21]

The date for the New York City election was set by the City Labor Department for December 15, 1961, and Professor Nathan F. Feinsinger of the Wisconsin Law School was named to conduct a public hearing to give all factions an opportunity to comment.[22] The professor then recommended three groups as qualified to vote: the Teachers' Union (with no state or national affiliation and which the Board of Education had long branded as communistic), the Teachers' Bargaining Organization (an *ad hoc* group composed of New York City education associations and affiliated with the NEA), and the United Federation of Teachers, supported by such public and academic leaders as Eleanor Roosevelt, Herbert Lehman, Paul H. Douglas, William H. Kilpatrick, John L. Childs, George S. Counts, Walter Reuther, and George Meany.[23] After a three-day election conducted by the Honest Ballot Association, the UFT was declared the winner, with the right to represent the city's more than 43,000 public school teachers for collective bargaining. With more than 20,000 votes, this was a smashing victory over the NEA group, which received only 9,770 votes, the Teachers' Union trailing with 2,575.[24]

The United Federation of Teachers was thus the first teachers' organization to win collective bargaining rights in a major city school system. The victory prompted the American Federation of Teachers, with its scanty 76,000 members, to issue a direct challenge to the National Education Association by

21 For it is said of the AFT that up to now it has been deficient as a professional organization, that it has no real program of certification or professional ethics, that it has never engaged in educational research. (Lieberman, *The Nation*, December 2, 1961, pp. 444, 447, 460.)

22 New York *Times*, November 4, 1961.

23 *Ibid.*, December 8, 1961.

24 *Ibid.*, December 17, 1961.

calling for a doubling of its membership within five years. The NEA, with its 812,000 members, countered with the slogan: "A Million or More for Sixty-Four." [25]

The year 1962 again brought turbulence in New York City. In its first experience with actual collective bargaining the UFT demanded a $53 million increase for salaries alone, and in addition about $45 million for improvements in educational facilities and working conditions. The salary range at the time was from $4,800 to $8,650 and the union sought a range from $5,400 to $9,500 in 14 years. Also $700 for all junior and senior high school regular teachers for "specialization." When the board countered with an offer of only $27 million the union's executive board recommended a city-wide strike on April 10, pending a vote of the membership. At a big meeting in St. Nicholas Arena on March 27, however, President Cogen urged that the union's objective was a contract and not a strike, and that the federation was ready to resume negotiations if the dealing could be in "cash and not soap coupons." Amid cheers and waving banners 5,000 teachers voted for the strike, nevertheless, unless they received an acceptable offer from the board. A strike by 30,000 teachers was thus predicted, while the board warned of the penalties of the Condon-Wadlin law.[26]

Meanwhile, serious national conflict was raging between the NEA and the AFT over the professional image versus the trade union as a way to achieve the professional status which every teacher craves. The federation warned that professional status is an empty phrase unless salaries and working conditions make teachers economic equals with other professionals, and that strikes may be necessary to achieve them. The NEA held that "the seeking of consensus and mutual agreement on a professional basis should preclude the arbitrary exercise of unilateral authority by boards of education and the use of the

[25] *Ibid.*, August 26, 1962.
[26] *Ibid.*, March 22, 24, 28, 30, 1962.

strike by teachers," and that "extreme differences" should be resolved by arbitration through a board of professional and lay groups.[27] "Economic sanction is our word for strike" a New Jersey delegate had declared at the NEA's hundredth convention in Denver in July, and Executive Secretary Dr. William G. Carr had warned teachers against joining unions, with the advice that "a public school is not a factory." AFT President Carl H. Megel retorted that the NEA had every reason to be "frightened," and reiterated the company union charge that the association was controlled by school administrators whom he equated with industrial employers. The NEA reply was that "teachers and school administrators are colleagues, not opponents." [28]

About the same time AFT President Megel was being challenged by a more militant faction within the organization, especially from New York City, which tried to unseat him in the voting for officers at the Detroit convention.[29] When Megel won by a narrow margin, New York *Times* education editor Fred M. Hechinger saw looming ahead the possibility of a three-way division of the nation's teacher representation: the NEA's type of professional association, a moderate teachers' organization, or a more militant and dissident one.[30]

Back in New York City, UFT President Cogen succeeded in postponing the walkout scheduled for April 10, 1962, for one day, and asked the city to reopen talks. But the running disputes between Governor Rockefeller and Mayor Wagner on the matter of state aid left issues so unresolved that some 20,000 teachers struck on April 11 and closed about 25 schools. The following day the Board of Education obtained a court order restraining the union from further action that would interfere with operations. Later the board said it would "with-

27 *Ibid.*, April 1, 1962.
28 *Ibid.*, July 4, 7, 8, 1962.
29 American Federation of Teachers, *Convention Proceedings* (abridged), August, 1960, pp. 75, 89.
30 New York *Times*, August 26, 1962.

hold general action" against teachers pending a review of the Condon-Wadlin law.[31] And by April 25, after the governor and the mayor had worked out a formula under which the state advanced more aid, the Board of Education resumed negotiations with the union.[32]

The negotiations were long and arduous, the main stumbling block being the board's demand for a no-strike contract that would end on June 30—the last day of the school year. Very wisely, the board appointed the counsel to the City Department of Labor, Miss Ida Klaus, to conduct the negotiations, and as a full-time director of staff relations to develop sound policies and carry on the day-to-day task of administering contracts and processing agreements.[33]

Under the new arrangement a collectively bargained contract was reached in September, 1962, and 8,698 union members against 920 voted to accept it, although it called for major concessions. "We consider this an overwhelming vote of confidence in the union by the teachers," declared Mr. Cogen. "The signing of the contract will put an end to the years of turmoil that have plagued the school system."[34] As demanded by the board the contract ran from July 1, 1962, to June 30, 1963, and contained a no-strike clause. On the other hand the salary range, effective July 1, was advanced to begin with $5,300 instead of $4,800, and to rise to a top of $10,445 from $9,450.[35]

In the country as a whole the AFT reported a membership of 56,156 in 428 locals in 1961, of whom slightly more than

[31] *MLR*, June, 1962, pp. 681–82.

[32] *Ibid.* Like the AFT the UFT was under a cloud at this time because of pending election of officers in which the more militant officers aimed to unseat President Cogen. But just as President Megel had won, so did President Cogen. (New York *Times*, May 1, 1962; August 27, 1962 [editorial].)

[33] Lawyer Klaus had been the chief author of Mayor Wagner's pioneer program for collective bargaining in municipal agencies, and U.S. Secretary of Labor Arthur Goldberg had called her to Washington as principal drafter of the federal labor relations code which President Kennedy promulgated. She had also been serving as a consultant to the school board. (New York *Times*, August 23, 1962 [editorial].)

[34] New York *Times*, September 17, 1962; October 2, 1962.

[35] *Ibid.*, October 4, 19, 1962; *MLR*, July, 1962, p. 902.

half were women—33,700.[36] But when we measure this advance in unionization against the nation's total of more than 1,700,000 noncollege teachers it is clear that the federation has much to do.

And now what is the state of unionization among college and university teachers, many of whom are so poorly paid that they have been called the proletarians of the professions? The American Association of University Professors (AAUP) with its 46,500 members is strictly a "professional" organization. Like the AFT with its 76,000 members, and unlike the NEA with a membership of some 813,000, it does not admit administrators to membership. It is concerned with the general advancement of the profession, such as the defense of academic freedom, tenure, and salary increases. So far it has nothing to do with collective bargaining, although it has taken no official position for or against the unionization of professors.[37]

As long ago as the late 1920s, Columbia University Professor John Dewey told a membership meeting of the New York City Teachers' Union Local 5 of the AFT "Why I Am a Member of the Teachers' Union." These were his words:

If the teachers today, especially in our larger centers, are not in the position of intellectual serfs, it is due more, I am confident, to the energetic and aggressive activity of the teachers' unions than to any other cause . . . the Teachers' Union was the first teachers' organization to protest against the Lusk Law [and] the bills introduced in the Legislature which would involve censorship of history teaching. . . .

We live in an industrial age and it is academic folly and mere phantasy to suppose that the conduct of public education can be divorced from the prominence which economic, industrial and financial questions occupy in all other phases of our social life.[38]

By 1935, Local 5 had accumulated about 2,000 members as well as a big headache over "Communist domination," and at

[36] U.S. BLS Bull. 1320, 1961, pp. 30, 62.
[37] Harold Seymour, "Divided, the Profession Weighs the Pros and Cons of Unionism," New York State Industrial Bulletin, January, 1962, pp. 17–20.
[38] The American Teacher, January, 1928, pp. 4, 5.

the AFT convention of that year, 700 members asked for revocation of the charter. When the convention refused the request, the protestants quit the Teachers' Union and formed the Teachers' Guild. Then in 1941, with Communist domination still strong, the AFT did revoke the Local 5 charter and gave it to the Teachers' Guild, which became Local 2.[39] Local 25 was also chartered as the only college teachers' union in the metropolitan area affiliated with the AFT. With Professor William Withers as president and Professor Dewey one of its prominent members, the new local resolved to refrain from all but strictly professional activities for at least one year. Nevertheless, along with Local 5 it passed out of existence. At its convention in 1960 the AFT resolved to establish a College and University Department with the aim of organizing College teachers, and today the federation has 24 locals in 12 states, probably none of which has been recognized as bargaining agent for the faculty, however. And there have been no strikes.[40]

It must be concluded, therefore, that up to now most college and university teachers are not disposed to join a union; and some believe that if the AAUP increases its pressure to improve the economics of the profession, there is little probability of unionism in the future.[41] On the other hand there is the view that, while this is not the time for the AFT to set up a corps of organizers, a likely outcome of the "tidal wave" of students which is expected to innundate colleges and universities in this decade will be the organization of college teachers into "something more formidable than the present American Association of University Professors." In fact, in a recent letter to the AAUP from the vice-president for the colleges of UFT

[39] New York *Times*, April 12, 1962.
[40] Seymour, "the Pros and Cons of Unionism," p. 18; American Federation of Teachers, *Convention Proceedings* (abridged), August, 1960, p. 67.
[41] Seymour, "the Pros and Cons of Unionism," p. 20; see also a discussion of "Professors, Physicians, and Unionism," by Professor Melvin Lurie in *Bulletin* of the American Association of University Professors, September, 1962, pp. 272–76.

Local 2 we learn that the New York City Community College has had a union shop for a decade.[42]

Nurses

In sharp contrast to the turbulent relations between unionized teachers and their professional organization, the American Nurses' Association (ANA) has developed a unique plan for collective bargaining with the employers of their members without subscribing to trade unionism. We have seen in Chapter 17 that in its 1962 convention the association supported the "courageous nurses" of several state associations who, by "orderly" action considered not in violation of their no-strike pledge, had resigned en masse to obtain better conditions of employment. But this, it was emphasized, was not an endorsement of nurses' membership in trade unions.

Apparently fearful of union inroads under the New Deal, the association had declared in 1937 that "in their professional organizations nurses have the instruments best fitted and equipped to improve every phase of their working and professional lives." [43] And in a special effort to meet the needs of members, the ANA convention of 1946 gave a prominent place to an economic security program aimed to secure reasonable and satisfactory conditions of employment for nurses while it assured the public of continued nursing service. In 1950 a no-strike policy was adopted. Now a plank in the association's platform reads that the ANA will "asssist nurses to improve their working conditions through strengthening economic programs, using group techniques such as collective bargaining." [44]

What is the procedure for realizing this unprecedented aim? We have a detailed analysis by a college professor who makes

[42] American Association of University Professors *Bulletin*, Spring, 1963, pp. 74–75; David Hamilton, "Will the College Teachers Organize?" I.U.D. *Digest*, Spring, 1962, p. 128.

[43] *MLR*, July, 1961, p. 699.

[44] American Nurses' Association, *Release, on Platform 1962–1964*.

it clear that the ANA neither engages in collective bargaining nor establishes minimum employment standards. This, he says, is the responsibility of the State Nurses' Associations, who negotiate contracts with employers when so authorized by the nurses involved. In 1960 there were 75 such agreements in effect involving 115 institutions and covering some 8,000 nurses in varying numbers from less than ten to 2,500. In some of these agreements there was a maintenance-of-membership provision which required all professional nurses to be members of the State Associations or become members within 30 days after the contract was signed. If they did not do so they were subject to dismissal by the hospital on request of the State Association.[45] Nurses are forbidden to be members of more than one collective bargaining group, but membership in another organization is not prohibited. Moreover, if their State Associations are not bargaining for them they are free to elect a trade union to do so while retaining association membership.[46] For example, an ANA officer tells this writer that nurses employed in United Mine Workers' hospitals are represented by that union's bargaining committee in order to receive their pensions.

Collective bargaining progress to attain economic security for nurses has thus been slow but steady, Professor Kruger notes. One obstacle has been the attitude of nurses themselves, who appear to confuse bargaining with unionism, which they view as unprofessional. Another is that employers continue to resist collective bargaining. They want complete freedom to determine employment conditions. As Professor Theresa Wolfson put it in an address to an ANA conference in 1960, "Hospitals are the last bulwark in our society to retain authoritarian administration." [47] A third difficulty is the lack of adequate legal protection for nurses. While no federal law bars them

[45] *MLR*, July, 1961, pp. 702–03.
[46] *Ibid.*, p. 701.
[47] *Ibid.*, pp. 704–05.

from bargaining collectively to improve their economic status, and few states have acted on the subject, the protective provisions of the National Labor Relations Board exempt nonprofit hospitals and publicly owned hospitals from coverage, and the NLRB has declined to assert jurisdiction over most proprietary hospitals.[48]

Today, of the nation's 550,000 professional nurses, some 169,000 are members of the American Nurses' Association. In light of the fact that only some 8,000 of these are included in collective bargaining agreements, it is probable that not many, if any, nurses outside the ANA have joined trade unions.

Social Workers and Librarians

Insofar as social workers and librarians have been organized into unions, it looks as though they have been gathered in by the relatively new but flourishing American Federation of State, County and Municipal Employees (AFSME).

SOCIAL WORKERS

It was not until 1930 that the United States Census Bureau classified social work as a distinct profession. But the American Association of Social Workers (AASW) had been created nine years earlier with one of its aims that of increasing salaries, the founders having been convinced that the prevailing level prevented attraction of properly trained personnel.[49] By

---

[48] *Ibid.* After a recent study of unionization of nonprofessional workers in nonprofit hospitals—employees in housekeeping, dietary, laundry and nursing service departments who are usually classified as aides, orderlies, porters, maids, and helpers—the investigator concludes (against the views of hospital managements) that the best way to prevent strikes is to permit employees to organize and bargain collectively. "Michigan's experience suggests," she says, "that hospital unions are not prone to strike when other avenues of settlement are open to them" and that their rights "can be fully protected without causing jeopardy to patient lives." (Estelle Hepton, *Battle for Hospitals*, Bull. 49 [New York State School of Industrial and Labor Relations, Cornell, New York], 59 pp.)

[49] Shlakman, "White Collar Workers and Professional Organizations," p. 220.

1933, in the depth of the depression, the Association recorded a membership of 7,500—six women to every one man.[50] It was at that time that some social workers openly questioned certain practices of the AASW, especially its preoccupation with "professionalism" and the domination by high-salaried executives. There were also new recruits who had not been exposed to professional discipline—numerous unemployed white-collar people who came into the service when the federal government assumed responsibility for unemployment relief. Hence a rank-and-file movement emerged which challenged the assumption of identity of interest between executives and practitioners, and leaned toward the labor movement. The prompt reaction of the national organization was that in 1935 its New York City chapter's Committee on Employment Practice declared that

[collective bargaining] is a tool that may reasonably be used wherever the employer-employee relationship exists. . . . For social workers, the strike will seldom be a feasible weapon because of the necessity of protecting the interests of clients. . . . We should not, however, rule out the method of the strike as inherently impossible. . . . We should only hold that the conditions must be exceptional and the client must be protected.[51]

And AASW responded further in 1945 when it declared that "the right of individuals to bargain collectively and to be represented by a union of their choice is recognized and approved by the Association." The union of their choice proved to be the United Office and Professional Workers of America (CIO), which the association president believed was performing useful work in extending collective bargaining and lifting work stand-

[50] Mary Clarke Burnett, "Training for Social Work," *Encyclopaedia of the Social Sciences,* XIV, 184, 186.

[51] Shlakman, "White Collar Workers and Professional Organizations," pp. 221–25; *The Compass,* American Association of Social Workers, "Standards of Employment Practice," November, 1935, pp. 16–17. For another point of view see Virginia P. Robinson, "Is Unionization Compatible with Social Work," *The Compass,* May, 1937, pp. 5–9.

ards, and the hope was expressed for "continued cooperation
with the U.O.P.W.A. in our many common concerns." [52] Only
five years later, however, this union was expelled by the CIO
for its left-wing activities, and began rapidly to disintegrate.
Hence, since the AASW was strictly a professional organization,
although sympathetic to unionism, the relatively few social
workers who wanted to retain union affiliation had to look elsewhere. And by that time the American Federation of State,
County and Municipal Employees (AFSCME) was ready to
receive them.

It was in 1932 that a small union of 5,000 Wisconsin state
employees—the American Federation of Government Employees—was at work to save the civil service of that state from
being abolished, and out of the success emerged the AFSCME,
which received a charter from the American Federation of Labor in 1936.[53] The organization was led by Arnold S. Zander,
who held a master's degree in city planning and a Ph.D. in public administration from the University of Wisconsin.[54] Dr.
Zander has been reelected president of the federation at every
convention since that time and the membership has grown to
more than 200,000 in 1,561 local unions, with an estimated potential of a million or more members. The union took a constructive step forward in August, 1956, when it achieved a
merger with the Government and Civic Employees' Organizing Committee, formerly of the CIO, which removed the ele-
ment of competition from the public employee field.[55] There
has been competition from the Teamsters, Building Service
Employees, and independent unions, however, and consider-

[52] Shlakman, "White Collar Workers and Professional Organizations," p. 225.
[53] American Federation of State, County and Municipal Employees
(AFSCME), The Public Employee, March, 1958, pp. 4, 12; and see Leo
Kramer's Labor's Paradox (New York, John Wiley & Sons, 1962), Chapter I.
[54] Business Week, "Unions Eye Municipal Employees," March 21, 1959, pp.
117–18.
[55] Ibid., p. 121; AFSCME, Convention Proceedings, 1958, p. 327.

able general opposition. Nevertheless, Professor John T. Dunlop of Harvard is reported to have tagged the federation "one
of the unions of the future." [56]

"We have standing against us an organization called the
United Public Workers of America, CIO" President Zander
told the delegates in a stirring address at the 1948 convention
of AFSCME. "We are seeking the same kind of members, ex-
cepting that we do not want the Communists. We draw the
line there, and I trust we will be able to find them before they
get in." He added that groups were falling away from the
UOPWA, "some of them coming over to us. The opportunity
to move in there and do a job is immediate. . . . The whole
world needs this organization." [57] Again at the convention of
1952 Zander declared that "we are going out from here to
build this Union so that we may have the kind of structure . . .
which our members can use in improving their working conditions . . . [and] their positions in society . . . in doing all the
things that need to be done in order to improve the machinery
of democracy in our country." [58]

Civic groups who oppose the AFSCME hold that the union
policy of seeking across-the-table salary increases harms attempts of state and city governments to recruit the most competent people; that "lobbying is the logical counterpart in public
employment to the right to strike." The retort of the federation to this reasoning is that "we believe in collective bargaining instead of collective begging." It condones a strike only
as a last resort, however.[59]

The AFSCME describes itself as something unique in American labor history—as "a national union of local government

[56] Wilson R. Hart, *Collective Bargaining in the Federal Civil Service* (New
York, Harper & Brothers, 1961), p. 135.
[57] AFSCME, *Convention Proceedings*, 1948, pp. 21, 23.
[58] *Ibid.*, 1952, p. 194.
[59] *Business Week*, "Unions Eye Municipal Employees," March 21, 1959, pp.
117, 120; Hart, *Collective Barguining in the Federal Civil Service*, p. 135.

employees." [60] Seventy percent of its members are blue-shirt workers such as street cleaners and garbage collectors. Twenty percent are white-collar people ranging from institution attendants and traffic officers to tax assessors and clerks. The remaining 10 percent are classified as professional. [61] Here are some social workers, psychiatrists, and a few librarians. Although teachers fall within this jurisdiction the federation says it makes no attempt to organize them because they have their own national union.

AFSCME leaders are not inclined to be greatly worried about competition from industrial unions because, they explain, two entirely different sets of law cover each group and no union can afford to maintain separate establishments—one to cope with the problem of public employees and another with those of private enterprise. Therefore most of the competitors are said soon to fade out. They say that even the Teamsters show signs of backing away, for since that huge organization could not give advice to public employees some of their locals in New England had come over to the AFSCME by 1959. [62] But the now 210,000-member federation is not without international factionalism. Its great emphasis upon democracy and "voluntarism," together with the fact that officers have no hold upon members under either the Wagner Act or the Taft-Hartley Act means that any member can disagree with the officers and can leave the union if he or she is not satisfied. [63]

It was with the cooperation of social workers who had been members of the UOPWA that AFSCME's Community and So-

[60] Leo Kramer, *Labor's Paradox*, p. 154.

[61] *Business Week*, "Unions Eye Municipal Employees," March 21, 1959, p. 120.

[62] *Ibid.*, p. 121.

[63] It appears that the 1960 convention of the AFSCME was rife with factionalism. See Kramer's *Labor's Paradox*, Chapter 3, and the critical review of this book in *The Public Employee*, January 18, 1963.

cial Agency Employees (CSAE) was formed in 1949–50 and in less than eight years thereafter the CSAE had grown from a handful of members to an organization of more than 3,200 in 82 chapters, including those of Philadelphia, Chicago, Detroit, Cleveland, and St. Louis. Its New York City Local 1707 had by that time organized most of the city's nonprofit, nongovernment community and social agencies, some 50 in all; and having reached a milestone in its efforts when it signed its first master contract in 1955, with ten group-work agencies affiliated with the Federation of Jewish Philanthropies, it could boast of the largest number of community agency employees in the United States.[64] Three years later, at the personal request of Governor Averell Harriman, Local 1707 averted a scheduled strike by signing a two-year contract with seven of the Jewish agencies which included a "career salary plan" for professional case workers as well as salary increases.[65] Today, CSAE Local 1707 has a membership of some 3,500—a third in social agencies. Of these about 300 are social workers and 700 are clerical employees, some 75 percent of whom are women.[66]

New York District 37 of AFSCME has city-employed social workers who choose to be unionized, but its 54 locals are largely made up of maintenance people and clerical workers and others. For example, it has maintenance employees in the Bronx Zoo, the Museum of Natural History, the Metropolitan and Brooklyn museums, Hayden and Coney Island planetariums. It also has hundreds of clerical and administrative employees of the New York City Transit Authority. The special objective of District 37 has been to organize city-wide clerical and administrative services and to win exclusive bargaining

[64] AFSCME, *The Public Employee*, May, 1957, pp. 20–21.
[65] *Ibid.*, April, 1958, p. 25.
[66] Information given to this writer by the office of Local 1707, March 4, 1963.

rights for them. It noted that clerical workers had not had a salary raise since 1954, but that before 1960 those in District 37 had received several jumps in their salaries.[67]

Gains for clerical and maintenance workers were also made by the Community and Social Agency Employees Local 1707 in 1958 when, as reported by the AFSCME's newspaper, it signed a contract with the New School for Social Research which included a 35-hour week for them. A 35-hour week and salary adjustments were also won in new contracts with the New York Society for Ethical Culture, and with Hadassah.[68] Other members of this growing local union include attorneys, psychologists, cooks, counselors, and fund raisers, as well as case workers.[69]

It was largely the so-called Little Wagner Act of March 31, 1958, that made possible the organizing strides in the New York metropolis. By this edict city employees were granted almost the same bargaining rights as workers in private industry—the right to join unions of their choices and exclusive bargaining rights for majority unions. It will be recalled, however, that under the State Condon-Wadlin law all state and city employees are subject to dismissal if they strike.

In the nation as a whole the field of public employees is largely unorganized, and the aspiring AFSCME has a gigantic task ahead. For the membership of more than 200,000 must be seen against the backdrop of upwards of 3,000,000 state and local employees exclusive of nearly 3,000,000 in state and local educational systems.[70]

Returning to the social workers, what can be said of the re-

[67] AFSCME, *The Public Employee*, November, 1959, pp. 10–11. After a four-day stoppage of 700 employees of the zoo, museums, and art galleries in 1958, District 37 and Mayor Wagner came to an agreement which brought substantial salary increases and correction of "inequities" in pay under new job classifications. (*Ibid.*, July, 1958, p. 15.)

[68] *Ibid.*, April, 1958, p. 33; *Ibid.*, July, 1958, pp. 30–31.

[69] *Ibid.*, May, 1957, p. 20.

[70] Everett M. Kassalow, "New Union Frontier: White-Collar Workers," in *Harvard Business Review*, January–February, 1962, p. 50.

lations between the AFSCME and their professional society—the National Association of Social Workers, which the AASW became in 1955 after a merger of seven organizations and which has 163 chapters throughout the nation? The answer is, according to officials on both sides, that there is not only friendly cooperation between the two bodies but that, while the great majority of the 105,000 social workers reported by the U.S. Women's Bureau (six out of ten of them women) identify themselves with agency executives (as do librarians), many of those who are union members are active in the NASW. Insofar as it has gone, therefore, the unionization of social workers differs from that of the teachers, who created their own national union, and from that of the nurses, whose professional organization takes care of their needs.

LIBRARIANS

When we come to librarians it is difficult to find a trace of unionism in the United States, and there seems to be little discussion of the subject. In fact, in New York City, faces go blank when one broaches the subject. In the general surge toward unionization after World War I, library unions were formed in five large eastern cities: in the Library of Congress and the Public Library of Washington, D.C., and in the New York, Boston, and Philadelphia public libraries. They were all affiliated with the American Federation of Labor. But the unions were not welcomed by the library executives. Here is the comment of the librarian of the Boston *Athenaeum:*

If these young women are to be taken at their own estimation in fixing salaries and assigning tasks and not on the judgment of the librarian, have we not reached a Russian standard of "self-determination" in the Boston Public Library? [71]

That unionization would mean intrusion into what was ex-

[71] Bernard Berelson, "Library Unionization," in *The Library Quarterly,* October, 1939, pp. 492–93.

clusively the chief librarian's province was one of the two major arguments against it. The other was that it was unprofessional and undignified. Nevertheless, the American Library Association became concerned about extending democracy into library administration, as well as about salaries, and at its conference in 1919 the New York union introduced two resolutions. One decried the discrimination against women in the profession, and the other called for improvement in salaries and working conditions, civil service status, the right to organize, union representation, and union-labor representation on library boards. Membership in the union was largely among the lower grades in library service, however; many of their statements were challenged by others, and the union fared badly in the library press. Moreover, we are told that, while there is no record of dissolution, none of these unions lasted beyond the early 1920s. That is, none but the Library of Congress union, which continued to exist, with more than 100 members in 1935. After that time it was weakened by internal dissention and in 1937 the AFL charter was surrendered and the organization disbanded.[72]

Since World War II, we are told, library unionism has become "a negligible portion of the submerged tenth of the American trade union movement, with about a dozen locals scattered from Butte, Montana, to Washington, D.C." Independent local staff organizations had become far more widely adopted than unions.[73] Librarians have increasingly identified themselves with the administration, and while they are dissatisfied with salaries and working conditions, very few seem to think of joining a union. This is particularly true, perhaps, of a metropolitan area like New York. Several years ago the AFSCME tried to organize New York City librarians but with

[72] *Ibid.*, pp. 495, 496, 503.
[73] Orme W. Phelps, "Organization of Employees, with Special Reference to Library Personnel," in *The Library Quarterly*, January, 1946, pp. 28, 31.

no success. On the other hand, its Detroit local brought Detroit Public Library employees into the union in 1949, and ten years later it was reported that the annual salaries of members had increased by more than $1,500 a year.[74] AFSCME has also organized a reasonably effective union of library workers and professionals in Milwaukee.

Office Employees

When we recall from Chapter 13 the technological revolution which office work has undergone in the past 60 years, with its high percentage of women whose duties range from typing to electronic-computer programming in small and in large offices and everywhere in the business world from insurance companies to manufacturing plants, it is certain that the Office Employees' International Union (OEIU) has had no simple task in its drive to organize them. In an address at the Union's fifth convention in 1953, former Secretary of Labor Frances Perkins remarked that here was "an experiment in a new field never before organized so far as I know, anywhere in the world." She stressed the peculiarly delicate relationship between office employees and managements where personal loyalty is important in handling the confidential matters of their firms. She noted also that 60 percent of OEIU members were women who held official union positions on both the national and local level.[75]

We have seen that some office workers received an introduction to unionism in the Summer School for Office Workers in the 1930s. It was in the next decade that the Office Workers' International Union was organized. It received a charter from the American Federation of Labor in 1945 when it started

[74] AFSCME, *The Public Employee*, November, 1959, p. 12.
[75] Office Employees International Union AFL, Fifth Convention, *Proceedings*, June, 1953, p. 210.

an active organizing campaign.[76] Hence, by 1949, the union's president, Paul R. Hutchins, reported that despite "the infamous Taft-Hartley Act . . . which enables employers legally to utter practically any type of anti-union statement as long as they do not actually threaten discharge or discrimination because of union membership or activity," the OEIU "has continued to move forward . . ." as a result of elections under the National Labor Relations Board. Mr. Hutchins said the union had more than 200 locals in the United States and Canada ranging in size from 15 or 20 to 3,000 members, and that the union had more than 500 collective bargaining agreements covering employees in almost every type of industry and trade: "mining, construction, manufacturing, wholesale and retail trades, finance, insurance, real estate, public utilities, transportation, broadcasting and the service industries." Noted among several examples of organizing success was that of a Cleveland copper company in which the OEIU displaced the United Office and Professional Workers.[77] The office is the nerve center of present-day industry, President Hutchins urged, and he was "amazed" to find that "organization has not destroyed or jeopardized the amicable relationship between management and worker but that on the contrary in many outstanding instances has enhanced such relationship." [78]

The OEIU convention of 1953 elected Howard Coughlin as its new president, and in his acceptance speech he said the union's goal was not only to organize office workers "who are on the average, the poorest-paid workers in the United States . . . but to secure for them the highest possible gains . . . in so far as wages, hours and working conditions are concerned . . . we will, without doubt, create the largest International Union

[76] *Ibid.*, p. 7.
[77] Paul R. Hutchins, "Office Workers are Organizing," *American Federationist*, October, 1949, pp. 8–9, 42–43.
[78] *Ibid.*, September, 1950, pp. 22–23.

of the American Federation of Labor," [79] a brave ambition in the light of more recent developments, as we shall see.

This was the decade of the introduction of electronic computers into the office, it will be recalled, and an interesting sidelight on the effects of mechanization was that, while it reduced the demand for routine workers, most of whom were women, the standardization of processes tended to displace work which had been peculiar to each firm, and this made women freer to choose employers. Nonunion offices were, therefore, sometimes obliged to compete with union offices where the new international union president was at work to achieve an economic status at least equal to that of factory workers. A major grievance among clerical workers was that the former gap in vacation policies, paid holidays, sick leave, and other benefits between them and factory workers had been closed through union activity in industry.[80]

Moreover, "our union, as a collective bargaining policy," Mr. Coughlin told a congressional committee during hearings on automation and technological change in 1956, "is insisting on bump-back provisions in layoff clauses." He meant, he said, that individuals who were displaced would be retrained by the company for the automated job, and those who had been promoted within the company "will be given the right to bump back in accordance with their seniority and qualifications." In the event of permanent layoff, "we are asking for and receiving a liberal severance-pay program. Through collective bargaining we can protect our membership who are touched by the introduction of electronic equipment. In unorganized offices there is no such protection." [81] In this field the union presi-

[79] Office Employees International Union, AFL, Fifth Convention, *Proceedings*, 1953, pp. 331, 333; Robert A. Bedolis, "Union Profile: The Office Workers," in *Management Review*, June, 1962, p. 14.

[80] *MLR*, April, 1956, p. 414; Kassalow, "New Union Frontiers," p. 47.

[81] U.S. Congress, Joint Economic Committee, Hearings, *Automation and Technological Change*, 1955, p. 217.

dent's chief concern was that abrupt technological changes might suddenly put a large number of people out of work, although he thought office jobs as a whole might even increase.[82]

Organization of office workers has been and continues to be a tough, uphill problem for the OEIU, which today has a membership of only some 53,000 in a total of some 9,000,000 clerical and kindred workers, according to the 1960 census. The various reasons are traceable. One of the barriers has been that, although small offices are beginning to use computer centers for some of their work, there are thousands of small offices throughout the country in which employer-employee relations are close. The women and girls are office-oriented, their interests employer-centered. Some hope to move into management positions and they want to learn all they can that might help toward promotion. These women place high value upon responsibility and harmony, upon prestige and status, and are averse to daring union maneuvers, strike threats, harsh bargaining, or strained management-employee relations.[83]

A few scattered groups of office workers have developed because of common and specific grievances, nevertheless, a research associate in the Industrial Relations Center at the University of Chicago recalls. One of the most prominent of these was the New York City Bookkeepers, Stenographers and Accountants Union (BS&AU) which claimed a membership of 3,000 in the early twenties, and which along with other unions of this type had been chartered directly by the American Federation of Labor as federal locals. By 1934 there were 34 such locals in the AFL, with the BS&AU in the lead. Then when the

[82] *MLR*, April, 1956, p. 416. A Bureau of Labor Statistics representative has noted to this writer that the number of office workers has declined about 25 percent in the last five years and that the prospect is that it will fall another four to five million in the next five years.

[83] Arthur B. Shostak, *America's Forgotten Labor Organization, a Survey of the Role of the Single-Firm Independent Union in American Industry* (Princeton University, Industrial Relations Section, 1962), pp. 56–57.

AFL refused to give this group a national union charter it turned to the Congress of Industrial Organizations and became the ill-fated United Office and Professional Workers' of America. The resulting competition stimulated the AFL to the extent of chartering 150 locals of office employees which became the OEIU. The new organization was a "strictly business" union which stressed the differences between white- and blue-collar people. The UOPWA was ideological in its approach, stressing the common interests of all workers; and it was in 1950, when it endorsed Henry Wallace as a presidential candidate, that the CIO discarded it. Many of its members then joined other unions rather than go unorganized.[84]

Identification of white-collar workers with management has become more tenuous in the larger offices where their jobs are rationalized, standardized, diluted, routinized, and noisy. Here, Ida Hoos reports that the environment increasingly resembles that of the factory, and the job content of the girl who punches cards or sorts checks by machine differs little from that of the girl who stamps out metal disks in a plant. Yet for the greater distinction they believe it gives them these girls cling to their "office complex." Many of them, along with tabulating-machine operators, have become staunch members of unions, however; and some managements, to offset the trend, have tried to appeal to prestige-hungry key-punch girls by calling them "machine bookkeepers." [85]

Furthermore, many companies, determined not to repeat former mistakes, now deliberately plan action to prevent the desire for unionization among their clerical workers, or at least to keep the unions weak. In a recent study of the National Office Management Association of 2,002 companies employing nearly half a million workers, only 6 percent were found

[84] Elinor Waters, "Unionization of Office Employees," *The Journal of Business*, October, 1954, pp. 285–86, 291.

[85] Hoos, *Automation in the Office*, 1961, pp. 82–83, 105.

to be fully or partly organized. Most of the firms had developed methods of handling grievances, had provided good physical conditions, reviewed salaries and fringe benefits at regular intervals. Half of them conducted training programs and provided written management policies.[86] The National Association of Manufacturers has also given collective attention to ways and means of providing satisfactions for those who work in offices and laboratories. Manufacturers realize all too well that the depersonalization of relations between them and the employees tends to turn attention to unions. "The heart of our efforts," they say, "lies in showing the employees that their company and their supervisors are really interested in what they are doing, and that they are considered to have a constructive part in the company's activties." [87]

Employees who hold better-paying jobs as a result of automation, such as computer operating and programming, may be less likely to organize because they have less to complain of, and because of the possibility that, when classified as professionals or executives, they will be excluded from bargaining under the Taft-Hartley law. The OEIU is reported to have won a recent victory in Buffalo, New York, however, when the National Labor Relations Board upheld the local union's contention that electronic data-processing occupations could be included in an appropriate bargaining unit.[88]

In the drive to unionize white-collar employees it is important to note that the forces which have made most office jobs

[86] Charles E. Ginder, "Unionization in the Office—a Report on a NOMA Survey," in *Office Executive*, January, 1961, pp. 11–14.

[87] Alfred G. Larke, "Spotlight on the Office Worker," in *Dun's Review*, April, 1957, pp. 42, 87. Professor Jack Barbash in an unpublished paper on "The Present Status and Future Course of the American Labor Movement," read at Oberlin College on October 18, 1962, has called this development "union-substitute strategy" in which management has the advantage under conditions of technological change. He warns, however, that the overhead cost of such strategy, the danger of overstaffing, and the industrializing of white-collar tasks could result in stirring up white-collar unionism.

[88] NLRB Case No. 3-RM-227 (1962).

more like those of the factory have been making the factory more like an office. In the automated plant, machine operators are no longer controlled by the speed of the machine but are monitors; and this, of course, further reduces the social distance between clerical and factory operators. The vertical unionization of many manufacturing companies has placed production and clerical workers under the jurisdiction of the same union where the "brotherhood" embraces everyone from those in accounting operations to the Class-C lathe operators.[89]

This development brings us to the most persistent organizing problem which the small OEIU has been facing—that within the house of labor itself, the determination of the industrial unions to increase their efforts to draw white-collar workers into their own organizations. It is significant that the employees of that 6 percent of the 2,002 companies in the National Office Management Association in 1960 were in unions affiliated not only with OEIU but with the United Automobile Workers, the United Steelworkers and even with the Teamsters and others.[90] Representatives of industrial unions insist that in the light of the decline of blue shirts their unions must organize white-collar people in some form or "we not only reduce our economic strength but we reduce our political strength." "We've got to grow. If we stand still we're dead." [91]

In a more recent analysis of the situation, the research director of the AFL-CIO Industrial Union Department voices the belief that there is enough flexibility in the labor movement and enough mutual interest among clerical, professional, and technical workers in big companies to make it probable that most of the serious organizing efforts of the 1960s will be made by the existing industrial unions. He holds that where

[89] Hoos, *Automation in the Office,* 1961, p. 82.
[90] Ginder, "Unionization in the Office," p. 14.
[91] AFL-CIO Industrial Union Department Conference, *Automation and Major Technological Change,* 1958, p. 21; "Why White Collar Workers Can't be Organized," *Harper's Magazine,* August, 1957, p. 45.

employees have been organized into entirely separate unions there have been "fairly sharp social cleavages" between them and the blue-collar people.[92] He has investigated the organization of white-collar workers in European countries where to some extent the formation of separate labor federations for them have been accepted, but he has come to the conclusion that this probably will not work in the United States. Here, he points out, economic power is basically organized along corporate lines and the white-collar worker who is employed by great corporations "will have to join together with his brother workers in production to be truly representative economically." [93]

The introduction of giant computers and other electronic devices in offices, continues Everett Kassalow, will generate group consciousness that will intensify the need for unionization. He cites a clause in the negotiated contract of the steelworkers with the American Can Company designed to help provide new jobs and training for office workers displaced by automation. Moreover, he suggests, as Ida Hoos has done, that it is easy to exaggerate the differences between blue- and white-collar people, and that once organized their collective bargaining and programs will doubtless be more similar than different. Major structural changes in labor organization will, therefore, be necessary. A special department for the new group should be set up at or near the top of the labor movement itself to take the place of the present arrangement in which representatives of manual workers' unions have most of the seats on the Executive Council. He concludes, *What will be called for over the next decade or two, if the job is to be accomplished successfully, is a veritable transformation of the institution itself."* [94]

[92] Kassalow, "New Union Frontiers," p. 49.
[93] AFL-CIO, Industrial Union Department Conference, *Automation and Major Technological Change,* 1958, p. 23.
[94] Kassalow, "New Union Frontiers," pp. 45, 51.

To all this the OEIU vehemently protests. Its director of organization has said that the union has recruited twice as many clerks through NLRB elections in the last four years as all the industrial unions combined. The union's President Coughlin sent complaints against Kassalow's plan to AFL-CIO President Meany and to Walter P. Reuther, who heads both the IUD and the United Auto Workers. Mr. Meany assured Mr. Coughlin of support of his union, but no reply came from Reuther,[95] who has recently been reported to be accumulating funds for an organizing campaign among office, technical, and professional people.

The trend toward industrial unionism for office workers has been explained by one observer as being the result of the relatively weak position of these people without the support of production workers. And this situation has prompted the OEIU to concentrate its efforts in organized industrial plants instead of in companies which largely employ white-collar workers. But here it faces the fact that office employees in manufacturing plants are aware of the industrial union and probably credit it with some of their gains. And they may be daughters, wives, or sisters of production workers. Also, industrial union organizers are familiar with both the industry and the particular company management, and so, if they are sophisticated, they may be able to make more effective appeals to the office people than can a white-collar union coming from outside.[96]

On the other hand, some office employees continue to appear to feel that belonging to a manual workers' union brings loss of status which they are spared if they join an independent union that enables them to keep in more friendly touch with their supervisors. Being thus free of "outsiders" they can

---

[95] A. H. Raskin, "2 Unions Compete to Enroll Clerks," New York *Times,* January 31, 1961.

[96] Waters, "Unionization of Office Employees," p. 288.

be "all in a family" together.[97] Howard Coughlin is aware that one of his organizing blocks is the interest of women in promotion. He says the union sometimes refers to women as "until" workers. "They are always working until they get married, until they have a baby, until the house is paid off, or until they retire." [98]

It is noteworthy in this context that in 1953, according to Elinor Waters' estimates, the OEIU-AFL had only 40,000 members in a total of 233,000 office workers in other white-collar international unions, including the Brotherhood of Railway Clerks (AFL), which had 130,000, and the Communication Workers of America (CIO) with 20,000. There were 76,000 of them in independent unions, and the industrial unions reported 240,000. Among these were 80,000 in the automobile workers union (CIO), 60,000 in the steelworkers union (CIO), 40,000 in electrical workers' unions (AFL and CIO), and 60,-000 in other organizations including the Teamsters. In all, by this estimate, 549,500 nongovernment office employees were in unions; and even this number represented only 13 percent of the eligible office force of 4.3 million.[99]

We have no comparable data on the unionization of the well over 9,000,000 clerical and kindred workers in 1960, 15 percent of all employees, more than two thirds of them women.[100] The Bureau of Labor Statistics reported not quite 53,000 members in the OEIU in 1961 and the union's president claimed 65,000 to 70,000 in late 1962.[101] But it still looks as though there are well over twice as many office employees in industrial and independent unions as are in the OEIU. Seventy percent of all

[97] *Ibid.,* 291.

[98] Robert A. Bedolis, "Union Profile: The Office Workers," *Management Record*, N.I.C.B., June, 1962, p. 20; U.S. House of Representatives, Hearings, *Equal Pay for Equal Work*, Second Session, 1962, p. 255.

[99] Waters, "Unionization of Office Employees," pp. 287–88.

[100] *MLR*, November, 1962, p. 1211; *U.S. WB Bull. 275*, p. 7.

[101] *U.S. BLS Bull. 1320*, pp. 24, 62; a letter to this writer from Howard Coughlin, December 21, 1962.

OEIU members are women, and it is possible that the proportion is as high elsewhere.

Telephone Operators

Telephone operators under the leadership of such women as Julia O'Connor and Mary Gannon have played no small role in the union activities of telephone employees. Yet telephone unions have never succeeded in attainting a collective bargaining system on a recognized national scale, largely owing to the determined resistance of Bell System companies, including their parent American Telephone and Telegraph Company, and to jurisdictional and ideological disputes among telephone workers themselves. Moreover, the dramatic advance of the dial system has impaired the effectiveness of union strike harassment. We have seen that by 1930 the Bell companies owned more than nine tenths of all dial telephones and nearly that proportion of those still operated manually, and that Secretary of Labor Frances Perkins declared that during the cutover from manual to dial the companies had set "an almost perfect example of technological change made with a minimum of disaster" for the operators. To hear of unsatisfactory industrial relations as employees became unionized thus comes as a surprise to the interested observer. Much of what follows up to the mid-century has been taken from Professor Jack Barbash's careful study of *Unions and Telephones.*[102]

The International Brotherhood of Electrical Workers (IBEW) —a craft union of linemen and cable splicers—was the early organizer of telephone operators. Only five operators' unions were found in 1909, and they were affiliated directly with the American Federation of Labor as federal unions outside the IBEW. Some were said to have been "more like social clubs

[102] See also Joel Seidman and Associates, *The Worker Views His Union* (Chicago University Press, 1958), Chapter 7.

than trade unions," and the IBEW had looked askance upon
women as members. They considered them flighty and un-
dependable, and declared that they joined a union only when
they needed help, then dropped out when the trouble was
over. But when the Commercial Telegraphers' Union began to
assert jurisdiction over the operators, the IBEW opened its
drive for them. Hence, the first permanent organization of
these girls within the IBEW was established in Boston in 1912,
and in the following year they conducted a strike to preserve
their organization. According to the electricians, however, the
high turnover among these young women required a "per-
petual motion" organizing campaign to keep the union alive.[103]

In 1915 a United States field investigator into wages and
conditions in telephone operating declared that, notwithstand-
ing her conviction that thorough organization of the operators
was essential, she was forced to conclude that "successful organization of telephone girls is practically impossible, or very
remote, under existing conditions." These conditions, said
Nelle B. Curry, were: a. the hostility of the companies to the
formation of unions; b. the youth and inexperience of the operators, since the vast majority of the girls left the service after
about two years; and c. the keen competition for positions.
The reasons given by the telephone companies for their resistance to unionism, she reported, were that as a public utility
their first duty was to the public. Therefore, obstructive measures such as strikes could not be tolerated. Also employers
were certain that a union composed of telephone girls would
be an irresponsible body.[104]

In the absence of the ability of the girls to organize and enforce just demands, Miss Curry recommended establishment of
a six-hour day and a minimum age of 18 years. She said the

[103] Jack Barbash, *Unions and Telephones, The Story of the Communications
Workers of America* (New York, Harper & Brothers, 1952), pp. 3–4, 19.
[104] Nelle B. Curry, U.S. Commission on Industrial Relations, Report, *Investigation of the Wages and Conditions of Telephone Operating*, 1915, pp. 6–7.

girls received slightly better wages than in other occupations, but because many of them had no other means of support she advocated a minimum wage of $55 a month. She added that the financial reports of the companies which showed large dividends to stockholders were partly accounted for by withholding a portion of the real earnings of more than 50,000 girls who worked under a severe strain and rigid discipline that caused many nervous breakdowns.[105]

Despite the predictions, however, so many operators joined the IBEW that this man's organization scarcely knew what to do with them. At first it chartered the girls as sublocals, but after seven years of protest against second-class union citizenship, operators' locals were created with dues one half those of the men and with half the voting strength of the men's locals at conventions. Even then the electricians began to fear that the operators would become so numerous that they would control the organization, or at least influence delicate issues of jurisdiction. As the executive board put it:

We think there can be no rule of ethics or of human right which requires men handling the sting of electricity to submit forever to the rule of telephone operators in their methods and conditions of work because they have tried that arrangement for a while.

The immediate problem was solved by establishing a separate Telephone Operators' Department, and staunch unionist Julia O'Connor became its president.[106]

During World War I the membership of telephone employees in the IBEW rose to its highest levels. The scarcity of workers together with the need for uninterrupted service tended to strengthen the bargaining power of all unions. Furthermore, the Wilson administration was sympathetic to labor organization, and the National War Labor Board, which was authorized to adjust labor-management disputes, undoubtedly

[105] *Ibid.,* pp. 5, 7–8, 9, 10.
[106] Barbash, *Unions and Telephones,* pp. 4–5, 8, 18.

influenced workers to join unions of their own choosing. But at the same time the board set up machinery for the selection of employee representatives, which seemed to have been a factor giving company unions a start. In fact, the IBEW charged telephone companies with deliberately disobeying or evading the order to deal with employees' representatives by forming "company-owned and controlled organizations or associations." [107]

When the war was over, manpower shortages and the friendly attitude of the government prompted many business executives to devise new tactics to combat the "menace of unionism," as we have seen in the case of office employees. For them the Bolshevik revolution in Russia made every strike appear to be a forerunner of an American revolution. And there were plenty of strikes. In 1919, the Bureau of Labor Statistics reported an upsurge of more than four million strikers—in steel and even among actors and policemen. For this reason, unions in big industry were violently suppressed by court injunctions, professional strikebreakers, and state militia. The open shop became the hallmark of industrial relations policy —already well known in the telephone industry and a "patent device for getting rid of the unions," declared Julia O'Connor.[108]

When properties were turned back by the government, company unions in the form of committees or associations were developed by American Telephone and Telegraph Company affiliates to enable them to deal directly with employees in matters affecting their common interests and performance. Few or no membership dues were collected, and there were no general meetings of employees. Officers' meetings were held on company premises, and the time lost in association meet-

[107] *Ibid.*, pp. 6, 7.
[108] *Ibid.*, pp. 7–9.

ings was paid for by the company, as well as all operating expenses. Professor Barbash declares that, in keeping with the social and economic climate of the period, the structural principle of these associations was atomatization—many small units isolated from one another. He also suggests that IBEW policy matched this principle all too well by dealing with its members not as craft unions with industry-wide coordination, but as telephone operators, cable splicers, and linemen bargaining with their local companies with no industry approach. As a result the IBEW, which "was not the best managed of unions," was beset with "secessions, rival organizations, conflicts over status and autonomy." [109]

The National Federation of Telephone Workers (NFTW) came into being as a rival of the IBEW during the New Deal era of the 1930s, and by 1939—two years after the National Labor Relations (Wagner) Act was declared constitutional—it had collected 92,000 members. By 1946 the number had mounted to 217,549. But having sprung from an atmosphere of company unionism, the new union provided in its constitution that "member organizations . . . shall remain forever autonomous. . . ." Therefore, while A.T. & T. refused to recognize the NFTW, the constituent unions had no trouble being recognized by the managements who, according to Barbash, continued to regard them as "our boys." [110]

Early national assemblies of the NFTW took a stand against strikebreaking, and the switchboard operators emphasized what they termed "public relations" objections to the use of the strike. Nevertheless, when in 1914 a midwestern union member was demoted to the status of operator after holding a position as service observer for 22 years, 60 percent of the company's operators declared a stoppage during peak evening

[109] *Ibid.*, pp. 8, 9, 13, 16–19.
[110] *Ibid.*, pp. 26–28, 30, 52.

hours, and the demotion order was rescinded. About the same time a strike of 500 operators was declared against a Dayton, Ohio, company's practice of importing girls from other states to work alongside the local operators. The union said the scarcity of local girls was due to the low starting rate, but the company held it had to bring people from places not so directly affected by the war in order to meet the pressing local need. Before the strike ended it had spread outside Ohio, and 10,000 telephone workers had left their jobs. It was only the intervention of the War Labor Board that prevented it from spreading further.[111] Among other strike movements in 1946, the Washington Telephone Traffic Union, led by its firebrand president, Mary Gannon, staged a one-hour sitdown against what she charged to be "sweatshop practices and a drive on the part of the company to break the union." A year later 3,000 Washington, D.C., telephone operators held a "continuous meeting" for eight days "until our grievance is settled." [112]

The first and only nationwide strike in the telephone industry occurred in 1947 when 350,000 NFTW members walked out. The aim, among other things, was to establish industry-wide bargaining and to gain wage increases. The A.T. & T. refused to yield on the industry-wide issue and offered to submit the wage dispute to individual local arbitration, which Joseph A. Beirne, who had been president of the union since 1943, said would create a crazy quilt of awards. Because of the dial system, however, the strike did not last long. The A.T. & T. estimated that normal service was being provided for 20,000,-000 of the 26,000,000 telephones, and after some wage concessions on the part of several Bell companies the dispute ended with little violence. During its course the A.T. & T. did not recede from its position that all agreements must be on a local ba-

111 *Ibid.*, pp. 40, 41–42.
112 *Ibid.*, p. 57.

sis with individual companies. In fact, according to Barbash, the aim was clearly to weaken or destroy any union that presumed to be the national bargaining agent for telephone workers.[113]

The 1947 strike had critically shaken the NFTW, and its convention of 1946 proved to be the last when, under the forceful leadership of Joseph A. Beirne, it forfeited its name in favor of the Communications Workers of America (CWA).[114] Electing Mr. Beirne as president, which it has done on every occasion since that time, the new organization held its founding convention in 1947. It met as a national union rather than as an assembly of many autonomous organizations, which now made divisions that maintained considerable free action but less than they had been accustomed to. Many leaders vigorously disapproved of this change of structure. In other words they dissented from the one-national-union idea. Also, almost simultaneously with the birth of the CWA, a Telephone Workers' Organizing Committee was formed by the Congress of Industrial Organizations as a rival organization, and telephone workers had to ponder over which one to join. Soon, however, with women as well as men on amalgamating committees, the two organizations merged under the name of CWA (CIO) and later CWA of the AFL-CIO of which Joseph Beirne became a vice-president and member of the Executive Council. The other rival IBEW withdrew its affiliation from the CIO and

---

[113] *Ibid.*, pp. 65, 68, 69–70. Within the NFTW there had been much concern about getting equal pay for equal work for women, especially during the shortage of men when women were assigned to some of their jobs. There was also a campaign for a "skilled" instead of a semiskilled classification for the operators. It was the NFTU that prompted the U.S. Women's Bureau to make a study of *The Women Telephone Workers*, including nearly half of the membership, which the Department of Labor published in Bull. 207 and is noted in Chapter 18 above. (U.S. WB, *Release*, April 25, 1945, p. 5; Barbash, *Unions and Telephones*, p. 46.)

[114] Barbash, *Unions and Telephones*, pp. 79, 88–89; Shostak, *America's Forgotten Labor Organization*, pp. 64–65; New York *Times*, Section 12, April 7, 1963, advertisement: "CWA: A Modern Union for a Modern World."

became independent. Later it, too, joined the family of AFL-CIO.[115]

Out of the CWA bargaining negotiations with the Bell companies in 1949 came a series of events which led to an investigation by a congressional subcommittee on *Labor-Management Relations in the Bell Telephone System*. Here, during two sessions in 1950, were long-drawn-out presentations and arguments from representatives of the companies and of the CWA. The exhibit on "The Telephone Worker's Wage Case," presented by Sylvia B. Gottlieb, Research and Education Director of CWA, noted the problems of the union, which represented 320,000 telephone workers, and its struggle to improve their wages and working conditions in the face of "a union-busting program" on the part of the Bell System, which controlled practically all of the telephones in the country. Miss Gottlieb compared the hourly earnings of telephone workers with those in other industries to show that telephone wages had lagged behind. "Today telephone workers are among the lowest-paid organized workers in the United States," she charged, yet "CWA is dealing with a company which represents the most powerful financial accumulation of wealth in the United States and probably in the world." "In addition to paying low wages," she added, "the Bell System has carved the United States into as many as 100 different wage areas" and "workers doing precisely the same work are paid different wages throughout the country." [116]

In refutation of these and other charges, and in support of the position that the autonomy the different Bell Companies

115 Barbash, *Unions and Telephones*, pp. 79, 91–92, 109, 111. In 1953 Mrs. Jennie M. Hills was elected president of the Detroit, Michigan, CWA local union, and she was also secretary-treasurer of that city's CWA Council.

116 U.S. Senate Eighty-first Congress Subcommittee Hearings, *Labor-Management Relations in the Bell Telephone System*, Second Session (G.P.O., 1950), pp. 842–45. Bell System low-wage abuses of operators, which Senator Morse called "a pure case of exploitation," had been aired at length by the General Counsel of the NFTU at the Senate Hearings on Equal Pay for Equal Work for Women in 1945, pp. 129–44.

rightly applies to labor negotiations, another exhibit of 41 pages presented copies of Bell System illustrated advertisements from various city newspapers to show that "Telephone Wages Are Good." "All things considered," said a Chicago *Sun-Times*, "telephone operators are among the best paid white-collar girls in their communities for comparable work or skill. . . . We are trying our best to bargain collectively and calmly with our local CIO leaders. It's rather difficult when, in effect, they hold a 'loaded pistol' at the meetings." "We want telephone employees to be well paid," said the *Louisville-Journal*, "and we have submitted proof that they are well paid." [117]

Among eight senators who signed the majority report of this investigation were Herbert H. Lehman, Wayne Morse, Paul H. Douglas, and Hubert H. Humphrey. Their conclusions were that "bad labor-management relations exist in the Bell Telephone System [and that] these relations appear to be getting worse." "If the Bell System truly desires good relations with the labor organizations representing the employees, as management witnesses profess it does . . . then it must deal honestly and in a forthright manner with the representatives of its employees. On the other hand, the unions must . . . assume correspondingly greater responsibilities to the employees they represent, and to the Nation they serve. . . . The subcommittee is not impressed with the claims of management that bargaining can be more effective on the departmental level." [118]

Considerable attention had been given during the hearings to Bell company strategy under the Taft-Hartley law of 1947, especially the provisions which the subcommittee said the Bell System was taking advantage of by coming to the bargaining

---

[117] U.S. Senate Subcommittee Hearings, *Labor-Management Relations in the Bell Telephone System*, Second Session, 1950, pp. 875, 877.

[118] *Ibid.*, First Session, pp. 31, 32, 34.

table "without any intention of actually participating in the bargaining process." Instead, "management negotiators will confer and discuss union demands for months without getting down to serious bargaining. . . . These strategies and tactics have resulted in strikes. This Nation cannot afford strikes in this system." [119]

The minority views, presented by Robert A. Taft, H. Alexander Smith, and Richard M. Nixon, held that the majority's finding "has very little support from the evidence," that in fact labor relations were "relatively good, and that such difficulties as have occurred have been as much the fault of CWA's officials' drive for a concentration of power in their hands as of the company." The minority report pointed out that less than half of the more than 500,000 telephone employees were members of the CWA, that many of the some 250,000 of them were covered by contracts negotiated by AFL and independent unions which the CWA was out to absorb in a single nationwide bargaining unit composed of all employees in the Bell System. "The practical effect of the majority recommendations would be the establishment of the CIO union as the national collective bargaining agency of every employee in the Bell System." "We believe it would be unfortunate to force Nation-wide collective bargaining in the Bell System at the present time, without full study of the problems raised by Nation-wide bargaining." "To summarize, if labor relations . . . were bad, the record would have shown more grievances, more arbitration cases, more strikes and work stoppages, a greater number of NLRB orders, fewer applicants for employment, a higher turn-over rate, and lower morale. By all these tests the labor relations must be satisfactory to the employees themselves." [120]

The struggle of the CWA to attain nationwide collective

[119] *Ibid.*, pp. 33, 34.
[120] *Ibid.*, pp. 35–47.

bargaining continues today, reports a professor of sociology in a recent analysis. Its fight is not only with the Bell System, says one observer, but with the independent unions, the largest of which is the Alliance of Independent Telephone Unions (AITU), which has a membership of 125,000 employees of Bell companies—more than half as many as the some 260,000 that the CWA claimed in 1960. The two groups differ basically over what the policy of the government should be toward Bell System labor relations, and this impairs friendship between them. The independent unions want to continue dealing with separate companies, and they ask government aid in loosening the "unifying influence" of the A.T. & T. over the "closely knit Bell System." In other words they ask for antitrust action. The CWA wants government aid in enforcing centralization in labor negotiations so that the A.T. & T. will have to act as the "real employer" and bargain with the unions on a national basis.[121]

Meanwhile, it appears that both management and union have been doing some rethinking in the wake of the last major strike in the spring and summer of 1955, when the union conducted an 11-week walkout against the Southern Bell Telephone Company, during which switchboard operators and clerical workers joined linemen and plant people on a day-and-night picket line in good and bad weather. And their behavior won public sympathy, according to President Beirne. But the union's hope for deterioration of service through lack of maintenance did not materialize, because the automated telephone system of Southern Bell went right on putting through calls. The union won some points at issue, reported Beirne, "and management's attitude towards us underwent a marked change." Hence, "Just as the strike experience foreshadowed a series of changes in the Bell System's relationships with the union of its employees, so also it drove home to us . . .

[121] Shostak, *America's Forgotten Labor Organization*, pp. 66–68, 138.

an appreciation of the need for different and better tactics to enhance our collective bargaining efforts. . . . Both sides have learned the very real and present dangers of coming up automatically to the 'brink.' We have gained mutual respect for a sense of reserve." [122]

To celebrate its twenty-fifth anniversary in 1963, the CWA published as an advertisement an entire section of the New York *Times* Sunday edition under the title, *A Modern Union for a Modern World.* To make collective bargaining more effective, it explains, the CWA now conducts major negotiations on two levels—national and local. On the national level major agreements are arrived at with units of the Bell and General Telephone Systems, which follow a combination of "pattern" and "local" bargaining, and its 160 contracts terminate in almost every month of the year.

The first major agreement of the year with a subsidiary of each of these large nationwide corporations forms a pattern for all succeeding settlements. The pattern establishes a floor below which no local group can go, but above which each group can seek to improve additional provisions for local wages and working conditions.

The result is, according to the statement, that stronger groups can help the weaker ones. Also that the unified and relatively uniform approach enables the union to bargain collectively on such matters as health insurance, pensions, vacations, and sick pay, as well as on wages and working conditions. Since 1951 average hourly earnings in the telephone industry have risen more than 60 percent.[123]

Collective bargaining is basically the art of seeking to live together on the job, say the writers of the newspaper piece. "The only thing in life that is constant is change," and "CWA

[122] Beirne, *New Horizons for American Labor* (Washington, D.C., Public Affairs Press, 1962), pp. 60, 63–64.
[123] New York *Times*, April 7, 1963, Section 12, pp. 10–11.

is not afraid of change." The bitterness and hostility of earlier years are recalled as compared to the "generous doses of common sense and experience" today: "In the telephone industry, collective bargaining has become a conversation between equal forces. Neither side dominates or controls the other, and each knows it couldn't if it wanted to. Recognition of that important fact has led to mutual respect and sensible progress." [124]

The CWA also boasts of an expenditure of $480,000 a year "to broaden and train the leaders who must administer the day-to-day problems of its 300,000 members." Two women are among its officers: Mary H. Hanson, New England District Director, and Elaine T. Gleason, Long Lines Director, both of whom began as telephone operators.[125]

Today the CWA has some 130,000 women members—operators and clerical workers, and President Beirne praises "their loyalties, energies and militancy [which] are equal to any displayed by their fellow male unionists." [126] The AITU has 54,000 women; and in four other unions with a collective membership of some 62,000 doubtless half are women, though we have no reports here.[127]

Salesclerks

We have seen that before 1900 salesgirls and women in retail shops felt a need of organization to improve their economic status, but that they turned from unionization to organization of the shoppers, who soon formed the Consumers' League, which worked for their protection by law. At the turn of the century these women behind the counter numbered 142,000—nearly a fifth of all salespersons. Today they are a

[124] *Ibid.*, pp. 3, 10.
[125] *Ibid.*, pp. 13, 15.
[126] Beirne, *New Horizons*, p. 39.
[127] *U.S. BLS Bull. 1320*, pp. 17, 30, 62–63.

million and a half strong and constitute two fifths of all sales
workers; and many of them are members of bona fide trade
unions.

Salesclerks are by far the most numerous among employees
in the retail trades, and there are several organizations which
claim them. The largest of these is the AFL-CIO Retail Clerks
International Association (RCIA) in which women account
for about 58 percent of the more than 340,000 members. In the
other major union—the AFL-CIO Retail, Wholesale and Department Store Union (RWDSU) with a membership of more
than 143,000, 45 percent are women.[128] Retail trade is one of
the fields in which the largest number of white-collar workers
are unionized—along with public service, communications, railroads, and the entertainment industry—but even here unions
have absorbed less than 10 percent of the nearly 5,000,000
nonmanagerial employees in the nation's retail businesses,
some 90 percent of them employing fewer than ten paid
workers.[129]

Most of the present-day bargaining units in retail unions
opened action in the period of the New Deal; but under a
banner of early closing the RCIA dates back to 1890, when it
was chartered by the American Federation of Labor. By 1905
its membership had mounted from 3,000 to 50,000, but after it
adopted a program of minimum wages and maximum hours
the number dropped to scarcely 5,000 in the 1933 depression.
Moreover, its aging leadership was challenged by a New York
City faction whose members the AFL expelled on the charge
of dual unionism. This was when the Retail Wholesale and
Department Store Union (CIO) was born. Since that time the
competition between the two national unions has been sharp,

[128] *U.S. BLS Bull. 1320*, pp. 28, 62.
[129] Raulston Zundel, "Conflict and Co-operation Among Retail Unions," in
Journal of Business, October, 1954, p. 301.

to say nothing of the jurisdictional battles with other organizations. Under this stimulus the RCIA expanded its scope to include for the first time the organization of department-store employees, and no small part of its relative but temporary success was due to support by the Teamsters in conjunction with their own campaign to organize department-store warehousemen and drivers. The Retail Clerks also had help from the Building Service Employees' International Union, which was increasing its efforts among the larger department-store elevator operators, porters, and maids. The Meat Cutters in their narrowly defined retail jurisdiction gave further aid.[130]

The RCIA was unique among AFL unions in its complete identity with the retail trades, and its heavy concentration in a few city centers from San Francisco and Seattle on the west coast to metropolitan New York and Boston. By comparison the RWDSU was an uneasy coalition of disparate elements ranging from warehousemen to wholesale and retail salespeople, and it was widely alleged to be Communist-dominated to the extent that the CIO invited its officers to resign. For both of these reasons dissident locals began to secede from the RWDSU in quick succession and the RCIA became the dominant union, with James A. Suffridge its energetic president. In 1960 its members numbered approximately 400,000.[131]

A basis for the success of RCIA is that it has become more and more an industrial union of workers who are employed midway between the white- and blue-collar type of job. Relations with customers will of course remain, but an increasing proportion of the work force is becoming materials handlers engaged in the back of the store unloading, stocking, and moving goods, and this means that the proportion of men to women is increasing. Retail trade as a whole is one of the most rapidly

130 *Ibid.*, p. 303.
131 *Ibid.*, pp. 304, 306.

expanding sections of the American economy, and according to Michael Harrington of the Fund for the Republic and the Center for the Study of Democratic Institutions,

in RCIA, one is in the presence of labor's newest giant. It is new in a double sense: Its admission to the ranks of the huge union organizations is a postwar phenomenon, and its structure, its character, and its composition are new in that they reflect the most recent developments of the American economy. This is a union which will be studied a great deal more as time goes on.[132]

The Retail, Wholesale and Department Store Union with its 64,500 members has not "withered on the vine" as it was expected to do. For example, as recently as 1961 its New York Macy store Local 1-S, in which women constitute some 80 percent of the membership, was very much alive, and was reported to represent the overwhelming majority of the 11,000 employees in the company's five metropolitan New York stores. Local 1-S boasts a two-year contract dated in April, 1961, in which a new "automation" clause was included for the office workers whereby 127 of the 130 employees who faced displacement by data-computing machines were retrained and reassigned by the store, the remaining three having asked for severance pay, either because they were reluctant to learn a new machine skill or because of an abiding dissatisfaction with the long journey to work. Other gains in the contract included higher minimum wages, pensions, sick benefits, and life insurance. More than 2,000 of Macy Local 1-S members have a history of at least 25 years of service on the job, and the average is 12 years of service.[133] The RWDSU now stands on a firm basis, but it is still only half the size of the RCIA, and

---

[132] Michael Harrington, *The Retail Clerks* (New York, Macmillan, 1962), pp. 4, 6, 84, 88–89.

[133] Norman L. Sobol, "Department Store Sales, Employment Effects of State's Population Increase," New York State *Industrial Bulletin,* October, 1961, pp. 7–11; *U.S. WB Bull. 285,* p. 63; *Business Week,* "Macy's Contract Pledges Retraining," April 29, 1961, p. 81.

far more localized. Harrington foresees the possibility of a merger between the RCIA and the RWDSU.[134]

Nevertheless, the department store appears for the most part to be a major piece of unfinished union business in the postwar drive, and conflicts over jurisdiction have bcen rampant. A bitter clash between RCIA and the Teamsters has been raging on the Pacific coast because of rival claims for people actively engaged in handling or selling merchandise, "or performing other services incidental thereto." [135] It is expected, however, that in the coming years cooperative efforts of the various competing groups will improve. Moreover, it is believed certain that unionized department store workers are likely to learn new techniques in meeting the public, especially in centers where a large number of the customers are union workers.[136] Up to now the RCIA, which has 198,000 women members, has been most successful in organizing food and drug stores, and the report comes that its Los Angeles Local 770 "considers its women members to be the back bone of the union." [137]

Summary and Conclusions

White-collar employees—professional and clerical, more than half of whom are women—remain the largest group of American workers outside the trade-union movement. And their organizations show no over-all growth. The United States Department of Labor estimates that there were 2.4 million of these people in unions in 1948 and only 2.2 million in 1960— a decline in the proportion of organized white-collar workers from 16 to 11 percent of their total number. Let us glance

---

[134] Harrington, *The Retail Clerks*, pp. 79–80.

[135] Zundel, "Conflict and Co-operation," p. 309.

[136] Sobol, New York State *Industrial Bulletin*, October, 1961, p. 11.

[137] Irving Bernstein, "Don't Count the Unions Out," in *Challenge*, November, 1961, p. 18; *U.S. WB Bull. 285*, p. 63.

back at the 60-year experience of the largest groups of women.
First the teachers.

We have seen that women have been active in teachers' unions since the turn of the century, and during World War I
the American Federation of Teachers (AFT) was born despite
opposition by the National Education Association and numerous state and local associations who considered unionization
unprofessional, and still do. The modern history of teachers'
unions appears to have opened during the inflation period following the last war when, in 1947, the federation of teachers
in Buffalo, New York, quit their classrooms for a week to win
salaries that they could live on with dignity. The lasting result
of their action was the Condon-Wadlin law, which the state
legislature promptly enacted, and which only now in 1963 has
been modified—a law which declares strikes by public employees to be illegal and penalizes those who disobey. But it
has yet to be enforced against teachers.

In 1960 the United Federation of Teachers (UFT) of the
AFT became a strong force in New York City. And in an election it defeated the National Education Association representatives and other nonunion groups to become the first union in
the country to represent all teachers in a major city. After a
one-day strike in 1962 this union signed a one-year contract
which ruled out strikes, but boosted the salary scale. This was
notable progress in teachers' unionization, but the fact remains
that the American Federation of Teachers has a membership
of only about 56,000 in a total of more than 1,700,000 who are
eligible. More than half of the union members are women, and
75 percent of all noncollege teachers are women. Very few
college and university teachers are in unions.

We find also that only a small percentage of our professional
nurses have collective bargaining agreements. But, unlike
teachers, those who have them have not won them by forming
trade unions. It is the State Associations of the American

Nurses' Association that do the bargaining for the few members who wish it. Only in case a State Association is not bargaining for them are they free to be represented by a trade union. This does not mean, however, that nurses may not receive the sanction of the ANA despite a no-strike policy when they take "orderly" action by resigning en masse to win improvements in their economic status, as they did in 1962.

When we come to social workers and librarians it is difficult to find any union members. And when we do find some they are in the young and rising American Federation of State, County and Municipal Employees (AFL-CIO) where only 10 percent are professional people, the others being manual workers, including garbage collectors, zoo and museum attendants, and nonprofessional white-collar employees such as clerical workers. The New York City local union reports about 300 social-work members, many of whom are in agencies affiliated with the Federation of Jewish Philanthropies. Librarians appear to scorn trade unions, with the notable exception of the Detroit Public Library.

Offices and office workers are ubiquitous in our twentieth century America. It is to be expected, therefore, that as blue-collar union membership ceases to grow, the officers would be bidding for office and other clerical workers. Should these people belong to an organization devoted solely to their interests like the Office Employees' International Union (AFL-CIO) or to an industrial union which has organized the production workers in the plant in which they are employed? Or if they feel the need of unionization, which most of them so far do not, can they maintain their status with management and have a better chance of promotion if they belong to an independent union and remain close to their supervisors "in the family"?

The answers to these questions remain largely for the future to decide, but at present the trend is in the direction of union-conscious office workers combining with manual employees in industrial unions where they may have close relatives or friends rather than isolating themselves in a union for office workers only. Large offices with their electronic computers have become more like factories and the close relation between employees and management is disappearing. At the same time, mechanized factories have been eliminating sweat and drudgery and calling for more skill and alertness; work is becoming less physical, more mental. Hence, union activity of factory workers has been closing the gap between themselves and office employees in the matter of vacation policies and other fringe benefits, to say nothing of wages—a development which tends to draw white-collar people into their unions for protection—a quarter of a million of them in all. And in white-collar unions, while OEIU still has fewer than 70,000 members, the Brotherhood of Railway Clerks and the Communication Workers of America have many more. In addition there are at least 76,000 in independent unions. Up to 1953, however, only 13 percent of the nation's office workers were in unions, and we find no account of the proportion having increased since that time.

Some telephone operators along with linemen and other employees were organized early in the century by the International Brotherhood of Electrical Workers, later by the National Federation of Telephone Unions, and more recently by the AFL-CIO Communications Workers of America (CWA) and the Alliance of Independent Telephone Unions (AITU), among a number of smaller organizations. But from the Bell Telephone Companies there was opposition to unions from the start, and in two federal investigations made 35 years apart the "closely knit Bell System" was called to account for low wages to operators, resistance to unions, and "bad labor-management relations" in general. It is most promising to discover, therefore, that since 1955, when the CWA precipitated its last major strike and found that the telephone system could operate without them, both union and management have been overcoming old-time hostilities and depending more upon "common sense."

Today the two largest telephone unions are reported to have an over-all membership of some 385,000, nearly half of them operators and clerical workers in a total of some 700,000 employees. Women have led strikes to gain a union foothold and wage increases, as well as protection for operators against wage-cutting. And in some local areas they have won. CWA President Beirne says, in effect, that in his organization if he had to choose between men and women as the best unionists he would choose women.

Unions of salesclerks, in which women account for about half of the membership, represent one of the largest accumulations of organized white-collar workers, although about nine tenths of the nearly 5,000,000 people remain outside unions. It seems likely that the number will increase considerably as more and more of the labor force are blue-collar workers. As with the telephone employees, there are two competing unions, but here both organizations are affiliated with the AFL-CIO. Up to now, department stores—with the notable exception of Macy's in the New York City area—appear to remain a challenge to union organizers.

A final look at white-collar unionism makes it clear that up to now it is far from a widely accepted policy in America, by either employers or employees. The obstacles are real. A union like the teachers', for example, suffers from three "handicaps": public employment, professionalism, and the large number of women who for the most part continue to be discriminated against in matters of status and salary.

Nevertheless, in some directions, it is certain that white-collar unions have made an impressive start. Seeds have been sown that may take root and grow as grievances accumulate and the need for union protection is increasingly felt. Indeed,

there are signs in this direction as forward-looking labor leaders strive to remain a potent balancing force in our technologically advanced democratic society. What seems significant is
the *nature* of the gains that have been made as employment
continues to rise in so many sectors of the economy. For the
gains, though modest, seem to imply that the unionization of
working white-collar men and women is not impossible.

PART V
Our Economy's Adjustments to Women's Work

CHAPTER 21
Protective Labor Legislation

In the great sweep of technology and woman's work during the past six decades, what measures have been taken to protect health and welfare and how effective have they been? Between the two world wars the United States Women's Bureau made an extensive study of the effects of protective laws in women-employing industries. And now, after the advances of technology since the Great Depression, there has been a new investigation of these laws. President Kennedy in December, 1961, established a 26-member Commission on the Status of Women to undertake a broad study of employment and wage policies affecting women, and to determine whether federal and state protective laws are accomplishing the purposes for which they were enacted or whether they should be readapted to changing technological, economic, and social conditions. Mrs. Eleanor Roosevelt was named chairman of the commission, and after her death Women's Bureau Director Mrs. Esther Peterson became acting chairman and Professor Richard Lester the vice-chairman. The final report of the commission was published in October, 1963.

Hours of Work

To be prepared for the new findings let us take a backward look. We have seen in Chapter 7 that nineteenth century discussion of the need for protective labor legislation included men as well as women, but that before the century's turn 14 states led by Massachusetts had enacted laws limiting the hours of women's work, together with some other regulations. We recall also that an Illinois court ruled that women had "natural equality" with men and so a maximum-hour law for them could not be based on sex alone. In 1900 we found a

Pennsylvania court establishing a new judicial philosophy by declaring valid a 60-hour-week law for women because of their potential motherhood and because they were "unable to endure physical exertion and exposure . . . that is not harmful to adult males."

The zenith of judicial reasoning in support of limiting women's hours was reached in 1908 when the nation's highest court affirmed an Oregon ten-hour law, saying of woman:

She is properly placed in a class by herself, and legislation designed for her protection may be sustained, even when like legislation is not necessary for men, and could not be sustained.[1]

Seven years later the same court extended its acceptance of hour regulation for women by validating an eight-hour-day, 48-hour-week law which California had enacted.[2] Thus, by 1920, 43 states, the District of Columbia, and Puerto Rico had passed maximum-hour laws for women. Thirteen of these jurisdictions had set a maximum eight-hour-day, a 48-hour week, or both. This extensive progress was a result of continuing efforts of citizens' groups, of technological progress, which increased the productivity of workers, especially during the war, and of the growing realization of alert employers that shorter hours caused less fatigue, less absenteeism, higher morale, and a lower accident rate.

Apparently it was for this reason that the southern state of Mississippi passed a law in 1912 establishing a maximum ten-hour day for *all* employees in manufacturing and repair, and that the supreme court of that state declared it a reasonable act within the police power of the state. "It is well known," said the justices,

that, in the work connected with the running of machinery, the operator is subjected to a mental as well as a physical strain. In many cases the nearness of machinery makes the work dangerous

---

[1] Muller v. Oregon, 208 U.S. 412 (1908).
[2] Miller v. Wilson, 236 U.S. 373 (1915).

in case of an overtaxing of the strength of the worker, or any lessening of his alertness. . . . In fact, when we consider the present manner of laboring, the use of machinery, the appliances, requiring intelligence and skill, and the general present day manner of life, which tends to nervousness, it seems to us quite reasonable, and in no way improper, to pass such law so limiting a day's labor.

Commenting upon the principle of liberty of contract and the inalienable rights of labor, the court added cynically but prophetically, "Some day, perhaps, the inalienable right to rest will be the subject of litigation." [3]

The Mississippi decision remained unchallenged, so it was not carried to the nation's high court. Like a free spirit it floated off to Oregon, where a ten-hour law for men and women in factories was passed in 1913 (allowing three hours a day overtime at time-and-a-half rates), and after two years of argument was affirmed by the Federal Supreme Court in a famous decision. Under the sponsorship of Louis D. Brandeis, Felix Frankfurter and Josephine Goldmark had compiled the winning brief, as Brandeis and Goldmark had done in the earlier Oregon case; and now again the court responded to the commanding weight of their contention that "the considerations that were patent as to miners in 1898 [in an eight-hour law in Utah] are today operative, to a greater or less degree, throughout the industrial system." The work of any person for more than ten hours a day is "injurious to the physical health and well-being of such person, and tends to prevent him from acquiring that degree of intelligence that is necessary to make him a useful and desirable citizen of the State." [4]

This was almost a quarter of a century before the passing of the Federal Fair Labor Standards Act, which placed a ceiling over standard hours for all interstate commerce employees,

[3] State v. J.J. Newman Lumber Co., 102 Miss. 802 (1912) and 103 Miss. 283 (1913).

[4] Bunting v. Oregon, 243 U.S. 426 (1917). The exhaustive brief in this case was published in book form entitled *The Case for the Shorter Work-Day* (National Consumers' League, New York, 1916).

but the Oregon decision certainly marked a turning point in that direction.

Women's nightwork was also being limited during these years. Massschusetts again led the way in 1890 and 1907, and in 1915 the New York court of appeals reversed an earlier decision by favoring prohibition of nightwork for women.[5] The bill had been drafted by the Factory Investigating Commission based on medical testimony which stressed the lack of privacy and quiet for sleep during the day and the fact that women spent much of the day doing housework instead of sleeping. Accompanying the bill was another elaborate Brandeis-Goldmark brief for the instruction of the judges— a 452-page summary of which was published by the National Consumers' League under the title of *The Case Against Nightwork for Women.* The New York decision virtually established the constitutionality of legislation against women working at night although it was not court-confirmed until nine years later.[6]

Minimum Wages

What now of legal action against women's unconscionably low wages, particularly in the "sweatshop trades"? Minimum-wage legislation for all sweatshop workers had started in New Zealand, Australia, and Great Britain before the State of Massachusetts took this country's first cautious step by enacting in 1912 a nonmandatory law for women that depended entirely upon public opinion for its enforcement. The National Consumers' League and the Women's Trade Union League had been vigorously active in forming a joint committee, including organized labor, to work for the law, and both the financial conditions of the industry and the cost of living were taken

[5] People v. Charles Schweinler Press, 214 N.Y. 395 (1915).
[6] Radice v. People, 264 U.S. 292 (1923).

into account in establishing minimum rates. In 1913 minimum-wage laws for women were enacted in California, Oregon, and Washington and in five other western and midwestern states: Colorado, Utah, Nebraska, Minnesota, and Wisconsin. These early nine were soon followed by eight others, including the District of Columbia, although the laws passed by Texas and Nebraska were repealed.[7]

The operation of these laws was hampered everywhere, however, by persistent attempts of employers to get them declared unconstitutional, and they soon succeeded. The reasoning was based on the principle that labor is a commodity and that to compel employers to pay a living wage was taking away their property rights. Moreover, the Nineteenth Amendment, which gave women the right to vote, had made them equal to men, hence they were as able as men to bargain for their wages. "The tendency of the times to socialize property rights under the subterfuge of police protection is dangerous," said Justice Van Orsdel of the circuit court of appeals of the District of Columbia in 1922, "and if continued will prove destructive of our free institutions."[8] In the next year, by the equivalent of a five-to-four decision in the historic *Adkins* vs. *Children's Hospital* case of the District of Columbia, the U.S. Supreme Court affirmed the lower court ruling, one judge who favored the legislation having disqualified himself.[9]

Following this pronouncement in those ebullient twenties, minimum-wage legislation lapsed into the doldrums, not to be resuscitated until after the Great Depression. Six more laws were declared unconstitutional by various state courts, and most of those that remained became inoperative. Thus, although court decisions in those early decades had revealed a

[7] *U.S. WB Bull. 247*, pp. 1–2; Donald E. Cullen, *Minimum Wage Laws*, New York State School of Industrial and Labor Relations Bull. 43, February, 1961, pp. 1 ff.

[8] 284 Fed. Rep. 613 (1922).

[9] Adkins v. Children's Hospital, 261 U.S. 525 (1923).

trend toward special protection for women, just as certainly did the tendency waver. There was considerable controversy on the subject among laymen as well as among some working women themselves, who asserted that too often the laws shackled instead of protecting them. "Give a woman a man's chance —industrially," they asked of legislators. The National Woman's Party opposed legal protection unless it included men as well. And in his presidential address to the American Association for Labor Legislation in 1916, Columbia University Professor Henry R. Seager declared that

there is no sharp dividing line between women wage-earners and men wage-earners as regards their helplessness in the face of diverse industrial conditions. . . . Is it reasonable to maintain that the health and vitality of the potential fathers of the oncoming generation are less essential to our national welfare? . . . Our judges appear to me to have been guided by a somewhat old fashioned attitude toward women rather than by sound reason. . . . There are many women wage-earners who do not need legislative protection, and there are, in my judgment, more men wage-earners who do need it.[10]

On the other hand, U.S. Secretary of Labor James L. Davis said in 1922 that there was no question as to whether women had a right to earn a living, but

at the same time all will agree that women in industry would not exist in an ideal social scheme. Women have a higher duty and higher sphere in life. Eve was the companion and helpmate of Adam and in every way his social equal, but it was for Adam to protect Eve and provide for their posterity. . . . I personally prefer to see a woman guiding the destiny of the nation—in the home.[11]

In the following year an official of the U.S. Department of Labor explained that legislation for women was an effort to bring women up to the point where industrial equality with men was more nearly possible. "The time will undoubtedly

[10] *American Labor Legislation Review*, March, 1916, pp. 93–94.
[11] James L. Davis, "Safeguarding the Mothers of Tomorrow," *Gazette* of Colorado Springs, November 5, 1922.

come," she added, "when women will need less special legislation than they do now, but until that time it is little short of criminal to deny them the opportunity for reasonable leisure and a living wage, which legislation alone can obtain for them." [12]

The Women's Bureau Investigation
into the Effects of Legislation, 1928

To clear the atmosphere as well as inform itself, the Women's Bureau, which had been established in the United States Department of Labor in 1920, made an intensive and scholarly inquiry into the effects of labor legislation so far enacted, and published a detailed 500-page report in 1928. At this time we can only scratch the surface of the major findings. One was that no evidence came to light that women had lost employment because they could not work as long as men. In fact, men's hours had often been reduced as a result of women's hour laws. However, a number of new occupations were noted that might have been open to women had they been permitted to work longer.[13]

"The majority of employers in industry consider nightwork to be even more undesirable for women than for men," ran the report, "and they would not employ women at night even if the law permitted." But again it was found that "in some establishments women would be employed at night if the law permitted, and in an even smaller number of cases increased numbers of women might be employed in the daytime, if they could work at night." [14] Several states prohibited or limited

[12] Clara Mortenson Beyer, "What is Equality?" *The Nation,* January 31, 1923, p. 16.

[13] *U.S. WB Bull. 65,* pp. 45–46, and see pp. 123–28.

[14] *Ibid.,* p. 47. It will be recalled that state laws against women working at night were found to be one reason for their not being promoted to the highly skilled occupation of programming and operating electronic computers.

women's nightwork on newspapers, and in New York the rebellion of the proofreaders, linotypists, and monotypists became a *cause célèbre,* which in 1921 brought their exemption
from the factory law of eight years earlier which had included
them. In Indiana, where these women worked at night, one
employer said, "Women are just as good as men. This is not
like a factory. Women are union members, have as good jobs
as men, and are paid the same. They are here to work. The
priority rule in the shop requires new employees to begin on
the night shift. A night-work law would cut women out of
these jobs on newspapers." [15]

Prohibitory legislation received adverse judgment from the
Women's Bureau. Here was "an outstanding example of possible discrimination against women resulting from labor legislation." The bureau saw no reason why Ohio women were not
allowed to drive taxicabs, or why in two states they were not
permitted to read gas and electric meters. On grinding, polishing, buffing, and acetylene and electric welding, women, some
of them highly skilled, were found successfully employed in
states that permitted them to do this work. In Michigan, however, where women had been employed in large numbers during the war, grinding and welding had been "men's jobs" and
men replaced women when the war was over. The prohibitions
in New York and Ohio had been passed before modern safe-
guards and improved machines had been installed, and they
had not been removed.[16] New York women had been prohibited in 1913 from making cores in foundries if the work was
done in the room where the cores were baked. Several other
states followed by limiting the weight of cores on which
women might work, as well as the temperature of the work,
and by requiring certain partitions and ventilation in the core-

---

[15] *Ibid.,* p. 179, and see E. F. Baker, *Protective Labor Legislation,* pp. 242–
44.
[16] *U.S. WB Bull. 65,* pp. 53–54, 225–26.

room. In many establishments coremaking was a new wartime occupation for women, but in others we have seen that they had been employed before World War I and that they had been so successful that they had "come to stay." In fact, five out of six firms said their work was equal to or greater than men's in quality and quantity.[17]

Nevertheless, there was opposition to having women make cores. The Molders' Union declared foundries "not a proper place for women" and expelled any member who gave instruction to women "in the foundry or at any branch of the trade." And the New York Factory Investigating Commission, which had presented that state's bill to the legislature, had also declared that "the foundry is no place for women" and that foundrymen "should cease to employ women in work not intended for them." But the Women's Bureau discovered that modern foundry corerooms had been entirely cut off from the melting and baking rooms and that the atmosphere was "as free of disturbing or harmful elements as an office room." Moreover, two out of three of the firms reporting on postwar conditions were continuing to employ women as makers of small cores. "Women have come to stay in the coreroom," one foundryman declared.[18] And this was of course music to the ears of women coremakers themselves, who had vigorously protested against being deprived of continuing to earn a living by the vocation for which they had been trained.[19]

Ballasted thus by scores of carefully presented tables and pages of explanations, the bureau's findings left no doubt of

[17] *Ibid.*, p. 240.

[18] *Ibid.*, p. 241.

[19] Baker, *Protective Labor Legislation*, pp. 264, 367–68. Today, 25 states have laws which prohibit some kinds of employment for women. Aside from their being kept out of mines in 17 states and prohibited from serving alcholic beverages in nine states, 11 states prohibit their employment in other places, occupations, or under certain conditions. These include New York State, which still prohibits women from making cores in a room in which the oven is also in operation, and Massachusetts, Colorado, and Minnestota, which place certain restrictions upon coremaking for women; *U.S. WB Bull. 285*, pp. 145–46.

the broad beneficial effects of protective laws for women before the advent of the disastrous 1930s. Nevertheless, in the eyes of some informed readers the study had given too little attention to the significant groups of women who lost job opportunities that World War I had opened to them. If the opportunities of only 2 percent of the 3,000,000 women included in the study had been cramped or wiped out by laws that benefitted 98 percent, this would be a 60,000 minority, who might have been considered pioneers marking the way to new employment goals and full economic enfranchisement, thus breaking down prejudice, which the war emergency had tended to soften. An example of the abiding enemy of women —prejudice—was found in the metal-trades industry in Michigan, which dismissed thousands of women after the war not because of legislation or because the work was too heavy, but because of the attitude of employers toward having women on machine work. "In no other industry studied," the Women's Bureau reported, "was there found such violent prejudice against women's employment because of the mere fact that they were women." Women were bad for the moral tone of the place generally, and married women should not be employed because of their home duties. The chief inducement for hiring women was that they cost less.[20]

Minimum Wages Again

The Women's Bureau did not investigate effects of wage legislation because the nation's Supreme Court had rendered it void. But there was a resurgence of demand for minimum-wage laws as a result of the unbelievably low wages paid to women and girls in the depression of the thirties. The Massachusetts Consumers' League, for example, found some shops paying as low as 1 cent an hour. Unscrupulous garment manu-

[20] U.S. WB Bull. 65, p. 220.

facturers hired young girls and paid them little or nothing for a "learning period," then discharged them and hired a new group of "learners." In Tennessee, textile-mill women were paid as little as $2.39 for a 50-hour week, and in Connecticut the Commissioner of Labor recorded more than 100 sweatshops hiring young girls for 60 cents to $1.10 for a 55-hour week. "The entire wage structure of the country was apparently condemned to disintegration," declared the United States Department of Labor.[21]

In the hope of circumventing the Supreme Court's minimum-wage decision, New York and several other states enacted a new type of law based on a "fair value" for service rendered as well as on the "cost of living." And under the pressure of the national emergency, Congress passed the National Industrial Recovery Act which may be fairly termed a minimum-wage law. One section of this law required employers to "comply with the maximum hours of labor, minimum rates of pay, and other conditions of employment, approved or prescribed by the President." In the covered industries, men as well as women were included in "codes of fair competition." But the NIRA lasted only two years. The Supreme Court pronounced it unconstitutional in 1935, and Congress repealed the provisions of the codes of fair competition. In the following year the high court also declared a New York law invalid, declaring that it found no essential differences between it and the one held unconstitutional in the Adkins case of 1923—that "any measure that deprives employers and adult women of freedom to agree upon wages, leaving employers and men employees free to do so, is necessarily arbitrary."[22]

Once again, therefore, minimum-wage laws were moribund.

[21] U.S. Bureau of Labor Standards, *Growth of Labor Law*, p. 120; U.S. Bureau of Labor Standards, Bull. 194, *Labor Laws and Their Administration, a Discussion*, 1957, p. 29.
[22] Morehead v. Tipaldo, 298 U.S. 587 (1936).

But a turning point had arrived. In 1936 the State Supreme Court of Washington held that state's minimum-wage act constitutional. And in the following year the U.S. Supreme Court gave it its blessing in a five-to-four decision on the ground that minimum-wage legislation was a proper exercise of the police power because "the exploitation of a class of workers who are in an unequal position . . . is not only detrimental to their health and well-being but casts a direct burden for their support upon the community. . . . The bare cost of living must be met." [23]

The Fair Labor Standards Act of 1938

New and more extensive patterns were also laid. On October 24, 1938, as we were emerging from the depression, the United States Congress passed the nation's first federal law on wages of men, women, and minors working in interstate commerce; and the Fair Labor Standards Act (FLSA) became a permanent law of the land when the Supreme Court declared it constitutional three years later.[24] This act is popularly known as the Federal Wages and Hours Act. It was the result of congressional determination not only to bolster the economy by spreading employment and increasing purchasing power, but to defend the interests of fair-minded employers by attacking competition based on substandard conditions. The act embodied three important variations from the pattern thus far typical of state minimum-wage and hour laws. It applied to a vast number of men as well as women and minors, it established a uniform minimum hourly rate of wages, and it required penalizing time-and-a-half pay for hours worked in ex-

[23] West Coast Hotel v. Parrish, 300 U.S. 379 (1937); *U.S. WB Bull. 267,* Part I, pp. 6–7; U.S. Bureau of Labor Standards, *Growth of Labor Law,* p. 122.
[24] United States v. F. W. Darby Lumber Co., 312 U.S. 100 (1941).

cess of 44 the first year, 42 the second, and 40 thereafter, thus improving upon Oregon's ten-hour law of 1914. The hourly rate of pay began with 25 cents, to be raised to 40 cents in 1945 and thereafter. The new act thus marked a decided shift in the philosophy of minimum-wage and hour legislation.[25]

Pressure for changes in the federal act began building up after World War II; and by amendment in 1949, Congress raised the minimum wage from 40 cents to 75 cents an hour, although political pressure and expediency resulted in narrowing the coverage by exempting switchboard operators at the smaller public exchanges, many employees in retail establishments, and others.[26] Then under pressure from organized labor the minimum was again boosted to $1.00 an hour, effective March 1, 1956; and Labor Day evening, 1961, became the date for a further rise to $1.15 an hour for some 24 million workers, to be increased to $1.25 in September, 1963.

Moreover, the 1961 amendments expanded the coverage of the act for the first time since its adoption. John F. Kennedy, then a senator, introduced a bill designed to embrace between six to 11 million workers; and after he became President he proposed to congressmen an extension of minimum-wage coverage to 4,300,000. The House reduced the figure to 1,300,000, but the final bill, which President Kennedy signed in May, 1961, added 4,086,000 newly covered employees—nearly half a million more than the number finally included.[27] On September 3, Labor Day, an estimated 3,624,000 more employees came under the act—in retail trade and service, telephone exchanges, seafood processing, and some others. For these new people a $1.25 minimum wage and 40-hour straight-time work

[25] U.S. Bureau of Labor Standards, *Growth of Labor Law*, pp. 124–25.
[26] *Ibid.*, p. 125; *MLR*, October, 1958, p. 1101; Robert D. Leiter, "Coverage Confusion under the Fair Labor Standards Act," in *Labor Law Journal*, February, 1962, p. 142.
[27] Leiter, "Coverage Confusion," p. 145.

week is being applied on a step-by-step basis over a four-year period.

The amendments thus raised the number of covered workers to a total of nearly 27,500,000, or approximately 42 percent of the employed civilian labor force and 39 percent of the total labor force. Workers now outside the coverage of the act include about eight million in retail and service trades and two million hired farm workers. Also exempt are executives, administrative and professional employees with salaries generally high enough to exempt them from the act, and employees of federal, state, and local governments.[28] The Secretary of Labor is expressly authorized to "define and delimit" these exempt classifications, and his definitions are said to have the force of law "so long as they are not set aside by the courts as arbitrary or capricious." [29]

It appears, however, that the coverage of the Fair Labor Standards Act can easily be further expanded if the Congress is so disposed. Prior to 1961, it covered people only if they were personally engaged in interstate commerce or in producing goods for interstate commerce. The business of the employer was not controlling. Now, all employees of a firm having annual sales of more than $1,000,000 and involved in interstate commerce are included. In other words the new law sets forth a dollar volume of business as the test of coverage, and extension of protection to additional millions of workers is possible by a simple reduction in the annual volume of sales necessary

[28] *Ibid.*, pp. 143, 147; U.S. Bureau of Labor Standards, *Growth of Labor Law*, p. 129n. Note also Leiter's charge of political pressures and expediency that were brought to bear before the amendments were passed which have made the "somewhat random basis of coverage . . . more obvious than formerly [and] have increased the complexities. . . . The coverage and exemption provisions of the statute . . . should be completely rewritten in order that clear principles and a sound policy are evident," this critic concludes (pp. 139, 150).

[29] Bureau of National Affairs, Inc., *The New Wages and Hours Law* (Washington, D.C., 1961), pp. 57–79.

for inclusion.[30] The exact impact of the 1961 amendments will not be clear, however, until much of the new language has been interpreted by the courts.

That the FLSA has had considerable effect in the entire economy seems clear from a recent study by the U.S. Bureau of Labor Statistics, which reports that the average work week in May, 1963, was 40.7 hours. A fifth of the people were working 49 hours or more (a high proportion of whom were self-employed); a fifth were working less than 35 hours, or part time (especially in retail trade and service industries such as education, entertainment, recreation, and private household work); and two fifths were working 40 hours, including office workers and blue-collar workers in factories. In nonfarm industries two fifths of all men were working 40 hours compared to 18 percent of the women. In the central age group (25–64 years) 45 hours was the average work week for men and 36 hours for women, a higher proportion of whom were on part time. Among full-time workers, however, nearly half of the men as compared to a fourth of the women worked more than 40 hours. More married than single women worked long hours, but the hours of both were exceeded by women who were widowed, divorced, or separated—those who were probably in greater need for income. The gradual decline in working hours per day and days per week has reflected a desire for more leisure time and, more recently, as a possible solution of the continuing high rate of unemployment.[31]

State Minimum-Wage Laws Today

As for wages in intrastate establishments, the blessing of the United States Supreme Court on the Washington State mini-

[30] *Ibid.*, pp. 1, 4; Leiter, "Coverage Confusion," pp. 149–50.
[31] *MLR*, August, 1963, pp. 925–34.

mum-wage law of 1937 had stimulated renewed legislative and administrative activity by the states. In the years 1937 and 1938 six jurisdictions enacted laws for the first time—Alaska, Kentucky, Louisiana, Nevada, Oklahoma, and Pennsylvania, and nine states validated, amended, or reenacted their laws. In 1939, Connecticut became the first state to bring men under coverage of its law, and soon, during the war years, New York, Rhode Island, Massachusetts, and New Hampshire did likewise.[32] In the 1950s, for the first time, Idaho, New Mexico, Wyoming, Vermont, and North Carolina enacted laws including men as well as women. Hence, by January, 1961, 35 jurisdictions had minimum-wage laws, not counting the federal act, and 15 of these applied to men as well as to women and minors. This left 17 states with no laws, while in many of the others the law was largely ineffective.[33]

To give greater assurance of protection to intrastate workers by rules which employers feel they must observe, 18 states now set statutory rates instead of depending upon administrative orders by wage boards. These rates vary from Alaska's $1.50 an hour (higher than the federal law), Washington's $1.15 and a $1.00 rate in nine states, to as low as 70 cents in other jurisdictions, including North Carolina.[34] It is worth noting that states can also establish higher minimum rates for those of their employees who produce for interstate industries if they desire to do so, for the federal act provides that if a state standard is higher the state standard shall prevail. During the years 1938 to 1949, while the federal minimum remained stationary at 40 cents, this provision enabled the states to set minimum rates for interstate employment in line with the rising cost of living. In recent years, however, the states

[32] *U.S. WB Bull. 267*, pp. 6, 9; U.S. Bureau of Labor Standards, *Growth of Labor Law*, p. 123.

[33] U.S. Bureau of Labor Standards, *Growth of Labor Law*, p. 126; *U.S. WB Bull. 285*, pp. 130, 137.

[34] U.S. Bureau of Labor Standards, *Growth of Labor Law*, p. 128.

have tended to concentrate on the intrastate trade and service occupations, including restaurants, stores, and beauty shops where the need for legislative protection has persisted because of generally low wages, long hours, and relatively little union organization.[35]

An "Equal-Pay" Law Is Needed

For the nation as a whole, although the FLSA had put a floor under wages for all interstate workers, it had said nothing about what women should be paid above the minimum. Only in the sixty-third year of our century did the Congress enact an "equal-pay" law. Preceding pages have shown that the principle underlying this move has deep roots, however. And as far back as 1870 Congress legislated that women clerks in the Treasury Department should be graded like men and should receive the same salaries.[36] In 1878 the Knights of Labor stated in the preamble of their constitution that one of the principal objects of their order was "to secure for both sexes equal pay for equal work." [37] And the final report of the Industrial Commission, which Congress created in 1898, included this statement:

The manifest fairness of the proposition that there should be equal pay for equal work must be its own justification. Its successful adoption would not only free men from the evil of lower wages by reason of the competition of women, but it would fix a standard of labor to which both men and women would be obliged to conform, and would bring about the fixing of wages on the only fair basis possible, viz., that of the quality of work performed.[38]

---

[35] *Ibid.*, p. 129; *U.S. WB Bull. 267*, pp. 3–4. On employment effects of minimum-wage laws, see also *Industrial and Labor Relations Review*, April, 1959, pp. 406–22, and January, 1960, pp. 254–73.

[36] Sumner, p. 240.

[37] Dorothy S. Brady, "Equal Pay for Women Workers," *Annals of the American Academy of Political and Social Science*, May, 1947, p. 55.

[38] U.S. Department of Labor, *Labor Information Bulletin*, "Senate 'Equal Pay' Bill Culmination of Decades of Federal Support of Principle," November,

It should be noted that this early declaration, which might have been written today, was made 14 years before the country's first minimum-wage law for women was enacted. Prevention of women's wages from undercutting the wages of men had indeed become a strategic goal to be gained, and quite as important as protecting women from incomes they could not live on. During World War I, when two to four million additional women were being brought into the labor force and while more states were passing minimum-wage laws, the Commission on Industrial Relations, which was created by Congress to inquire "into the effect of industrial conditions on the public welfare," recommended that both public opinion and legislation recognized "the principle that women should receive the same compensation as men for the same service." In 1917, the chief of the Bureau of Ordnance of the War Department issued to arsenal commanders and all manufacturers filling war contracts General Order 13, which included the provision that "the standards of wages hitherto prevailing for men in the process should not be lowered when women render equivalent service." In the following year the War Labor Conference Board stated this principle which the National War Labor Board applied in more than 50 cases that came before it in the handling of industrial disputes.

If it shall become necessary to employ women on work ordinarily performed by men, they must be allowed equal pay for equal work and must not be allotted tasks disproportionate to their strength.[39]

In New York State in 1919 the Machinists' Union was continuing to organize women who had been replacing men in machine shops during the war so that they would be in a posi-

---

1945, p. 5. It will be recalled that it was in the same decade that wise Commissioner of Labor Carroll D. Wright forecast equal pay for equal work for women.

[39] *U.S. WB Bull. 196*, pp. 17–18; Brady, *Annals*, p. 53.

tion to demand "equal pay for equal work." The union was unalterably opposed to women's entrance into new occupations as underbidders, the leaders declared, but their official opinion was that "we have no objection to women working in the machine industry, *provided,* they receive equal pay for similar work." [40] And it was in 1919 that the automobile state of Michigan (also Montana) enacted the nation's first equal-pay law, ineffective though it proved to be. For nearly 25 years these were the only states with such laws.[41]

In the depth of the depression new impetus was brought to the equal-pay movement. Michigan made her law more specific with the hope of preventing disastrous effects of differences between women's and men's rates. Most of the National Recovery Act codes for industries established the principle of equality in minimum rates, and we have seen that in the Fair Labor Standards Act of 1938 Congress provided for fixing minimum rates of millions of workers regardless of sex.

In 1940 a Michigan State court validated that state's law which held that "any employer of labor in this state, employing both males and females . . . who shall pay any female engaged in the manufacture or production of any article of like value, workmanship and production a less wage by time or piece work, than is being paid to males similarly employed . . . or in any employment formerly performed by males, shall be guilty of a misdemeanor." The word "similarly" had a definite meaning, the court explained, and in this statute it meant "substantially alike."[42] Two years later under another direction of the court, when women were being called to play a vital role

[40] New York State Department of Labor Bull. 93, *The Industrial Replacement of Men by Women in the State of New York,* 1919, pp. 43–46.
[41] *U.S. WB Bull. 285,* p. 138.
[42] General Motors Corporation v. Read et al., 294 Mich. 558; 293 N.W. 751 (1940); U.S. Congress House Committee on Education and Labor, Hearings, *Equal Pay for Equal Work,* 1962, p. 42.

on the industrial front, the War Labor Board directed the General Motors Corporation and the United Automobile Workers to include an equal-pay provision in their new agreements— one for which the union had contended for many years. Any disputes arising on the question of quality, quantity, or comparability of work, the board said, should be finally determined by an arbitrator appointed by the Board. Hence the board's General Order No. 16 authorized employers voluntarily to raise women's wages to those of men "for work of comparable quantity or quality on the same or similar operations" without applying to the board for advance permission, as was generally required for wage increases.[43]

It was after these rulings by the National War Labor Board, which were in line with the Michigan court decision of 1940, that the national campaign for equal pay for equal work really began, during the exigencies of the war. In 1945, senators Claude Pepper, Democrat of Florida, and Wayne Morse, Republican of Oregon, introduced Senate Bill No. 1178 into the Seventy-ninth Congress—a bill which established a pattern for those that followed in every congressional session.[44] The bill declared it an unfair wage practice for employers: a. to pay females a lower rate of wages than or had been paid to males for comparable work; b. to replace females with male employees except where the layoff or discharge was for good cause or on the basis of a seniority system; and c. to discriminate against employees for exercising rights or privileges under the act. In recognition of the problem of determining the meaning of "comparable work" the bill proposed establishing industry committees patterned after those used in the early years of the FLSA to consider the problems of eliminating wage-rate dif-

[43] U.S. Congress, Hearings, 1962, p. 337; *U.S. WB Bull. 196*, pp. 17, 24; *MLR*, September, 1946, p. 389.

[44] Alice K. Leopold, "Federal Equal-Pay Legislation," *Labor Law Journal*, January, 1955, pp. 8, 21, 27; *U.S. WB Bull. 243*, p. 2.

ferentials based on sex. The administration of the act was to be in the hands of an Equal Pay Division of the Women's Bureau.

A number of labor leaders testified in favor of the bill. It is "absolutely essential" said a representative of the United Electrical, Radio and Machine Workers of America (UE), CIO. It is "an extremely important legislative measure, not only for the 300,000 women members, but the 450,000 men within the UE. . . . Since the . . . bill can act on a national basis, it removes the question of competition, since all companies will have to eliminate discrimination." [45] A committee of 42 national organizations, including management representatives and unions, had joined to sponsor the bill. Three days of hearings were held, and although the bill was favorably reported by Senate and House committees it did not come to a vote.[46]

At hearings on Representative Helen Gahagen Douglas's bill on the "Women's Equal Pay Act of 1947," a member of the National Association of Manufacturers recalled that his organization had taken an official stand on the subject in 1942, and that the board of directors had approved the recommendation of the association's industrial relations committee, which said in part:

There is little difference between men and women as regards their satisfactory performance in industry. Sound employment and personnel practices are applicable to both men and women and no emphasis should be placed on any distinctions between them as workers.

In the matter of wage policies we advocate the principle of equal pay for equal performance by women.[47]

A coordinator of the Fair Practices Department of the UAW-

---

[45] Hearings before a Subcommittee of the Committee on Education and Labor, U.S. Senate, *Equal Pay for Equal Work for Women*, 1945, pp. 161, 167.

[46] Leopold, "Federal Equal-Pay Legislation," p. 21.

[47] Hearings before Subcommittee No. 4 of the Committee on Education and Labor, House of Representatives, *Equal Pay for Equal Work for Women*, 1948, p. 252.

CIO also made a strong plea for equal pay at these hearings. "During the war in most of our UAW-CIO plants, women performed all kinds of operations in the production of war implements to win the war and to win the peace," he told the Eightieth Congress. "We also found that . . . the women . . . proved they had the ability to produce the quantity and quality of the type of work which was being requested by management throughout the country." But when the union went into negotiations for a new agreement, he continued, the company said that henceforth certain jobs would be performed by women exclusively and no men would be needed. The union negotiators were able to end the job freeze, however, by reminding the employers of the Michigan equal-pay law, although that law "is not everything we would like it to be. It is weak." The union speaker cited an example in one plant where a 16 cent differential between men's and women's wages was paid "for the same or comparable work," adding that "after VJ-Day the company hired only women and refused to hire men, and many of them veterans." We needed a federal law, he urged, because there were only about seven states that had any kind of equal-pay-for-equal-work laws on their statute books.[48]

In the Eighty-third Congress, 1954, Ohio Representative Frances P. Bolton's bill on equal pay would establish procedures and remedies similar to those in the FLSA. Although by that time 13 states and Alaska had so-called equal-pay laws, she noted that few were free of loopholes, and they varied in both their provisions and their effectiveness, some containing provisions which could be used to defeat the major purpose of the law. And no state attempted to eliminate inequalities between rates paid for so-called men's and women's jobs. "The problem we face as a free Nation dedicated to justice and opportunity for the individual," said the congresswoman, "spreads

[48] *Ibid.,* pp. 174–75.

itself out before us as the exigencies of living continue to force women into the labor market. . . . It seems to me that it is a question with which this Congress must deal in the very near future." [49]

The Equal Pay Act of 1963

Congress did deal with it in the years 1962–63, though it took more than a year to finish the job. At House hearings on the administration's bill in April, 1962, Mrs. Eleanor Roosevelt declared that women were being employed in place of men because they could be hired at cheaper wage rates. She noted that under the FLSA, which set a floor under wages and a ceiling over hours, women could not be used to undercut men's wages at the minimium level. "But something more is needed, and that is a law to prevent undercutting by women of wages above the minimum." [50] Although 22 states now had so-called equal-pay laws, she said they were inadequate and some even lacked enforcement provisions. The states must continue their efforts on intrastate cases, she urged, for "individuals employed by concerns in intrastate commerce are often among the lowest paid of our work force . . . people who work in laundries, the hotel and restaurant workers, hospital employees." [51]

James B. Carey, secretary-treasurer of the Industrial Union Department, AFL-CIO, and president of the IUE, reminded the congressmen that the number of women in the labor force in the coming decade would increase by 25 percent as compared with 15 percent for men, that in many states labor commissioners are prevented from taking effective action to compel compliance with their "equal-pay" provisions. This gave the advan-

[49] Leopold, "Federal Equal-Pay Legislation," pp. 9–10, 22.
[50] U.S. Congress, House Hearings, Committee on Education and Labor, *Equal Pay for Equal Work*, March and April, 1962, pp. 171–72.
[51] *Ibid.*, p. 225.

tage to the employer, just as it did in states which had no such
laws, making it necessary to have one statute for the entire
nation.[52]

In a long and impassioned plea, Caroline Davis, director of
the UAW Women's Department, recalled that for 25 years her
union had been in the forefront of the effort to establish equal-
pay provisions in their contracts with employers. She urged
that "unequal pay is a form of cheating whose victims include
widows and orphans. . . . Each day until the equal pay bill is
passed and provision is made for its enforcement, hundreds of
thousands of women will be paid less than they are entitled to
and they need." [53]

The National Association of Manufacturers put into the record again its statement established in 1942 advocating the principle of equal pay for women.[54]

Mrs. Emma Guffey Miller, chairman of the National
Woman's Party, which was urging an equal-rights amendment
to the Constitution, "devoutly hoped" the bill would be passed
and that no future Congress would repeal it. Chairman Zelenko
reassured her by saying he was "quite confident that the law
will never be repealed, once it is enacted, unless they repeal
women." [55]

Secretary of Labor Arthur Goldberg declared that favorable
action on H.R. 8898 and H.R. 10226 was "particularly urgent
in view of the forecast that by 1970 we will have 30 million
women in our labor force as compared with an average of 24¼
million . . . during 1961." "You can imagine today what would
happen to our country, its productivity, its position in industrial and other production, in commerce, if 24 million women
were withdrawn from the labor force. That is inconceivable,
and since the women are partners in our labor force, it seems to

[52] *Ibid.*, pp. 171–72.
[53] *Ibid.*, pp. 337, 340.
[54] *Ibid.*, p. 161.
[55] *Ibid.*, p. 142.

me that the elementary rule of equity requires that they be full partners. . . . Here as the New Frontier of our defense the women are playing an extraordinarily important part in vital work." [56]

Assistant Secretary of Labor and Director of the Women's Bureau, Mrs. Esther Peterson added that

the increase in women's employment, the responsibilities of women for their own support, and often also for the support of others, their performance during two World Wars, and the vital contribution made by women to the Nation's economy today—all these factors testify to the basic unsoundness of paying wage differentials based on sex. The time has come to put an end to this practice through enactment of the bills before you.[57]

So went the testimony of dozens of people in favor of the bill. Some placed the emphasis upon women's need for fair wages. Others stressed the necessity of protecting men's wages from being undercut by women competitors. Altogether, the arguments convinced the Congress to the extent that both the Senate and House approved the bill. They differed on the language to be used, however, and the close of the session was too near to afford time to resolve the differences in joint conference.[58]

But the time had come to enact a federal equal-pay-for-equal-work bill. It was as though the staunch and persistent adherents of the legislation had been climbing a steep and rocky mountain and were now at last reaching the top. Senator Patrick V. McNamara of Michigan and Representative Edith Green of Oregon introduced the administration's bill in February, 1963. On May 17 the Senate approved it by a voice vote after it had been studied by the Committee on Labor and Public Welfare, which straightened out kinks that had been causing controversy. Six days later the House approved the bill,

[56] *Ibid.*, pp. 10, 18–19.
[57] *Ibid.*, p. 26.
[58] *Christian Science Monitor*, February 18, 1963.

having also made slight amendments as to language, which the Senate accepted rather than risk further delay. The document was sent to the White House on May 28 and President Kennedy signed it with 19 pens on June 19, 1963. The Department of Labor estimated that some 8,000,000 women would be affected.[59] Many will be left out, of course, because the law includes only those under the FLSA.

The Equal Pay Act of 1963 is an amendment to the Fair Labor Standards Act of 1938. Since it affects all workers in interstate commerce rather than only women, it is to be administered by the Wages and Hours Division of the Department of Labor. The wording of the law is especially interesting in view of all the earlier failures to reach agreement on how "equal work" should be interpreted, or how it could be measured. Under the amendments, no employer of persons working or producing in interstate commerce may pay more to one sex than to the other, generally, "for equal work on jobs the performance of which requires equal skill, effort, and responsibility, and which are performed under similar working conditions." Exceptions will be allowed where a seniority or a merit system is in force, or where earnings are measured by the quantity or quality of production. Differentials based on any other factor other than sex are also permissible. Employers may not cut the pay of men to effect a payroll balance between the sexes; and any wages owing to an employee which have been withheld in violation of the law will be considered "unpaid minimum wages" or "unpaid overtime compensation," collectible from the employer. The new statute is to become effective one year after its enactment except where collective bargaining contracts are in force. In such cases up to another year is allowed for adjustments.[60]

---

[59] New York *Times*, May 18, 23, 1963; June 11, 1963.
[60] *Ibid.*, May 29, 1963; for the full text of the law see *Monthly Labor Review*, August, 1963, p. 947.

The problems of enforcing the equal-pay law will be numerous and complicated, especially perhaps in the southern states, none of which are among the 22 that have enacted equal-pay laws.[61] Questions that come to mind for the long run include at least these two: will the law cause replacement of women by men where men are available for the same jobs? Will the principle of equality extend from wage rates to job advancements that carry more women to supervisory and executive posts? It may be also that the courts will have something to say about the latest amendments to the Fair Labor Standards Act.

Summary and Conclusions

In the twentieth century sweep of industrial technology, the development of protective labor legislation in America has tended toward protecting the worker as such rather than the woman worker only. In fact, minimum-wage legislation, which began in New Zealand and Australia for all employees, was acceptable for women by the Supreme Court only as we emerged from the Great Depression. One year later the Fair Labor Standards Act of 1938 was passed, which established minimum rates for men as well as women; and in recent years the states have increasingly followed this pattern. A floor under wages has been considered important not only to protect workers, but as a stabilizing force in our dynamic economy.

The states were more successful in limiting women's working hours and in prohibiting nightwork and some occupations with court approval. It was agreed at the time that females were in a class by themselves and could not endure physical exertion and exposure that did not harm men. But many who devoted themselves to getting these laws passed could not have been in sympathy with the Secretary of Labor's declaration in the 1920s, after women's participation in production for the war,

[61] For the list see *U.S. WB Bull. 285*, p. 139.

that in an ideal society women would not be in industry but
"would be guiding the destiny of the nation in the home."
Women were in industry to stay, nevertheless, and hour laws
to protect them from extreme exploitation were essential.
Moreover, the State of Oregon in 1914 decided this was true
for the fathers as well as the mothers of our children, and the
ten-hour law for all workers in factories was validated by the
Supreme Court. Some employers, too, were noticing that
shorter hours reduced fatigue and accidents and boosted morale. The Women's Bureau discovered in the late 1920s that
men's hours had been reduced in many places as a result of the
hour laws for women.

In an exhaustive investigation of the effects of legislation,
the Women's Bureau found that millions of women had benefitted by the protection of state laws, but that thousands had
been deprived of jobs because of them. Probably this was a
necessary price to pay for the sake of the majority, many of
whom were carrying the double load of homework and paid
work, but it raised questions about preventing the minority
from loosening the long grip of tradition by moving out of the
congested woman-employing industries into new jobs that
would have been open but for the laws, or by retaining those
jobs they had held successfully as emergency substitutes for
drafted and enlisted men. Rather than be bothered about re-
strictive laws, employers had found it simpler to employ men
when they could get them.

But though prejudice lingered on, the forces of the depression and of World War II, together with the rise of automatic
technology, brought telling changes for women and their work
as their numbers in the labor force continued to swell. The Fair
Labor Standards Act made minimum wages and maximum
hours the same for men and women engaged in production for
interstate commerce, but there were industrial disputes as a

result of the hiring of women at the minimum rates, which undercut men's higher wage scales. In the war decade the National War Labor Board told employers to raise women's wages to equal those of men for comparable work without asking for the permission otherwise required.

It was then that Congress began to be bombarded with requests for equal-pay-for-equal-work legislation. We have reviewed the arguments in favor of the bills as they were presented in congressional hearings beginning in 1945—statements from parties socially and economically as far apart as the National Association of Manufacturers and the Automobile Workers' Union, along with those of scores of organizations, groups, and individuals, including Mrs. Eleanor Roosevelt and Arthur Goldberg, then Secretary of Labor. In one way or another, all who testified urged that women should have equal wage rates for comparable work because it was just, and because men's wages must be protected. So, finally, in May, 1963, the Senate and House agreed on the language to be used on the subject of comparable work, and the President signed their bill on June 10, which made equal-pay-for-equal-work the law of the land, to become effective in one year. The Department of Labor estimates that some eight out of more than 23 million women will be covered.

Whether and to what extent the new law will cause tradition and prejudice against women at work to be overridden, and what the courts will have to say of its validity, will be discovered only in the years to come. Much depends, of course, upon the growth of the economy, full employment of the available labor force aided by greater geographical and occupational mobility, vocational training and guidance, and improved employment service. And the trend in this mid-century is in the direction of shorter hours of the work week and work year, and probably of the work life for all employees. These developments, together with the lessening of occupational hazards and the improved working conditions which our technological society affords, suggest that protective labor legislation may play a smaller role in the future than in the past. But doubtless there will always be less advantaged workers—more women than men perhaps—who will need legislative protection from employer abuses.

CHAPTER 22
Summation, Adjustments,
Special Problems

Looking back over 16 decades of technology and woman's work, it is clear that, as occupations have moved out of the home, women have been moving after them. Before the Industrial Revolution they did economically productive work on the farm and in the house while they raised their families. Since that time they have been gradually recapturing lost positions in a man's world—pushed and pulled by the driving forces of science and technology, wars, and education. As two British authors cogently remind us, "If women are today leaving their homes to set out on a new road to work, this is a road which will take them 'back home' to their proper place in the community."[1]

Summation

The fact that women were available at lower rates than men undoubtedly gave them work opportunities they would not have had otherwise. For they were a new economic factor and they accepted whatever they were paid. Then as they moved into new occupations their wage was likely to be determined by what they received elsewhere rather than by what men were receiving, so that the custom of paying lower wages to women persisted. "So true it is," conjectured John Stuart Mill a hundred years ago, "that everything which is usual appears natural."[2]

When the invention of the principle of interchangeable parts made mass production and the subdivision of labor possible,

[1] Alva Myrdal and Viola Klein, *Women's Two Roles: Home and Work* (London, Routledge, 1956), p. 189.
[2] Mill, p. 27.

there were semiskilled and unskilled job openings for women and girls on the simpler machines which required little training—only patience in performing repetitive tasks, often also finger dexterity. It was men, not women, who were serving apprenticeships in line for promotion. Most young women were expecting to be married and have children. During the two world wars, however, women surprised employers by performing "men's jobs" in the factory and the office, and in some jobs they were kept on after the men returned from the battlefields. In others, as in the aircraft industry, they proved to have been only marginal or secondary workers to be taken on and let off according to the special need for them.

Employers are accustomed to using women to reduce costs, and at times women have been effective union strikebreakers. Office women have a tendency to be employer-centered. Most of them have an aversion to unionism, and managements are making conscious efforts to keep them in this mood. But now as mechanized offices become more like factories, and as white-collar people outnumber blue-collar workers for the first time in our history, it is possible that we shall see a rise of white-collar unionism in an effort to win wages and fringe benefits, which production workers have achieved.

In 1930 the number of feminine office workers had doubled. There were more than in the factories and for the first time they outnumbered men. There continues to be an insatiable demand for secretaries, stenographers, and typists; and now the electronic computer, which is revolutionizing office procedure, is bound to affect woman's work in yet unpredictable ways.

So far, practically all of the highly skilled occupations of programming for the computer—those of preparing for and operating automatic data-processing machines—have been held by men. Managements have been reluctant to pay the high price for training women because of the probability that they would not stay long, and because the expensive computers are likely

to be used during night hours when many states forbid women
to work. On the other hand the New York State Department of
Labor pronounces programming especially suited to women
because of their attention to details; and a United States Secretary of Labor has predicted that during the 1960s business and
industry will overcome their "quaint inhibitions" about hiring
women. Already there are a few outstanding women mathematicians at work in the field of programming; and the programming staff in one industrial laboratory is reported to be two-
thirds women. The whole innovation is so new that one can
only conjecture what women's future role will be. It seems entirely possible, in view of the persistence of prejudice, that
many women will be employed on routine tasks connected with
the computer, but that their chances for promotion will remain
rather slim.

The history of the education of American women and of their
role as teachers is a spectacular example of the weight of tradition and prejudice. The education of girls would be "inconsistent with the design thereof," and an educated wife was "an infringement upon the domain of man." But when Jeffersonian
liberals introduced free elementary schools, young women who
had been learning while they wove and spun in the Lowell
cotton mills were employed to teach the children because they
could be had at a fraction of what men who were going into
business and skilled trades received. In the years after the Civil
War more and more women became public school teachers,
and state school superintendents pronounced them better than
men. Their low salaries, moreover, were a boon to taxpayers.
Meanwhile, as early as 1837, Oberlin College had opened its
doors to four women, and other institutions gradually followed
this lead.

There was great question about the advisability of a college
education for women, however. It was contended that they
were mentally inferior and would be entirely unable to meet

the standards set for men; that they were too frail to withstand the physical strain of higher learning; that overstudy would give them brain fever, and if they lived and were able to have children the children would be sickly. Furthermore, coeducation was inadvisable because women in the classroom would distract the men, men would not like having them around, there was not enough money for both, and the admission of women would lower the reputation of the institution.[3] Psychologists and psychoanalysts urged that "the luxury of intellect" comes only after nature's first claim upon women; and as late as 1950 one male president of a woman's college advocated "truly feminine" education for daughters. Yet tests indicated greater differences within each sex than between them, and sociologists advocated education in family living for men as well as for women.

The views of the sociologists appear to have been supported by recent developments. Higher education has not destroyed femininity, or produced sickly children, or distracted men from their studies when women are in their classes. In fact we are told that more than half of our university students between the ages of 22 and 34 are married—an estimated 800,000 of them in the nation as a whole. Indeed, American universities have been increasingly providing living quarters for married students, equipped with day-care arrangements for the children. In 1961, according to the United States Office of Education, campuses were providing for 47,780 married couples.[4] Men's colleges and universities have also been "going co-ed," and women's colleges are making it possible for women to come back to classes as their children grow older.

It was especially under the pressure of World War II, when great technological changes were demanding more brain power, more scientific training, more engineers, that many of

[3] Newcomer, pp. 25–32.
[4] New York *Times,* January 16, 1964, Special Education Survey, p. 77.

the myths about women were shattered. Rensselaer Polytechnic Institute broke a 116-year tradition by admitting some women as students and instructors. There were WACs and WAVES. And as more men were drawn into military service more women were taken on to relieve the shortage of teachers in mathematics and related subjects in colleges and universities as well as in secondary schools. Many of these opportunities have continued since the war. One example is that of an outstanding woman mathematician who was engaged in the National Defense during the conflict and who has been selected as Dean of Graduate Studies at the City University of New York.

The number of women schoolteachers rose from approximately 835,000 in 1950 to nearly 1,300,000 a decade later. Since that time improved salaries have brought more men into teaching so that by 1962 the number of women had fallen by several thousand and they comprised 70 percent of all noncollege teachers instead of the earlier 75 percent. About a fifth of the teachers in colleges and universities in 1960 were women. New teaching devices have been introduced into classrooms in various degrees throughout the nation—team teaching, television, teaching machines, and programmed textbooks, but like the computers they are all so new that it will take some years before they are perfected and integrated into our educational system. In time they may eliminate the unqualified people whom the scarcity of schoolroom teachers has made it imperative to employ, but they will never displace good men and women teachers on any level in this age of revolutionary change.

Unionization is almost unknown on college and university campuses today, but in the public schools the American Federation of Teachers has made some progress, and nearly 34,000 women comprise something over half of its membership. However, because such affiliation is considered unprofessional, few more than 3 percent of the nation's teachers are in unions. A larger proportion of New York City teachers are now unionized and their recent strikes and near strikes have made newspaper headlines. Gradually women's salaries have been raised to equal those of men on the same teaching level, although the higher teaching and administrative posts are far more often held by men.

Nurses have had much in common with teachers—lack of status, low salaries, poor working conditions. They have not scorned unionization as a means of lifting their economic status, and they have not followed the example of those teachers who embraced it. The American Nurses' Association has developed its own unique plan for collective bargaining. Both teachers and nurses are important members of the Peace Corps at work in underdeveloped countries.

And now, as we again look back to the time when Alexander Hamilton first called women into the "more important work" of tending machines in cotton mills, we recall the implication that society would have to make the necessary adjustments. And so it is time to ask what adjustments has society made? To what extent has the "sanctity of tradition" been dissolved? What are the remaining "cultural lags"? To what extent can working men and women be judged by the same standards? What are the special problems of employed women today?

Adjustments and Lags

PROTECTIVE LABOR LEGISLATION

We have seen that the passage of the Federal Fair Labor Standards Act, with its recent amendment on equal pay for equal work, stresses the nation's realization that in this day of automation and other technological changes, which replace brawn with brain and dexterity and release more and more workers from dangerous and dirty jobs, the sex of the worker has become less important than his or her experience, ability, and training. But the woven fabric of tradition and prejudice does not easily unravel. Much state legislation continues to apply to women only, and the United States Women's Bureau discovered 35 years ago that some of those laws were keeping perhaps 60,000 women from being continued in jobs they had performed successfully during World War I, or from newly opened jobs. For as long as there are regulations on the basis of sex alone, employers who are customarily prejudiced against hiring women will often take on men when they can find them whether or not they are better or even as good workers, and whether or not the women need the work.

The recent report of the President's Commission on the Status of women makes forward-looking recommendations: the Federal Fair Labor Standards Act should be extended to workers in hotels, motels, restaurants, and laundries, in more of the retail establishments, in agriculture, and in nonprofit organizations; and premium pay for time in excess of eight hours a day and 40 a week should be included. State legislation applicable to both men and women should be enacted or strengthened to apply to all types of employment and provide minimum-wage levels for intrastate workers approximating the minimum under the federal law. There should also be greater flexibility in state laws to avoid discrimination against women. For example, fixed limits on weight lifting do not take into account individual differences; and while nightwork is usually undesirable for both men and women, regulation to prevent abuse rather than prohibition is preferable.[5] Thus, there is plenty to do to overcome the cultural lags in the protection of American workers.

FAMILY LIFE

Ironically enough it is wars as well as technological progress and education that have brought economic opportunities to women by breaking down prejudices against hiring them, and

[5] *American Women*, pp. 36–39.

thereby changing the very nature of family life. After the last world war the number of married women at paid work exceeded the number of single women for the first time; and by 1958, 80 percent more married women in the labor force had children under 18 years of age than in 1949. Today some of the children of almost 3,000,000 mothers are less than six years old. Yet the multitude of household innovations—from vacuum cleaners to packaged foods, TV dinners and baby-sitters—have reduced homemaking to a part-time job as soon as the youngest child is in elementary school. Nevertheless, many problems in family administration remain to be solved to help women who are both homemakers and wage earners, and social groups are seeking to determine society's responsibility.

A recent publication by the United States Department of Health, Education, and Welfare is a revealing account of what education should be doing along these lines. The real problem of the woman in her dual role is "decision-making" in conference with her husband, this bulletin says. And here she needs help in such matters as dividing responsibilities among the family members; guidance and care of the children; maintaining health and caring for the sick; management of food; provisions for clothing, housing, furnishing, and equipment; planning for recreation and leisure; management of money. In this study of 153 pages we learn that home-economics teachers, supervisors, and school administrators are planning to give more attention to home management in public schools and in adult education programs; and that suggestions for further study of the nature of the problems can often be learned by listening to high school students, to children at play, or to husbands shopping for groceries. Several vocational high schools are already offering a one-year or one-semester home-management course as a part of the general education program, and in some places such courses are available for those in occupational training on a post-high school level. As would be expected, one of the hurdles to be jumped is the resistance or lack of interest in these programs; and it is of high importance to have well-qualified teachers, which we have seen is in itself a problem everywhere in academic life today.[6]

But what arrangements are being made for the care of children of working mothers? What these mothers want is assurance that their children will be "in good hands," that the services will be operated at convenient times in terms of the mother's work and shopping arrangements, and sufficiently flexible to cope with special circumstances arising out of such situations as day and evening shift work. Another important point is that the facilities be conveniently located. These mothers marry and have children in their twenties, and one of the deciding factors on how much employers make useful adjustments to employ them depends on "how hungry the market is."

Studies by the Children's Bureau stress the "quiet revolution" through which the family is going. Husbands in middle-class families are no longer considered sissies if they help with such domestic tasks as taking clothes to be washed, shopping, dishwashing, and baby-tending. In fact in 1958, of 5,073,000 children under 12 years of age (children of 2,873,000 women who were employed full time), 58 percent were being cared for at home: 802,000 or 16 percent by fathers who were employed at different times from those of the mothers, or were unemployed, or were not in the labor force; about 30 percent by other relatives, a substantial number of whom were less than 18 years of age; and 12 percent by nonrelatives. Relatives and neighbors cared for 22 percent of the children away from home, and of the remaining 20 percent unclassified arrangements were made for 600,000, and 400,000 were expected to take care of themselves when they returned from school—known as "latchkey children." Husbands of women in domestic

[6] U.S. Department of Health, Education, and Welfare, Office of Education, *Management Problems of Homemakers Employed Outside the Home*, 1961, Parts I and II *passim*.

or other services took care of children to a greater degree than those of mothers in any other occupation; and except for men on the farms the least care of these little people was by professional and managerial fathers. In the South a relatively small proportion of children were provided for by fathers—9 percent as compared to 16 percent for the nation as a whole and 24 percent in the North Central States. Children of mothers in clerical and sales occupations were more likely to have care away from home.[7]

Too many children today lack good day care, the President's Commission on the Status of Women declares. "If the family is to continue to be the core institution of society as it has been for many centuries, new and expanded community services are necessary. . . . The gross inadequacy of present child-care facilities is apparent." All communities should have child-care services for children of all kinds of families who may require day care, after-school care, or intermittent care. Costs should be met by fees scaled to parents' ability to pay. Since passage of the Revenue Act of 1954, working mothers have been aided in financing care of children and disabled dependents by deductions from federal income tax liability, but no account is taken of the number of children. Moreover, the present limits on the joint income of husband and wife above which deductions are not allowable are now too low, inasmuch as median incomes have increased from $5,336 in 1954 to $7,188 in 1961, which means that at present the majority of working couples are ineligible for deductions. At the low end of the scale a new hard core of disadvantaged people, many of them women with children, has been forming in American cities. "We have by no means done enough to strengthen family life and at the same

[7] U.S. Department of Health, Education, and Welfare, and Children's Bureau Bulletin 378, *Child Care Arrangements of Full-Time Working Mothers,* 1959, Summary and pp. 3, 14–15, 18–20; Children's Bureau Bull. 382, *Children of Working Mothers,* 1960, pp. 1, 13–15, 26.

time encourage women to make full contribution as citizens," declared President Kennedy. "It is appropriate at this time . . . to review recent accomplishments, and to acknowledge frankly the further steps that must be taken. This is a task for the entire Nation." [8]

PART-TIME WORK

For many years part-time has characterized the work pattern of many women with household responsibilities; and this form of employment is becoming increasingly important for the modern woman who wants to increase the family income, "keep her hand in" while the children are growing, and find relief from social isolation. In April, 1962, there were more than 6,000,000 women working part time (less than 35 hours a week)—29 percent of all women employed in nonagricultural enterprises. Large numbers of these were working in private households, retail stores, restaurants, beauty parlors, and other personal service establishments, in hospitals, at telephone switchboards, at typewriters, in libraries, offices, and classrooms.[9]

Part-time work is said to be undesirable in manufacturing industries because of the difficulties in meeting the needs of women with young children and because it makes too many extra demands upon the supervisory staffs. Here as elsewhere it is often true that one whole-time worker accomplishes more than two part-time people who must catch up on each others' threads. Insofar as businessmen are willing to help solve the

[8] *American Women,* pp. 1, 18, 19, 20–22, 66. An October 20, 1963, a *Release* by the Children's Bureau under the aegis of the Department of Health, Education, and Welfare reports that 41 states now hold approved plans to establish or expand day-care services for children during the fiscal year 1964 with an appropriation by Congress of $4,000,000. The report says there are now nearly 9,000,000 working mothers. Dr. Ellen Winston is the nation's first Commissioner of Welfare.

[9] *U.S. WB Bull. 285,* pp. 57–58.

problems of married women, they might accept these disadvantages, but prejudices die hard. On the other hand, a lawyer proprietor of a large firm says he has gone into the business of placing part-time women since a former employee of his firm who left to have a baby came back to meet an emergency in getting out a brief and did it with great success.

Another successful experiment is worth relating in some detail. It is the imaginative plan of a midwestern mutual insurance company, organized in 1947, whose business expanded so rapidly that it was cramped for space. Pending construction of larger quarters it inaugurated a "working mothers' night shift" geared to attract women with work experience who had left their jobs to be married and have a family. The response to the call was so immediate that the quota of 50 women was filled within a week, many applicants being turned away. For a number of reasons these women were glad to have the work: 1. the hours were convenient—from 6 P.M. to 10 P.M. nightly, while husbands were at home and could look after the children; 2. the added income was not needed to keep the wolf from the door but for extras, including better medical care and education for the children and added payments on the house or car; 3. the desire to keep their business skills alive so they could more readily resume full-time work as soon as family responsibilities permitted; 4. escape from household routine for a few hours during the evening. The atmosphere was informal and the women were permitted to dress as they pleased. Between eight and nine o'clock they were given a 15-minute "break" for free beverages and pastry, with second helpings. They received most of the usual fringe benefits, including Blue Cross and Blue Shield.

The gains for this company from the working mothers' night shift were reported to be equally rewarding. There were savings in making use of the building many extra hours. Operations were smoother in that the night shift could clear away the day group's backlog of processing records so that a fresh start could be made each morning. Owing to the superior aptitudes of the women, the quantity and quality of their work was high, in some cases higher than that of the day shift, and only first-line supervision was needed. When the more difficult tasks required training in the daytime classes, the company reimbursed the women for the expense incurred for baby-sitters. The whole arrangement proved so successful that it was not only made permanent, but plans were laid for extending the night shift to include commercial college students, who would probably be given daytime positions when their schooling was completed.[10]

Doubtless there are many more developments such as these, and they lend credence to the forecast that by 1975 the number of women on part time will have expanded more than 75 percent compared to about a 50 percent advance in the number working full time.[11]

Part-time and free-lance work is thus undoubtedly an excellent temporary solution for young wives and mothers who want to resume some sort of career later on, and there should be cooperation by unions and employers in solving the problems it presents so that these women can be integrated into the labor force. For as long as women are regarded as helping hands only, the difficulties of those who attempt to have both a career and a family will be perpetuated. Marginal workers who are called when needed and disposed of at will seldom receive promotions. The imperative need for both men and women is for our affluent society to achieve a status of full employment so that all who wish to work for pay can find suitable jobs despite

[10] N. Beatrice Worthy, "Part-Time Working Mothers—a Case Study," Division of Personnel Administration, National Industrial Conference Board, *Management Record*, September, 1960, pp. 17–19.
[11] *U.S. WB Bull. 273*, p. 1.

displacements as a result of technological change. At the average age of marriage a woman today has a half century or more ahead of her and in a large proportion of these years she will be free for full-time employment.

Special Problems of Women

The abiding special employment problems of women revolve about the fact that, with all the advances which science and technology, war emergencies, and education have brought to them, it is they who bear the children so that their work is bound to be interrupted. No longer is it a question of *can* they do the work, for today the Census Bureau reports some women holding jobs in every one of the 479 individual occupations. And former President Eisenhower has been quoted as saying that women have the brain, the heart, and other qualities desirable in a President of the United States, but that they have the good sense to resist the job.[12] The basic fact is that, while no young man considers marriage as a fundamental project, the great majority of young women put marriage and family first and work second. The typical life pattern of the woman at work is that she will go to school or take some temporary job until she marries (today one in every four women is married by the age of 18); she will have two to four children in her twenties, and return to work when the last child is in school. This means that she will begin again just about where she left off, while in the meantime the young man has been going ahead, receiving promotions, higher pay, and various other forms of recognition. Perhaps this is a major reason why more women are not in administrative positions.

More and more women who go to college also marry before graduation or very soon thereafter. And we have seen that universities are providing housing on their campuses for the in-

12 New York *Times*, January 14, 1954.

creasing number of young married couples, some with provision for care of their children. But when the wife receives
her diploma, her first job is that of child care, and perhaps part-
time work to help her husband win an advanced degree or get
started in business. If she manages to fill a full-time job she
cannot be considered permanent because she does not know
what she is going to do. Her husband may be assigned to a
position in another city, which will require a change of resi-
dence, and a "good wife" to a businessman is one of his chief
assets.

For various reasons, therefore, the employed woman is a
greater risk than the employed man. She may have talent, but
the sincerity of her interest is usually in doubt. For this reason
many employers do not open executive training programs to
women because they consider the expense of their training for
more than routine jobs to be unjustifiable. Graduate schools
which offer expensive training also feel disinclined to pay for
education of women so that they may become better mothers.
These customs mean, of course, that in both the business and
the academic world exceptions are not often made for women
who do not marry or do not let marriage interfere with their
careers, partly because there is no way of knowing in advance
of which women this will be true.

Not a few women have risen to high places, some of whom
have been noted in previous pages of this volume. And Dr.
Lillian Gilbreth, "the world's greatest woman engineer" and a
"genius in the art of living," mother of 11 children, all of whom
are college graduates, is another distinguished example. Jane
Addams was awarded the first Nobel Peace Prize to an American woman, and today's newspaper headlines report women
"firsts" in "men's jobs" all the way from astronaut to high bank
officer, film editor, and town planner. But all of these women
are considered unique, and when they leave their positions
they are usually replaced by men. Their experience does not

alter the fact that women—like Negroes and other minority groups—are judged collectively rather than as individuals. The resulting attitude toward women—that they are secondary members of the labor force—remains relatively unchanged. An executive in one company seems to have put it in a nutshell when he declared, "She would be a . . . vice-president by now if she wore pants." [13]

The situation in an important sector of the academic world has been brought home by two professors in a recent book on *The Academic Marketplace.* Here we are told that faculty women are not taken seriously in liberal arts departments of major universities where so much depends upon prestige and personal relations among the members. It is explained that this discrimination against women is "not because they have low prestige but because they are outside the prestige system entirely" and can be of no use to a department in getting replacements with whom the department can live—those who are *persona grata* to every member of the group. (In other words it appears that women do not qualify because they cannot "play ball.") For this reason, these authors hold that women scholars cannot look forward to a normal professional career. They are careful to point out that this custom is part of a much larger pattern which determines the utilization of women in our economy, that it is not peculiar to the academic world, but that "it does blight the prospects of female scholars." [14] We leave other examples to the reader.

Women's place in the economic world thus remains confused. Some women want the old ways, others welcome the new, but most women are in between. On leaving school the

[13] Frances M. Fuller and Mary B. Batchelder, "Opportunities for Women at the Administrative Level," *Harvard Business Review*, January–February, 1953, p. 120.

[14] Theodore Caplow and Reece J. McGee, *The Academic Marketplace* (New York, Basic Books, 1958), pp. 17–18, 111, 134, 226.

ambitious young woman finds that custom and prejudice bar her from many occupations and assign her a subsidiary role in most others so that she cannot have a career on equal terms with men. She also finds that the crux of her problem lies in the desire to combine the satisfactions of having a vocation outside the home with the role of wife and mother, although she has probably accepted the masculine view that her home activities are dull and trivial. This cultural conditioning of women's sense of inferiority has entered so deeply into their outlook on life that it has too often induced what many men regard as "typical female behavior"—unreasonable demands and over aggressiveness, inconsistencies, small-mindedness. Women, to say nothing of men, are said not to like working for a woman because she takes things too personally and pays too much attention to details whereas a man is more objective and leaves details to his subordinates to work out in their own ways. Insofar as these charges are true, here is a fault that must be faced and overcome. Up to now women administrators have been so few that they are more conspicuous than men, and so are more closely watched. Both men and women cite some women for whom they enjoy working, and of course the number will increase as women are recognized for their individual merits. "Bread-winning is no longer a monopoly of men, and home-making should no longer be a monopoly of women." [15]

Indeed, may we not look forward to the time when the fact is generally recognized that in most respects women have far more in common with men than society has yet been willing to accept, that men and women are more alike than different, that they are complementary rather than opposite. "Love," in the penetrating words attributed to Saint Exupery, "does not consist in gazing at each other, but in looking outward in the same direction." Perhaps, in line with the late President Ken-

[15] Myrdad and Klein, *Women's Two Roles*, p. 161.

nedy's suggestion in his Independence Day address at Philadelphia in 1962 for razing tariff walls in the changing commerce between politically free nations, the developing relations between men and woman may overcome the cultural lags and bring forth a "Declaration of Interdependence"—in the home and in the market place. Surely in this age of revolutionizing technology more and more education is the most promising route.

BIBLIOGRAPHY

Abbott, Edith. Women in Industry: A Study in American Economic History. New York and London, D. Appleton & Company, 1910.

Abbott, Edith and Sophonisba P. Breckinridge. "Employment of Women in Industries," *Journal of Political Economy*, XIV (1906), 14–40.

Alderfer, E. B. and H. E. Michl. Economics of American Industry. New York, McGraw-Hill Co., 1957.

American Women, Report of the President's Commission on the Status of Women, Washington, D.C., 1963.

Andrews, John B. and W. D. P. Bliss. History of Women in Trade Unions. Vol. X. Report on Condition of Woman and Child Wage-Earners in the United States, Washington, Government Printing Office, 1911.

Baker, Elizabeth Faulkner. Protective Labor Legislation. New York, Columbia University Press, 1925.

—— Displacement of Men By Machines. New York, Columbia University Press, 1933.

—— Printers and Technology. New York, Columbia University Press, 1957.

Barnett, George E. The Printers. Cambridge, Mass., 1909.

Bogart, Ernest Ludlow. Economic History of the American People. New York, Longmans Green & Co., 1930.

Clark, Victor S. History of Manufactures in the United States. Vol. I, 1607–1860, Vol. II, 1880–1893, Vol. III, 1893–1928. New York, Peter Smith, 1929.

Commons, John R. "American Shoemakers, 1648–1895: A Sketch on Industrial Evolution," *Quarterly Journal of Economics*, Nov., 1909.

Diebold, John. Automation: The Advent of the Automatic Factory. New York, D. Van Nostrand Co., 1952.

—— Automation: Its Impact on Business and Labor, May, 1959. National Planning Association Pamphet No. 106.

—— "The Application of Informal Technology," Annals of the American Academy of Political and Social Science, March, 1962, pp. 35–45.

Elsbree, Willard S. The American Teacher. New York, The American Book Co., 1939.

Hoos, Ida Russakoff. "When the Computer Takes Over the Office," *Harvard Business Review*, July–August, 1960.

—— Automation in the Office. Public Affairs Press, Washington, D.C., 1961.

Jacobson, Howard Boone and Joseph S. Roucek, eds. Automation and Society. New York, Philosophical Library, Inc., 1959.

Kaempffert, Waldemar. A Popular History of American Invention. Vols. I and II. New York, London, Charles Scribner's Sons, 1924.

Lahne, Herbert J. The Cotton Mill Worker. New York, Farrar and Rhinehart, 1944.

Meyer, Annie Nathan. Woman's Work in America. New York, Henry Holt and Co., 1891.

Michael, Donald N. Cybernation: The Silent Conquest. A Report to the Center for the Study of Democratic Institutions, Fund for the Republic, Inc., 1952.

Mill, John Stuart. The Subjection of Women. New York, Frederick A. Stokes, 1911.

Monthly Labor Review, U.S. Bureau of Labor Statistics:

Dec., 1930, "Wages and Hours of Labor in Rayon and Other Synthetic Textile Manufacturing, 1930," pp. 150–56.

Dec., 1931, "Technological Changes in the Cigar Industry and Their Effects on Labor," pp. 11–17.

Feb., 1932, "The Dial Telephone and Unemployment," pp. 235–47.

March, 1932, "Displacement of Morse Operators in Commercial Telegraph Offices," pp. 501, 514.

Jan., 1938, "Mechanical Changes in the Woolen and Worsted Industries, 1910–1936," pp. 58–93.

May, 1939, "Earnings and Hours in the Manufacture of Full-Fashioned Hosiery, 1938," pp. 1147–71.

June, 1939, "Earnings and Hours in the Manufacture of Seamless Hosiery, 1938," pp. 1388–1403.

Dec., 1941, "Hours and Earnings in the Cigar Industry, 1940," pp. 1514–1537.

Jan., 1942, "Earnings and Hours in Manufacture of Cigarettes, Chewing and Smoking Tobacco and Snuff, Dec. 1940," pp. 184–205.

Sept., 1942, "Employment of Women in Wartime," pp. 441–45.

Sept., 1942, "Effect of the War on Textile Employment," pp. 446–58.

Dec., 1942, "War Work of the United States Women's Bureau," p. 1183.

April, 1943, "Women's Work in Wartime," pp. 551–65.

Aug., 1943, "Employment of Women in Petroleum Refineries," pp. 1–4, 7.

Oct., 1943, "Women Workers in Two Wars," pp. 650–71.

Sept., 1944, "Employment in Airframe, Engine, and Propeller Plants, November 1943–June 1944," pp. 475–80.

May, 1945, "Postwar Employment Prospects for Women in the Hosiery Industry," pp. 978–989.

Sept., 1946, "Equal Pay for Women Workers," pp. 380–389.

Dec., 1947, "Women Workers and Recent Economic Changes," pp. 666–71.

May, 1952, "Education Through White Collar Workshops," pp. 508–510.

June, 1955, "A Review of Automatic Technology," pp. 637–44.

Aug., 1955, "Labor Turnover of Women Factory Workers, 1950–1955," pp. 893–94.

Apr., 1956, "Factors in Industrial Relations Prospects," p. 414.

Apr., 1956, "Changes in Teachers' Salaries in City Public Schools, 1953–1955," pp. 427–28.

Oct., 1958, "Two Decades of the Fair Labor Standards Act," pp. 1097–1106.

June, 1959, "Earnings in Synthetic Fibre Manufacturing, October 1958," pp. 653–58.

Oct., 1959, "Armour-Meatpacking Unions Provision," pp. 1109–10.

Jan., 1960, "Union Membership, 1958," pp. 5–6.

Jan., 1960, "Comparative Job Performance of Office Workers by Age," pp. 39–43.

Nov., 1960, "Earnings in Cigarette Manufacturing, May 1960," pp. 1193–96.

Jan., 1961, "White Collar Employment: I Trends and Structure," pp. 11, 15.

Feb., 1961, "White Collar Employment: II Characteristics," pp. 139–47.

May, 1961, "Earnings in the Cotton Textile Industry, August 1960," pp. 479–85.

June, 1961, "Earnings in Synthetic-Textile Manufacturing, August 1960," p. 620.

July, 1961, "Wages in Candy Manufacturing, November–December 1960," pp. 937–39.

July, 1961, "Wages in the Dress Manufacturing Industry, August 1960," p. 744.

July, 1961, "Bargaining and the Nursing Profession," p. 704 (by Daniel H. Kruger).

Nov., 1961, "Meat Packing and Other Food Products," pp. 1246–47.

June, 1962, "Developments in Industrial Relations," pp. 681–82.

July, 1962, "Industrial Relations—Teachers," p. 802.

Nov., 1962, "The Occupational Structure of U.S. Employment, 1940–1960," pp. 1209–13.

Aug., 1963, "Hours of Work in the United States and Abroad," pp. 925–34.

Nathan, Maud. The Story of an Epoch-Making Movement. New York, Doubleday, Page & Co., 1926.

National Manpower Council. Womanpower. New York, Columbia University Press, 1957.

Newcomer, Mabel. A Century of Higher Education for American Women. New York, Harper & Bros., 1959.

Smuts, Robert W. Women and Work in America. New York, Columbia University Press, 1959.

Sumner, Helen L. History of Women in Industry in the United States, 1910. Vol. IX. U.S. Bureau of Labor Report of Condition of Woman and Child Wage-Earners in the United States. Washington, D.C., 1911.

U.S. Bureau of Labor. Report on Condition of Woman and Child Wage-Earners in the United States, 1915:

Vol.   II. Men's Ready-Made Clothing, 1911
III. The Glass Industry, 1911
IV. The Silk Industry, 1911
V. Wage-Earning Women in Stores and Factories, 1910
IX. History of Women in Industry in the United States, 1910
X. History of Women in Trade Unions, 1911
XI. Employment of Women in the Metal Trades, 1911
XII. Employment of Women in Laundries, 1911
XVIII. Selected Industries, 1913

U.S. Bureau of Labor Standards. Growth of Labor Law in the United States. 1962.

U.S. Bureau of the Census. Statistics of Women at Work, based on unpublished information derived from the schedules of the Twelfth Census, 1900. Government Printing Office, 1907.

U.S. Bureau of Labor Statistics Bulletins:

175. Summary of the Report on Condition of Woman and Child Wage-Earners in the United States. 1915.

178. Wages and Hours of Labor in the Boot and Shoe Industry: 1907 to 1914. 1915.

180. The Boot and Shoe Industry in Massachusetts as a Vocation for Women. 1915.

532. Wages and Hours of Labor in the Cigarette Manufacturing Industry. 1930.

604. History of Wages in the United States from Colonial Times to 1928. 1934.

660. Mechanization and Productivity of Labor in the Cigar Manufacturing Industry, by W. D. Evans. 1938.

662. Productivity of Labor in the Cotton-Garment Industry, by Nahum I. Stone. 1938.

663. Wages in Cotton-Goods Manufacturing, by A. F. Hinricks, 1938.

1126. Occupational Outlook in the Printing Occupations. 1953.

1241. Automation and Employment Opportunities for Office-Workers. 1958.

1255. Occupational Outlook Handbook. 1959.

1267. Directory of National and International Labor Unions in the United States. 1959.

1276. Adjustments to the Introduction of Office Automation. May, 1960.

1287. Impact of Automation, a collection of 20 articles about technological change from the *Monthly Labor Review*, Nov., 1960.

1294. Earnings and Supplementary Benefits in Hospitals, Mid-1960. 1961.

1300. Occupational Outlook Handbook. 1961.

1306. Industrial Wage Survey—Communications. Oct., 1960.

1320. Directory of National and International Labor Unions in the United States, 1961. March, 1962.

U.S. Bureau of Labor Statistics Reports:

40. Knit Outerwear. July, 1953.

41. Knit Underwear. July, 1953.

90. Wage Structure Series 2, Woolen and Worsted Textiles. April–May, 1952.

109. A Case Study of a Large Mechanized Bakery. 1956.

116. Wage Structure, Men's and Boy's Shirts (except work shirts) and Nightwear. Feb., April, and Oct., 1956. (Studies of the Effects of the $1.00 Minimum Wage.)

117. Wage Structure (in Selected Areas), Cigars, Canning and Freezing, Raw Sugar, Tobacco Stemming and Redrying, 1955 and 1956. (Studies in the Effects of $1.00 Minimum Wage.)

122. Wage Structure, Women's and Misses' Coats and Suits. Feb., 1957.

129. Wage Structure, Seamless Hosiery. April, 1957. (Studies in the Effects of the $1.00 Minimum Wage.)

133. Wage Structure, Footwear Industry. April, 1957.

134. Wool Textiles, Wage Structure, Part I, Yarn and Broadwoven Fabric Mills; Part II, Securing and Combing Plants. 1957.

137. Automatic Airline Reservation System. July, 1958.

140. Wage Structure, Men's and Boy's Suits and Coats. March, 1958.

167. Wage Structure, Cigarette Manufacturing. 1960.

168. Wage Structure, Miscellaneous Plastics Products. Jan.–Feb., 1960.

171. Earnings of Communications Workers. Oct., 1959.

184. Wage Structure, Cotton Textiles. August, 1960.

U.S. Bureau of Labor Statistics. Studies in Automatic Technology: No. 1: A Case Study of a Company Manufacturing Electronic Equipment. 1955. No. 2: The Introduction of an Electronic Computer in a Large Insurance Company, by Kenneth G. Van Auken, Jr. 1955.

U.S. Department of Labor. The American Workers' Fact Book. 1960.

U.S. Women's Bureau Bulletins:

12. The New Position of Women in American Industry. 1920.

28. Women's Contributions in the Field of Invention. 1923.

50. Effects of Applied Research Upon the Employment Opportunities of American Women. 1926.

65. The Effects of Labor Legislation Upon the Employment Opportunities of Women. 1928.

66. History of Legislation for Women in Three States, Parts 1 and 2, *passim.*

73. Variations in Employment Trends of Women and Men. 1930.
83. Fluctuations of Employment in the Radio Industry. 1931.
88. The Employment of Women in Slaughtering and Meat Packing. 1932.
100. The Effects on Women of Changing Conditions in the Cigar and Cigarette Industries. 1932.
110. The Change from Manual to Dial Operation in the Telephone Industry. 1933.
115. Women at Work. 1933.
120. The Employment of Women in Offices. 1934.
159. Trends in the Employment of Women. 1928 to 1936.
194. Your Questions as to Women in War Industries. 1942.
196. "Equal Pay" for Women in War Industries. 1942.
199. Successful Practices in the Employment of Nonfarm Women on Farms in the Northeastern States. 1944.
203–5. As Practical Nurses and Auxiliary Workers on the Nursing Team. Revised, 1953.
204. Women's Emergency Farm Service on the Pacific Coast in 1943. 1945.
207. The Woman Telephone Worker. 1946.
218. Women's Occupations Through Seven Decades. 1947.
223–1. The Outlook for Women in Science. 1949.
223–4. The Outlook for Women in Mathematics and Statistics. 1948.
223–5. The Outlook for Women in Architecture and Engineering. 1948.
232. Women's Jobs—Advance and Growth. 1949.
236. Women in Higher Level Positions. 1950.
243. Report of National Equal Pay Conference, March 31– April 1, 1952. 1952.
247. State Minimum-Wage Laws and Orders, July 1, 1942– March 1, 1953. 1953.
251. Progress Toward Equal Pay in the Meat Packing Industry. 1953.
253. Changes in Women's Occupations, 1940–1950. 1954.
254. Employment Opportunities for Women in Professional Engineering. 1954.
256. Training Mature Women for Employment. 1955.

263. Women Mathematicians and Statisticians. 1956.

267. State Minimum-Wage Laws and Orders. 1959.

270. Careers for Women in the Physical Sciences. 1959.

271. Careers for Women in Retailing. 1959.

273. Part-time Employment for Women. 1960.

274. Training Opportunities for Women and Girls. 1960.

275. 1960 Handbook on Women Workers. 1960.

276. Today's Women in Tomorrow's World. 1960.

285. 1962 Handbook on Women Workers. 1963.

286. Women Telephone Workers and Changing Technology. 1963.

Ware, Norman J. The Industrial Worker, 1840–1860. Boston and New York, 1924.

Willett, Mabel Hurd. The Employment of Women in the Clothing Trade. Doctor's Dissertation. New York, Columbia University, 1902.

Wolfson, Theresa. The Woman Worker and the Trade Unions. New York, 1926.

Woody, Thomas. A History of Women's Education in the United States. Vols. I and II. New York, 1929.

Wright, Carroll D. The Industrial Evolution. New York, Charles Scribner's Sons, 1895.

Index

Actuaries, 263

Adams, Arthur S., quoted on television, 291

Addams, Jane, 439

Aerologists, 265

Agricultural age, 3

Aircraft manufacture, 199–201, 209, 426

American Association of University Professors, 280, 348, 349

American Council on Education, 291

American Nurses' Association, 62, 312–24; on collective bargaining, quoted, 350–52, 388–89, 430; membership, 352

American Red Cross, 62

American Tel. & Tel. Co., 246; attitude on unionism, 371, 374–77, 381

American Women's Education Association, quoted on nursing, 62

Anthony, Susan B., cited on women compositors, 39n; 41, 42; woman's rights movement, 59

"Astronauttes," vii; 269–70; see also Dr. Louis Lasagna

Automatic selling, 254

Automation, vii, 202–03, 205; defined, 206–07; some effects in factory, shop, and office, 210–11, 212–37, 254–55, 381; requires more education, 210; in nursing, 322; see also Computers; Steelworkers, contract on; Teaching

Baby-sitters, 110, 111, 273, 276

Bacteriologists, 278

Bagley, Sarah, quoted on life at the Lowell mills, 15; 88–89

Barbash, Jack, cited on white collar unionism, 366n; 371; quoted on telephone unionism, 375, 377

Barnard, Henry, 56

Barnard College, 274, 286n

Barton, Clara, 62

"Battle of fibers," 144

Beecher, Catharine E., quoted on teachers, 58

Beirne, Joseph A., 376, 377, 381; quoted on women as union members, 383; see also Communication Workers of America under Labor Unions

Bell, Alexander Graham, quoted, 68

Bell Telephone System, 238–46; attitude on unionism, 371–83, 391

Beyer, Clara M., 88, quoted, 94

Bindery, 47–48, 77, 181–83, 209

Blue-collar workers, 217, 256, 262, 367

Blyth, John W., quoted on effect of teaching machines, 303–04

Bookkeepers and accountants, 78, 213, 216, 221

Brandeis, Louis D., 397, 398

Brooks, John Graham, 66

Bruner, Jerome S., quoted on the programmed textbook, 308

Bunting, Mary I, 273–74, quoted on education, 330

Caplow and McGee, quoted on women professors, 440

Career women, 253; see also Marriage and Career

Carey, James B., on women in the labor force, 417

Carey, Mathew, quoted on employing women, 9; 40, 63

Carnegie Corporation, 274, 304–05

Cartwright's power loom, 143

Cellulosic and noncellulosic fibers, 125; see also Silk and synthetic fiber manufacture; Rayon; Nylon

Census, U.S., classifications, viii–ix; Bureau's use of machines, 212–13, 219

Center for Programmed Instruction, 304, 309

Chemists, 277

Children, at work, 5–6, 18–19, 21, 23, 25, 28–29, 35–36, 60; Horace Mann on its regulation, 88; care of, 235, 316, 428, 432–33, 439

Cigarette manufacture, 36–37, 162, 168–70, 208

Cigars, household industry, 32; subdivision of the craft, 34; union action, 33, 35; women's employment, 32–35, 52, 162–68, 208; handmade, 34, 162–63; automatic machines,

Cigars (*Continued*)
162–63; further mechanization, 166–67
City University of New York, 264
Civil War period, 20, 23; uniforms, 25; nursing, 62; saleswomen, 64
Clerical workers, 74, 212–28, 233–37, 241, 247–56; number, 335, 370; attitude on unionism, 336, 364–65, 369–71, 391
Clothing, 20–21, 24–27, 52; changing nature of, 143, 151–52; women's employment, 148–52, 203, 208; *see also* under Labor unions; Amalgamated Clothing Workers of America; International Ladies' Garment Workers' Union
Cogen, Charles, 342, 345; quoted on teachers' union contract, 347
Coit, Eleanor, 338
Colleges and universities, women teachers, 279; University of Chicago President Harper quoted, 280; status, 440
Columbia University, on engineers, 264
Communism, 286, 354, 355, 359, 374, 385; in teaching, 344, 348–49
Computers (data-processing machines), 213, 218–37, 256, 263, 268, 368, 390; women's employment on, 259, 263, 268, 363, 426–27
Conant, James B., cited, 285–86n; 326
Condon-Wadlin Law, 341, 342, 345, 347, 358, 388
Consumers' League, New York, 65–66, 92, 249, 251; National, 398; Massachusetts, 404–05
Cooper Union, 72
Core-making, 196, 402–03
Cornell University, 272
Cotton textile manufacture, Lowell and Waltham mills, 8–17; expansion in the South, 116–17, 143–44; New England at its peak, 115; women's occupations, 116–17, 124; conversion to rayon, 124; *see also* Textiles
Coughlin, Howard, cited on office employment, 237n; 362–63; quoted on women, 370
Coxe, Tench, 6

Craft vs. Industrial Unionism, 336, 367–71, 375
Cryptographers, 263
Cultural lags, 85, 270–71; 430, 431, 442
Curry, Nelle B., quoted on telephone operators, 372–73
Cybernation, 254–55

Dall, Caroline, quoted on woman's rights, 59
Data-processing machines, *see* Computers
Daughters of St. Crispin, 30–31
Davis, Caroline, quoted on equal pay, 418
Davis, Mrs. Jefferson, quoted on nursing, 62
Dentists, 277
Department stores, 64–67, 249–56
Deutsch, Helene, 261, 277
Dewey, John, quoted on team teaching, 288; quoted on unionization of teachers, 348; 349
Diebold, John, on teaching machines, 304
Displacement of women by men in the factory, 208; textiles, 17, 19, 20, 22; clothing, 25, 27, 29; dairy products, 49; printing, 46, 178, 180
Domestic and personal service, 8, 54–55, 76; decline in, 109–12; *see also* Baby-sitters; Housekeepers; Laundresses
Domestic system, 3–4
Douglas, Paul H., quoted on the Bell Telephone System, 379
Dunlop, John T., quoted on the AFSCME, 355
Durable-goods manufacture, beginnings of, 24, 49–51, 76–77; 194–205, 206, 209–11

Edison, Thomas Alva, 194–95
Editors and reporters, 277
Education of women, 57–59, 215; commercial and business school, 72–73; required by automation, 210–11; saleswomen, 252–53; higher level, 259–60; for engineers, 268–69, 272–76; prejudice against, 280; demand

for, 325–27, 331–32, 442; history of, 427–29

Eisenhower, Dwight D., quoted on prejudices against women, 268, 325, 438

Electric energy opens more jobs for women, 24, 67, 194

Electric lamp manufacture, 195, 203

Electric machinery, 194; employment on, 197–98, 201–03, 209, 267–68

"Electronic nurse," 312, 328

Electronics, 198, 208, 209, 212–37; radios, 198, 209

Engineers, 264–69, 278; Society of Women, 266, 268

Equal pay for equal work: early demands for, by cigar makers, 33; by compositors, 40–41, 43; for teachers, 58; in government offices, 73; advocated by, Commissioner Wright, 83; Knights of Labor, 411; War Department, 412; Machinists' Union, 412–13; employers beginning to observe equal pay, 201, 325, 402; Michigan law, 413–14, 416

Equal pay for equal work: the national campaign for: Pepper-Morse bill No. 1178, 414, 423; United Electrical Workers, quoted, 415; Helen Gahagan Douglas bill, 415; UAW quoted, 415–16, 418; Frances P. Bolton's bill, 416; Eleanor Roosevelt, quoted, 417, 423; James B. Carey, 417; Caroline Davis, quoted, 418; National Association of Manufacturers, quoted, 415, 418, 423; National Woman's Party, 418; Arthur Goldberg, quoted, 418–19; 423; Esther Peterson, quoted, 419

Equal Pay for Equal Work Act of 1963, the McNamara-Green bill, 419; approved by Senate and House, 419–20, 423; signed by President Kennedy, 420, 423; coverage and content of, 420–21, 423

ERMA, 218, 221

Eurich, Alvin C., quoted on teaching technology, 287–88

Fair Labor Standards Act of 1938, on minimum wages, 118, 138n; on

hours, 387; described, 406–09; amended by the Equal-Pay-for-Equal-Work Act, 416–17, 420–21, 422; coverage, 406–09, 420, 430–31

Fall River cotton manufacture, 10n

Family life, labor-saving inventions for, 59; changes in, 87, 111; Dr. Mirra Komarovsky quoted, 261–62; education for, 428, 432; "quiet revolution" in, 433; President's Commission quoted, 434; President Kennedy quoted, 434–35, 442

Farm workers, 3, 53, 99–109; out migration, 101–04; family farms, 102–03, 108–09; worth of a farmer's wife, 102–03; push-button farming, 103; part-time operations, 104; bookkeeping, 104; decline in women's employment, 109; see also Migratory workers

Fathers' changing role, 111, 261–62; 433–34, 442

Feed-back, see Automation

Female Labor Reform Association, 15, 16, 88–89

Flemming, Arthur S., quoted on women engineers, 267

Food manufacture, 48–49, 185–86; canning and preserving, 186–88; meat processing, 188–89; confections, 189–90; bakery products, 190–91; beverages and dairy products, 191

Footwear manufacture, 27–30, 156–60, 208; see also Daughters of St. Crispin

Ford Fund for the Advancement of Education, 283, 287, 289, 292, 302–03, 326–27

FOSDIC, 219

Fotosetter, 175

Frankfurter, Felix, 397

Friends of Domestic Industry, 9

Gainfully employed women in 1900, 75–79

Gallatin, Albert, 6, 9

Gannon, Mary, 371; quoted on telephone operators, 376

Gibbs, Katherine, school, 217

Gilbreth, Lillian, 439

Gilman, Charlotte Perkins, quoted on woman's progress, 79

Godey's Lady's Book, 59

Goldmark, Josephine, 397, 398

Government Printing Office, 175

Hadassah, union contract, 358

Hamilton, Alexander, Report on Manufactures, quoted, 3–6; 8, 430

Hansen, Alvin H., quoted on education, 259

Harper, William R., president of the University of Chicago, quoted on prejudice against women on college and university faculties, 280

Harrington, Michael, quoted on the Retail Clerks International Association, 386; 387

Harvard University, 265, 271, 283–84, 289, 330

Hechinger, Fred M., 330, 346

Hollerith, Herman, 212–13

Hoos, Ida, on white-collar unionism, 365, 368

Hopper, Grace, mathematician, 265

Hosiery manufacture, 134–42; labor organization in, 136; seamless replacing full-fashioned, 141–42

Hours of work, at Lowell mills, 13; of saleswomen, 249, 251, 252; legislation on, 88–95, 153; 395–98; in Fair Labor Standards Act, 406, 409, 420; the trend, 421–23

Housekeepers, 110, 111

Housewives, see Married women; *see also* Family life

Howe, Elias, the sewing machine, 24–25

Hughes, Dr. Charlotte, quoted on surgery for women, 277

Hughes, Everett C., quoted on nurses' stories, 320–21, 327

Humphrey, Hubert, quoted on the Bell Telephone System, 379

Hunter College, 295

Hutchins, Paul R., quoted on office unionism, 362

IBM computers, 218–19, 226–27, 232

Immigration, to the cotton mills, 15, 23; to the clothing industry, 26; to

the tobacco industry, 32; increase in, 77, 89; laws against, 115–16

Industrial vs. craft unionism, 179, 367–71

Interchangeable parts system, 5, 24, 76, 194, 218, 425–26

Jewish Philanthropies, Federation of, 389

Johns Hopkins Medical School, *see* Dr. Louis Lasagna

Jung, Carl G., 261

Kassalow, Everett, quoted on organizing white-collar workers, 368

Kay's flying shuttle, 3

Kelly, Florence, 66, 95

Kennedy, John F., Senator, 277, 407; President, 395, 407, 420, 423; quoted on family life, 434–35, 441–42

Keppel, Francis, quoted on teaching, 284; founder of team teaching, 289–91

Key-punch operators, 233–34

Klaus, Ida, lawyer, 347

Knights of Labor, *see* Labor Unions

Knit-goods manufacture, 20–21, 127–42; union-management agreement on technological change, 133–34; *see also* Hosiery manufacture

Komarovsky, Mirra, quoted on fathers in the family, 261–62

Komoski, P. Kenneth, quoted on teaching machines, 304–05

Korean War period, 266, 325

Labor unions

Actors and Artists of America, 339

Air Line Pilots Association, 339

Amalgamated Clothing Workers of America, xii, 154–56

American Federation of Hosiery Workers, xii, 136

American Federation of State, County, Municipal Employees (AFSCME) xii, 352–61, 389; *see also* Arnold S. Zander

Automobile, Aircraft and Agricultural Implement Workers' Union, United (UAW) 204, 367, 369;

quoted on equal pay for equal work, 415–16

Bookbinders, International Brotherhood of, xii, 182n

Bookkeepers, Stenographers and Accountants Union (BS&AU), 364–65

Boot and Shoe Workers Union, 159–60

Building Service Employees' International Union, 354, 385

Cigar Makers International Union, on employment of women, 33–35, 93, 162–65

Communication Workers of America (CWA), 370, 377–83, 390–91; see also Joseph A. Beirne

Doll and Toy Workers, International Union of, 204

Electrical, Radio and Machine Workers, International Union of (IUE), on equal pay, 417

Electrical, Radio and Machine Workers of America, United (UE), quoted on equal pay for equal work, 415

Electrical Workers, International Brotherhood of (IBEW); telephone operators, 371–75, 377–78, 390

Garment Workers of America, United, 154

Hospital unions, 352n

IUD (Industrial Union Department, AFL-CIO), quoted on organizing white-collar workers, 336, 367–68; on equal pay for equal work, 417–18

Knights of Labor, 31, 411

Ladies' Garment Workers' Union, International (ILGWU), xii, 153–56

Machinists, International Association of, on equal pay for equal work, 412–13

Meat Cutters and Butcher Workmen of North America, Amalgamated, 385

Mine Workers of America, United, 351

Molders and Foundry Workers Union, International, 403

Office Employees International Union (OEIU), xii, 237n, 361–71, 389; see also Howard Coughlin

Office and Professional Workers of America, United (UOPWA), 353–54, 356–57, 365

Papermakers and Paperworkers, United, quoted on organizing white-collar workers, 336

Printing Pressmen and Assistants Union, International (IPP&AU), xii, 46, 179

Railway Clerks, Brotherhood of, 370

Retail Clerks International Association (RCIA), 383–87, 391

Retail, Wholesale and Department Store Union (RWDSU), 384–87

Shoe Workers of America, United, 150–60

Steelworkers of America, United, 335, 367, 370

Teachers, American Federation of (AFT), 340, 343–49, 388

Teachers, United Federation of (UFT), 342–43, 346–47; 349–50, 388

Teachers' Guild, 342, 349

Teachers' Union, 343

Teamsters, Chauffeurs, Warehousemen and Helpers, International Brotherhood of, 336, 354, 367, 370, 385, 387

Telegraphers' Union, Commercial, 372

Telephone Unions, Alliance of Independent (AITU), 381, 390

Telephone Workers, National Federation of (NFTU), 375–77, 390

Textile Workers Union of America, xii, 114n, 121, 126, 132

Textile Workers Union, United, 114, 121–22

Tobacco Workers' International Union, 167–68

Typographical Union, International (ITU), 41–42, 172–76; see also Augusta Lewis

Lambert, Sam M., quoted on education, 286–87

Larcom, Lucy, quoted on New England girlhood, 13–15; cited on education, 55n

Lasagna, Dr. Louis, quoted on "astro-nauttes," 269–70
Laundresses, 110
Leather products manufacture, not footwear, 160
Lehman, Herbert H., quoted on the Bell Telephone System, 379
Leisure time, 409
Lewis, Augusta, quoted on conditions for women in the composing room, 43
Librarians, 277, 332; attitude toward unions, 356, 359–61, 389; *see also* AFSCME under Labor Unions
Little Wagner Act of 1958, 358
Livermore, Mary, quoted on woman's place, 84–85
Lowell Cotton mills, 9–17, 58; working conditions, 69; 427
Lowell, Mrs. Charles Russell, 66
Lyon, Mary, Mount Holyoke Female Seminary, 58

McClellan Committee revelations, 336
McIntosh, Millicent C., quoted on marriage and career, 274, 276
McIver, Charles, quoted on women teachers, 56–57
Macy's department store, 64, 253–55; unionism in, 386, 391
Man-made fibers, 151; *see also* Silk and synthetic fiber manufacture; Rayon; Nylon; "Battle of fibers"
Mann, Horace, quoted on the status of women, 56; on regulation of child labor, 88
Marriage and career, 274, 276, 332, 439, 441
Married students, 273, 428, 438–39
Married women at paid work, viii; cigar making, 32, 34, 35; teachers, 60, 282, 286; Carroll D. Wright quoted, 84, 86; Mary Livermore quoted, 85; in offices, 212, 215, 235; telephone operators, 241; saleswomen, 247, 249–50, 252; housewives, 262; engineers, 267–68; demand for, 276–77; more than single women, 432; part-time work, 436–37; family before work, 438–39
Martineau, Harriet, women's seven occupations, 39, 55–56, 170

Mass production, key to, 24
Mathematicians, 262–63, 277, 325, 427
Mead, Margaret, quoted on "sex-typing," 270–71
Meany, George, 343, 369
Megel, Carl H., president, American Federation of Teachers, 346
Metals and Machinery manufacture, 196–97, 204, 404
MICR, in banking, 221–22
Migratory workers, 104–08
Mill, John Stuart, 59; quoted on woman's place, 85–86; quoted on woman's wages, 425
Mills College, 261
Morse, Samuel F. B., quoted, 67
Morse, Wayne, quoted on the Bell Telephone System, 379; equal-pay-for-equal-work bill, 414
Mott, Lucretia, woman's rights, 59
Mount Holyoke College, 58
Mule spinning, 10, 15, 17; replaced by frame spinning, 116

National Association of Manufacturers, quoted on clerical work, 366; quoted on equal pay for equal work, 415, 418; 423
National Defense Education Act of 1958, 286, 325
National Education Association (NEA), investigation of teaching and a "goal salary schedule," 284–87, 300, 326, 331; on unionization of teachers, 340, 343–46, 388
National Industrial Recovery Act, 405
National Labor Relations (Wagner) Act, of 1935, 338, 375
National Labor Relations Board, 366, 373–74
National Recovery Act (NRA), 413
National Trades' Union, quoted on woman's place, 84
National War Labor Board, on equal pay for women, 412, 414, 423
National Woman's Party, 400, 418
Negroes, tobacco strippers, 161, 208; key-punchers, 234; nurses, 319, 327–28; 440
Newspaper strike in New York City, 176n

New School for Social Research, union contract, 358

New York Mercantile Inspection Act, 249

New York School of Social Work, 329

New York Society for Ethical Culture, union contract, 358

New York University, admits women, 271–72

Nightingale, Florence, quoted on nurses' morals, 61; at the Crimean War, 61; nursing established as a profession, 312

Nixon, Richard M., quoted on the Bell Telephone System, 380

Non durable-goods manufacture, textiles, 8–23, 113–47; clothing, 24–27, 148–56; footwear and other leather products, 27–31, 156–60; tobacco, 31–37, 160–70; printing and publishing, 37–48, 170–85; food, 48–49, 185–91; other, 191–93

Nonelectrical machine manufacture, 203, 210

Northrup, James, automatic loom, 113–14, 143, 208

Norton, Mildred McAfee, quoted on the status of women, 262

Nurses and nursing, 16–17, 59, 79; early status, 55, 60, Florence Nightingale quoted, 61; birth of the profession, 61–63, 312–313; problems and developments, 313–24, 327–28, 430; in the Peace Corps, 329; collective bargaining, 350–52, 430; see also American Nurses' Association; Florence Nightingale

Nylon, 126, 144

Oberlin College, admits women, 58, 259, 427

O'Connor, Julia, quoted on the Bell Telephone System, 374

Office machines, 212–37, 366–67

Office Management Association, National (NOMA), to prevent unionization, 365–67

Office workers, summer school for, 338, 361; attitude on unionism, 369–71, 426; see also Stenographers, typists, secretaries; White collar workers; Office Workers' International Union

Ogburn, William Fielding, the "cultural lag," 85

O'Neill, Eugene Frank and Lawrence H., quoted on teaching, 263–64

Parent-Teachers' Association (PTA), 275

Part-time work, unclassified workers, 110; clerical workers, 222; preferred by many at times, 271; for more mature students, 276; teachers, 284, 289; nurses, 316; nonfarm workers, 409; 435–38

PBX, 238

Peace Corps, 328–30, 430

Peplau, Dr. Hildegard E., quoted on automation in nursing, 323–24

Perkins, Frances, quoted on displacement of telephone operators by the dial system, 240n, 371; quoted on unionizing office workers, 361

Peterson, Esther, President's Commission on the Status of Women, 395; quoted on equal pay for equal work, 419

Philadelphia Trades' Union, quoted on woman's place, 84

Physicians and surgeons, 277

Plastics, 127, 146, 193

Prejudice and tradition on women's employment: teaching, 57, 280, 440; shoemaking, 158; effect of state laws, 171, 404, 423, 431; printing, 178; married women, 215; President Eisenhower quoted, 268; programming computers, 427; college education, 428–29; 441

Pressy, Sydney L., quoted on teaching machines, 299, 311

Printing and publishing, a family enterprise, 37–39; early attitude toward women, 37–48 passim; the Linotype arrives, 44; women's employment, 77, 170–85 passim, 208–09, 401–02; see also Bindery; Specialty printing

Programmed instruction, teaching machines, 298–305; programmed textbooks, 305–10, Goldstein and Gotkin quoted, 309–10; see also

Programmed instruction (*Continued*) Teaching Machines; Programmed textbook

Programmed textbook, 305–10, 429; described by Homme and Glaser, 306; publishers' concern, 308; Bruner, Jerome S., quoted on the textbook of the future, 308; Rourke, Robert E. K., quoted on new textbooks, 308–9; Goldstein and Gotkin, on advantages of, 309–10

Programming for computers, men preferred, 221, 229–30; the process, 228–29, 231; qualifications for, 229n, 230–31; training for, 232, 268, 272; successful women, 232–33, 259; Grace Hopper, executive, 265; women's role uncertain, 426–27

Proofreaders, 45n, 176

Protective labor legislation, New Hampshire, 89; Massachusetts, 15, 90–91, 95; New York State, 92–95; Illinois, 95; Pennsylvania, 96; U.S. Women's Bureau analysis of effects, 401–04, 422; advocated for fathers, 400; trend, 421–24; prejudicial to employment, 230, 426–27; *see also* Fair Labor Standards Act; Equal Pay for Equal Work Act

Radcliffe College, 271, 330–31

Raushenbush, Esther, quoted on educating mature women, 274–76

Rayon, 120, 123–24, 143

Rees, Mina Spiegal, mathematician, 233, quoted on national defense, 264; 429

Rensselaer Polytechnic Institute, accepts women, 262, 272, 325, 429

Reuther, Walter, 369

"Right-to-work" laws, 335–36

Roosevelt, Eleanor, chairman of President's Commission, 278, 395; quoted on equal pay, 417; 423

Rutgers University, Mrs. Helen M. Marston trains mathematicians, 272–73

Saleswomen, vii, 63–67; number in 1900, 78; encouragement and exploitation, 241, 247–56; care of their children, 434; *see also* RCIA and RWDSU under Labor unions

Sarah Lawrence College, 274–76

Scientific management, 213–14

Seager, Henry R., quoted on protective legislation for fathers, 400

Secretaries, 215, 216–18, 237

Seven College Vocational Workshops, 274

Sewing machine, introduction of, 24–25

"Sex-typing," 263, 270–71, 332

Shaver, Dorothy, president of Lord & Taylor, 253

Sholes, Christopher Latham, quoted on his typewriter for women, 70–71

Shriver, Sargent, quoted on the Peace Corps, 328–30

Silk and synthetic (man-made) fiber manufacture, 21–23, 117–18, 120, 122–27; "battle of fibers," 144

Skinner, B. F., quoted on teaching machines, 298–303, *passim*

Slater, Samuel, "father of American cotton industry," 5, 8

Smith, Alexander, quoted on the Bell Telephone System, 380

Social workers, vii, 277; American Association of (AASW), 352–54, 359; Community and Social Agency Employees (CSAE), 356–57; New York District 37, AFSCME; National Association of Social Workers (NASW), 359; *see also* AFSCME under Labor unions

Southern expansion in textile manufacture, 116–17, 143–44, 208

Special problems of women, vii, 438–42

Specialty printing, 179–81, 209

Spicer, Verona A., teacher, 263–64

Spinner, Francis Elias, cited on bringing women into government offices, 71n

Sputniks, 268, 286, 325, 326

Stanford University, 330–31

Stanton, Elizabeth Cady, women's rights, 59

Statisticians, 263, 277

Status of Women, 4n, 12, 54; Horace Mann quoted, 56; status in 1900,

80–87; 215, 259, 278, 391; President's Commission on, ix, 278, 395, quoted on child care, 434; turning points, 15, 23, 76, 95–96, 398, 406

Stenographers, typists, secretaries, 71–74, 78, 212–18, 237, 337, 426; see also White-collar employees; Office workers

Strikebreakers, cigar making, 33–34; printing, 39, 41; 77, 426

Student restlessness, 330–31

SUPRAD, 289–91

Sweatshops, 26, 28, 152–54, 398, 405

Taft, Robert A., quoted on Bell Telephone System, 380

Taft-Hartley Act of 1947, 335, 356, 366, 379–80

Taylor, Frederick, scientific management, 213

Teachers, vii; Lowell mills, 12–14, 16; 55–60, 79; 259–60, 312, 320; status of, 280–82, 326, 430; salaries, 284, 285, 287, 345, 347, 427, 430; importance of, 310–11, 326; in colleges and universities, 279, 427–28; see also Teachers under Labor unions; Teachers in unions

Teachers College, Columbia University, 316–17

Teachers in unions, 281, 326, 339–50, 388; Norwalk strike, 340; Buffalo strike, 341, 388, New York City strike, 341–43, 346; salaries, 347, 429; see also Teachers under Labor unions

Teaching machines, described, 298–305, 312, 327, 429; see also B. F. Skinner; Sydney L. Pressy; John W. Blyth

Team teaching, 288–91, 327, 429; Dean Francis Keppel, founder, 289–91; Franklin School experiment, 289; Helene M. Lloyd, pilot project, 290

Technicians, 277, 313

Technology of teaching, 288–310, 429; see also Team teaching; Television; Teaching machines; Programmed textbook

Telegraph operators, 67–69, 70, 244–45

Telephone operators, vii, 67–70, 211; effect of dial system on, 239–46; unionism, 371–83, 390–91; Julia O'Connor, 371, 373, quoted, 374; Mary Gannon, 371, quoted, 376; Sylvia B. Gottlieb, 378; Mary H. Hanson, 383; Elaine T. Gleason, 383; Wages, 372–73, 378–79; see also Communication Workers of America (CWA); Telephone Unions; Alliance of Independent (AITU); Telephone Workers, National Federation of (NFTU)

Teletypesetter, 209

Television, 201–3, 209–10, 219; 276–77, 288, 291–98, 312, 327, 429

Telstar, 246, 263, 276

Tenement-house labor, regulation of, 92–93

Tennessee Valley Authority, women engineers, 265–66

Tereshkova, Valentina, astronaut, vii, 269–70

Textiles, substitute for, 145–46; women's employment, 147, 203, 208; relative decline of, 208; see also Cotton textile manufacture; Woolen and worsted manufacture; Silk and synthetic fiber manufacture; Rayon manufacture; Knit goods manufacture; "Battle of fibers"

Theobald, John J. and the United Federation of Teachers, 342–43

Thomas, M. Carey, quoted on women's education, 59; 260

Thorndike, Edward, 300

Tobacco, manufactured, 35–36, 160–62, 170; snuff, 36, 170; see also Cigars; Cigarette manufacture

TOR Education, Inc., on store employees' training, 256

Travell, Dr. Janet, 277

Triangle Waist Company fire, 152

Twenty-Nine College Cooperative Plan, 283–84, 326

Typists, see Stenographers, typists, secretaries

Uni-Tote, automation of sales accounts, 255–56

UNIVAC, 218, 233
U.S. Women's Bureau, investigation of legislation effects, quoted, 401–04, 431; see also *Bulletins* in Bibliography

Varityper, 172–74
Vassar College, 262
Vocational Education Act of 1946, 268

WACs, 263, 325
Wages, shoebinding, 28; cigar making, 33; tobacco, 36; printing and publishing, 41, 43, 47; watchmaking, 50; teaching, 55, 427; saleswomen, 63; "wages of sin," 66; why less than men's, 80–83, 425, 438; cotton textile manufacture, 117n; hosiery manufacture, 138n; clothing manufacture, 150, 153; minimum wage laws, 398–401, 404–411; equal pay legislation, 411–24
Wald, Lillian, 62
Waltham cotton mill, 10–11
Washburn, Governor, quoted on limiting hours for men as well as women, 90–91
Watch and clock manufacture, 49–51, 77, 195–96, 204, 210
Watson, James C., quoted on women in watchmaking, 50
WAVES, 233, 262, 265, 325, 429
Weaving, 15, 16, 19, 113, 115n; silk and synthetic textiles manufacture, 122–23; see also Northrup automatic loom
Wellesley College, 262
Western Union Telegraph Company, 67
White-collar employees, 63, 78, 184, 211; number exceeds blue-collar workers, 217, 335; attitude toward unionism, 337, 365, 369–70, 384, 387, 389, 390–91, 426; "must be organized," 336, 367, 368; see also Teachers; Nurses; Social workers; Librarians; Office workers; Saleswomen; Stenographers, typists, secretaries; Telephone operators
White, Lynn, Jr., quoted on women's education, 261

Whitney, Eli, cotton gin, 4; principle of interchangeable parts, 5, 24, 76, 194, 218, 425–26
Willard, Emma, quoted on women's education, 58
Wolfson, Theresa, quoted on white-collar unionism, 337–38, 351
Woman's Party, see National Woman's Party
Woman's place, viii, 7; in 1900, 83–87; 261–62; Secretary of Labor James L. Davis quoted, 400, 422; Alva Myrdal quoted, 425, 441; 430, 441–42
Woman's rights movement, 59; see also National Woman's Party
Woman suffrage, 59, 215, 280
Women in labor unions, ix; cigar making, 33–35; clothing manufacture, 154–56; meat processing, 189; 336–37; see also Labor unions
Women's colleges, 273–76, 325–26; Big Seven, 260, 331
Women's Douglass College, 272
Women's employment in 1900, 51–52, 75–79
Women's Trade Union League, 65–66, 338
Woolen and worsted manufacture, 17–20; competition from rayon and synthetic fibers, 121, 144–45; southern expansion of, 120–21; collective bargaining agreements, 121–22
Wright, Carroll D., quoted on women's occupations, 51; on saleswomen, 65; on women's wages, 83; on women's employment, 86–87; 412n

Yale University, quoted on education for women, 272
Young Women's Christian Association, 72

Zander, Arnold S., quoted on the American Federation of State, County and Municipal Employees (AFSCME), 354–55
Zelenko, Herbert, chairman of the subcommittee on labor of the Committee on Labor and Education, quoted on equal pay bill, 142